On Loyalty and Loyalties

On Loyalty and Loyalties

The Contours
of a Problematic Virtue

John Kleinig

OXFORD
UNIVERSITY PRESS

OXFORD
UNIVERSITY PRESS

Oxford University Press is a department of the University of Oxford.
It furthers the University's objective of excellence in research, scholarship,
and education by publishing worldwide.

Oxford   New York
Auckland   Cape Town   Dar es Salaam   Hong Kong   Karachi
Kuala Lumpur   Madrid   Melbourne   Mexico City   Nairobi
New Delhi   Shanghai   Taipei   Toronto

With offices in
Argentina   Austria   Brazil   Chile   Czech Republic   France   Greece
Guatemala   Hungary   Italy   Japan   Poland   Portugal   Singapore
South Korea   Switzerland   Thailand   Turkey   Ukraine   Vietnam

Oxford is a registered trade mark of Oxford University Press
in the UK and certain other countries.

Published in the United States of America by
Oxford University Press
198 Madison Avenue, New York, NY 10016

Library of Congress Cataloging-in-Publication Data
Kleinig, John, 1942–
On loyalty and loyalties : the contours of a problematic virtue / John Kleinig.
p.   cm.
Includes bibliographical references and indexes.
ISBN 978–0–19–937126–6 (pbk. : alk. paper) — ISBN 978–0–19–937125–9 (hardcover : alk. paper)
1. Loyalty. I. Title.
BJ1533.L8K54 2014
179'.9—dc23
2013040821

1   3   5   7   9   8   6   4   2

Printed in the United States of America on acid-free paper

CONTENTS

ACKNOWLEDGMENTS

It was not until 1989 that I began exposing my moral struggles with loyalty to an academic audience. But the issues on which I had been brooding went back to the Sturm und Drang of adolescence and had resurfaced from time to time as I confronted the realities of my social and domestic life. The opportunity and incentive to formalize what had been mostly particularized and practical deliberations came somewhat unexpectedly in 1986 with my move to John Jay College of Criminal Justice. I was expected to develop courses in police ethics, and, as I reflected on their content, I quickly became convinced that for police, as well as their public, the ethical and practical problems of divided and competing loyalties ranked among their most challenging and troubling. Through a consideration of those, I was permitted a more general philosophical entrée to the issues of loyalty with which I had been personally confronted. By providing a venue for their discussion from which I was detached, issues of police loyalty offered a check on musings that had been clouded by my own past experiences. But the equipoise did not hold for as long as I anticipated. As I attempted to structure these diverse perspectives and influences into a coherent whole, I found myself, a resident alien, witness to the World Trade Center tragedy and a participant in its aftermath. For a time at least, it became difficult to maintain the balance that expresses itself as: on the one hand . . . , but on the other. . . . As I now complete this long-overdue discussion, however, I am modestly hopeful that I can offer a fair appreciation of loyalty's strengths and weaknesses—of why it is a problematic virtue.

The development of my ideas has been slow. Although some part of that can be imputed to other commitments, my slow progress has also reflected a growing sense of the complexity of the issues and shifts in my own position. My earliest deliberations were strongly colored by Harry Blamires's contention that loyalty was a "sham virtue," invoked only to give a patina of moral respectability to conduct that could not otherwise stand on its own moral feet. Much of what I initially saw of loyalty's functioning in policing contexts seemed to confirm that impression. It was reinforced by some of my reading about the McCarthy years and the exploitation of loyalty oaths. On a practical level, there is still much to be said for Blamires's invective. As I got deeper into the issues, however, I came to think that loyalty needed to be rescued from its detractors no less than its exploiters. Police ethics provided a valuable context for that reconsideration. The more I probed into police ethics as well as my own experience, the more I came to the view that loyalty had been improperly maligned as well as neglected (at least by my professional colleagues). In the course of that reflection, George Fletcher's reaffirmation of loyalty provided a stimulating defense, even though I found myself uncomfortable with a number of his theoretical underpinnings and elaborations. Much later, Simon Keller's lively but more skeptical critique left me unsatisfied for quite different reasons.

The written project progressed in fits and starts. An early opportunity for extended reflection presented itself when I was a Fellow in what was then the Harvard University Program in Ethics and the Professions (1990–1991). Although my focus there was almost exclusively on loyalty as an ethical problem for police, the program allowed me the luxury of reading more widely, and my fellow "PEPy," Ross Cheit, introduced me to Albert Hirschman's wonderfully suggestive *Exit, Voice, and Loyalty*. A sabbatical leave in 1993–1994, split between Ben Gurion University and the Australian National University, enabled an expansion of that material, along with other projects that were then engaging me. A big boost occurred in 1997–1998, when I was a Rockefeller Fellow in the University Center for Human Values at Princeton University. There I was able to accumulate a large amount of material and had the freedom to revise, draft out, and present several papers that have been important to this final version. For all these opportunities I am enormously grateful. Nevertheless, I remained unable to construct either a theoretical or organizational framework for my thinking. The more I familiarized myself with the terrain, the more it kept expanding and the more elusive a structure became. A second sabbatical in Fall 2001 enabled me to fulfill that structural purpose. Little did I realize that it would be punctuated by the deconstructive attacks on the World Trade Center (which I witnessed from my Manhattan terrace) and the Pentagon. Context may not be everything, but it counted for something. Though these events made writing almost impossible, they illuminated some of the issues in unanticipated ways.

In the aftermath, the manuscript remained dormant for some years, with occasional but limited opportunities to teach and write on the topic. After 2004, however, an ongoing involvement with the Centre for Applied Philosophy and Public Ethics (CAPPE), Charles Sturt University, in Canberra, enabled me to do some work on it. Nevertheless, it required a further sabbatical in 2009, once again split between Israel and Australia, to complete a full draft, revised during a further sojourn at CAPPE and further revised in New York and Canberra in 2010–2012.

Along the path, I have appreciated the various opportunities I have had for presenting my developing ideas. Among the venues that were receptive to my presentations (if not to my views) were the PhD Program and Colloquium, the Graduate

School and University Center, CUNY; the Philosophy Department, Ben Gurion University, Israel; the Philosophy Program, Research School of Social Sciences, Australian National University, Canberra; the Political Philosophy Colloquium, Princeton University; the New York Chapter of the Society for Philosophy and Public Affairs; the Fortunoff Colloquium, New York University; the Centre for Professional Ethics, University of Central Lancashire; the Provost's Lecture Series, John Jay College of Criminal Justice; the Institute of Criminology, University of Cambridge; the Association for Practical and Professional Ethics; the Australasian Association for Applied Ethics; the Centre for Applied Philosophy and Public Ethics; the philosophy colloquia at Charles Sturt University, Wagga Wagga; Latrobe University; Monash University; the University of Western Australia; and an informal group of philosophical colleagues in New York.

Many individuals have also passed on their comments, sometimes in conversation, sometimes in formal discussion, sometimes in writing: Jeff Blustein, John Cooper, Bob Ewin, George Fletcher, Yehuda Gellman, Elise Hedemann,Virginia Held, Frances Kamm, Tziporah Kasachkoff, Simon Keller, Marvin Kohl, Julian Lamont, Michael McChrystal, Graeme McLean, Stephen Nathanson, Ross Poole, Joseph Raz, Bernard Reginster, the late Dita Shklar, Sam Souryal, Tatanya Valland Ducran, Andrew von Hirsch, Alan Wertheimer, Susan Wolf, and Robert Young. Jerry Gaus kindly agreed to look over an almost complete draft over Summer 2010, which he did with his colleagues, especially Julia Annas and Tom Christiano. Their acute criticisms, along with those of various anonymous referees, have been very helpful to my final revisions. My apologies to those I have overlooked.

Some earlier attempts to grapple with these issues have been published in "Loyalty in Public Service" *The Public Interest* (RIPA, Queensland) 1, no. 3 (June 1994): 10–11; *The Ethics of Policing* (Cambridge University Press, 1996), ch. 4; "Police Loyalties: A Refuge for Scoundrels?" *The Professional Ethics Journal* 5, no. 1–2 (Spring–Summer 1996): 29–42; "Professional Loyalties," *APA Newsletter on Philosophy and Law* 98, no. 1 (Fall 1998): 77–83; "Police Violence and the Loyal Code of Silence," in *Violence and Police Culture*, ed. Tony Coady, Stephen James, Seumas Miller, and Michael O'Keefe (Melbourne University Press, 2000), 219–234; "The Blue Wall of Silence: An Ethical Analysis," *International Journal of Applied Philosophy* 15, no. 1 (Spring 2001): 1–23; "Whistle-Blowing," in *Encyclopedia of Crime and Punishment*, ed. David Levinson (Thousand Oaks, CA: Sage, 2002), vol. 4, 1706–1708; "The Problematic Virtue of Loyalty," in *Policing a Safe, Just and Tolerant Society: An International Model for Policing*, ed. Peter Villiers and Robert Adlam (Winchester, UK: Waterside, 2004), 78–87; "Loyalty," *Stanford Encyclopedia of Philosophy*, August 2007; revised July 2013 (http://plato.stanford.edu/entries/loyalty/); "Patriotic Loyalty," in *Patriotism: Philosophical and Political Perspectives*, ed. Aleksandar Pavkovic and Igor Primoratz

(Aldershot, UK: Ashgate, 2008), 37–53; review of Simon Keller, *The Limits of Loyalty* (Cambridge: Cambridge University Press, 2007), *Notre Dame Philosophical Reviews*, April 29, 2008 (http://ndpr.nd.edu/review.cfm?id = 12983); "Judicial Corrosion: Outlines of a Theory," *Criminal Justice Ethics* 31, no. 1 (May 2012): 19–30; and *The Ethics of Patriotism: A Debate* (New York: Wiley-Blackwell, 2014), with Igor Primoratz and Simon Keller. I am grateful for permission to draw on these materials, though the views presented here sometimes differ from those previously published.

INTRODUCTION

Loyalty is a word which has worked vast harm; for it has been made to trick men into being "loyal" to a thousand iniquities, whereas true loyalty should have been to themselves—in which case there would have ensued a rebellion, and the throwing off of that deceptive yoke.[1]

Mark Twain was no great friend of loyalty—at least of loyalty as I understand it. He puts his finger on one of its troubling dimensions, one that I will need to address in this study. Nevertheless, what he characterizes and affirms as "true loyalty," I am inclined to characterize as integrity. So, not only its problematic status but also its conceptual contours will occupy my attention in what follows.

In a poll of moral opinion that was taken before the terrorist attacks on the World Trade Center and Pentagon, Alan Wolfe observed that "of all the virtues presumed to have been lost in America, loyalty generally took pride of place."[2] Wolfe's observation was intended to cover the full range of loyalties—from personal to patriotic, familial to organizational, and religious to professional. Some of this loss he attributed to a wistful individualism, the sense that in this modern day and age "one has to look out for oneself." Such individualism expressed the nostalgia of *Bowling Alone*, of lost community and diminished social engagement.[3] Yet, because it also indicated a certain self-reliance and independence, the loss, though felt keenly, was nevertheless experienced ambivalently.

---

[1] *Mark Twain's Notebook*, ed. Albert Paine (New York: Harper, 1935), 199.
[2] Alan Wolfe, *Moral Freedom: The Impossible Idea That Defines the Way We Live Now* (New York: W. W. Norton, 2001), 23. What that attack revealed was that loyalty had not been lost so much as displaced or—for a time—relegated.
[3] The phrase comes from Robert Putnam's *Bowling Alone: The Collapse and Revival of American Community* (New York: Simon & Schuster, 2000).

But no less than its loss or, as we might now think, its temporary relegation, loyalty itself generates feelings of ambivalence. The belonging that locates one within a community may also cloy, censor, and suffocate, and, as Twain recognizes, the support and security given by loyal others may issue in compromising expectations and base collaboration. Loyalty may be something of a neglected friend but, because of its excesses, a dangerous enemy.

It is with this Janus-faced character of loyalty—loyalty as something to be nurtured yet resisted—that this study is primarily concerned. Unlike many other virtues, such as justice, generosity, and integrity, loyalty seems to have as many critics as supporters, and even some of its friends are wary of its potential for overreaching. What is it, then, that might lead us to think, on the one hand, that "the ideal of loyalty is at the heart of commonsense morality,"[4] that the loss of loyalty is a significant social loss, and that betrayal is an egregious and shameful moral failure, and, on the other hand, that the demands of loyalty represent the very antithesis of an acceptable moral outlook, that loyalty is a sham and slavish virtue and a cloak for immoral collaboration?

As I hope will become clear, this inquiry is not about a marginal and parochial or even phony virtue but implicitly and explicitly engages with some of the most central and difficult problems of moral philosophy. Tensions between community and individuality, sentiment and reason, universalism and particularism, deontology and consequentialism, and virtue and obligation quickly appear on the philosophical radar screen, and though I do not engage with them all in detail, they are never far away.

Loyalty does not exist as a free-floating virtue, to be fostered indiscriminately, but especially and primarily (albeit controversially) within certain associational contexts such as friendship, family, tribe, country, organization, and religion; hence the title: *On Loyalty and Loyalties.* The study of loyalty forces us to confront the extent to which various associational ties should figure in our lives. Is patriotic loyalty a political virtue of the highest order—something to die for—or does it represent, as Samuel Johnson memorably put it, "the last refuge of scoundrels"?[5] How far, if at all, should we favor family over friends? Are tribal loyalties discriminatory, even racist? Is the virtuousness of loyalty contingent on the legitimacy of the associational ties to which it is related? The study of loyalty, I claim, is also a study of the ties that should bind.

Before I attempt to address these issues, however, it is useful to reflect on the general neglect of loyalty in philosophical inquiry, a neglect that is sometimes reflective

---

[4] Philip Pettit, "The Paradox of Loyalty," *American Philosophical Quarterly* 25, no. 2 (April 1988): 163.

[5] James Boswell, *The Life of Samuel Johnson, LL.D* (London: Macmillan, 1900), vol. 2, 115.

of its problematic character. There are notable exceptions, to be sure, such as Josiah Royce's idealist treatise, *The Philosophy of Loyalty*.[6] But Royce's study, though influential among a group of Roycean devotees, generated little independent interest in loyalty. Only recently has there been a shift of focus and the emergence of a significant philosophical literature on loyalty.[7] Several reasons can be advanced for this neglect and renewal of interest. Although some relate specifically to loyalty, others reflect more general philosophical preoccupations. I begin with the latter.

First, a great deal of moral philosophy over the past two centuries has construed morality as a system of rules and principles and viewed moral theory as an attempt to provide a statement of and rational grounding for such rules and principles. The idea of morality as centrally—or even significantly—concerned with virtues and ideals, with character and commitment as well as conduct, has only recently (especially since Elizabeth Anscombe's provocative 1958 essay, "Modern Moral Philosophy") reclaimed the attention it once had in philosophical reflection.[8]

A second factor was the first half of the twentieth century's philosophical preoccupation with moral theory rather than the concrete problems of human life—with metaethics rather than normative ethics (and even then with metaethics understood in a particular way). Until the social upheavals of the late 1960s returned Anglo—American moral philosophy to its traditional engagement with vital practical concerns, moral philosophers left to novelists, poets, playwrights, and others the task of working through the hard practical decisions that humans must sometimes confront.[9] It is no accident that a good deal of the still relatively meager discussion of loyalty has been generated by the practicalities of whistle-blowing in commercial/industrial, professional, and governmental/bureaucratic organizations. More recently, resurgences of religious, ethnic, and nationalistic fervor have generated a renewed

---

[6] (New York: Macmillan, 1908), available online at www.archive.org/details/philosophyloyal-00roycuoft. See, however, the recent Roycean study by Mathew A. Foust, *Loyalty to Loyalty: Josiah Royce and the Genuine Moral Life* (New York: Fordham University Press, 2012).

[7] See, for example, Andrew Oldenquist, "Loyalties,"*Journal of Philosophy* 79, no. 4 (April 1982): 173–193; Marcia Baron, *The Moral Status of Loyalty* (Dubuque, IA: Kendall/Hunt, 1984); George Fletcher, *Loyalty: An Essay on the Morality of Relationships* (New York: Oxford University Press, 1993); and Simon Keller, *The Limits of Loyalty* (Cambridge: Cambridge University Press, 2007).

[8] G. E. M. Anscombe, "Modern Moral Philosophy," *Philosophy* 33, no. 124 (January 1958): 1–19. I should note, however, that though this study focuses on what I take to be an important virtue, I do not take it to be a study in what has recently come to be termed "virtue ethics." The virtues have been sorely neglected, but I doubt whether we should make them the linchpin of ethical theory.

[9] Various classics of Western literature turn on issues of loyalty. See, for example, *Agamemnon*; the various novels of Joseph Conrad, including *Lord Jim*, *Heart of Darkness*, and *Typhoon*; and John Galsworthy, *Loyalties*.

philosophical interest in patriotic and national loyalties. Sixty years ago—during the McCarthy years—a similar opportunity to explore the claims of (patriotic) loyalty was all but ignored by philosophers. The discussion was left to political theorists.

A third factor has been more pervasive. The liberal tradition, with its individualistic tendencies, has backed away from social theories friendly to the claims of loyalty. Indeed, Kenneth Minogue has suggested that liberalism may almost be defined as a settled aversion to making the mistake of demanding excessive loyalty. What Minogue means by "excessive loyalty" is probably to be understood as any commitment to social arrangements that jeopardize individual autonomy. Minogue postulates that "the history of the modern state, from its beginnings in the sixteenth century, may be viewed as a centuries-long experiment in loosening the bonds of loyalty demanded from the subjects."[10] On one account, it is the autonomous individual, the rational chooser, prior to and only contingently involved in communal relations, who reigns supreme. Custom and tradition, hierarchy and social order, and the obligations of loyalty traditionally associated with them have been replaced by contract, with its self-assumed obligations. This liberal urge to "economize on loyalty" has had repercussions for other institutions (for example, the family) that have sought to influence conscience and choice. And, it might be argued, it is only as we have begun to recognize the personal and social fragmentation fostered by an excessive individualism that we have been prepared to appreciate and reconsider the virtue of loyalty.

A fourth factor is to be found in the partiality of loyalty—the fact that loyalty appears to be owed not *generally* but to *particular* people or groups. We have become deeply immersed in a tradition of moral thinking that construes morality as an overcoming of personal and partial concerns and that characterizes moral development as the replacement of these with a universalizable concern. Whether it is a Kantian commitment to acting according to maxims that we can will to be universal laws or a consequentialist pursuit of the greatest good, philosophers have frequently characterized moral deliberation in a way that does not easily accommodate the partial and personal character of loyalty. Although we are sentimentally drawn to "our own" and those to whom we are close in time and space, it is said that morality is constituted by a deindividualization of sentiment, an abstraction from what is immediate and proximate, and an attachment to what is universal.[11] The favoring of and commitment to one's family, friends, and country over those of others, when their being *one's own* appears to be the only way they differ from those of others, does not sit comfortably

---

[10] Kenneth Minogue, "Loyalty, Liberalism and the State," in *Lives, Liberties and the Public Good*, ed. George Feaver and Frederick Rosen (New York: St Martin's Press, 1987), 203.

[11] See David Hume, *Treatise of Human Nature*, ed. L. A. Selby—Bigge (Oxford: Clarendon, 1888), 582; John Grote, *An Examination of the Utilitarian Philosophy*, ed. Joseph Bickersteth Mayor (Cambridge: Deighton, 1870), 94.

with a tradition that emphasizes the universalizable, impersonal, or impartial nature of moral concern.

A fifth factor, often related to the foregoing, has been the prevalence of utilitarian thinking in postindustrial moral philosophy. Whatever specific account one gives of the burgeoning of consequentialist and especially of utilitarian theorizing in morality, such tendencies have seemed inimical to the apparently self-sacrificial and nonmaximizing element within loyalty. This is notoriously exhibited in William Godwin's example of a burning house in which Archbishop Fénelon and his own mother (or sister) have been trapped, and from which he can rescue only one. Whom should he rescue? Godwin opts for the Archbishop, as someone who is likely to contribute much more to the general happiness: "What magic," he asks, "is in the pronoun 'my,' that should justify us in overturning the decisions of impartial truth?"[12]

Each of the foregoing reflects more general social and/or theoretical concerns that impact on the status of loyalty rather than problems that are specific to it. Loyalty, on such views, might seem to have been merely a victim of those larger movements of thought that affect so much of our social and intellectual endeavor. But many have also seen loyalty itself as a problematic virtue—or not even a virtue at all. In that perception may lie further reasons for its neglect, if not outright rejection.

First, although loyalty seems central to much commonsense morality, it also features in a good deal of commonsense immorality. After the Watergate scandal, the loyalty of Gordon Liddy and John Mitchell generated about as much admiration as the honor among thieves.[13] Patriotic and religious loyalties, for all their soul—stirring qualities, are frequently jingoistic, exclusionary, and even terroristic. The loyalty of police officers, doctors, and lawyers to their fellows often strikes us as arrogantly self-serving or narrowly tribalistic. Even the impressive loyalty of legal professionals to their clients can appear insensitive to the public interest. Those who demand loyalty most may deserve it least. As a colleague once put it: "When an organization wants you to do right, it asks for your integrity; when it wants you to do wrong, it demands your loyalty."[14] It is easy to be left with the feeling that, like certain

---

[12] William Godwin, *Enquiry Concerning Political Justice* [third ed., 1798], photographic facsimile, ed. F. E. L.Priestley (Toronto: Toronto University Press, 1946), vol. 1, 127. See D. H. Monro, "Archbishop Fénelon versus My Mother," *Australasian Journal of Philosophy* 28, no. 3 (December 1950), 154.

[13] We should not assume that this means *no* admiration. The subsequent fate of these and other Watergate conspirators suggests that, in the long run, the loyal rogues may have been more successfully reintegrated than those (e.g., John Dean) whose moral qualms (or self-interest?) led them to act in ways considered disloyal. Whistle-blowers (allegedly, the "disloyal") do not generally do well, even if they are thought to have been justified in their claims.

[14] Aaron H. Rosenthal, former Assistant Chief, NYPD.

other supposed ideals (for example, neutrality, balance), loyalty too easily becomes the refuge of rogues and hypocrites.

This moral ambiguity or Janus-like quality that loyalty exhibits, and its seeming intensification of the good or evil with which it is associated, has almost certainly affected its status, even when the elements of good character have attracted the interest of moralists and moral philosophers. Justice, courage, compassion, kindness, generosity, benevolence, and love appear to have a less ambiguous claim to our support and inculcation.

Second, some writers have wanted to go even further and see in loyalty something *essentially* corruptive or subversive of morality. Harry Blamires, for example, writes that "whenever the virtue of loyalty is quoted as a prime motive or basis for action, one has the strongest reasons for suspecting that support is being sought for a bad cause."[15] He refers to it as a "sham" or "pseudo-virtue exploited to give a bogus moral flavour to amoral or immoral actions." For Blamires, appeals to loyalty do not constitute a reason for action *apart from* the propriety of the actions for which loyalty is invoked (in which case, he suggests, such appeals are redundant). They give a disingenuous patina of moral rectitude to that which lacks moral merit. They exploit the language of bondedness, fellowship, connectedness, and commitment to "justify" participation in evil causes.

Third, as noted earlier, it is argued that appeals to loyalty as a motivation to moral conduct are redundant.[16] Moral motivation is rooted in morally appropriate reasons for action. If some act is worth doing, then it is worth doing because of the particulars of the act it is—say, defending one's country, zealously supporting one's clients, sticking with a friend, and so on. In other words, there is a presumption that one's country is worth defending, that there are good reasons for defending clients, and that one's friend is worthy of one's support. No reason for doing these things is necessary beyond those reasons that make them worth doing. One does not need to appeal to some further consideration—such as loyalty one owes—as a basis for supporting them in the ways indicated. Appeals to loyalty are morally otiose.

Fourth, acting out of loyalty can appear to be a case of acting without an appropriate reason. If I am asked to justify some act of loyalty, it would seem that the only response I can give is that the object of the act was in some sense *mine*: I had no reason

---

[15] Harry Blamires, *The Christian Mind* (London: S.P.C.K., 1963), 24. He concludes: "Loyalty is a key concept in modern life; and it does enormous damage to our moral fibre."

[16] Cf. Blamires: "Loyalty is in itself not a moral basis for action. Loyalty to a good man, a good government, a good cause, is of course a different matter. But in these cases, where one stands by a man, or a government, or a cause, because it is good, one is standing by the good. The basis of action in these cases is moral in that one is serving the good; and thus the concept of loyalty is redundant," ibid., 24.

to give to *A* rather than *B* apart from the fact that *A* was particularistically *mine*—my friend, my relative, my countryman, and so on. Referring to Andrew Oldenquist's distinction between loyalties and ideals, Marcia Baron writes:

> If my reason for defending my country is democratic, then, he [Oldenquist] says, "I have not a loyalty but an ideal," for "what I am committed to is a kind of thing, not some particular thing." I have a genuine loyalty only if I am dedicated to *X* under the description "my *X*"; otherwise I would have to say, any other *X* of the same kind (e.g. any democratic country) would have an equal claim on me. But what kind of reason is "Because it is mine"? If to act loyally is to act with a special regard for something because it is mine—only because it is mine—loyalty seems at best silly.[17]

Fifth, without necessarily imputing disreputable motives to those who defend it, loyalty may be seen as an essentially discriminatory "virtue." Loyalty to *my own* in distributing benefits—jobs, opportunities, and so forth—deprives those who are not my own. Consider, for example, how the old boy network provides access to some and denies it to others. The claim need not be that "others" are inferior, but simply that they are not "of us," not one's own. The magic of "my" and "our" does not work for "your" or "their." On a broader level, loyalty plays into the hands of different forms of tribalism—discriminatory divisions between in-groups and out-groups, a problematic psychological need to define ourselves against the Other.

Sixth, loyalty seems to invite or even require heteronomy, a renunciation of responsible decision making. Morally responsible action is action undertaken on the basis of one's best judgment of what is appropriate. The loyalist, however, appears to give herself over to the cause or object of loyalty without any thought or consideration to whether this object's particular expectations or demands might be justifiable. In speaking of the loyal cause to which one should aspire, Royce writes:

> Let this [cause] so possess you that . . . you can say . . . "I am the servant of this cause, its reasonable, its willing, its devoted instrument, and being such, I have neither eyes to see nor tongue to speak save as this cause shall command." Let this be your bearing and this your deed. Then, indeed, you . . . have won the attitude which constitutes genuine personal dignity.[18]

---

[17] Baron, *The Moral Status of Loyalty*, 6, referring to Oldenquist, "Loyalties," 175.
[18] Royce, *The Philosophy of Loyalty*, 106; cf. 120. Royce, it should be noted, sees the cause's devotee as reasonable, reflecting his own belief that the process of determining one's cause—the object of loyalty—is a rational one: "all of the higher types of loyalty involve autonomous choice" (119). Nevertheless, in pledging loyalty, one may appear to immunize oneself against later reconsideration.

Joseph Agassi has argued that appeals to loyalty manifest and encourage an unseemly dependence, a sacrifice of autonomy and rationality to the object of loyalty.[19] And what Graham Greene celebrates as "the virtue of disloyalty" is a breaking free from the shackles of conventional thought, an insistence on making up one's own mind and treading one's own path.[20]

Seventh, it is sometimes contended that loyalty should not be seen as a virtue at all, but simply as a sentiment and therefore deserving of no special attention. Because expressions of loyalty are generally associated with strong feelings, some take it to be merely an affective bond whose expression in deeds of loyalty is the outward manifestation of what is essentially an internal attachment. The resistance that bonds of loyalty often manifest to both argument and prudence may seem to confirm this view.

And eighth, though this is at best a tendency, loyalty has often been associated with conservative rather than liberal or progressive causes. It is often complained that the presidential years of George W. Bush were marked—and corrupted—by a culture of loyalty, one in which competence took at best a second place. *All the President's Men*, whether Nixon's or Bush's, were expected, first and foremost, to be loyal, an expectation that led not only to poor judgment but also to secrecy and cover-ups. As a political and personal virtue, loyalty was overrated—a defense of the status quo and corrosive of good judgment.

These points are not always stated or discussed separately, but individually and cumulatively they offer a challenge to the "commonsense" claims of loyalty and help to explain the problematic status that loyalty has acquired as an object of ethical interest or element in a good life.

In the chapters that follow, I explicate this problematic character of loyalty in greater detail, indicating its roots while defending what Pettit sees as the commonsense

---

[19] Joseph Agassi, "The Last Refuge of the Scoundrel," *Philosophia* 4, nos. 2–3 (April–June, 1974): 315–317:

> When an appeal is made for patriotism, for any loyalty, it is because reasonable arguments have been tried and failed. This is so because loyalty at times when it is supportable by other considerations is simply redundant and is thus usually not evoked [*sic*: invoked?]. Logically, the question is not, do we ever have to be loyal, but rather, is loyalty a sufficient force to impose obligation on us [?] . . . The reason . . . for not seeing loyalty—to spouse, friend, or tribe—as a special category, is the claim that the burden of responsibility lies in the individual, that *better a responsible individual who errs than a dependent one who is told to do the right thing and does it*. This is, I think, the statement contested by those who demand loyalty: they require precisely the abdication of one's own judgment in preference for that of the tradition and the group.

[20] The title of Greene's acceptance speech for the 1969 Hamburg Shakespeare Prize.

account. I seek to marry that commonsense account with a full acknowledgment of the moral hazards to which it is prone and that I have sought to identify in the preceding points. I do this, first, via a general discussion and defense of loyalty—insofar as it is amenable to such—and then track its contours and acceptable limits within some of its primary associative contexts.

In the first part, I address some of the more general questions prompted by loyalty—problems of boundary, foundation, and status—and seek to develop an account of loyalty that shows not only why it is important to human association and flourishing but also the features that make it corruptible and dangerous. In chapter 1, I offer a workable account of loyalty as perseverance (especially in the face of self-serving temptations) in the conditions that sustain relationships whose objects have come to be valued for their own sake. This is filled out in chapter 2, where I connect loyalty with a range of other dispositions, qualities, and practices with which it is commonly associated either for comparative (fidelity, allegiance, constancy, devotion, integrity, and solidarity) or oppositional (disloyalty, betrayal, and faithlessness) purposes. In chapter 3, I outline the distinctive contribution that loyalty makes to a virtuous human life—its role as an associative glue. Chapter 4 provides an approach to its justification. The discussions of chapters 3 and 4 leave partially unaddressed the problem of loyalty's particularity—the tension between the oft-touted impartiality of morality and the partiality of loyalist obligations. That issue is discussed in chapter 5. The thesis of chapter 6 is that loyalty need not be complaisant or heteronomous. Nor is it an unconstrained virtue, the topic of chapter 7. These chapters defend an appropriately characterized loyalty against some of the main criticisms that have been canvassed in the preceding pages.

In the second part, I deepen the earlier discussion by reviewing some of loyalty's primary sites—particular *loyalties*—noting how loyalty may not only enhance its associational embodiments but also distort and threaten them. I make no claims to completeness: the various associations I review represent only some of those within which loyalty might reasonably be fostered. The associational list is not arbitrary, however. It reflects the fact that our identities tend to be partially characterized by reference to our associational involvements, and the list focuses broadly on those that are most likely to be significant as bearers of our identities and as constituents in a good and flourishing life. In chapter 8, I explore the association with which loyalty is most intimately connected—friendship. The bonds of family loyalty are tracked in chapter 9. In chapters 10 and 11, I show how loyalty operates in organizational and professional contexts. Chapters 12 and 13 separate out the frequently interwoven themes of what I characterize as tribal/nationalistic and patriotic loyalties. And finally, in chapter 14, taking as my focus the biblical story of "the binding of Isaac," I consider the problem of absolute loyalty.

PART I

Loyalty is usually concretized in what I refer to as loyalties, but, because it may be shown wherever there are associative bonds, we might speak of it in general. Part I of this study focuses on the generalities of loyalty as an active disposition. I distinguish it from the other personal attributes and practical dispositions to which it is related or with which it is to be contrasted and then explore its normative status, the challenge it poses to certain forms of universalism, and finally consider some of the general normative constraints that apply to it. Although most of the associative relations that will be addressed in part II already make an appearance here, their fuller discussion will be held over until then.

1

TOPOGRAPHY

We breathe the word "loyalty" and immediately a sentimental warmth floods our minds. We get the emotional kick which properly accompanies decisions made in the interest of noble causes. Our complacency is cheaply earned.[1]

Is it? Harry Blamires thinks of loyalty as no better than a sentimental attachment to supposedly noble causes—a "pseudo-virtue exploited to give a bogus moral flavour to amoral or immoral actions." Although he is not alone, we may ask whether what is here proffered as loyalty may not be a degraded version. Has its exploitation marred it like a strip-mined landscape? My purpose in this and the next few chapters is to delineate the conceptual contours of loyalty and see how it is most usefully characterized and why, despite its detractors, it remains important to human flourishing and a good life. In this chapter, I provide what I represent as conceptual topography; in the next, I shift the metaphor by locating loyalty within a larger neighborhood of concepts. That foreshadows a more explicit and extended account of its underlying rationale in chapters 3 and 4.

Few of our everyday concepts have the precision and clearly defined functions of surgical instruments. They are more like pieces of modified terrain, distinctively featured and identifiable, but with conventionalized "natural" boundaries and somewhat irregular contours. There may be a highest point and a lowest point, but there will not usually be a single high or low point. These terrains were not always shaped as they are, and their contours may alter in the future.

Concepts have histories. They evolve. Unlike vanishing ripples or the constantly shifting swell of an ocean, however, their contours are generally stable enough to be mapped. Nevertheless, unlike a wilderness tract, shaped primarily by impersonal

[1] Harry Blamires, *The Christian Mind* (London: S.P.C.K., 1963), 24.

and arbitrary forces, our social concepts reflect the constraining influence of human purposefulness in altering contours and modifying elevations. The enterprise is one of social topography.

We can do some archaeological excavation for clues about how concepts came to have their present configurations, and we can review the various factors and social pressures that even now modify them as we describe how they "are." Following a brief archaeological study, I offer a topographical map of what I take to be loyalty's current configurations.

ARCHAEOLOGY

Loyalty has its philological background in Old French (*loialté, leialté, lealté*), which in Middle French became *loialté* and in Modern French *loyauté* (meaning, primarily, "faithfulness to obligations").[2] Its remoter roots are to be found in the Latin *lex* (law) and *legalis* (pertaining to law).

The connection with law (*lex*) has become severely attenuated, although there are some obsolete adjectival uses in which *loyal* meant something like "legitimate"—a "loyal child" was one born in wedlock, "loyal money" was legal tender, and "loyal cloth" was cloth that met a legal standard for quality. And we sometimes still refer to the "loyal toast," in which allegiance to the monarch (originally, the source of law) is affirmed. Residues of this quasi-legal framework are also found in its substantive form, in the oath or pledge of fealty or allegiance sworn by a vassal to his lord. Loyalty to the lord was constituted by faithful adherence to the liege or sovereign.[3]

Loyalty is now used much more broadly to refer to persevering commitment to some associational object. Indeed, Sophie Bryant plausibly suggests that if we wish to explore the term's philological underpinnings, we should take the French *loi* as its base rather than the more remote *lex*.[4] *Loi* and its derivative *loial* had a more general meaning than *lex*, referring broadly to that which ought to be obeyed, hence *loialté* as faithfulness to obligations. Although these obligations may be seen as natural (as

---

[2] The earliest uses—from the eleventh to twelfth century—are feudal, having to do with vassal-to-lord and lord-to-vassal relations.

[3] With such a meaning, *loyalty* has an earlier semantic cognate in the biblical Hebrew *chesed*, often translated as "faithfulness" or "covenant loyalty" to characterize a person's or people's fidelity to the terms or conditions of its relationship with God *(YHWH)*, the source of *torah*. See Katharine Doob Sakenfeld, *Faithfulness in Action: Loyalty in Biblical Perspective* (Philadelphia: Fortress Press, 1985).

[4] Sophie Bryant, "Loyalty," in *Encyclopedia of Religion and Ethics*, ed. James Hastings (Edinburgh: T. & T. Clarke, 1915), vol. 8, 183. Perhaps, however, as the following note suggests, even *lex* could have such overtones.

in a family or among friends), they may once have been more formal, indicating some compact between two parties.[5]

As with many social concepts, developed over time, accretions have resulted in a somewhat complex "metastable" idea that embodies several loosely connected elements.[6] Such complexity threatens fragmentation, as one set of uses focuses on, say, the personal dimension of loyalty's attachments, another on its motivational side, a further set on the persistence that loyalty displays, and yet another on its self-sacrificial character. Whereas it is the conformist quality of conduct that constitutes it as loyal for some, for others it is a passionate attachment and/or devotedness. And whereas the unquestioning attachment of a dog is paradigmatic of loyalty for some, for others loyalty is a quality of character for which dogs are ineligible.[7]

MAPPING THE CONTOURS

In providing a topographical map, I consider first its general composition—whether loyalty should be seen as a sentimental attachment, a practical disposition, or type of conduct.

Sentimental Attachment?

As Blamires's remarks suggest, loyalty's frequent association with strong occurrent feelings—an intense devotion to its objects—is sometimes taken to suggest that it is primarily a sentimental or emotional attachment, an affective bond whose expression in loyal deeds manifests outwardly what is essentially an inner feeling or attitude.[8] The resistance that appeals to loyalty frequently display to both argument and prudence may seem confirmatory.[9] Loyalty may therefore be thought to stand in need

---

[5] "À la base du mot *lex* il y a une idée de convention, de contrat exprès entre deux personnes ou deux groupes. . . ." *Dictionnaire étymologique de la langue latine: histoire des mots*, ed. Alfred Ernout and Antoine Meillet, 4th ed. (Paris: Librairie C. Klincksieck, 1959), 353.

[6] Ruth B. Cochran, "Some Problems with Loyalty: The Metaethics of Commitment," *Dialectics and Humanism* 17, no. 3 (1990): 203.

[7] Associated with that may be normative factors that lead to what Walter B. Gallie termed "essentially contested concepts," in which topographical debates will be colored by competing normative frameworks. See his eponymous article in *Proceedings of the Aristotelian Society* 56 (1955–56): 167–198.

[8] See, for example, R. M. MacIver and C. H. Page, *Society: An Introductory Analysis* (New York: Rinehart, 1949), 146; James Connor, *The Sociology of Loyalty* (New York: Springer, 2007).

[9] Simon Keller develops this into a general thesis about political and other loyalties. See *The Limits of Loyalty* (Cambridge: Cambridge University Press, 2007). See also Hume's remark, that loyalty is a virtue holding "less of reason, than of bigotry, and superstition," in *Treatise of Human Nature*, ed. L. A. Selby-Bigge (Oxford: Clarendon, 1888), 582.

of explanation more than justification. That is, how do we come to have such feelings, and what function do they serve?[10]

It is not surprising that loyalties are generally associated with strong feelings, because our primary loyalties are to objects with which we often strongly associate or identify ourselves—our friends, families, country, and so forth. Such identifications can be expected to have an affective component. Even when our loyalties are to associations of lesser significance (say, sporting teams), the attachment is likely to have an affective side. But the affectivity of loyalty is not its central or determinative constituent. One can have strong feelings of loyalty without being loyal. The weak-willed Peter emotionally affirms his "loyalty unto death" but, as the story goes, soon denies any association with the one to and for whom his feelings were expressed.[11]

Nevertheless, the affectivity associated with loyalty is not merely contingent. It is awkward to characterize a person as loyal if she lacks *any* affective attachment to the object of her loyalty. Normally, loyalty to a spouse encompasses not only an effective disposition to act in certain specifiable ways but also an affective attachment to the other. Consider, however, the case of a wife who, despite her husband's indifference and chronic infidelity, *and her own consequent loss of affection*, nevertheless remains loyal to him out of a belief that, having pledged herself for better or worse, she continues to owe it.[12] Do we want to speak of loyalty here, or is it better seen as a case of fidelity? I am inclined to think the latter, because the focus is on the vow rather than the person. Nevertheless, characterizing it as loyalty is not entirely implausible.[13]

---

[10] Once we have understood that, we might then ask whether and to what extent such feelings should be encouraged. R. E. Ewin, who implicitly takes what Hume says as a sufficient reason for denying that loyalty is a virtue, sometimes speaks of it as "an emotional bond, not a calculating form of commitment." In Ewin's view, "the person who acts only after calculating that the act is owed as a matter of loyalty is, to that extent, not typically a loyal person," in "Loyalty: The Police," *Criminal Justice Ethics* 9, no. 2 (Summer–Fall 1990): 12. In "Corporate Loyalty: Its Objects and Its Grounds," Ewin writes: "Loyalty is, fundamentally, an emotional attachment and an emotional reaction to its objects: insofar as one's actions are entirely explicable in terms of cool, clear reason, one's actions are not a display of loyalty," in *Journal of Business Ethics* 12, no. 5 (May 1993): 389.

[11] Matthew 26:33–35, 69–75. "Loyalty unto death" is a common paraphrase rather than a direct translation. The disloyalty was such that its repair required more than a simple apology. See John 21:15–18. If this is simply interpreted as weakness of will on the part of someone otherwise loyal, then perhaps a better example is provided by Judas.

[12] Even though the exact nature of the obligations associated with such loyalties may be a matter of debate, they are likely to include forbearance from publicly humiliating him or from talking behind his back when it would be convenient and perhaps opportune to do so, by remaining sexually faithful when it is tempting to be otherwise, and by being there for the spouse during the hard times—sickness, sorrow, and poverty—as well as the good ones.

[13] In such cases, we might be tempted to claim that the loyalty is to an institution (marriage) rather than to a person, even though it manifests itself as loyalty to a particular person.

Or consider various role-based loyalties—for example, the loyalty of a lawyer to his client or a public servant to her minister. The lawyer and public servant may have only feelings of contempt for those they serve. Does this make it inappropriate to speak of their loyalty? Maybe, though one might argue in such cases that the affective loyalty has been transposed to abstractions—that is, to the ideals of zealous advocacy (on behalf of clients) or civil service.[14]

We expect loyalty to be associated with some feeling for the object of loyalty. In this respect, it is similar to gratitude. Both are practical virtues, exhibited in action and to particular others. If we *are*, we may *feel* grateful to another. Such a feeling is neither constitutive of nor irrelevant to the genuineness of the gratitude. It anticipates opportune expression. And just as the child who does not feel grateful when gratitude would be appropriate is somehow deficient, so, too, the loyalty of a person who lacks loyal feelings for an object of loyalty is also—absent a special story—deficient in some way.[15]

Motivational Constraints

The inwardness associated with loyalty has a further dimension, for the active expressions that are centrally constitutive of loyalty must also be appropriately motivated. A person who steadfastly suffers criticism about her spouse merely to avoid jeopardizing an inheritance is not behaving loyally (or, for that matter, disloyally). A person who keeps a friend's confidences simply because the opportunity for betrayal does not arise does not thereby show loyalty (or, for that matter, friendship). The Hall of Fame pitcher Don Sutton cynically put it thus: "Loyal? I'm the most loyal player money can buy." To act loyally, one must act *for the sake of* the object of loyalty (albeit under a particular description—for example, friend, family member, fellow countryman) and not out of, say, self-interest. In sticking by the other, the loyalist must not disregard the interests—or perhaps the wishes—of the object of loyalty at the center of his or her concern. There must be some commitment to preserve, secure, or even further the interests of the object of loyalty.

Simon Keller appears to take issue with this last point. In distinguishing five forms of loyal expression—what he refers to as loyalty in concern, advocacy, ritual,

---

[14] The same might be said of police officers who remain loyal to a rogue officer by refusing to say anything that would incriminate him. Even though they may feel nothing or only contempt for the officer, they may stick loyally by him or her. Are they loyal to the officer or passionately committed to a certain ideal: "never hurt a fellow officer"? We will later review some difficulties associated with the idea of loyalty to abstractions.

[15] Or perhaps the deficiency is with the loyalty rather than the person. The phenomenon of affectless loyalty may help to explain the marginal status that is sometimes accorded to professional loyalties. Is the lawyer's loyalty to a client loyalty in the full sense? See chapter 11.

identification, and belief[16]—Keller claims that although loyalty in concern (say, that which a parent shows toward a child) will involve a prioritizing of the interests of the object of loyalty, this is not (or at least need not be) the case with other forms of loyalty. For example, the person who defends Al Gore at a dinner party (loyalty in advocacy) or recites the Pledge of Allegiance (loyalty in ritual) is not ipso facto seeking to advance the interests of the object of loyalty. This is true enough. A range of explicit motivations for loyal conduct is possible. What is critical is not that one is explicitly motivated to advance or prioritize the interests of the object of loyalty, but only that one's conduct includes a concern not to jeopardize those interests.

Perseverance

In addition to the issue of an appropriate motivation, the conduct that exemplifies loyalty will exhibit a certain form of perseverance. There are generally two elements to perseverance—*persistence* in an attachment despite the *difficulty* it involves. Loyalty to a friend is paradigmatically constituted by an ongoing refusal to reveal confidences, by sticking up for the friend when others are maliciously attacking her, by responsiveness when the friend's needs are great, and so on. But more than that, it involves a willingness to hang in there for the friend, to refuse to jeopardize the friend's interests, despite inconvenience, temptation, or even the burdensomeness of doing so.

Not every case of unselfish perseverance in a commitment qualifies as loyalty. If I keep my promise to return a book and do so despite an unanticipated storm, I show perseverance but not necessarily loyalty. The telos of loyalty is not the fulfillment of an obligation (in the face of hardship) but securing or at least refusing to jeopardize the interests of its object as part of expressing and/or furthering an association.[17] Most often, the kinds of commitments that undergird loyalty refer—at least indirectly—to associations that are, rightly or wrongly, important in a worthwhile life. Our primary loyalties are to friends, families, professions, organizations, ethnic groups, and countries, associations that we generally consider important to our human well-being.

The perseverance of loyalty is often said to be self-sacrificial. There is something to that. Loyalty is not a fair-weather virtue. The loyal person perseveres in her commitment despite the costliness of doing so, whether the cost is that of resisting temptation or the pressure to further or maximize one's narrowly framed interests. The language of self-sacrifice may sometimes be too strong. The friend who always remembers to send a birthday card, even when contact has been minimal, shows herself to be a loyal friend in the sense that she overcomes the tendency we have to

---

[16] Keller, *The Limits of Loyalty*, 3–11.

[17] Nevertheless, even though pledges of fealty may make us think that loyal adherence is somewhat like, and is justified in the same way as, the keeping of promises, there are important differences.

self-preoccupation.[18] Yet no dramatic self-sacrifice is involved. Sidney Axinn, who emphasizes the self-sacrificial dimension of loyalty, does so because he is occupied with patriotic loyalty—in which something close to self-sacrifice may be expected.[19]

May one be loyal even though one has never been tested? If one thinks of the virtues as involving a disposition to act, then it is possible for a person to be *disposed* to conduct herself loyally in the absence of any occasion to do so. True, we might have no reason—that is, no basis in experience—to attribute loyalty to her. But that does not amount to a conceptual problem. Nevertheless, some oddity would be involved, not only in the case of loyalty but also of other virtues. It would be misleading to call a person courageous (or otherwise) had there never been an occasion to show courage. A disposition is not an action, but in the absence of an occasion for its expression in action, we have no reason to claim that it would manifest itself in action when an occasion presented itself. At the point of testing, any such disposition could be overborne by weakness of will or duress. Indeed, part of the point of saying that a person has a particular virtue is to say that in the face of some reason to do otherwise, the person has shown the disposition to be effectual.

Associative Identification

Loyalty, then, is a practical or realized disposition to deny oneself for the sake of an associational other. What do I mean by an associational other? Many have observed the social identification that exists between the subject and object of loyalty. That to which one is loyal is that with which one in some measure identifies oneself. My loyalty is to what I identify with as *mine*—to *my* friend, *my* tribe, *my* company, *our* country, and so forth.[20] There is something irreducibly first personal (singular or plural) about loyalties.

There is, however, more than one sense in which something may be mine, my own, or ours. My spade is *conventionally* mine; it is my property or at least the one I use.

---

[18] Perhaps such a friend shows herself as loyal only in a minimal sense, and, in fact, she may be only minimally loyal. If a subsequent request for assistance is turned down or very grudgingly responded to, we may be inclined to discount the loyalty. Nevertheless, the gesture may well betoken much greater loyalty—a preparedness for some form of self-sacrifice. My thanks to Susan Wolf for this example.

[19] Sidney Axinn, "Loyalty and the Limits of Patriotism," in *Political Realism and International Morality: Ethics in the Nuclear Age*, ed. Kenneth Kipnis and Diana T. Meyers (Boulder, CO: Westview Press, 1987), esp. 242–246.

[20] John Ladd makes the point by saying that it is "conceptually impossible to be loyal to people in general (to humanity) or to a general principle," in "Loyalty," in *The Encyclopedia of Philosophy*, ed. Paul Edwards (New York: Macmillan and Free Press, 1967), vol. 5, 97. Leaving aside (for the present) the question of loyalty to principle, Ladd overstates his point. Insofar as I can construe humankind as my kind, it is possible to be loyal to humanity. If given an incentive

I have certain conventional entitlements to it. I may also have a sentimental attachment to it and even take good care of it. But the issue of loyalty does not arise simply by virtue of ownership or entitlement. My trash is also mine. It is *causally* my own. I have produced it and, by virtue of this, may even have some responsibility for what happens to it. I may dispose of it carefully. But it is not mine in a sense that is likely to raise the issue of loyalty. My job is *contractually* mine in the sense that I am paid for work that I do. The contractual relationship I have with an employer entitles me to remuneration for my services. There may be no loyalty involved, however: my interest in it may be merely instrumental. My friends and family, however, may be *relationally* or *associatively* mine. In associative relations, there is a certain identification of oneself with the other, often one in which one sees one's identity as being partially constituted by the relation.[21] That is, in giving a characterization of myself to others, I might well include my salient friendships and family connections in that characterization, along with my ethnicity, citizenship, religious affiliation, and so on. It is not that one loses one's identity in the others with whom one identifies oneself, but that these relationships figure in one's interests to the extent that the others' interests come to have a significant place in one's own.

This identification with associational others can be seen as coming to care for them for their own sakes, an empathetic involvement with them that adds to the significance of one's life. Even if the interests of the other are not always one's own interests, their satisfaction or nonthwarting may well become one of one's own. As it is argued by those who have propounded what is sometimes termed an ethic of care, in identifying with the associational other, one also opens oneself to the other to learn

---

to surrender humans to an alien power, loyalty to my kind may lead me to refuse. In Mary Wollstonecraft Shelley's nineteenth-century novel *Frankenstein*, there is a scene in which Dr. Frankenstein's creature demands a female companion for himself. Frankenstein refuses:

> I created a rational creature and was bound towards him, to assure, as far as was in my power, his happiness and well being. This was my duty; but there was another still paramount to that. My duty towards the beings of my own species had greater claims to my attention because they included a greater proportion of happiness or misery. . . . I refused, and I did right in refusing, to create a companion for the first creature. (New York: Pyramid Books, 1957), 187.

Ignoring the consequentialist cast of these remarks, they might be taken to display the loyalty to humankind that Ladd finds conceptually impossible.

[21] In the special case of friendship, however, the connection is more likely to be expressed in relational terms than in terms of identification. For more on this issue, see Dean Cocking and Jeanette Kennett, "Friendship and the Self," *Ethics* 108, no. 4 (April 1998): 502–527; and Michael O. Hardimon, "Role Obligations," *Journal of Philosophy* 91, no. 7 (1994): 333–363.

from and—to a degree—be guided by the other. The other becomes a source of one's own self-realization, as well as the object of one's concern.[22]

It may not always be easy to determine whether the first-person connection is conventional, causal, contractual, or associative. The job that is mine may be contractually mine, but it may also be associatively mine if the work that I do is intrinsically fulfilling and I come to have a core interest in the profession's or organization's well-being.

Ordinarily, one's family will be associatively one's own. One will value it and one's connection to it for its own sake and will have an interest in acting in ways that preserve and advance its interests. Very likely, one's parents and siblings will be individually seen as one's own in that same associative sense. But sometimes one's family or particular members of it may be one's own only in a causal sense. One will be biologically connected to its members as sibling or parent or offspring but without any sense of associative identification. In such cases, even though loyalty may be expected by others, it is not likely to be acknowledged by oneself and may not even be warranted.

Partiality

Those with whom one is associatively connected—as *one's* friends, family, colleagues, or fellow citizens—also tend to be the objects of partial or preferential treatment.[23] The objects of such preferential treatment need not be *worthy* of it—though they will most likely be *valued* by those who consider themselves loyal.[24] One may be a loyal gang member or loyal Nazi as well as a loyal friend and colleague. Misplaced loyalty is not less loyalty for that. All that is required for loyalty is that the objects be seen as "constitutively" *one's own*—that one in some sense identifies with them in the sense of being committed to them, and that carries with it the protection or furtherance of their interests.

How are we to construe the partiality of loyalty? Is it simply affirmative and supportive, or might it also be exclusionary and oppositional? Real-life loyalties are often exclusionary and oppositional. Jingoism and chauvinism abound in the political sphere. In *Stickin'*, his swashbuckling defense of loyalty, James Carville suggests that

---

[22] See, for example, Nel Noddings, *Caring: A Feminine Approach to Ethics and Moral Education* (Berkeley: University of California Press, 1984); and, more recently, Virginia Held, *The Ethics of Care: Personal, Political, Global* (New York: Oxford University Press, 2006).

[23] Though not in every case. If my child is in my class, assigning a preferential grade because she is my child would be out of place.

[24] Sometimes it may not be clear what is valued—the particular object of loyalty or the general association that is supposedly exemplified in the particular case. Sometimes police officers are loyal to fellow officers even if—because of what they have done—those particular officers are no longer valued by others. Nevertheless, because of the (almost) absolute importance accorded to backing up a fellow officer, others will remain loyal to them.

the "stickin' with" of (especially political) loyalty goes hand in hand with "stickin' it to" others.[25] But how deeply does the exclusionary and oppositional dimension of loyalty go? It can be expected in cases in which some other object competes for my loyalty or threatens the object of my loyalty, and I must oppose it to assert my loyalty. That oppositional stance often characterizes party politics.

Fletcher suggests that loyalty is necessarily oppositional or exclusionary. Loyalty claims are triadic:

A can be loyal to B only if there is a third party C (another lover, an enemy nation, a hostile company) who stands as a potential competitor to B, the object of loyalty.[26]

But that is surely too strong. To be loyal, A may not have to favor B *against* C. A need have no alternative C in mind or view when he loyally favors B. And certainly A need not be antagonistic to C in favoring B. Though patriotic loyalties have often been jingoistic, it is no part of the *idea* of loyalty that one opposes oneself to another. Nor, except in special circumstances, need it be part of patriotic loyalty. My attachment to my country need not involve any comparison with or derogation of others' countries. If my country is poor, I may choose to practice my skills there rather than migrate to a more lucrative position in another country. Indeed, for all my patriotism, I may hope that others feel about their country in the way that I feel about mine. The same is true of other loyalties: the loyalty I have to my own family need not involve the criticism, downgrading, or undermining of others or their families; the loyalty I have for my university or profession does not require that I think them better than others' universities or professions. Only in limited circumstances will loyalty to what is mine *require* opposition to yours.

What Fletcher's contention inadequately responds to is loyalty's foul-weather background. As we noted earlier, there is generally a personal cost or sacrifice associated with acts or expressions of loyalty. When loyalty is shown, and usually when it is called for, there will be some disadvantage, burden, or loss for the loyal party.[27] This

---

[25] James Carville, *Stickin': The Case for Loyalty* (New York: Simon & Schuster, 2000), esp. 51–60. It is no accident that *Stickin'* was a follow-up to his *We're Right, They're Wrong: A Handbook for Spirited Progressives* (1996).

[26] George P. Fletcher, *Loyalty: An Essay on the Morality of Relationships* (New York: Oxford University Press, 1993), 8.

[27] The cost to self that is involved in acts of loyalty may not always compromise self-interest in a narrow, selfish sense. One's loyalty to a great cause may be expressed in one's willingness to sacrifice the interests of one's family. Their interests are bound up with one's own, though not narrowly. Here, for the sake of what is seen (whether rightly or wrongly) as a higher loyalty, a lesser loyalty is sacrificed. But because it is a loyalty that is sacrificed, there is a significant cost to self (as well as, of course, to others).

cost may take the form of refusing a rival or competitive *C*, but it may also involve no more than a sacrifice of one's comfort, convenience, or advantage. My loyalty to IBM may be shown by my holding on to or even purchasing additional shares when there is a general downturn in the market, and not only when I hold on to my Coca-Cola shares when some rival company makes an aggressive bid for the company. My loyalty to a friend may be shown when, despite the inconvenience involved, I write him a supportive reference or testify on his behalf. In other words, *A* can be loyal to *B* only if there is a cost (whether that cost arises from some competitive third party, *C*, or the effort required to favor *B*).

The partiality of loyalty is not simply discriminatory, but imperfectly obligatory. The loyal person does not act in a merely preferential way, or even in a way that is believed to be permissibly preferential; she must believe herself *obligated* to act preferentially.[28] With associative relations come obligations of partiality. In this sense, loyalty is a normative idea. Whether such partiality is obligatory all things considered may depend on an assessment of the worthiness of its object or of its worthiness in relation to other objects. The loyal Nazi will believe himself to be obligated in certain ways—though we can assume that they are not morally determinative obligations. And whether any legitimate obligation of loyalty is *overriding* may depend on other obligations and circumstances. Loyalty to a family member may, for example, have to give way to other expectations if the issue to be resolved is an academic grade or appointment.

In some associations, obligations of loyalty will be integral to the associative relationship. In others, and more commonly, the development of loyalty and its attendant obligations will be only contingent. In the former associative relationships, obligations of loyalty will be intrinsic to their character; in the latter, obligations of loyalty will ordinarily be acquired only when one comes to identify with the object as associatively one's own. Obligations of loyalty are internal to what are sometimes

---

[28] I am not suggesting that it is *the sense of obligation* that *motivates* the loyal behavior, or even some explicit reference to the loyalty. The paradigmatically loyal person will be motivated by a concern for the object of loyalty as one to whom he is committed. Loyalty is most impressively shown if one's reason for acting is not the loyalty one owes but the commitment one has to the object of loyalty. As Bernard Williams remarks regarding the person who, in rescuing his wife, is motivated not merely by the thought that it is his wife, but that in such circumstances it would be morally permissible to rescue one's wife: such a person has "one thought too many," in "Persons, Character and Morality," reprinted in *Moral Luck: Philosophical Papers 1973–80* (Cambridge: Cambridge University Press, 1981), 18. Nevertheless, appeal to the object of the association may not always carry the day, and one may sometimes have to remind oneself of the loyalty one owes. Even more problematic is the desire that one see oneself or be seen as a loyal person—a form of motivation that Williams elsewhere refers to as moral self-indulgence. See "Utilitarianism and Moral Self-Indulgence," reprinted in *Moral Luck*, 45.

termed *end-friendships*. Friendships without loyalty fail as end-friendships. Obligations of loyalty are not generally integral to membership of a team or organization.[29] Teams or organizations may or may not (though often do) seek our loyalty; they may or may not reasonably expect our loyalty (though they sometimes do); if we identify with them such that they become associatively *ours*, then ipso facto and with previously noted caveats in mind we acquire obligations (of loyalty) to them as part of what that association means to us.

Not every associative obligation will be an obligation of loyalty. Spousal abuse violates an associative obligation to the other but does not ordinarily constitute a failure of loyalty. Obligations of loyalty have as their social context an environment in which parties to the association are likely to encounter internal or external inducements to endanger or harm interests that are integral to the association and whose resistance will be costly. But spousal abuse, though disruptive, is not usually motivated by factors that are relevantly self-serving. It is more likely to be an expression of anger or frustration or of some defect of personality. Although the prohibition on spousal assault may function to preserve such relationships, that is not its purpose. It instantiates a general prohibition on assaulting others, whether or not we are associatively bonded to them. A key element in obligations of loyalty, however, is the affirmation or reaffirmation of our relational bonds with others. That is why disloyalty—even if it does less overt damage to a person than assault, may nevertheless be more destructive of the relationship. When expressing loyalty, one acts in ways that intentionally affirm, sustain, or strengthen the association that is expressive of one's loyalty.[30] The associations that loyalty sustains require a certain overcoming of self-interest. One gives oneself to the other in a way that is not simply instrumental. Narrow self-interest, however acceptable in other circumstances, is corrosive of loyalty and is the essence of disloyalty (which, of course, is not to deny that loyalty may usually be in a person's overall interest).

Although we might speak generally of the obligations associated with loyalty as "obligations of loyalty," they will normally have diverse and particularized instantiations. Obligations of loyalty to one's spouse are likely to include an obligation to give her some kind of public support (or at least to refrain from publicly criticizing her), observance of sexual fidelity, an obligation to provide care for her in hard times, and so on, especially in circumstances in which it might (appear to) be prudent, advantageous, or tempting for one not to fulfill such obligations. Loyalty to one's organization

[29] Any membership will carry obligations with it. What may be only contingent are the obligations that are expressive of the associational commitment that loyalty exemplifies.

[30] This does not imply complaisance. One may constitute a loyal opposition. The other's interests may not be identical with the other's wishes: a loyal friend will let one know when one is being stupid.

might include obligations to work for change from within the organization should it fall short of its ideals or mission, to have the organization's interests at heart (rather than just one's own ambitions) in working for it, to refrain from disclosing its competitive secrets, and so on, again in circumstances in which it might (appear to) be prudent or advantageous for one to renege on such obligations.

As I have already suggested, obligations of loyalty, though sufficient to justify preferential treatment of their object, need not be overriding. They are defeasibly sufficient. The Jewish woman who sleeps with a Nazi officer so that her child may be spared the gas chamber may not fulfill the obligation of loyalty she has to her husband (and the child's father). Apart from the duress involved, we might argue that the child's interests take precedence. But neither is the woman *dis*loyal to her husband. When obligations of loyalty are overridden by higher (or what are perceived as higher) or situationally more demanding obligations (including higher loyalties), we do not speak of disloyalty being shown.[31] There are limits to what loyalty can demand. Disloyal conduct is constituted by deviation of a more mundane kind— when some form of narrow self-interest, self-advancement, or self-assertion motivates the departure. In the unlikely event that the women sleeps with the Nazi officer simply to indulge some passion, we will consider her culpably disloyal; if she does it to save her own life or some priceless works of art, however, we might consider her disloyal, albeit excusably (though not thereby justifiably) so.

I have claimed that loyalty to another will involve partiality toward or preferential treatment of that other. However, it should be remembered that loyalty to another is not the exclusive vehicle of sustainable partiality. Partiality may be grounded in recompensive considerations such as the need to compensate or express gratitude, or in certain voluntaristic acts, such as promises. Even in relations of love and friendship, the partialities that are integral to them extend beyond those that fall under the umbrella of loyalty. If I have a spare theater ticket and offer it first to my friend or lover, the partiality, though generally unexceptionable, is not an expression of loyalty.

The obligatoriness of loyalty need not be construed morally. Nor need loyalty be seen in exclusively moral terms. Although the constituents of character are likely to have moral dimensions, not every manifestation will have direct moral implications. Not every virtue is a moral virtue, and even those virtues that we consider to be morally important may be shown in circumstances that lack direct moral significance. We may admire a person for his loyalty to the New York Mets but not necessarily see that as expressive of moral virtue. His loyalty will be shown in buying a season's

---

[31] Even so, because the obligations of loyalty are preferential, the person who sets aside those obligations to meet a higher obligation might owe the other party an apology or at least an explanation.

ticket to the Mets games, in attending games even when the weather is inclement, in supporting the team even when it is having a bad season, and so on. Not every association whose persistence depends on the loyalty of its membership has straightforward moral importance. Nor does every ingredient in a good life carry moral import.

Some loyalties may be good to have because institutions depend on the persevering commitment of their members or supporters. And healthy institutions of those kinds may be good things to have without their being morally significant. To the extent that we consider the institutions worth having, we will value loyalty to them.

WHO CAN BE LOYAL?

I have for the most part assumed that, when A is loyal to B, A is a person—or, if not a person in some straightforward sense, then a quasi person or collectivity. But the subjects of loyalty have sometimes been cast more broadly, and eloquently so. In particular, dogs are asserted to be capable of—and even exemplars of—loyalty. Provocatively, but perceptively, Leslie Green refers to loyalty as "the canine virtue"—and thus something to be wary of as well as admired.[32] In its advertisements, Mercedes Benz once featured a dog and its master with the caption: "Loyalty. (You expect it from your dog. But from your car dealer?)."[33]

Other writers, however, have been more cynical about the exemplary loyalty of animals. "There is no doubt," writes the Viennese satirist Karl Kraus, "that a dog is loyal. But does that mean we should emulate him? After all, he is loyal to people, not to other dogs."[34] Yet even Kraus might be taken to attribute loyalty (albeit of a non-exemplary kind) to dogs. Fletcher is less concessive: animals cannot be loyal because they cannot betray.[35] At one level, the point is well taken. George Vest's "Tribute to the Dog" emphasizes that whereas one's patiently reared children may turn against one, one's faithful dog will not. But why not? Is it that the dog resists the temptation to look to its own interests? Or is it because the well-trained dog lacks the capacity/freedom, the will, or calculative self-interestedness to do otherwise, whatever other "personal" characteristics may be attributed to it? It may, of course, be questioned

[32] Leslie Green, "Loyalty, Security and Democracy," in *National Security: Surveillance and Accountability in a Democratic Society*, ed. P. Hanks and J. D. McCamus (Quebec: Éditions Yvon Blais, 1989), 116.

[33] One of its many incarnations can be found in the *New York Times Magazine*, April 18, 1999, 115. But see also George Graham Vest's lyrical "Tribute to the Dog," a nineteenth-century speech nominated by William Safire as the best speech of the second millennium and reprinted in "Faithful, Even in Death," *New York Times Magazine*, April 18, 1999, 72–73.

[34] Karl Kraus, *Half Truths and One-and-a-Half Truths: Selected Aphorisms*, ed. and trans. Harry Zohn (Montreal, Quebec: Egendra Press, 1976), 109.

[35] Fletcher, *Loyalty*, 9–11.

whether genuine loyalty requires a capacity for betrayal. Might it be possible to imbue animals with dispositional characteristics for which the language of virtue will be appropriate, even though their manifestations will not reflect judgments of appropriateness that would be expected in adult humans having those same dispositions? The dog that refuses to leave its master's body, eventually dying of starvation, may be showing its loyalty, albeit not in a completely appropriate way.[36] Perhaps animal loyalty (like animal courage) should evoke our admiration without the animal being deemed morally praiseworthy.[37] As I shall suggest later, unless what Aristotle calls *phronesis* or practical wisdom can be attributed to animals, what are taken to be the lineaments of loyalty will be somewhat lacking in moral virtuousness. Canine loyalty is closer to exemplifying what Aristotle speaks of as a "natural" rather than "full" virtue—not instinctive, perhaps, but lacking in judgment.

TO WHAT CAN ONE BE LOYAL?

In characterizing loyalty as an associative virtue, I have sided with those who view the objects of loyalty as persons, collectivities, or quasi persons. In common parlance, we speak more loosely. We talk of loyalty to principles, causes, ideas, ideals, professions, religions, ideologies, nations, governments, parties, leaders, families, friends, regions, racial groups—indeed, as Milton Konvitz puts it, of loyalty to "anyone or anything to which one's heart can become attached or devoted."[38] But despite this plethora of objects, well entrenched in common speech, there is much to be said for the more restrictive position, at least as a way of understanding what is central to loyalty's conceptual contours. According to this more restricted view, the central or

[36] In Japan, *chūjitsu*, usually translated as "loyalty," is most commonly exemplified by the story of Hachikō, an Akita dog. See "Faithful Old Dog Awaits Return of Master Dead for Seven Years," *Asahi Shimbun*, October 4, 1933. I am grateful to Cory Evans for this reference. See also Mayum Itoh, *The Truth of the Life and Legend of the Most Famous Dog in Japan* (Amazon Kindle, 2013).

[37] There are other questions as well. Is it true that domestic (and perhaps other) animals lack a capacity for betrayal? Or if they have the capacity for both loyalty and betrayal, perhaps it is to be distinguished only in regard to the sophistication of the contexts in which it might be shown. To the extent that they manifest such capacities, is it an outcome of their association with humans? I shall not attempt to resolve these issues here. For the present it is enough that we see what is at issue. Nevertheless, to the extent that animals are presented as exemplars of loyalty, the charge that loyalty is a heteronomous virtue is likely to gain in credibility—unless, of course, they are accorded moral personalities. See Stephen R. L. Clark, "Good Dogs and Other Animals," in *In Defense of Animals*, ed. Peter Singer (New York: Harper & Row, 1985), 41–51.

[38] Milton Konvitz, "Loyalty," in *Encyclopedia of the History of Ideas*, ed. Philip P. Wiener (New York: Scribner, 1973), vol. 3, 108.

critical objects of loyalty are personal—individual persons; personal collectives such as family, ethnic group, or national group; or quasi persons such as organizations or professional communities. Some writers, though, are even more restrictive and limit the scope of the personal to individuals or groups of personal acquaintance.

Although I would dispute his opening phrase, John Ladd claims that "in our common language, as well as historically, 'loyalty' is taken to refer to a relationship between persons," either individually or collectively.[39] Marcia Baron lends her support: "Loyalty [is] to certain people or to a group of people, not loyalty to an ideal or cause. . . . When we speak of causes (or ideals) we are more apt to say that people are committed to them or devoted to them than that they are loyal to them."[40] Even Royce, whom they criticize, may not stand too far from this centrally personalized understanding of loyalty. Although he characterizes the object of loyalty as a cause, Royce understands by a "cause" something that inter alia unites the individual "with other persons by some social tie."[41] True, he does not focus on individuals or collectivities as such, but only as they embody some transcendent or superpersonal goal—most generally, that of "loyalty to loyalty." But even that superpersonal goal is interpersonally embedded: "a cause is a possible object of loyalty only in case it is such as to join many persons into the unity of a single life."[42] And in his later work, *The Problem of Christianity*, Royce writes: "I now say that by loyalty I mean the *practically devoted love of an individual for a community*."[43]

Michael Walzer also expresses some skepticism about loyalty to ideals, though his doubts are psychological rather than conceptual. He suggests that what appears to be loyalty to an abstraction usually turns out to be loyalty to particular people: "Concomitants to principles are usually also concomitants to other men, from whom or with whom the principles have been learned and by whom they have been enforced."[44] Loyalties are strongest, he believes, where the personal objects of loyalty are clearest.

I noted earlier the tendency for complex social terms to evolve in diverse ways, some emphasizing one feature and others some other feature. Loyalty is like that. By focusing on different features of loyalty, we can talk not only of loyalty to friends and families (and other collectivities) but also of loyalty to moral principles, self,

[39] John Ladd, "Loyalty," 97.

[40] Marcia Baron, *The Moral Status of Loyalty* (Dubuque, IA: Kendall/Hunt, 1984), 6.

[41] Royce, *The Philosophy of Loyalty*, 25.

[42] Ibid., 107.

[43] (New York: Macmillan, 1913), vol. 1, xvii. Note, though, that the Roycean community is no mere collection of individuals but has a reality that transcends—without dissolving—the lives of its constituent members.

[44] Michael Walzer, *Obligations: Essays on Disobedience, War, and Citizenship* (Cambridge, MA: Harvard University Press, 1970), 5.

brands, loyalty, and prayer books. Nevertheless, despite the more expansive suggestions of common speech practices, I believe our primary understanding of loyalty is best served by the more restrictive account. Most of our core loyalties—loyalties to members of our families, to our friends, and even our religious and national loyalties—are loyalties to people, individually or collectively, and, as Walzer observes, they also seem to be our strongest (or at least most resilient). Police managers know all too well that those who press for police to place their loyalty to ideals or the organization above loyalty to partners or fellow officers often seem to be engaged in fruitless admonition, and not just because of the sanctions associated with disloyalty to a fellow officer. If it belongs anywhere, loyalty seems to belong most naturally and powerfully in the contexts of those to whom one is personally, communally, or otherwise associatively related.

We cannot, of course, use what may appear to be a psychological phenomenon to establish a piece of normative conceptualization. The point, however, is that the role played by loyalty, insofar as it is conceived as a virtue, is primarily that of securing the integrity of certain human associations—friendships, familial relations, ethnic connections, and patriotic bonds, not in the abstract but through their particularized exemplifications. It has that role by virtue of our human sociality—the importance that associative relations have for our flourishing—and focuses first and foremost on those associations that are important to our flourishing. The burden of part II of this study will be to make that more explicit. No doubt what is substantively the same perseverant virtue is also important to ensure ongoing support for more abstract ideals and values, but though this support can be advanced under the aegis of loyalty, it is probably just as effectively characterized using the language of devotion, commitment, dedication, and steadfastness.

Associational and moral integrity are not unconnected. Morality, after all, is the central coinage of our varied human associations, mediating our relations as humans and as humans who stand in more particularistic relations (family, friends, and cultural group). Associational life provides the milieu for our development and flourishing as the particular humans we are. As that which secures those particular relationships, loyalty will not only constitute an important moral virtue but also figure importantly in the education of virtue.

There is a deeper point that helps to explain why we move so readily from loyalty to people to loyalty to ideals and other abstractions. Implicit in personal loyalties is a presumption that the objects of such associations embody values that contribute to and enhance those associations. That is, my relationships with my friends, family, and country also embody certain presumptions about what they stand for, normative presumptions that are reflected in the fact that I acknowledge and retain the particularistic relationship that I have with them. My loyal support is given to those whose associational values are presumed to be largely consistent with my own.[45] But, as we too often see, the others with whom we are joined fail or cease to realize the values that make association with them the valuable or valued thing it is presumed to be, and we are forced to confront and even to reconsider our loyalty to them.[46] Our nation may show itself to be discriminatory or improperly aggressive toward others; a parent may abuse a child; a husband may cheat on a wife; a friend may violate unspoken but expected norms; a business partner may enter into an inappropriate business relationship. In such circumstances, we will be confronted with painful choices. We may rationalize the situation, even to the extent of adapting to it; we may seek to recall the other to the values presumed to have been compromised. We may break off the association, seeing the violated norms as being too important to allow for its continuation.

When situations such as these arise, we realize that although our loyalties are particular, the particulars that are the objects of our loyalty are appropriate objects of that loyalty only in certain roles or under normatively charged descriptions. In cases of radical change on the part of the object of loyalty, our loyalty, to the extent that we may still speak of such, may be displaced onto less personal bearers of those values. Thus medieval writers were led, by the abject failure of the personal objects of their loyalty to embody the qualities of character—the values—that would sustain that loyalty, to distinguish between loyalty to an office (kingship) and loyalty to the king (as officeholder). The distinction was intended to undercut the charge of subversion— the allegation that anyone who challenged the king ipso facto threatened to rend the fabric of society. And so, too, may the focus (or at least the normative object) of our loyalties be shifted from associations that concretely express justice to the principle of justice. The embedded values will now be deemed the bearers of our loyalty.[47]

The basic point, perhaps, is this. At their most fundamental or primitive level, loyalties are to others—to others as associational objects. But these loyalties are

---

[45] As I have already pointed out, it is not my claim that associations will always coalesce round acceptable values. The friendship of racists and Mafiosi may center on base values. Nevertheless, even here, for their members to consider the association worth preserving and for the association to survive, there is likely to be a core provided by values essential for productive human interaction. Note, nevertheless, "Sammy the Bull" Gravano's complaint that under John Gotti Jr. the Mob no longer maintained its old-time criminal values, hence his disenchantment. See Peter Maas, *Underboss: Sammy the Bull Gravano's Story of Life in the Mafia* (New York: HarperCollins, 1997).

[46] The point is not that the association is formed because of those values—that they constitute the point of the association—but that the valued association is presumed to be infused with those values.

[47] Cf. Herbert A. Bloch, *The Concept of Our Changing Loyalties: An Introductory Study into the Nature of the Social Individual* (New York: Columbia University Press, 1934), 51–52.

not normatively neutral connections but normatively invested unions in which the others with whom we associate ourselves are not only valued but presumed to embody values with which we are broadly comfortable.[48] If those values change, or if we discover that the values actually embodied in the object of loyalty are other than we thought they were, this is likely to impact on the value of the association for us and hence on our loyalty. The spouse or friend or god with whom we profess a bond no longer meets the presumptions that were taken to infuse that bond. We may seek to restore the associational object to what we presume it represented, we may proclaim that our loyalty is ultimately to the values that we had (wrongly) presumed were embodied in and perhaps exemplified by the object of our loyalty, or we may adjust our own values so that we can retain our association with the personal object previously thought to embody them.[49] In the last case, there will be a trade-off between the continuing value that the association will have for us and the value that has been shown to be lacking. This is how the estimable and important value of loyalty among police becomes the corrupted and corruptive loyalty of the blue wall of silence.

Although we value the associations we have with others, both intrinsically and instrumentally, we do not value them independently of their embodiment of certain values. From time to time, those loyalties can be severely tested—for example, when the valued association no longer exhibits the values that we presumed were implicit in it. Consider the situation of parents who have reason to believe that their child may have been involved in a heinous crime. Where do their obligations lie or lie most decisively? In loyalty to their child or in their commitment to the regime of retributive justice that (we may presume for present purposes) seeks to assure for victims the respect that is due to them? There may be no simple either–or answer to such a question, but its resolution may change either or both the parents and the relationship.

Of course, loyalty is only one factor to be taken into account in determining how we are to respond to associative others. The person we may no longer wish to assist as a friend remains a human being, and that humanity may call forth a helping response from us, even a sacrificial one. And even if we remain loyal to someone who has bitterly disappointed us, that loyalty may take a different form. The parents who refuse to shield their child from the consequences of his actions may nevertheless visit their child in prison.

---

[48] As I make clear later (chapter 13), these do not need to be seen as values "from a neutral point of view." See Simon Keller, "Patriotism as Bad Faith," *Ethics* 115 (2005): 574.

[49] A nice example of this is found in Galsworthy's *Loyalties*, in which Mabel, Dancy's young wife, on learning that her husband has been less than honorable in stealing a large sum of money, nevertheless pledges her continued loyalty to him—even though previously she could not have countenanced that he might have been guilty of the deed.

CONCLUDING NOTE

Given that some of loyalty's problems have arisen from misunderstandings about its nature and scope, I have endeavored to provide enough conceptual clarity to circumvent some of the criticism to which it has been subject. At the same time, I hope to have identified some of the sources of its problematic nature. Loyalty, I have claimed, is centrally constituted by perseverance in the conditions undergirding our relationship to an object that has come to be valued for its own sake—perseverance motivated by a concern for the object of the relationship and resistant to various self-interested temptations or personally advantageous alternatives. Although this may not encompass every form of loyalty—loyalty to brands and the loyalty of loyalty programs and dogs—it exemplifies a type of loyalty on which those more exotic expressions draw.

2

NEIGHBORHOOD

Loyalty specializes in respect of the object of service, fealty in respect of faith to the pledge. Of these the latter is more necessary to virtuous character, and so it has been judged by the common sense of mankind, as the testimony of language shows.[1]

In the last chapter, we endeavored to trace the contours of loyalty without any particular concern for how it might connect with related practically realized dispositions. Are loyalty and fidelity the same? What about loyalty and integrity? How do we distinguish loyalty from constancy and solidarity? In this chapter, we focus on connections, comparisons, and contrasts—sources of confusion and contributors to loyalty's problems. No less important, I seek to place loyalty in its larger social place before considering, in chapters 3 and 4, more extended reasons for giving loyalty something like the place that common sense accords it. The division of chapters is somewhat artificial, as the topics are intermingled, and therefore the division of material is heuristic rather than logical.

I first distinguish loyalty from its closest neighbors—faithfulness, fidelity, allegiance, fealty, steadfastness, constancy, devotion, solidarity, and integrity. I then consider some of its wayward relatives—disloyalty, betrayal, treachery, and the more particularized expressions of treason, adultery, idolatry, and apostasy—before offering an account of the social underpinnings or presumptions of loyalty: its neighborhood culture.

Most thesauri link loyalty with faithfulness, fidelity, allegiance, fealty, steadfastness, constancy, devotion, solidarity, and integrity, and though these terms are sometimes used interchangeably with loyalty, they often reflect subtle and confusing

---

[1] Sophie Bryant, "Loyalty," in *Encyclopedia of Religion and Ethics*, ed. James Hastings (Edinburgh: T. & T. Clarke, 1915), vol. 8, 184.

differences. The conceptual clarification that follows will help us to understand not only what is special about loyalty but also what contributes to its problematic character.

CLOSE NEIGHBORS

Unless Sophie Bryant is correct in thinking that loyalty's earliest associations were political,[2] its closest neighbors are *faithfulness* and *fidelity*—almost family members. When the compilers of the *Oxford English Dictionary* give as loyalty's primary sense "faithful adherence to one's promise, oath, word of honour, etc.,"[3] we are to infer from this that loyalty presupposes a self-assumed obligation and is therefore constituted by perseverance in that preexisting commitment.

However, a review of the contexts in which we speak of loyalty suggests that this account, if not contentious, is lacking in nuance. In a provocative but thoughtful article, R. T. Allen suggests that by tending "to assimilate it to faithfulness to a promise," most contemporary discussions of loyalty "omit what is distinctive of it," namely, "keeping faith with that to which one has prior obligations."[4] He contends that even Royce, by focusing on "*chosen* causes," confuses "loyalty" with "faithfulness."[5]

Significantly, and perhaps as evidence of loyalty's "essential contestability," Allen's claims form part of his larger protest against "the modern view of man as a self-defining subject who has autonomously to invent his own law or way (*tao*), for the universe presents none to him."[6] By contrast, Allen maintains that the demands of loyalty are undergirded by commitments derived from associations that are not self-assumed. He has in mind the traditional loyalties to family and social group that are expected and acquired by virtue of the community within which we are nurtured. Even though we will most likely come to affirm what we are already communally obligated to do, as the rite of confirmation does for baptism, such expectations predate those generated by self-assumed obligations. It is the ancestral communal

[2] Ibid., 187. In that case, allegiance and fealty would be its closest relatives.

[3] Bryant also views loyalty as a particular specification of faithfulness (ibid., 184).

[4] "When Loyalty No Harm Meant," *Review of Metaphysics* 43, no. 2 (December 1989): 281, 288. Allen takes *fidelity* and *fealty* to be synonymous with *faithfulness*.

[5] Ibid., 289. He sees "Royce's general outlook [as] symptomatic of the devaluation and misinterpretation of loyalty, even in the very act of making it the supreme principle of morality" (290).

[6] Ibid., 281. Allen articulates this larger project in "Rational Autonomy: The Destruction of Freedom," *Journal of Philosophy of Education* 16, no. 2 (1982): 199–207. There are important affinities between Allen's position and that of Andrew Oldenquist in his provocative "Loyalties," *Journal of Philosophy* 79, no. 4 (1982): 173–193.

associations that impose obligations of loyalty; it is not self-assumed obligations that create communal associations.

Allen's account makes the discussion of loyalty a site for what he sees as two contending conceptions of human being—one in which human personality is deeply embedded in concrete social networks and in which identity and the personal obligations of loyalty predate the so-called determinations of autonomous agency, and another that views the individual as a self-defining agent whose associations with and obligations of loyalty to others are self-chosen. Although I believe that Allen captures something important here, to which I will return at the end of this chapter, I doubt whether we are confronted with a simple either–or. Some of our loyalties are likely to be (initially, at least) unchosen, but others reflect commitments that we have consciously made: loyalty may be as appropriately directed to my wife or university as it is to my family.

In the case of fidelity, Allen's contrast might seem to be even stronger. It is plausible to posit a communal dimension to loyalty that is only contingently present in the case of fidelity. Fidelity is shown to one's word, whereas one is generally loyal to a person or group with which one is closely associated. Fidelity is to articulated commitments, whereas loyalty is to an associational other. Infidelity—thought of as a violation of the traditional marital vow to sexual exclusivity—thus tends to be narrower in scope than disloyalty. Although the distinction is not hard, it suggests that loyalty inhabits some larger associational space. The relevance of this will become clearer later in the chapter.

Judith Shklar suggests a different contrast between loyalty and fidelity. Loyalty, she claimed, "is given to groups, [whereas] individuals may and do receive our fidelity." Yet she also allows that "causes, be they moral, political, or aesthetic, demand loyalty, [whereas] friendship calls for fidelity."[7] Whatever her exact position, her intention was to exclude merely personal relationships from the proper objects of loyalty. On the surface, at least, this division seems implausibly prescriptive. Loyalty is just what we expect and receive from our friends. What may lie behind Shklar's contention, however, is a distinction between commitments that are relatively open-ended and those that are more tightly circumscribed. It may be thought that the personalized, face-to-face character of friendship will find its expression in specific expectations and commitments, whereas the commitments associated with causes and the groups associated with them will be less explicit. But that does not seem quite right, and it may well be that Shklar's point reflects the fact that many invocations of loyalty are group based.

---

[7] Judith Shklar, "Obligation, Loyalty, Exile," *Political Theory* 21, no. 2 (May 1993): 184. The paper was published posthumously, unrevised. In an earlier work, *Ordinary Vices*, Shklar had no problems with the idea of loyalty in friendships.

OLD NEIGHBORS

Relations between loyalty, *allegiance*, and *fealty* go back a long way. *Allegiance* (from Old French *ligeance*; cf. *lige* = liege) originally referred to the obligation (generally of fidelity or devotion) that a vassal or subject owed to his liege lord or sovereign, whereas *fealty*, an old English term (from the Old French *feaute*, *feelte*, and Latin *fidelitas*), referred to the fidelity or faithfulness usually sworn or pledged by a vassal to his lord.

> The giving of allegiance is in effect a vow to serve; the standard case of loyalty coincides, therefore, with the standard case of fealty in which a pledge of service is given, as, for instance, by oath of allegiance to a king, by marriage vows between two persons, or by acclamation—and vote—in tribal assemblies when law was promulgated and accepted thus. The standard cases are the same, but in the development of thought the two ideas differ. Loyalty specializes in respect of the object of service, fealty in respect of faith to the pledge. Of these the latter is more necessary to virtuous character, and so it has been judged by the common sense of mankind, as the testimony of language shows.[8]

Bryant's concluding normative reflections return us to the earlier thought that whereas faithfulness and fidelity are most closely associated with adherence to a commitment or pledge, loyalty has associational overtones and is shown primarily to people. As to why fealty might be thought "more necessary to virtuous character," we might refer again to the medieval distinction between loyalty to the king and loyalty to the idea of kingship. Whereas the latter presumes certain normative expectations, actual kings may fall short of them. Loyalty to people, only loosely connected with broader normative constraints, may lead or be taken to commit one to roguish behavior.

FRIENDLY NEIGHBORS

The ideas of *steadfastness* and *constancy* focus on the perseverant aspect of loyal commitment. The steadfast person manifests a certain firmness or resoluteness of purpose. Although steadfastness is implicit in loyalty, it is broader in scope. My steadfastly sticking to a task that I have set for myself would not normally constitute loyalty to it. Constancy is not easily distinguishable from steadfastness, though its

[8] Bryant, "Loyalty," 184. She goes on: "the free development of fealty by self-discipline to social ends, and of loyalty as a particular case, may be studied in the literature of chivalry and romance."

focus is more likely the affections. The affections of the friend who displays constancy are settled, firm or resolute, invariant or unchanging. In constancy, there is little suggestion of Sturm und Drang, whereas loyalty, often a foul-weather virtue, is frequently wrenching in its demands. Loyalty is typically displayed when storms arise; constancy is as effectively shown when the weather is clear. Constancy is a quality of character that reflects internal rather than external conditions. There is, moreover, often a sustaining passionateness about loyalty that is absent from constancy. There is an evenness about constancy that is not implied by loyalty. The fickleness of inconstancy is to be contrasted with the betrayal signaled by disloyalty.

The idea of *devotion* captures the wholeheartedness frequently associated with loyalty. It is characterized by a profound, earnest, and full attachment, commitment, and dedication to some object, as suggested by its linguistic connection with the making of a vow. But the objects of devotion are not identical with the objects of loyalty. It would be odd to be loyal to some of the objects to which one may be devoted (one's work or collecting stamps, for example) .

Some authors have made a more substantive point about the respective foci of loyalty and devotion. As noted earlier, Marcia Baron believes that when the object of a loyal-like commitment is an ideal or cause, it is better to speak of devotion. Loyalty, she argues, has people as its object.[9] Certainly this account captures the associational significance of loyalty, though the fact that its personal objects are normatively constructed creates the frequently exploited space for loyalties to be subsequently transferred to values that are embedded within them.

The associational character of loyalty might incline us to think that it has close affinities with *solidarity*. As a practical matter, that is often the case. Calls for solidarity often draw on the loyalties of those to whom the appeal is made. Yet solidarity and loyalty need not have much to do with each other—at least at a conceptual level.

There are many social goals that cannot be achieved by individuals working alone and, if they are to be achieved, require the cohesive strength that a group can provide. They need, in other words, group solidarity. Solidarity is constituted neither by likemindedness nor by concern for the group as such but by the joint pursuit of certain social goals.[10] Although solidarity may be reinforced if members of the group in question also have some loyalty to it, people may demonstrate solidarity without having any loyalty to it. The associative ties that loyalty exemplifies—care for the associative

[9] Marcia Baron, *The Moral Status of Loyalty* (Dubuque, IA: Kendall/Hunt, 1984), 6. Tributes to "X, devoted husband and father" and references to what is sometimes spoken of as "Marian devotion" in Catholic theology suggest that one may be devoted to people as well as to ideals—not that Baron's formulation of the distinction rules out this possibility.

[10] See, for example, Avery H. Kolers, "Dynamics of Solidarity," *Journal of Political Philosophy* 20, no. 4 (2012): 365–383.

object as such—differ significantly from the purposive ties that solidarity exemplifies and requires. What those bound by solidarity care about is what the group is seeking to achieve, and they recognize the importance of grouping to achieve it. Such people need not care at all for the association that the solidarity group constitutes. The ends of those who constitute them are, in a sense, external to the group that is the means for achieving them. Whereas the obligations of those who are loyal members of a group is to the group itself—the ties that make it that group—the obligations of those who display solidarity are to the purposes for which the groups exists, and to the group only insofar as it is a means to achieving them.

Loyalty and *integrity* will hardly appear obvious candidates for close and friendly neighbors if we responded knowingly to the cynical remark that when an organization wants us to do right it asks for our integrity but that when it wants us to do wrong it demands our loyalty. Less jaded reflection, however, suggests that the contrast is somewhat contrived.[11] Loyalties are more than emotional attachments or complaisant yieldings to an external object. As Thomas Wren observed in regard to the police, because loyalty is itself viewed as obligatory, loyal conduct will be internal to the maintenance of a police officer's integrity rather than compromising of it.[12] If integrity is viewed—roughly—as keeping faith with one's principles (that is, remaining integrated), the duty to be loyal to fellow officers is likely to be included among those principles. To be sure, the scope of loyal obligations and their weight relative to others that a person has will need resolution. Nevertheless, integrity is here an intimate of rather than a stranger to loyalty. One's integrity will be challenged only if there is an unresolved conflict between one's duty of loyalty and other principles to which one is committed.

Joseph Raz ventures a closer relationship between loyalty and integrity when he speaks of integrity as "loyalty to one's pursuits and relationships."[13] On this understanding, loyalty to one's commitments is tantamount to maintaining one's integrity. In both cases, there is a practical perseverance in one's commitments. It makes for greater analytic clarity, however, if we distinguish loyalty from integrity. Whereas the focus in loyalty is on maintaining one's *associational* commitments, the focus in integrity is more broadly on the coherence and realization of a diverse group of

---

[11] The opposition arises in part because we construe integrity narrowly as "honesty" and police loyalty as observing "the blue wall of silence," which may often involve dishonesty. Integrity has broader meanings, and loyalty is identified only cynically with what is in effect blind or absolute loyalty.

[12] Thomas E. Wren, "Whistle-Blowing and Loyalty to One's Friends," in *Police Ethics: Hard Choices in Law Enforcement*, ed. William C. Heffernan and Timothy Stroup (New York: John Jay Press, 1985), 25–43.

[13] *The Morality of Freedom* (Oxford: Clarendon, 1986), 355. For several interpretations of the phrase "loyal to one's convictions," see Bloch, *The Concept of Our Changing Loyalties*, 52.

commitments. Here, as in other cases already noted, the complex core of loyalty has occasioned extensions in more than one direction.

But even if distinguished, loyalty and integrity are likely to be closely connected. As Raz notes, the commitments that figure in integrity will include the associational commitments that are the focus of loyalty. Jeffrey Blustein further observes that

> persons of integrity are faithful to their core commitments, to those commitments, in other words, that have a privileged status in their lives because they reflect what is most important to them and give them reasons for living. The immediate object of the commitment is a principle, cause, ideal, person, country, or the like with which they identify themselves and which they cannot betray without betraying themselves, and their commitment to the maintenance of their own integrity is parasitic on these other commitments. . . . The constitutive loyalties of persons of integrity can be relatively narrow or quite wide. Their loyalty may be to their friends, loved ones, or family; to their profession or country; or wider still, to the whole of humanity.[14]

In other words, as Wren had already noted, in maintaining our loyalties, we are also likely to be maintaining our integrity, and in maintaining our integrity, we are likely to retain our loyalties. But this does not require an identification of loyalty with integrity.

Is it possible to be disloyal without losing one's integrity? One might think not. When one betrays what is acknowledged to be an identity-conferring commitment, then along with the betrayal will also come a loss of integrity. But consider a case in which people violate *expectations* of loyalty that they do not themselves own. Suppose they give secrets to a foreign power, thus attracting the charge of disloyalty, even though they do not acknowledge any special attachment to their own country. Indeed, they may feel that their country's political system has betrayed the reasonable expectations of most of its citizens. Something like that, presumably, was true of Julius and Ethel Rosenberg and others whose ideological commitments placed them at odds with the imputed duties of their citizenship. Though they were regarded as disloyal, and perhaps rightly so to the extent that they professed otherwise, no loss of integrity may have been involved by way of a breach of personal commitment.

Do we want to say that those who should owe loyalty, but do not, act disloyally when they act to undermine the interests of the object to whom their loyalty is owed? We may, though I think that we do so by extension from cases in which loyalty is

---

[14] Jeffrey Blustein, *Care and Commitment: Taking the Personal Point of View* (New York: Oxford University Press, 1991), 231.

seriously professed but not shown. We may be reluctant to say the same in cases in which it is more controversially claimed that loyalty is owed: in such cases, we may see the charge of disloyalty simply as a moral bludgeon—a convenient way of condemning what may have been, for example, a legitimate act of whistle-blowing.

NEIGHBORHOOD DELINQUENTS

Loyalty's delinquent neighbors are well represented. There is a rich vocabulary of disloyalty, betrayal, faithlessness, infidelity, treason, treachery, and apostasy, rich enough to provide an interesting challenge to those who see something fundamentally suspect about loyalty. If loyalty is so problematic (which is not to deny that it has problems), why do we generally think so disparagingly about those who are disloyal? Where do those who can be characterized in these ways go wrong? We will later have more to say about some of these failures of loyalty. Here, though, I make a few preliminary observations concerning their conceptualization.

Disloyalty is not coextensive with *betrayal*, for one may betray without being disloyal. It is possible to betray someone unwittingly, whereas disloyalty requires a specific kind of motivation. If I convey information about a friend to someone I mistakenly believe to be friendly to that friend, I may betray the friend, though my betrayal does not constitute disloyalty.[15] I may even be negligent in conveying the information, but mere negligence does not rise to the self-servingness or self-assertion that is generally associated with disloyalty.[16]

More, however, needs to be said about the self-servingness or self-assertion involved in disloyalty. There is a better case for accusing a person of disloyalty if he professes loyalty but does not manifest it than if he makes no pretense of loyalty *even if we believe that he owes it*. The ideological traitor who professes loyalty is covering himself—protecting himself from exposure—even if the reasons for his betrayal are ideological, whereas the ideological traitor who makes no pretense of loyalty, even if we think he owes it, is not motivated by the factors that give disloyalty such a bad name. The badness of disloyalty is closely associated with the factors that motivate it.

I am resistant to making the charge of disloyalty too easily. As George Fletcher observes, "the worst epithets are reserved for the sin of betrayal" or, as I would say,

---

[15] Even here there are subtleties. The coughing child may betray *the presence of* the refugees to those who are pursuing them; the child does not betray the refugees.

[16] Judith Shklar understands betrayal much more broadly to include cases in which a conflict of loyalties or clash between loyalty and principle is resolved by giving one loyalty precedence over another or some principle precedence over a loyalty. To the extent that the person or collectivity that misses out *considers itself* betrayed, she accepts that some betrayal—albeit a morally ambiguous one—has taken place. See *Ordinary Vices* (Cambridge, MA: Belknap/Harvard University Press, 1984), 141.

disloyalty.[17] And I think we preserve that insight best if we recognize that behind disloyalty there is usually a particularly corrosive motivation—willful self-servingness or self-assertion in the context of an associational commitment rather than, say, the sacrifice of that commitment to some supposedly higher claim. That will not please those who think of ideologically based treason as a pernicious form of disloyalty—though in the worst cases some form of deception (hypocrisy) is likely to be involved rather than an open defiance of the betrayed regime.

Self-servingness may take a number of forms. At its most crass and probably most common, the disloyal person is like the corrupt person who uses public office for private gain. It differs in that what is exploited is not public office but the object of an associational bond. I betray my country, company, or friends for money. On such an account, Benedict Arnold was disloyal, but Robert E. Lee was not. It is for this reason that when whistle-blowers are accused of disloyalty, as they almost inevitably are, self-serving motives are imputed—advancement within the organization, revenge,[18] or other selfish disregard for associational bonds. But more sophisticated forms of self-assertion may also attract the charge of disloyalty. Sometimes "doing it my way" may undermine the conditions governing an associative relationship, and the self-assertion involved shows scant regard for what enables the association to survive.[19]

Apart from the general claim that disloyalty is self-servingly or self-assertively motivated, it is not easy to specify the conditions under which either disloyalty or betrayal may occur. To a significant extent, they seem to depend as much on the expectations of the parties to the association as on the broad conditions specifying the type of association. As Blustein observes:

> What constitutes disloyalty to our friends and loved ones varies from case to case, since to a large degree the bases and expectations of every friendship and love relationship are different. In general, a loyal friend does not violate the trust

---

[17] George P. Fletcher, *Loyalty: An Essay on the Morality of Relationships* (New York: Oxford University Press, 1993), 41.

[18] I distinguish revenge from vengeance. Whereas the latter is often morally motivated, my seeking revenge reflects *my hurt*.

[19] Piers Benn asks whether forgiveness may sometimes constitute disloyalty. Assume that the close relatives of a murdered person decide to forgive or at least "quasi-forgive" the murderer; see "Forgiveness and Loyalty," *Philosophy* 71, no. 277 (July 1996): 369–383. If the murderer has repented and thus affirmed the worth of the murdered person, no disloyalty may be involved. But even if it is possible for the victim to unconditionally forgive the murderer, it would constitute disloyalty for the family to offer such forgiveness in the absence of the perpetrator's repentance (382): "Loyalty to others, even when they are dead, steadfastly asserts their worth, especially against the implicit denial of such worth which is embodied in acts of murder" (381). Loyalty can be shown, even if the person is no longer with us, because the interests that were constitutive of the previous association or relationship persist after death.

established by the friendship, but the conditions under which such trust is violated cannot be spelled out in the abstract.[20]

As Blustein implies, there is more than one dimension to this variation. It may be a function not only of the type of association but also of the character or personalities of its participants. Where, as in friendship, friendships vary in their nature, depth, and quality, there may be different normative expectations. But differences of personality may also figure significantly in what is seen as a breach of trust. What one person considers as undermining his interests another may not find at all threatening. The public criticism that *A* feels undermined by may not be at all worrisome to *B*.[21]

As argued, disloyalty is critically related to the motives that one has for violating a trust—particularly those characterizable as self-serving or, more broadly, self-asserting. Concretizing them may be more difficult. Is it disloyalty if it is for what one deems a higher purpose? In what does an appropriate higher purpose consist? When David Kaczynski reported to the FBI the suspicions he had about his (Unabomber) brother, Ted, many accused him of disloyalty. Even though Ted no longer had close relations with other members of his family, it was thought that Ted had done nothing *to them* that forfeited his claim to their loyalty: it was not *for David* to go to the FBI. But this suggests what I will later challenge, namely, that the associational goods linked with familial relationships override all universalistic claims. The challenge is to distinguish the effects of mere self-assertion from those of assertions of universalistic import—motives that undermine and motives that override.

Betrayal, disloyalty, faithlessness, and so forth are general terms. But within particular associational contexts, they have their context-specific analogues and half-relatives, such as treason, sedition, adultery, idolatry, heresy, and apostasy. To some of these we return in later chapters.

NEIGHBORHOOD VALUES

As Blustein noted, associations such as friendship manifest a level of *trust* between or among those who are party to it. Maybe some level of trust is required in most human interactions—even those that exist between prison officers and their charges. But is it reasonable to see a greater level of trust operative in associations that foster bonds of loyalty? To what extent does loyalty presuppose trust and its close relative, *trustworthiness*? And what kind of trust or trustworthiness is involved?

---

[20] Blustein, *Care and Commitment*, 232.
[21] One may see some similarities between disloyalty and violations of privacy. What one person regards as violative of her morally necessary space may be untroubling to another.

Trust involves more than a prediction that others will have regard to one's interests in their dealings with one: one may be able to make such predictions on the basis of others' fear. Trust is a form of reliance on the competence and trustworthiness of the other. In trusting, one makes oneself vulnerable to them. To be trustworthy is to be disposed and competent to take into account the interests of those with whom one has dealings. For the most part, it is important that a person be willing and able to trust others (at least trustworthy others), for an inability or unwillingness to trust others is crippling in both casual and associative relations. An unwillingness to trust others tends to cripple our capacity to function as human beings. Nevertheless, trust that does not take appropriate account of the trustworthiness of its object can easily corrode into gullibility or bad faith, and displaying trustworthiness without any assessment of whether the trusted object is worthy of being trusted easily degenerates into a blind obedience.[22]

Generally, loyalty requires trust in the object of loyalty. Why be loyal to someone one does not trust? If A is loyal to B, and A cannot count on B's loyalty to A, or at least on B's regard for A's interests, why should A remain loyal to B? Is such loyalty blind? What value can the association continue to have for A if B is not to be trusted? Why should A have any obligation to remain in associative relations with B? The answers to such questions may not always be simple. Consider, for example, the case of a child who has violated his parents' trust by committing serious criminal offenses. He is charged and convicted. Does—or should—their loyalty now evaporate? It may, and in some cases maybe it should. But it might also continue, and it might be right that it do so. In pledging their continued loyalty, the parents may affirm their love for *their* son by doing what they can to assist him at trial and afterward and by assuring him that they will be waiting for him when he is released. He's *our* son, they say; we cannot give him up. It is not that they trust him—he has shown himself to be untrustworthy—but he has a certain relationship with them, and they are not prepared to deny its importance to them despite what he has done. The parents need not be in denial about what their son has done, but by virtue of their relationship to him, they see beyond this violation of their trust. In such cases, one might presume some redemptive hope on the part of the parents—that their son will eventually come

---

[22] There is a delicate balance here. Not trusting someone until she has shown herself to be trustworthy may foreclose the possibility of a worthy relationship, and not showing oneself to be trustworthy until another has shown herself to be worthy of one's trust may be equally destructive. Many relationships require a measure of vulnerability on the part of the parties involved. Reading relational signals is an important part of making one's way in the world. See also R. M. Adams, "The Virtue of Faith," in *The Virtue of Faith and Other Essays in Philosophical Theology* (New York: Oxford University Press, 1987), 9–24.

good. But it is sometimes only hope—rather than trust or even blind trust—that is operative in such cases.

Consider also the case of a defense lawyer who may be loyal to her client even though she does not trust him. The lawyer is likely to hold (1) that every one accused of a crime has a right to legal representation, (2) that she will hold what occurs in their transactions in the strictest confidence, and (3) that her representation should be zealous. The defendant's expectations of loyalty may of course go too far (if, for example, condonation of perjury is anticipated), or the lawyer's loyalty to the client may be overridden by more demanding expectations (if, for example, the defendant reveals that he plans to kill a specified other).[23] No doubt there is a consequentialist point to such professional loyalty—to maximize the attorney's ability to provide an effective defense. What the attorney needs, however, is not to trust the client but to trust that the client will convey enough to enable "the effective assistance of counsel."

No doubt some associative relationships are more dependent than others on trust in the trustworthiness of those involved. In addition, given that particular relationships tend to involve a variety of trust expectations, they may be able to survive certain systematic failures of trust. A spouse may accommodate the infidelities of a partner if the partner lives up to other associational expectations. If there are other compensating values in the relationship, a person may put up with a friend's chronic lateness, despite the friend's continued assurances that he will be there on time.

Nevertheless, as a relationship approaches the closeness of friendship, it becomes harder to see how the association can survive a lack of trustworthiness where that constitutes a pattern of significant disloyalty. A, routinely betrayed by B, may continue to see B as or call B a friend, but there is something pathological about this— perhaps A considers it important to his social persona that B be seen as a friend. It would be pushing it to say that friendship continued to exist between them. The reason is that friendship is centrally concerned with trust, and the loyalty that is integral to friendship is grounded in the trust and trustworthiness of the parties involved.

In other natural associations, such as families, loyalty may continue in the face of significant breaches of trust, just because those associations are seen as sources of distinctive and significant goods. But in artificial associations, such as corporations, which frequently foster loyalty to themselves, lack of trustworthiness by one of the parties is likely to be met by lack of trust and a loss (forfeiture) of loyalty. Mutuality is generally a feature of stable loyalties.

---

[23] See *Tarasoff v. Regents of the University of California*, 17 Cal. 3d 425, 551 P.2d 334, 131 Cal. Rptr. 14 (1976).

It is worth adverting to another way of conceiving the connection with trust. In maintaining loyalties, we help to maintain the social fabric (of trust) within which human personality—our own and that of others—may flourish. For most of us, although our interactions with others possess a certain utility, a supportive social life provides an essential context of well-being. More than that, however, we are social beings, and the society of others is for most of us a condition for our doing many of the things that we value. It is a condition not only in the sense that the cooperative trust of others is causally required if we are to achieve of our goals but also in the sense that many of our valued projects are social in character.

Such social connections are often fragile. Along with our sociality we have a tendency to self-interested advantage taking. Building and maintaining loyalties helps to secure us against self-interestedness of that kind. The fostering of loyal dispositions and the formation of various associational loyalties helps to create the fabric of social trust we need to draw on the support of others, as well as to engage them in valued forms of social intercourse. Admittedly, this does not follow from loyalty per se. Certain kinds of clannishness may be disruptive of wider social trust. We need loyalty, but we also need that loyalty to be developed in the context of acceptable associative relationships. Here we see how some loyalties may work against others, an issue to which we will later return.

A person who is disloyal cannot be trusted to sustain (certain) associational commitments in the face of self-interest and other temptations to self-assertion. Although it does not strictly follow that disloyalty in one sphere (say, the political) will indicate disloyalty in another (say, the marital), nevertheless, the fact that someone is prepared to jettison commitments for self-interested reasons in one sphere might make us concerned about what he or she would be prepared to do in other spheres. Such a person will show himself or herself to be willing to abandon acknowledged commitments to associational others for self-serving reasons.[24]

NEIGHBORHOOD AND WIDER CULTURE

I noted earlier Allen's attempt to distinguish loyalty from faithfulness by reference to the optional or nonoptional character of the associations. One is born into a family, country, or even religion and, as an automatic member, may be expected not only to fulfill the various obligations associated with it but also to be loyal to it. In such cases,

---

[24] Given earlier suggestions about loyalty *owed*, the point may need to be stated more carefully. Someone who is deemed politically disloyal may be so characterized by others even though he does not identify with the country of his citizenship. Those who, with Kim Philby, spied for the Soviet Union, were ideologically disenchanted with the West. They were traitors but probably not disloyal in the sense of being motivated by narrow self-interest or self-assertion.

loyalty, unlike mere faithfulness, bespeaks associational obligations that predate the capacities for self-assumption. It is not that one cannot develop loyalties in relation to self-assumed associations but that such loyalty, unlike faithfulness, does not presume a capacity for self-assumption at the time at which the associational connection is forged. What is more, in Allen's view, these obligations of loyalty reflect a central feature of our humanness. We are not merely creatures who enter into associations, but we are creatures of associations, particularly of those associations to which our loyalties are likely to be most readily anticipated and felt most strongly.

This suggests that loyalty has its roots in a particular conception of human sociality—one to which I have already adverted in the previous section. Human persons do not emerge from the womb fully endowed. Nor do they become so merely by surviving long enough—like seedlings that eventually grow to maturity. Mill's romantic liberal metaphor of human nature as a tree, needing only room in which to grow, is intended "to apply only to human beings in the maturity of their faculties."[25] To develop, use, and maintain their distinctive powers, humans must pass through a long and, to some extent, structured process of learning. Only so are they able to display and further the characteristic marks of personality—speech, rationality, moral sensitivity, and so on. Such learning necessarily takes place in a social environment.[26] Language is learned, emotions are shaped, will is focused and strengthened, reason is developed, and moral sensibility is cultivated largely through the complex social interactions of childhood and adolescence. Even in adulthood, our lives tend to be articulated in joint or communal projects and activities, and our satisfactions are frequently rooted in communal experience. In a very important sense, then, our *human* or *personal* identity is to be construed in social terms.

Beyond these general requirements for distinctively human life, our *individual* identities tend to be even more narrowly structured. We do not grow up to be replaceable generic persons, but as members of particular families and ethnic groups, speakers of particular languages, citizens of particular states, inheritors of a particular culture and its traditions, friends with particular people, and so on. All these particular relations, traditions, ambitions, and the like may—and generally do—become ours, not only in some possessive sense, but in the more deep-seated and constitutive sense that we conceive of ourselves in terms of them. They are not simply general

---

[25] J. S. Mill, *On Liberty*, chapters 3, 1. Nevertheless, Mill is also clear that parents and others have significant responsibilities so far as the rearing of their children is concerned.

[26] This is not simply a matter of practical necessity. It is not just that we will starve and die if we are not cared for. Rather, the qualities that constitute us not merely anthropoid but human persons have much to do with our ability to relate to others in certain ways. That is why so-called wolf children and their like are such anomalies and why we do a great wrong if we bring up a child in a cage as though it were a pet.

facts about us, as is the fact of our being members of the species *Homo sapiens*, or even specific facts about us, such as our having gray-green eyes or hairy chests, but they are things that can be and usually are represented as partially constitutive of our particular individuality. They are features of our being with which we identify ourselves.[27] Although our association with them does not ordinarily amount to losing or finding ourselves in them, it is likely that the connection will have significant normative consequences: we may have some responsibility for the acts of the associative other and feel shame or pride in what the other does.

It is to these various constitutive associations that we develop our loyalties. They are integral to our humanity and individuality, valued not only for their benefits but also because in some measure we understand and express ourselves through them. Our loyalty, insofar as it sustains our attachment to and support for them in the face of more self-assertive individualistic possibilities, serves, therefore, to secure them.[28]

It is true that among the associations to which our primary loyalties are attached will be those to which Allen says we owe our loyalty independently of our prior consent and agreement. And such attachments are generally—or at least initially—heavily freighted with sentiment. Our loyalties to them are not easily dislodged. As sexually abused children know, the secrets of their abusive relationship are not revealed without significant emotional cost. It is partly for this reason that loyalty is often construed as a natural, nonrational, irrational, or even bad faith attachment. However, that it may be corrupted in this way is not to say that it lacks a sound social rationale.

Stability is not fixity, and we should not confuse the centering and stabilizing value of loyalty with stagnation. Social structures, traditions, groups, and individuals are generally evolving, and to the extent that they conduce to the development of our individuality or that we confront them as autonomous beings, we can have some measure of control over the extent of our identification with them and therefore loyalty that we have to them. Even if, because of our loyalties, the cosmopolitanization of our reasoning is discouraged, they need not discourage it in a way that undermines the expansive capacity for deliberation that fosters cosmopolitan tendencies. Deliberation always brings with it the risk of defection, but it may also serve to renovate

---

[27] Cf. John Dewey, *Human Nature and Conduct: An Introduction to Social Psychology* (London: Allen & Unwin, 1922), 59, 80 et seq. There is, however, no implication in this that we ought to accept some social status quo. To the contrary, see also D. H. Fisher, "Loyalty, Tolerance, and Recognition: Aspects of Morality in a Multicultural Society," *Journal of Value Inquiry* 31, no. 3 (1997): 343–344.

[28] In seeing atomistic individualism as a characteristic of liberalism (*Loyalty*, 15, 11), Fletcher overlooks its strong communitarian strands. See Gerald F. Gaus, *The Modern Liberal Theory of Man* (New York: St. Martin's Press, 1983).

and strengthen the bonds we have acquired by enabling us to appreciate more adequately the value that particular associational ties have for us. As Mill recognized, unless there is opportunity for associational commitments to be tested, they will be held dogmatically rather than vitally.[29]

A liberal institution need not be the conscious creation of those who are embraced by it. Nevertheless, among the characteristics it fosters must be those reflective virtues that enable its members to review and, if necessary, reshape such an institution in response to the challenges of its broader environment. Even if loyalty to family and tribe are unselfconsciously developed through the normal processes of socialization, they can be refined and expressed remedially if they are also sites for self-development. Loyalty may keep us from jumping Theseus's ship, but it is fully compatible with measured yet extensive overhauls as we travel the high seas.

CONCLUSION

What we see from this conceptual tour through the social neighborhoods in which loyalty resides is that it has a distinctive and important role in the lives of associative beings such as ourselves. Loyalty not only reminds us of our connectedness but also operates to affirm and reinforce it. It does so in the face of internal or external influences that incline us to act in self-advantaging ways that are associatively disadvantaging. In the next two chapters, we will consider whether, given some of the problems that have already become evident—particularly in its frequently prereflective development—loyalty should be conceived of as a virtue and, if so, how it might be justified.

[29] In his powerful critique of censorship. See *On Liberty*, chapter 2.

3

STATUS

It is ironic that the virtues of loyalty, discipline, and self-sacrifice that we value so highly in the individual are the very properties that create destructive organizational engines of war and bind men to malevolent systems of authority.[1]

Stanley Milgram touches a sensitive nerve. Loyalty seems to be both revered and feared. My own sympathies, as should be clear, are more positive than negative, yet the uses to which loyalty has been put demand that we consider its status. Is it a practical disposition of no inherent worth that gains whatever value it has from the use to which it is put? Or worse, is it a disposition that, all things considered, we should seek to discourage? Can a disposition that is so easily manipulable be considered a virtue worth fostering?

In this chapter, I take some steps toward an answer to these questions by focusing, in particular, on whether loyalty can be seen as a virtue. My procedure is first to offer a broad account of the virtues and then to consider two arguments—those of R. E. Ewin and Simon Keller—designed to show that loyalty falls short of qualifying as a virtue. Then in chapter 4, I explore various rationales for its being accorded the status of a virtue.

VIRTUES

Is loyalty a virtue? There are at least two interconnected ways of interpreting the question. First, is loyalty, as an attribute of persons, the kind of attribute that could be considered a virtue? And second, if it is, is it a real virtue? The first question is

[1] Stanley Milgram *Obedience to Authority: An Experimental View* (New York: Harper, 1974), 188.

49

about the formal properties of loyalty—whether it has properties appropriate to the virtues—and the second concerns the rationale that would establish its claims as a genuine virtue. Here we will focus on the former question, leaving much of the discussion of the latter until the next chapter. To the extent that we can justify loyalty's claims as a genuine virtue, we will have gone a long way to establishing its desirability, because, whatever else we may want to say about the virtues, we regard them as excellences or goods, and a virtuous person as an admirable or good person to be.[2]

Both questions are difficult and controversial. The first gets us into some of the disputes that encouraged Hume, where possible, to avoid the term.[3] It also confronts us with the wide diversity of senses in which the term is employed: what Aristotle saw as the defining features of a virtue leaves us with a different ensemble from that delineated by Kant. The second confronts us with the broad and controversial normative assumptions that inform the inventorying of virtues. The four cardinal virtues of classical theory—justice, courage, prudence, temperance—differ strongly from the three central theological virtues, faith, hope, and love. Nietzsche assailed many traditional Christian virtues as constitutive of a "slave morality," and Hume likewise had little time for what he called the "monkish virtues."[4] I will not descend too deeply into these black holes of controversy; it is important, nevertheless, that we recognize they are there.

Should we, perhaps, advert to the tendency of those who proclaim the importance of virtue to be as much as if not more concerned with the vices? Even Aristotle, who sees virtues as means between extremes, sees virtues as hedges against vices. This may appear to ring particularly true of loyalty, where the vice of disloyalty is probably to be avoided more than the virtue of loyalty is to be cultivated. As J. L. Austin might have put it, disloyalty sometimes appears to "wear the trousers."[5]

That said, I want first to look at the virtues generally, noting their diversity and features, before considering where loyalty, to the extent that it is a virtue, might belong.

When speaking about "the virtues," we usually have the so-called *moral* virtues in mind, though classical writers in particular used the term more broadly to include

---

[2] This is not to imply that a person who had a single virtue would be a virtuous person or would be a good person to be. Whether we view the virtues equally or hierarchically, one virtue without the moderation of other virtues is likely to leave a person gravely deficient.

[3] David Hume, *An Enquiry Concerning the Principles of Morals*, ed. Tom L. Beauchamp, (Oxford: Oxford University Press, 1998), appendix 4.

[4] Hume's catalogue, which included "celibacy, fasting, penance, mortification, self-denial, humility, silence, solitude," (ibid.) did not comprehend loyalty but illustrates how dispositional practices that have the form of virtue may nevertheless be disputed as genuinely virtuous. For discussion, see William Davie, "Hume on Monkish Virtues," *Hume Studies* 25, nos. 1–2 (April–November 1999): 139–154.

[5] From J. L. Austin, *Sense and Sensibilia* (Oxford: Oxford University Press, 1962), 70.

intellectual virtues (such as thoroughness, open-mindedness, and imaginativeness). The more inclusive approach is probably to be preferred: it also spares us certain nit-picking disputes about whether a particular virtue is a moral one and what we should say about so-called moral virtues when they are exercised in nonmoral contexts. Aristotle, whose contribution to the study of the virtues remains central, linked them via *phronesis*—itself a virtue—understood as the virtue of practical wisdom. For him, the virtues constituted a cluster of character traits that are moderated and exemplified through the judgmental offices of *phronesis*.[6] Otherwise, as we will see, they may be displayed in inappropriate ways.

Virtues are excellences of character in the sense that they are partially *constitutive of* what it is good for a human to be. In the case of the moral virtues, they are also partially constitutive of human goodness. To be a good person is, inter alia, to be a virtuous person.

Collectively, the virtues will be *good for* their possessors, even though particular virtues and virtues in particular cases may not work well for their possessor even if exercised wisely. Selflessness may expose one to danger, and the courage that serves to ensure one's security may also jeopardize it.[7] This is salient to the issue of loyalty, because the loyalty that one shows to one's family or country or god may result in one's death. Nevertheless, even though it is not because of their goodness for their possessors that virtues are good, it would be strange were they not connected to human flourishing in some fairly robust way. In what way? There are several possibilities. One would be to say that each virtue is for an individual person's good, even though it may not work to that person's advantage in some particular case. A different generalization is that even if it is not true of each person that a particular virtue will be good for him or her, it is generally good for people that they acquire such virtues. Or, further, even if in particular cases the justifiable exercise of a virtue may not work for a person's good, its possession will work for the collective good. For present purposes, I doubt whether it is necessary that we resolve these (and some other) ambiguities and controversies. It is not part of my purpose to provide a comprehensive account of the virtues—just enough of an account to locate loyalty.

As well as having value for individuals, the virtues possess a social value, even though their social value does not constitute their goodness. Because of the interpenetration of individual and social life, the virtues would lose much of the value they have as constituents of individual goodness were they not also to have social value. This should probably make us skeptical of drawing too firm a division between the

[6] Aristotle, *Nicomachean Ethics*, bk. VI.
[7] As I indicate later, there may be a social dimension to this. Courage may help to secure the larger social world of which one is a part, even though one's courage (say, that of a firefighter) may jeopardize one's individual security.

so-called self- and other-regarding virtues (prudence, equanimity, and circumspection versus justice, compassion, and veracity).

I have construed the virtues as excellences of persons.[8] As such, they include character traits or dispositions to recognize certain considerations as having normative significance for decision making, as well as the disposition to act in response to this recognition. That said, there is more to the virtues than the disposition to perform virtuous actions. To be a virtuous person is to be a certain sort of person—one possessing certain interests, sensibilities, desires, attitudes, and perceptions, as well as a disposition to act in certain kinds of ways. Virtuous dispositions are deeply woven into the multiple threads of a person's life. Such character traits are constituents— albeit not immutable ones—of the identity of the person they characterize and thus provide reasons for action. Thus a courageous person is one who confronts danger in a certain way—not, say, out of a devil-may-care attitude or panic but with prudent composure.

Characterizing the virtues in this way requires that we confront problem cases in which particular virtues seem to go awry—standardly, the apparently courageous Nazi. Do we claim (1) that whatever else we want to say about the Nazi, he is not courageous; (2) that courage is not always a virtue; (3) that in cases such as this the goodness of courage is subverted by its association with other facets of the Nazi's character; or (4) that although courage is a virtue, in such cases it does not constitute a good-making characteristic? The relevance for loyalty is clear: we might as easily have said the loyal Nazi. Some writers would go further: they would not speak of a courageous Nazi, whereas they would speak of a loyal Nazi, and for this reason would not count loyalty as a virtue. We now turn to two accounts of loyalty that question its status as a virtue. Along the way, we will address the problem case we have just outlined.

LOYALTY AS LESS THAN A VIRTUE

R. E. Ewin

On the basis of his own particular theory of the virtues, R. E. Ewin argues that loyalty fails to qualify.[9] His thesis, in brief, is that although loyalty plays an important—and

---

[8] I allow that to encompass certain collectivities while remaining agnostic about how the personhood of collectivities should be unpacked.

[9] Ewin has written four articles on the topic: "Loyalty: The Police," *Criminal Justice Ethics* 9, no. 2 (Summer–Fall 1990): 3–15; "Loyalty and Virtues," *Philosophical Quarterly* 42, no. 169 (October 1992): 403–419; "Loyalties, and Why Loyalty Should be Ignored," *Criminal Justice Ethics* 12, no. 1 (Winter–Spring 1993): 36–42; and "Corporate Loyalty: Its Objects and Its Grounds," *Journal of Business Ethics* 12, no. 5 (May 1993): 387–396. I shall use the *Philosophical*

perhaps indispensable—part in the motivation of virtuous conduct, it does so without itself being a virtue. Loyalty, he writes, is to be understood as "the instinct to sociability that keeps us from the radical form of the Hobbesian natural condition, the war of each against all";[10] it functions to bind us to various others in a way that subordinates our own interests to whichever others are the object of the particular loyalty. Loyalty is a sentimental bond that "makes possible the acceptance of moral prohibitions and requirements that are generally regarded as necessary for social life. . . . If morality is the working out of peaceful relations between people, then loyalty is at the start of it."[11] But, he says, this is not sufficient to qualify loyalty as itself a virtue.

Ewin's seemingly innocuous observations, that loyalty may be well or badly placed and that once in place it is hard to shift, provide a good entrée to his position. It is, he notes, possible to be a loyal Nazi no less than a loyal friend.[12] Moreover, there is something about loyalty, once a loyalty has been formed, that hinders or discourages an assessment of its object: "to some extent, at least, loyalty requires us to suspend our own independent judgements about its object."[13] Ewin goes even further to claim that loyalty requires not merely the suspension of our judgment but even "the setting aside of good judgement. . . . Failure to follow good judgement is not just a possibility when an issue of loyalty arises; willingness *not* to follow good judgement, at least some of the time, seems to be part of what it is to be loyal."[14] If we now link this with the observation (one we have already encountered in Allen's discussion) that many of our significant loyalties (say, to family, tribe, and country) tend to be acquired in the course of early socialization and are not chosen as the result of a conscious deliberative process, we will appreciate that even at the point of their acquisition, many loyalties will not be subject to reflective review. Loyalties may easily be misplaced, and, once misplaced, they are secured against corrective scrutiny.

Quarterly article as my primary source. In an earlier book, in which he first develops his theory of the virtues, Ewin allows that loyalty is a virtue, albeit, as he notes, "an odd virtue" (*Cooperation and Human Values: A Study of Moral Reasoning*, Brighton, Sussex: Harvester Press, 1981, 177, 212). Although a few of my arguments are ad hominem (in Locke's sense, *An Essay Concerning Human Understanding*, bk. 4, ch. 17, sec. 21), I will take Ewin to be articulating a more widely held—but seldom developed—position.

[10] Ewin, "Loyalty: The Police," 4.

[11] Ibid.

[12] A point that Ewin makes against John Ladd, "Loyalty," *The Encyclopedia of Philosophy*, ed. Paul Edwards (New York: Macmillan and Free Press, 1967), vol. v, 98.

[13] Ewin, "Loyalty and Virtues," 403.

[14] Ibid., 411, 412. In "Corporate Loyalty: Its Objects and Its Grounds," he writes that "the jingoistic slogan, 'My country, right or wrong' is an extreme version of this setting aside of judgment, but some degree of it is involved in any case of loyalty" (388).

Ewin believes that these two features of loyalty undermine its virtuous pretensions, for genuine virtues are internally linked to some idea of good judgment (*phronesis*). Courage, for example, involves reasonable judgment about the risks to be taken in relation to the values to be achieved. A person "who dives from a third—floor window into a bucket of water simply to entertain his guests is foolhardy, not courageous."[15] And the person who undertakes great risks for an immoral cause shows daring rather than courage.[16] Ewin concedes that courage may sometimes lead us astray and that our courageous intervention may assist an assailant rather than his victim. But this failure differs from that associated with misguided loyalty. In the case of misplaced courageous intervention, an assessment of what would have been proper to the situation would have taken place. With loyalty, however, no such judgment is required (or even encouraged). It is promiscuous with respect to its objects. Any judgment we might make concerning the worthiness of its object will be external to the loyal support. It is not a requirement of our purported loyalty's being genuine loyalty that we have first judged it to be reasonable with respect to its object. All loyalty requires is that we lend our support.

This, Ewin contends, is not to deny that loyalty serves an important social function. As social beings, we develop through social activity, and some of the significance that our lives have for us is derived from our place within particular social frameworks. If the enterprise of becoming the particular individuals we are is to work out successfully, it is essential that we develop qualities of character appropriate to the forms of social life that we come to value. Those are the virtues. But we can develop these qualities *only because we are already drawn to each other and have a natural tendency to bond with each other*. We are not merely *social* beings, bound by contractual relations, but also *sociable* beings. "Sociability . . . is necessary to human life."[17] And such sociability, Ewin claims, is "at the core of loyalty," which he characterizes as "our willingness to stick with the group":

> Willingness to stick with the group matters because it is the rawest expression of people's social nature: without such a willingness groups would not be formed and we should all be isolated asocial atoms. The only relationships between us would be contractual relationships.[18]

Despite the importance of a "desire to be and remain with the group," it fails to constitute loyalty as a virtue, for the groups to which one belongs and the individuals

[15] Ewin, "Loyalty and Virtues," 405.

[16] Ibid., 414, 415.

[17] Ibid., 419.

[18] Ibid., 418–419. Merely contractual relationships, he reminds us—a point he argues in earlier work—fail to provide an adequate basis for human cooperation.

to whom one becomes committed may pursue nefarious as well as beneficial social goals, and we may thus just as easily acquire loyalties that are evil as those that are good. Loyalty lacks the constraint of good judgment.

There is much to commend in Ewin's account. Nevertheless, it suffers from significant deficiencies that I group under three headings.

A Defective Account of the Virtues

In the absence of a fully developed account of the virtues of my own, it may seem presumptuous to quibble with Ewin's theory of the virtues. Nevertheless, his account strikes me as misleadingly restrictive.

I accept that all the virtues embody some kind of good judgment (*phronesis*), but I dispute whether they do it in exactly the same way or whether loyalty should do it in the same way as virtues such as kindness, justice, or even courage. The virtues display considerable diversity. Take, for example, sincerity and conscientiousness. Like loyalty, these may attach themselves to unworthy causes, but they do not thereby lose their claim to be virtues. Of course, there is a question whether they are virtues when attached to bad causes or if, as virtues, they are commendable when so attached, but that is not usually enough to dissuade us from seeing them as default virtues—traits and practical dispositions that it is good for us to have. Sincerity and conscientiousness may not be the most central or substantive of the virtues ("sincerity is not enough"); nevertheless, they have an important role to play in a person's life. Wise judgment is particularly important in ensuring that they appropriately shown. Such practical wisdom, the ability to make situationally relevant judgments, comes with age and experience and helps to ensure that the sincerity and conscientiousness that are appropriate for a person to acquire are vested in appropriate tasks. The same can be said of loyalty. Practical wisdom is shown not only in determining what loyalty requires but also in ensuring that it is rightly directed.

We might advert to a distinction sometimes made between executive virtues or virtues of the will and substantive or positive virtues. Whereas the former (such as courage, patience, industriousness, tolerance, and self-control) keep us from going wrong, the latter (such as honesty, kindness, generosity, justice, compassion, and wisdom) represent ways of going right. Whereas virtues of the will safeguard us against their corresponding vices, the substantive virtues are just good things to have.[19] Add this to

[19] See Robert C. Roberts, "Will Power and the Virtues," *Philosophical Review* 93, no. 2 (April 1984): 227–247. I am currently prescinding from a further possibility, namely, that rather than representing two kinds of virtues, this distinction characterizes two rival conceptions of virtue. I am also assuming that the distinction is exclusive, an assumption that strikes me as dubious: it seems possible to see honesty, justice, and compassion, for example, as virtues that overcome some form of unacceptable partiality, and not simply as good dispositions to have.

the corrective character of virtues—what Aristotle characterized as their constituting a mean between extremes—and we get an account of loyalty that is much more congenial to its characterization as a virtue. As Philippa Foot puts it, many virtues stand "at a point at which there is some temptation to be resisted or deficiency of motivation to be made good."[20]

If we are attracted to the foregoing distinction, loyalty will best be seen as an executive virtue that secures our associational commitments and obligations against associationally destructive self-interest or self-assertion.[21] That is, it preserves our relational and associational commitments in the face of inconvenience and risk (whether generated by opposition or competition or personal circumstances), despite the personal or private advantage that there would be to our abandoning them. Loyalty is called upon and is appropriately displayed when our associational commitments conflict with narrowly personal or private interests: *fidem secunda poscunt, adversa exigunt.*[22] It is called upon, not qua loyalty, but simply as the determination to secure (or persevere in) the conditions of our association when it would be more advantageous or less costly to sacrifice the objects of our association to self-interest of a narrower kind. At the same time, unless practical wisdom is also displayed in the choice of associational objects, then loyalty—like sincerity and industriousness—may be misdirected.

An Unsatisfactory Discussion of Hard Cases

Consider Ewin's discussion of the loyal Nazi. He correctly sees that there is no contradiction in speaking of a loyal Nazi. But what follows from that? Ewin believes that whether loyalty is a good or bad thing depends exclusively on the object of the loyalty: "a loyal Nazi is a possibility but not a good thing."[23] And that disqualifies loyalty as a virtue.

In response, let us begin with the harder case of an apparently courageous Nazi. One option—Ewin's—is simply to deny the possibility: the Nazi may be daring but, because the characteristic he displays is inappropriate to its object, what he displays cannot be characterized by using the language of virtue. At first blush, this is counterintuitive. The character trait that the Nazi displays in his anti-Semitic activity is the

---

[20] Philippa Foot, *Virtues and Vices* (Oxford: Oxford University Press, 1978), 8.

[21] I shall continue to use this way of talking about the "temptations" or "deficiencies" or "passions" from which loyalty preserves us. It is not to be interpreted too narrowly, as referring to a single specific passion. But neither is it to be interpreted too broadly, such that every interest of ours is understood as an expression of self-interest and every assertion of ours is understood as an assertion of self.

[22] "Prosperity asks for fidelity; adversity exacts it" (Seneca, *Agamemnon*, l. 934).

[23] Ewin, "Loyalty and Virtues," 411.

same character trait he would display in defending his child against a marauding wolf pack or in rescuing an injured German civilian under fire. That is, he shows prudent composure in a situation that elicits fear. In the latter cases, it would constitute courage, and in one of them at least, he does it qua Nazi. Does it become something else— such as daring—just because the object is undesirable? Perhaps we would argue so were the Nazi himself to give a different normative characterization to his object. Were he to see his conduct under the description of bigotry or murder, neither he nor we would see it as an appropriate site for the virtue of courage. When one recognizes oneself as doing something one ought not to be doing, then we are unlikely to see any room at all for the virtuous doing of it. But of course the Nazi does not see what he is doing in that way. He believes his cause to be righteous. However, it does not follow that we who see what he is doing as wrong cannot regard him as courageous, even if perversely so.

To relieve the pressure on courage, Ewin's strategy is to suggest that we might characterize the Nazi's conduct as daring, a less positive characteristic. But daring is not a less positive version of courage: the person who is daring *embraces* danger, something that the display of courage does not require.[24] Daring is not merely a less positive characteristic; it is a different one.

A second option sees courage in much the same way that Ewin views loyalty— as good or bad, depending on the object or circumstances of its manifestation. At first blush, there are problems with this in both cases. If courage is a virtue, is its expression not always virtuous, at least insofar as that to which it is applied is characterizable as courageous? When used to further the Nazi cause, even though it may have the effect of multiplying the evils associated with that cause, does it stop being virtuous? Do we want to say that it is not a virtue in the Nazi, because of the context in which he manifests it, or is it rather that any virtue may be perverted? A sincere Taliban may wreak more moral havoc than one who is moved by crass political considerations. Although being an *x* person, where *x* refers to some virtuous character trait (say, loyalty, courage, or conscientiousness), may not be sufficient to qualify one as a good person, because one may also need to be *y* and *z* (say, tolerant and compassionate), is it plausible to see *x*-ness as having a variable value, depending on what it is associated with?[25] Perhaps: we shall return to this.

---

[24] Even on his own account, Ewin seems to draw the wrong conclusion. The virtues involve good judgment. Courage involves reasonable judgment about the risks to be taken in relation to the values to be achieved. The courageous Nazi may have distorted understanding of the value that he is seeking to achieve, but his judgment about the risks in relation to those particular values may be quite reasonable (in a means-end sense). This is not like the foolhardy person who dives off the high tower into a pail of water.

[25] Lurking behind all this are problems about the unity, singularity, and compatibility of the virtues that (for now) I wish to dodge until chapter 7. There is an ambiguity in the reference to "the unity of the virtues." Reference to "the singularity of the virtues" generally picks out the

A third option would allow that the Nazi is genuinely courageous—as he may be loyal—but claims that the goodness of his being courageous is outweighed by the evil of his commitment to a hateful program. Like a sincere, conscientious, reliable, or industrious Nazi, the courageous or loyal Nazi goes about being what he is in a certain way. His devotion to evil ends does not detract from his goodness in respect of his having these other traits; instead, we focus on the more substantive evil of his Nazism. Linda Zagzebski puts it this way: Were the courageous Nazi to repent of his evil cause, he would have less moral distance to travel in becoming a good person than if he were not courageous.[26]

Zagzebski's point can be granted. But the argument to which it is yoked underplays the way in which the Nazi's courage exacerbates (and is not merely outweighed by) the evil of his anti-Semitic cause. His courage makes his criminality more potent, not less. Is it enough to argue that if we distinguish the evil of what he does from his evilness in doing it, the virtuousness of his courage will not be compromised, because it is in his commitment to Nazism, not in his courage that his evilness resides? No. The fact that the Nazi cause is furthered by his courageously doing what he does indicates that something has gone seriously awry when courage is associated with such ends.

A fourth option would allow that courage or loyalty is always a virtue but argues that in some cases it is not praiseworthy. It is not praiseworthy because, although it reflects the characteristics that make it the particular virtue it is, its application is unwise. On this view, we would not praise the Nazi qua Nazi for his courage or loyalty, even though courage and loyalty as virtues are ordinarily praiseworthy. Gregory Trianosky, who adopts something like this view, claims that a (moral) virtue is a "normative power"—a trait that has a "potential for contributing to the overall moral worth of the life of its possessor."[27] But whether it actually does so will depend on the context of its expression. Foot makes the similar point that, though a virtue, courage may not be a virtue in a particular person because of the ends to which it is directed.[28] Although it is right to see particular virtues as having features that give them their distinctiveness, their object as well as their form needs *phronesis*. This

doctrine that each virtue includes the others such that they all reduce to one. "The compatibility of the virtues" refers to the doctrine that no virtue, properly understood, will come into conflict with any other virtue. I am myself somewhat drawn to a version of the unity of the virtues that might be dubbed the "complementarity of the virtues," namely, that to be adequately realized, the virtues need to modify or constrain each other.

[26] Linda Zagzebski, *Virtues of the Mind: An Inquiry into the Nature of Virtue and the Ethical Foundations of Knowledge* (Cambridge: Cambridge University Press, 1996), 93–95.

[27] Gregory W. Trianosky, "Virtue, Action, and the Good Life: Toward a Theory of the Virtues," *Pacific Philosophical Quarterly* 68, no. 2 (June 1987): 133.

[28] Foot, *Virtues and Vices*, sect. 3.

option harks back to Aristotle's distinction between natural and full or complete virtues, the former constituting the building blocks of the latter.[29] Although Aristotle tends to treat the former as instinctive rather than underdeveloped, the distinction captures something that is probably true of all the virtues. We acquire them as part of our early upbringing, but only later do we acquire the *phronesis* that will enable us to employ them wisely. This is particularly—though not exclusively—true of some of our important loyalties, which are acquired early, before we have the discretion to manifest them wisely.

On this account, although a Nazi who showed courage in rescuing his daughter might reasonably be praised for it, this would not be the case when it was shown in rounding up Jews. In characterizing him as a courageous person, we want to annotate it in some way lest it be taken as unqualified praise. Although he is a better person because he possesses rather than lacks courage, it would be better still were his courage associated with worthwhile ends. Were the Nazi's political activities the only context in which he displayed courage, we would consider it pathological.

Although I am drawn to this fourth option, it is only as the least problematic one. Ewin himself is troubled by his recourse to the second option and shows some ambivalence when he comes to discuss the case of a disloyal (and cowardly?) Nazi—one who reneges on his commitment to exterminate Jews and Gypsies. Is it good or bad to be a disloyal Nazi? Is a disloyal Nazi one whose disloyalty is good because Nazism is such a bad thing, or is a disloyal Nazi one who has all the evil associated with being a Nazi plus the added one of being disloyal? We should expect Ewin to opt for the former rather than the latter: if the goodness or badness of loyalty depends on its object, one would also expect that to be true of disloyalty. But in fact Ewin favors the latter. He says of the disloyal Nazi that "his disloyalty is one reason we should never trust him even if later he willingly comes over to our side. He is the sort of person who might sell us out, too, since he has previously shown a willingness to sell out what he believes in."[30] So if disloyalty is an additional minus, why is loyalty not a virtue, albeit one that is not commendable when associated with Nazism?

Ewin is not oblivious to the problem, for he adds a qualification: whether the Nazi's disloyalty should be seen as an added minus will depend on *why* he was disloyal. If it was for self-serving reasons, the disloyalty *will* be a further strike against him. But if, on the other hand, the Nazi

is disloyal because, despite his convictions, he is, as he sees it, weak-willed and squeamish and simply cannot stand the thought of putting all those Jews and

---

[29] Aristotle, *Nicomachean Ethics*, bk. VI, ch. 13.
[30] Ewin, "Loyalty and Virtues," 404.

Gypsies into gas chambers, then his disloyalty reflects the presence in him of some virtue, even if of an incompletely formed virtue that he does not want to admit to.[31]

As it stands, the explanation fails to convince. If the problem is weakness of will, it is just as likely to manifest itself should he come over to "our side." He is in no fundamentally different position from the person who sells out the party for private gain. And squeamishness by itself does not help. Were the Nazi's squeamishness to have arisen from his recognition that innocent human beings were being murdered, it might reflect well on him. But squeamishness may have various sources, only some of which express moral sensitivity. Does the fact that I would be squeamish about being an executioner show an inchoate recognition that what I am doing is wrong, even if I believe that someone is a vicious killer who deserves to die? Would my being squeamish about killing a chicken, mouse, or cockroach or picking up a dead spider express a belief that it was wrong to do any of these things? Whether it is good not to do these things seems to be separable from any mere feelings of squeamishness. More needs to be said.

Let us grant what may be suggested by Ewin's wording, that although the Nazi is committed to his position, his squeamishness and failure to follow through on his anti-Semitic purposes reflect an underlying humanitarianism. Does this manifest disloyalty of a good kind? In cases in which people are conflicted like this, it is very difficult to know how to describe their conduct. Nevertheless, I would be reluctant speak of the Nazi's acts as disloyal—even though other Nazis might well characterize them in that way. This is because—like murder and unlike lying—disloyalty functions as a sufficiently closed moral concept[32] to incline us to handle apparent exceptions by redescribing them rather than merely qualifying them. Graham Greene notwithstanding, acting disloyally is just about always wrong and, when prompted by moral considerations, what would otherwise be characterized as disloyal is not appropriately characterized in this way.[33] Moreover, loyalty and disloyalty are not exclusive opposites. Those whose conduct forfeits our loyalty, so that we now refuse to stand by them as a loyal person would, cannot—simply by virtue of that—complain of our disloyalty. Only in cases in which our failure to stand by them, when it might be expected of us, is motivated by self-regarding or idiosyncratic concerns will the absence of loyalty properly constitute disloyalty. The Nazi who is moved by an underlying humanitarianism not to carry through with his

---

[31] Ibid., 418.

[32] See infra, note 39, and accompanying text.

[33] Graham Greene's celebration of "the virtue of disloyalty" is better seen as a defense of Socratic gadflyism than of disloyalty.

genocidal responsibilities is not pandering to self-interest or a private vision but is torn, however inchoately, between commitments, and he must choose which to honor.

Ewin feels the weight of the case against disloyalty, because in a later article he does not hesitate to say that disloyalty is *always* a vice.[34] But to sustain this claim and avoid the implication that loyalty is a virtue, he asserts that in the case of disloyalty a *further* vice is also involved. Thus, a person who leaves a firm to take up a better offer elsewhere is not disloyal *unless* he also steals his old firm's commercial secrets or does something else of a despicable nature.[35] It is only by virtue of his dishonesty (or whatever) that his lack of loyalty is to be characterized as disloyalty: "we will consider something to be disloyalty only if it can also be described as *another* vice too."[36] I do not know what to make of this. Is the disloyal person guilty of one or two vices, in the case in question, of both dishonesty and disloyalty, or of only one vice, dishonesty, which, because of the circumstances in which it occurs, can also be characterized as disloyalty? This is not quite the same as a case of dishonesty, which, because of the circumstances in which it occurs, also reflects ingratitude (stealing from one's parents). Ingratitude can stand as a vice in its own right. But leaving aside this puzzle, it is to be doubted whether disloyalty is always partnered by another vice or, when it is, whether its vicious character is parasitic on the other vice. A friend who deliberately passes to my enemy (publicly available) information about me, so that the enemy can take advantage of me, need not do anything that is improper beyond being disloyal; if that disloyal friend also tells lies about me, that displays a further vice; it is not the vice that makes the disloyalty vicious.

Loyalty and the Sacrificium Intellectus

Ewin states that loyalty requires a suspension or setting aside of good judgment and that any judgments we make about the worthiness of objects of loyalty are essentially external to the loyalty.

Loyalty certainly requires a sacrifice of convenience, some subordination of private vision, or risk to well-being. But this does not amount to a sacrifice of good judgment. A courageous act may also involve inconvenience or risk taking. In the case of courage, we judge the ends as worth the inconvenience or risk. Is this not also the case with loyalty, in which the objects of certain associations are judged sufficiently

---

[34] Ewin, "Corporate Loyalty," 387–388.

[35] This is much too strong. If loyalty has been expected and/or professed, all that is really required for considering leaving for another job as disloyalty is that it be seen as detrimental to the firm's interests.

[36] Ewin, "Corporate Loyalty," 388. Ewin acknowledges in a footnote that this is "a piece of speculation" for which he "leaves the reader to try examples."

worthwhile to warrant a cost to immediate self-interest or private assertion? Good judgment is not exhausted by the claims of self-interest or prudence. Ewin gives the example of an employee whose loyalty is expected to manifest itself in a willingness to stick with the firm in both good *and* bad times, and not only in good times but also when better times are elsewhere to be had:

> In the world of commerce, in which one would think it appropriate that judge-ment be exercised on commercial grounds, the loyal executive sticks with the company even when a better job offer comes along from another company; and if it is a better job offer then good commercial judgement would dictate that he take it. Failure to follow good judgement is not just a possibility when an issue of loyalty arises; willingness *not* to follow good judgement, at least some of the time, seems to be part of what it is to be loyal.[37]

This mistakenly assumes that an appropriate decision about whether to stay with a firm is a simple matter of self-interested calculation. Not that Ewin makes it a matter of economic calculation simpliciter; nevertheless, in making such decisions a relatively narrow form of self-interest or advantage is taken to be the predominant consideration. But the decision to stay with a firm not only will ordinarily include self-interested benefits but also will be influenced by the values that the executive holds and wishes to be maintained when making decisions of this kind. There are values served by remaining where one is despite the advantages of moving (a com-mitment to what the firm is about and recognition of the effect that one's leaving may have on the firm's success, viability, and so forth), and these may justify the execu-tive's loyally remaining where he is. This is not a sacrifice of good judgment, but a form it can take.

But even if we accept that an executive who sticks with the firm sacrifices a cer-tain measure of economic and other self-interest, it is no part of the internal logic of loyalty that radical self-sacrifice is required. As we will see in chapter 7, there is an implicit proportionality between the object of loyalty and the demands that loyalty appropriately makes of us, in just the same way as we might see propor-tionality between the object of courage and the courage that might be expected of us.

I therefore disagree with Ewin's claim that an important difference between loy-alty and his paradigmatic virtues is that whereas we no longer speak of dispropor-tionate courage as courage but as rashness or foolhardiness, we are still prepared to refer to excessive and blind loyalty as species of loyalty. I doubt whether our rich

---

[37] Ewin, "Loyalty and Virtues," 411–412.

vocabulary of "virtuous excess" can be used to draw such conclusions.[38] I may not speak of someone as excessively courageous; however, there is no barrier to judging someone to be generous or kind to a fault or overly solicitous or conscientious. And as Portia recognized, a justice not tempered with mercy is excessive even if no less just for that reason.[39] If a person expresses a particular virtue to a disproportionate degree, it does not automatically become something else.

Even more to the point, whether a virtue incorporates good judgment loosely or tightly has more to do with the ways in which we have differentiated our vocabulary of the virtues than with a particular disposition's status as a virtue. Value concepts vary in their openness. Consider the ways in which we characterize act-kinds: both *murder* and *lying* normatively characterize the act-kinds with which they are associated. But whereas murder is a closed moral concept, lying is much more open.[40] If a killing is thought to be justified, we do not use the vocabulary of murder but of homicide. White lies, on the other hand, have an established place in our moral vocabulary. Though lies are bad, we signal a qualification of their default disvalue by characterizing them as white. So, too, with loyalty, which, as with sincerity and conscientiousness, can be excessive, misplaced, or blind without losing some of the characteristics that make it a virtue. In some cases, our concepts are so open that we simply allow the context to provide the normative corrective—the person who steals an enemy's secrets is not ipso facto thought to have done something wrong.

Finally, although Ewin focuses on the good judgment internal to the virtues, we should not overlook the responsiveness of loyalty to external judgments. If it is brought to a person's attention that his loyalty has been placed in an object that is unworthy of it, he may be brought to see the object as no longer deserving of his loyalty. If it is brought to someone's attention that some object is worthy of loyalty, loyalty might be said to be deserved or owed. Loyalty's openness to the acceptance of judgments concerning an object's worthiness strongly suggests that it is grounded in certain normative presumptions about its objects and, moreover, tied to deliberation.[41] It is no part of the logic of loyalty that we shield our loyalties from appraisal,

---

[38] Gary Watson, "Virtues in Excess," *Philosophical Studies* 46, no. 1 (1984): 57–74. Cf. Montaigne: "Those who say, there is never any excess in virtue, forasmuch as it is not virtue when it once becomes excess, only play upon words" (*Essays*, trans. Charles Cotton, ed. William Carew Hazlett [1877], vol. vi, ch. 29, "Of Moderation," www.gutenberg.org/files/3586/3586.txt).

[39] Shakespeare, *The Merchant of Venice*, act iv, sc. 1. Or consider Jean Racine: "Une extrême justice est souvent une injure" (*La Thébaïde ou Frères ennemis*, act iv, sc. 3).

[40] The distinction between open and closed moral concepts is developed by Julius Kovesi, *Moral Notions* (London: Routledge & Kegan Paul, 1967).

[41] Once again, these normative presumptions need not embody values "from a neutral point of view."

though the circumstances in which we form loyalties may sometimes make their appraisal psychologically difficult, and, in the absence of specific reasons to the contrary, it is not incumbent on us to subject them to scrutiny. What occupies professional philosophers need not burden every liberal person. If, perhaps too often, we refuse to expose our loyalties to critical appraisal, that is a deficiency in ourselves—in *our* loyalties, not in loyalty.

Simon Keller

Like Ewin, Keller begins with the emotive dimension of loyalty and develops his account of displays of loyalty out of that. As we have seen already, he characterizes loyalty as "the attitude and associated pattern of conduct that is constituted by an individual's taking something's side, and doing so with a certain sort of motive: namely, a motive that is partly emotional in nature."[42]

I have already indicated some of my reservations regarding this account—in particular, that although Keller rightly sees in loyalty a "pattern of conduct," he sees it only as *associated* with an "attitude" that he construes as loyalty's core. Moreover, whether the motive for acting loyally is "partly emotional in nature" has some contingency about it: when I take my friend's side because he is my friend, my motivation may or may not be partly emotional. To the extent that it is, it is likely that this will simply reflect the degree to which my identification with the object of loyalty is an emotional one. I return to this point because, as with Ewin, how one initially conceives of loyalty has important implications for the problems that are said to beset it and the status it is ultimately accorded. In chapter 1, I sought to provide an account of loyalty that is rich enough to accommodate its core cases; Keller, on the other hand, provides an account that is thin enough to comfortably accommodate every case in which we might want to speak of it. Whereas Keller sees questions about the value or virtuousness of loyalty as independent of an account of what it involves, I see the normative and definitional considerations as intertwined.

That said, Keller explicitly takes up the issue of loyalty's value and virtuousness. He structures his argument round three concerns—whether loyalty is a value, whether it is a virtue, and the credibility of communitarian arguments for according it some form of normative centrality. I briefly track these arguments before responding to them.

(1) *Loyalty's value*: First, that loyalty *can* be valuable Keller does not deny. Indeed, he goes so far as to say that "we should be very happy that we do not live in a world

---

[42] Simon Keller, *The Limits of Loyalty* (Cambridge: Cambridge University Press, 2007), 21; cf. also 152.

without loyalty."[43] But loyalty's being valuable does not make it a value. Even if loyalty is a value, it may be only one value among others and, in some cases, should give way to other values. Indeed—and this bears on his central point about loyalty being valuable without having value—in many cases, loyalty generates from within itself the competing values that detract from it. Thus, insofar as loyalty disposes us to bad faith by tempting us to compromise epistemic integrity, we have a reason for not considering it valuable for its own sake.

Keller recognizes that many consider loyalty an intrinsic value, along with health, happiness, equality, respect, justice, integrity, beauty, and truth.[44] He contends, however, that whatever we find valuable in loyalty we can have without valuing loyalty. His argument is revealing. It turns in part on his parsing of two responses to the following situation. A distressed friend calls late at night, asking you to pick her up and drive her home. You agree to do so, despite the considerable inconvenience involved. On one account, you are moved by the fact that she is your friend, and you do not wish her to be placed in harm's way. On the other account, as someone who values loyalty, you realize that loyalty demands that you assist her. Here, Keller observes, you treat loyalty as a value, whereas in the former case you act "for the sake of your friend, not for the sake of loyalty."[45] Although Keller acknowledges that on the second reading you may still be said to have acted loyally when you act for the sake of your friend, nevertheless, because you do not act out of loyalty, you therefore need not treat loyalty as a value. As I have previously argued, however, valuing loyalty does not require having it in mind as the motive for one's action at the time of acting. Just as the person who acts courageously or generously does not have it in mind that he is acting courageously or generously in so acting, so, too, the person who acts loyally does not usually have it in mind that he is acting loyally (or out of loyalty) when doing so. Indeed, the person who has it in mind that he is acting out of loyalty is the person for whom loyalty to the object may not have deeply embedded itself. Valuing loyalty for its own sake does not require valuing loyalty as a motive. In this case, what we value in valuing loyalty is the friend with whom we are in relationship and to whom we seek to be responsive when our relationship is put to the test. In that our loyalty consists.

In a similar vein, Keller argues that to enjoy what is valuable about loyalty we need not value loyalty. The example he provides—friendship—is, I believe, particularly ill-suited to his case. He notes how, in a mutual friendship, each friend values the other, does things for the other, and is probably improved by the association.

---

[43] Ibid., 145.
[44] Ibid., 147. He does not intend this as an uncontroversial list.
[45] Ibid., 148.

Each, moreover, may reflect on the general value that friendship has for those who participate in friendships. But in doing so, he suggests, "valuing friendship [as well as a particular friendship] is not the same as valuing loyalty, even though friendship essentially involves a kind of loyalty."[46] It is not the same, but if one did not value friendship—or a particular friendship—one would not value the loyalty that this form of association embodies. Although one might want to argue that one does not value loyalty as such because one does not value it in other relationships—civic, organizational, and commercial—that is not to say that it is not valued for its own sake in the relationships in which one does value it. It would be odd to say: "Not only do I not value loyalty in civic, organizational, and commercial relationships, I do not value it in friendship either." True, it would also be odd were friendship the only relationship in which loyalty was valued. Although loyalty as we find it in varied relational and associational contexts differs in significant ways—as indeed the associational connections differ in significant ways—it is something of a stretch to think that loyalty is so thin that it is not valued in itself in many of the other relationships in which it is found.

The fact that our loyalty can be given to objectionable causes weighs with Keller as it does with Ewin. There is nothing about the loyalty of a Nazi to be valued for its own sake. But the conclusion does not follow without further argument. The mere fact that loyalty can be given to objectionable causes no more shows it to be lacking in value than the fact that sincerity, conscientiousness, and generosity lack intrinsic value because they can be shown toward inappropriate objects. What is by default a value may lose it when inappropriately displayed.

(2) *Loyalty's virtuousness*: Second, in his critique of loyalty as a virtue, Keller correctly recognizes that referring to someone as loyal simpliciter is odd—loyalty is generally vested in some associative object. Nevertheless, attributing loyalty to someone may be a way of indicating that she generally takes her associational connections seriously and can be depended on to fulfill their expectations. Should we encourage such a trait in the same way that we might want to encourage honesty and fortitude? Keller thinks not—though once again the plausibility of his position depends substantially on the plausibility of his initial understanding of loyalty. He doubts whether he would want his child to acquire the character trait of loyalty because, as he puts it, someone who has that trait "sounds a little too much like someone who is undiscriminating, and whose emotional attachments to particular entities play too much of a role in determining how she will live her life."[47] So conceived, loyalty differs substantially from the account I have offered in which it is construed as perseverance

---

[46] Ibid., 150.
[47] Ibid., 157.

in an intrinsically valued association in the face of self-serving alternatives. No doubt loyalty as I have construed it will sometimes go wrong because of ill-chosen associational relations. Nevertheless, the disposition to persevere in such circumstances is worth acquiring. Along with it, no doubt, we should learn discretion (*phronimos*) in the associative bonds we form and retain. We should be no less discriminating about the objects of our loyalty than about the objects of our generosity. As I have already suggested, loyalties may be forfeited because the objects of our loyalty show themselves to be unworthy of it or, alternatively, we may adopt an oppositional role in loyalties that we deem to be justified overall. What is critical to the nurture of children is not whether they develop a capacity for loyalty (and, presumably, certain loyalties) but that they develop a whole range of virtues that will moderate one another. We want them to develop discretion, tolerance, fairness, temperance, courage, and integrity as well as loyalty. Keller states that "to be loyal by nature is to be inclined to form loyalties just for the sake of having loyalties,"[48] but that is no more correct of loyalty than of other virtues—courage and tolerance may be equally problematic if not accompanied by wisdom or moderated by other virtues.

To Keller's credit, he does not find much to admire in the person who is completely lacking in loyalty—"who has no feelings of loyalty, does not value loyalty, is not loyal to anything."[49] He believes that we should feel sorry for such a person, though he suggests that whether being devoid of loyalty should be seen as a *moral* failure might depend on the story we tell about how that came to be. He imagines a situation in which a person develops a strong sense of right and wrong; is well-meaning, generous, and compassionate; and motivated by universal values but lacking in the kind of special relationships that are breeding grounds for loyalties. Though we may wish not to be such a character, we could have no justifiable moral complaint: "He could be a conscientious and upright member of the moral community, a person with whom you can deal—if not a person with whom you can be friends."[50] As Aristotle would observe, however, lacking a capacity for friendship seriously limits one's ability to have a good life. Such a person, moreover, would also be deprived of many other special relationships—familial and tribal bonds, bonds to a profession or to organizations of which he might be a member, bonds to local community and country, all capable, even if not unreservedly, of enriching one's human experience.

(3) *Loyalty and human associativeness*: Third, some of my latter arguments draw on considerations that Keller seeks to accommodate in a chapter on "communitarian arguments for the importance of loyalty." These were largely bracketed in his

---

[48] Ibid., 158.
[49] Ibid., 158.
[50] Ibid., 160.

discussion about the value and virtuousness of loyalty that, he considers, absent the communitarian arguments, to be merely "presumptive." Yet, given my understanding of loyalty as a critical associative virtue, these so-called communitarian arguments are central. Or, perhaps better, some understanding of the importance of associational life to human flourishing and morality is critical to understanding loyalty's importance. I say "perhaps better" because, although Keller appreciates the significance of communitarian considerations to the case for loyalty, he construes them in ways that leave the loyalist short.

Briefly, he advances and critiques four arguments:[51] (1) *The Argument from the Metaphysical Self*, which holds that, because we are constituted by our membership in various communities, failure to be loyal to them would amount to self-alienation; (2) *The Argument from the Ethical Self*, which holds that, because our moral consciousness is developed within and articulated through a particular community, failure to develop loyalty to that community will result in moral collapse; (3) *The Empirical Argument*, which holds that people who lack loyalty to their communities are likely to be alienated from themselves and others; and (4) *The "Morality as Loyalty" Argument*, which holds that morality is a matter of loyalty to others as members of some group or other.

This is not the place to provide a detailed review of Keller's arguments. I agree with a good deal of what he claims, though I think that there runs through his critique of each a similar deficiency—what I have characterized as an overly thin conception of loyalty as primarily an "emotional attachment."[52] Let me illustrate. In relation to "the argument from the metaphysical self" Keller argues that it fails because "it moves too quickly from the claim that humans are essentially members of particular communities to the claim that humans are alienated or self-denying if they are not loyal to those particular communities." He goes on to point out that "there are ways in which a person can be fully aware and accepting of her membership of a community without being loyal to it."[53] Now, it is certainly true that from mere membership of a particular community—say, growing up in an Iowan town in the United States—one need not be alienated from oneself if one feels no attachment to the town, the state, or even the United States. One may come to see the town as rigid and intrusive, the state as backward and insular, and the country as arrogant in its exceptionalism. Such a person will not be alienated from herself even though no loyalty is felt toward the communities. Indeed, she may think that loyalty to the communities of which she is a member would be self-alienating. If there is a sound basis for these views about the

---

[51] Ibid., chap. 8.
[52] Ibid., 180.
[53] Ibid., 164–165.

places of one's membership, we might think the person justified in not recognizing any bond of loyalty to them. If there is no basis for such views, however, and these *are* communities of identity, we might wish to argue that people who acknowledge no loyalty display some form of moral deficiency. Such people will fail to acknowledge their metaphysical debts to the communities that have been formative of the persons they have become. They will feel no obligation to vote or participate in civic or state activities and no interest in defending or otherwise contributing to the country of their citizenship. The associations to which they owe their being and identity have no existential claim on them. It is not simply that they lack an emotional tie to their communities. Even if they feel some sort of emotional tie, they do not express it in the communal obligations that come from being formed by the communities of which they are a part. Loyalty is constituted by perseverance in the associational ties (and attendant obligations) that develop through membership in such formative communities. In such cases, loyalty should be a natural outgrowth of the intrinsic valuing of that with which one has come to identify as one's own. What Keller fails to accommodate is the fact that one's community may be conceived of in more than one way and that whereas mere membership may not lead to self-alienation in the absence of loyalty, identification in the absence of loyalty is likely to involve self-alienation.

It is appropriate to conclude with a comment on Keller's view about the status of disloyalty. Unlike Ewin, who has to account for the uniform vice of disloyalty, Keller believes that just as loyalty may sometimes be bad, disloyalty may sometimes be good. Whistle-blowers provide him with the opportunity to argue that disloyalty may sometimes be justified. The justified whistle-blower can claim that the company whose confidential information she disclosed "did not deserve [her] loyalty," meaning not that she was "not really disloyal" but that her disloyalty was justified.[54] Our intuitions differ. I argue (later at greater length) that the whistle-blower can reasonably claim that because the company had forfeited its claim to her loyalty, she was not acting disloyally. This is implicit in the common attempt in which, to show the disloyalty of whistle-blowers (and *therefore* their moral wretchedness), whistle-blown companies seek to associate such whistle-blowing with self-serving or other base motives. Their response to whistle-blowing is to discredit the messenger. As I have argued, what is distinctive about disloyalty and differentiates the disloyal person are the operative motives for the associational breach. Disloyalty, as Keller argues at length, affronts a normative relational expectation. It can be canceled, however, if the associational other, by being unwilling to address its breach of the public trust, has violated the understanding that underwrote the association. The whistle-blower no longer owes it her loyalty. That is not disloyalty, even justified disloyalty.

---

[54] Ibid., 202.

CONCLUSION

Not only does loyalty satisfy the formal requirements of a virtue but also it operates like a virtue, serving, as many virtues do, as a check on tendencies that interfere with our interactions with others. In particular, it counters tendencies to self-assertion in associative relations that are important to our flourishing. Insofar as we enter into associative relations that are morally suspect, loyalty may come to have a more problematic cast. I have, however, argued that one source of its seemingly problematic character—conceiving of it as primarily an emotive bond—undercharacterizes it and fails to appreciate some of the conceptual and moral resources that are available to those who are loyal. Moral hazards there are, but not insuperable ones.

4

RATIONALE

Loyalty . . . tends to unify life, to give it centre, fixity, stability.[1]

I have sought to defend loyalty against critics who see its core as an emotional attachment and have argued, on the contrary, that loyalty has a good claim to being a virtue. This, however, may not be enough, given the diversity and contestability of various catalogues of virtues. Nietzschean virtues do not sit comfortably with Christian ones, and so we need to consider what might inform the virtues and whether the supposed virtuousness of loyalty is sustainable within the broadly liberal framework that I have presumed. As noted in the introduction, a number of writers have expressed doubts about the compatibility of loyalty and liberalism, thus contributing to its problematic character.

The self-assertion or self-interest that loyalty curbs is not inherently wrong. In many contexts, self-interest is a perfectly acceptable reason for action: indeed, the furtherance of our personal interests and ambitions is an important ingredient in our flourishing as humans. Loyalty, however, constrains self-interested conduct, and it is reasonable to ask why. Why should I put myself out to help a friend, defend my country, advance my profession, preserve my ethnic heritage, or serve my corporation? We already have some clues in the generally social nature of human life and flourishing, and the formation of identities, but in this chapter, I want to develop my account in contrast to several others that have gained traction. Among these alternative accounts are those that justify loyalty as a debt of gratitude, as necessary to the preservation of socially useful institutions, as a self-protective mechanism that secures institutions that have become part of one's identity, as owed to associations as a matter of fair play, or as an expression of a natural duty to support just institutions.

[1] Josiah Royce, *The Philosophy of Loyalty* (New York: Macmillan, 1908), 22.

I reject these accounts and argue instead that the associational ties that claim our loyalty are valued for what is considered to be their inherent worthwhileness and not because they are owed or because of some individual or social benefit they secure. The point is not that a person must consciously have the worthwhileness of the association in mind but that, if pressed on her maintenance of the association, that person will point to the intrinsic value it has *for her*: this is *my* friend, *my* profession, and *my* country.

It is not that the associations to which we are loyal lack benefits for us or that we do not owe them anything, but that loyalty and its obligations do not concern such benefits or other obligations of institutional membership. Loyalty is concerned with the intrinsic (rather than merely instrumental) value that the objects of certain associational ties have or have come to have for us. The other arguments, even if they are successful in establishing institutional obligations, fail to establish the obligations that we associate with loyalty.

The first three arguments are commonly advanced in discussions of political obligation, and in that context, they are often criticized. But they might also be advanced as arguments for (political) loyalty, or patriotism. As arguments for political obligation, they fail for a variety of reasons, but as arguments for (political) loyalty, they fail for essentially the same reason—namely, their failure to distinguish between what one may be politically obligated to do and obligations of political loyalty.

THE DUTY OF GRATITUDE

The idea that obligations of loyalty are properly expressions of gratitude gets much of its plausibility from a consideration of our involvement in what are generally experienced as beneficial associations—family, tribe, and state. By the time we can reflect on such connections, we are likely to be told that much of what we have and are is the result of what they have contributed and that therefore we owe some self-sacrificing commitment to them as a matter of loyalty.

Let us assume that under certain conditions of benefaction, debts of gratitude are incurred and that certain expressions of gratitude, sometimes amounting to tangible support, are owed.[2] Should we characterize these as obligations of loyalty and their fulfillment as manifestations of gratitude?

---

[2] On gratitude generally, see Terrence McConnell, *Gratitude* (Philadelphia: Temple University Press, 1993). He suggests the following as necessary conditions for having a debt of gratitude:
1. The benefit must be granted voluntarily, intentionally, freely, and not for disqualifying reasons [for example, putting the beneficiary in the benefactor's debt];
2. The benefit must not be forced (unjustifiably) on the beneficiary against his will;

I do not believe so. An obvious first point is that, whatever other obligations it may generate, gratitude as such does not generate obligations of loyalty. The brutalized Jew left by the roadside on the way to Jericho may well have owed a debt of gratitude to the Samaritan who went out of his way to attend to his needs.[3] But the obligation in question was not an obligation of *loyalty*. Should the Samaritan have subsequently found himself in a position to need the assistance of the Jew he had aided (or even some other Jew or other needy person), gratitude might well have dictated that assistance be forthcoming, but not as an expression or obligation of loyalty. The Jew and Samaritan were strangers, and the Samaritan's compassionate behavior neither created nor invited friendship or some other association that might have involved loyalty. Loyalty has no grip independently of an association to be served. There are obligations of gratitude and obligations of loyalty, and even if from time to time they might come together and be satisfied in similar ways, their underpinnings are very different.[4]

But what about gratitude in institutional contexts? Might obligations of loyalty be the appropriate grateful response to institutional benefaction? The long-standing tradition, stretching back at least to Socrates, that grounds patriotic or at least political obligations in gratitude might suggest an affirmative response:

> Are you not grateful to those of us Laws which were instituted for this end, for requiring your father to give you a cultural and physical education? ... Then since you have been born and brought up and educated, can you deny ... that you were our child and servant, both you and your ancestors? ... We have brought you into the world and reared you and educated you, and given you and all your fellow citizens a share in all the good things at our disposal.[5]

As Locke and others have pointed out, the parental analogy fails as an argument for political obedience.[6] But even were this problem circumvented, the argument would

---

3. The beneficiary must accept the benefit (or would accept the benefit if certain impairing conditions were corrected);
4. It must be the case that the person to whom gratitude is owed provided a benefit or through great effort or sacrifice tried to provide a significant benefit

(ibid., 44).

[3] Luke 10:30–37

[4] It is, for example, very likely that acts of disloyalty will also express ingratitude, since the disloyal member of the association will have been a beneficiary of the relationship.

[5] *Crito*, 50d–51d.

[6] See John Locke, *Second Treatise of Civil Government*, sects. 66, 69. Richard Kraut and A. John Simmons, however, suggest that the Socratic argument can be rephrased to avoid Locke's criticism. See Kraut, *Socrates and the State* (Princeton, NJ: Princeton University Press, 1984), 145; Simmons, *Moral Principles and Political Obligations* (Princeton, NJ: Princeton University Press, 1979), 183.

fall short. It would probably fall short of establishing traditional political obligations; it would almost certainly fall short of establishing obligations of loyalty. True, obligations of loyalty need not be obligations of obedience, and so from the fact that the argument from gratitude cannot be used to establish obligations of obedience, it does not automatically follow that the obligations it may be used to justify may not also be obligations of loyalty. Nevertheless, there is a fundamental difference between the obligations associated with loyalty and those associated with gratitude. Obligations of gratitude are recompensive, whereas obligations of loyalty are associative. Obligations of gratitude are owed because certain benefits are—or ought to be—appreciated, and a grateful response is owed. Obligations of loyalty are owed because the object of the association in which the parties stand is valued for what it is, and it is reasonable to expect that the preservation of the conditions under which the associative relation exists is called for. Traitors may be ungrateful, but treason is not primarily a form of ingratitude.

THE DUTY OF FAIR PLAY

Several contemporary writers have attempted to account for political and patriotic obligations by appealing to a duty of fair play.[7] The basic ingredient is a beneficial cooperative enterprise whose successful outworking requires that its participants constrain themselves in certain ways. It is only appropriate that those constraints be fair. Unlike the voluntarist or social contract tradition of political obligation, the fair play approach does not require some act of consent. If it works for obligations of loyalty, it will work for those associations into which one has entered without consent. Nor is the argument a consequentialist one. Even though it refers to the sharing of burdens of cooperation as the price to be paid for sharing its benefits, it does not assert that the benefits that come from cooperation justify the obligation; rather, it is the fact that one is a participant in a cooperative arrangement.

However, as critics of the fair play argument have pointed out, it is not always clear that the concrete institutions to which the argument is intended to apply—the state, families, and so forth—are properly describable as mutually beneficial and fair to all those who are party to them, that they are more beneficial and fairer than alternative schemes, that receiving benefits from them is tantamount to accepting them, or what obligations might actually follow from any such acceptance. What does seem

---

[7] The argument, however, can be found in the *Crito*. Contemporary proponents have included H. L. A. Hart and John Rawls. See Hart, "Are There Any Natural Rights?" *Philosophical Review* 64, no. 2 (April 1955): 185; Rawls, "Legal Obligation and the Duty of Fair Play," in *Law and Philosophy*, ed. Sidney Hook (New York: New York University Press, 1964), 9–10; see also Rawls, *A Theory of Justice* (Cambridge, MA: Belknap/Harvard University Press, 1971), sect. 18.

clear, though, is that the obligations are unlikely to be those associated with loyalty. The sorts of obligations usually said to follow from the fair play argument have to do with playing one's part in ensuring that the burdens required to produce the cooperative scheme's benefits are fairly shared. Although obligations of loyalty may help to ensure that the benefits of the cooperative scheme are sustained, they are not directed primarily at the benefits but at the value that the object of the association has for its participants. For participants who have become loyalists, the object of the association has come to mean something more than the benefits it enables.

A NATURAL DUTY TO SUPPORT JUST INSTITUTIONS

John Rawls, who advances a fair play theory,[8] also argues for a natural duty to support just institutions, and this, too, has been invoked to support institutional loyalty. The argument, briefly, is that when just institutions exist and apply to us, we should do our share to support and comply with them; when they do not exist, we should assist in their establishment, especially when doing so will cost us little.[9] His argument for such a duty has recourse to the veil of ignorance behind which people would choose the rules that should structure their public interactions.

To the extent that this argument is at all acceptable, it is crafted for political institutions. Justice might well be the primary virtue for such institutions. But for many of the associations that seek, and to which we might give, our loyalty, justice, though not irrelevant, is not the dominant virtue. There is, moreover, a peculiarity to the political argument that bears explicitly on the issue of loyalty. If the argument is taken to ground one's political obligations, it is not clear how it might ground support for *one's own* polity rather than *any* just institutions.[10] Perhaps the argument is not intended to support any such particularity, only political obligation in its most general sense. But to the extent that that is so, it will fall short of a defense of loyalty, whether political and otherwise.[11] One's loyalty is owed, if at all, to the polity one considers one's own, and not to any that might be considered just.

---

[8] Which Rawls retains for "those who have assumed favored offices or positions, or have taken advantage of certain opportunities to further their interests," in *A Theory of Justice*, 350.

[9] *A Theory of Justice*, 351. The appeal to a natural duty may take several forms, and Rawls's is only one. Five "natural duty" theories are discussed in Kent Greenawalt, *Conflicts of Law and Morality* (Oxford: Clarendon, 1987).

[10] See Simmons, *Moral Principles and Political Obligations*, 147–152; also John Horton, *Political Obligation* (London: Macmillan, 1992), 104–105.

[11] There might, of course, be pragmatic reasons for supporting proximate rather than distant just institutions. They are closer, and I am more likely to be affected by them. Although such considerations would not be sufficient to establish a distinctive duty, they might ground some kind of preferential treatment for one's own polity. Indeed, Rawls himself sometimes suggests

All three arguments considered so far fail to address the loyalty that may be associated with the institutions to which such arguments are directed. At best, they offer support for limited obligations, which, even if included among the obligations of loyalty, are not required by such arguments as obligations of loyalty. I now consider at greater length two arguments that focus specifically on loyalty before turning to what I consider to be its most compelling support.

RESTORING BENEFICIAL INSTITUTIONS

In *Exit, Voice, and Loyalty*,[12] his modern classic of political economy, Albert Hirschman develops an argument for the recuperative value of institutional and organizational loyalty. Hirschman's focus is somewhat broader than his subtitle—*Response to Decline in Firms, Organizations, and States*—suggests. His intention is to accommodate *all* kinds of social groupings—families, educational and religious institutions, political parties, trade unions, voluntary organizations in general, government bureaucracies, and international corporations—though he does not extend his argument to friendships.

Hirschman's base contention is that institutional decline is an ongoing problem, an endemic tendency in organizations. But he disputes the exhausting and crisis-ridden expectation of classic market-oriented economic theory that, whenever organizational or institutional deterioration occurs, other associations will and indeed should rise to fulfill the expectations of consumers or participants, thus optimizing the distribution of social resources. Hirschman believes that there exists an "organizational slack,"[13] a space within which even market-sensitive institutions can weather downturns and recuperate without the "social losses and human hardship" of extinction that classic economic theory appears to predict as the inevitable result of institutional decline.[14]

Potentially recuperative responses to decline or failures may take one of two general forms—"exit" and "voice"—and these may be exercised either separately or

that those who retreat behind the veil of ignorance are not completely anonymous human beings but members of particular societies. So their obligations will be society-specific rather than universal. Jeremy Waldron seeks to adapt this argument to particularistic ties in "Special Ties and Natural Duties," *Philosophy & Public Affairs* 22, no. 1 (1993): 3–30.

[12] Albert O. Hirschman, *Exit, Voice, and Loyalty: Response to Decline in Firms, Organizations, and States* (Cambridge, MA: Harvard University Press, 1970). See also his "Exit, Voice, and Loyalty: Further Reflections and a Survey of Recent Contributions," *Social Science Information* 13, no. 1 (1974): 7–26.

[13] Hirschman, *Exit, Voice, and Loyalty*, 10ff.

[14] Ibid., 3. Nor should we forget—as indeed Hirschman does not—that in some organizations, especially monopolies and government bureaucracies, decline can be weathered almost indefinitely.

together. Hirschman believes that traditional economic theory has focused almost exclusively on the exit response, whereby consumers or participants no longer associate themselves with the retrograde institution. As a consequence of such exit, the institution may be alerted to significant decline and thus be given an incentive to pull itself together and improve its performance. Alternatively—and this is the particular risk of an exit response—the institution will eventually collapse. Voice, however—that is, the critically constructive expression of dissatisfaction—has been the predominant concern of political theorists. Members and supporters of political parties generally voice their disapproval of what they see as significant decline, seeking their parties' reform, and exercise their exit option—if they exercise it at all—only after their voiced concerns have not been heeded.

As Hirschman recognizes, there are many institutions for which exit is impossible or possible only at great cost[15] and for which voice constitutes the only significant means whereby they may be goaded into betterment. In addition, he contends that for many other valuable social institutions, especially those allowing for relatively easy exit, there would be considerable benefit were a greater place given to voice. Such institutions are capable of conferring considerable social benefits,[16] and it is better that they be maintained, improved, and restored than that they be allowed to decline and even collapse.

Judging when voice is appropriate and exit better is a complex matter. In a discussion we can leave to one side, Hirschman devotes some attention to the factors that will show one or the other or some particular combination of them to be the most appropriate. More apposite at this point is his contention that our social life has been impoverished by an overconcentration on exit. This is not only because exit (even when possible) may not always be recuperative, when voice may be, but also because voice frequently offers a socially preferable response. Our institutional life would be strengthened more often were we to try to work for improvement from within rather than exiting and thus leaving it to chance whether the institution will get the message and have sufficient opportunity and resources to renovate itself.

It is with regard to internally generated recuperation that loyalty serves an important function. Effective voice may require loyalty. Those who develop loyalty to the institutions with which they are associated will have a reason to stay and work for change from within, rather than opting out—as a self-interested calculator would do. Not only does the loyalist give the organization more breathing space—that is, an increased opportunity for reform—but also the commitment felt by the loyalist

[15] States and families would be prime examples. But consider other social institutions such as rail systems or postal services or the electricity supply companies.
[16] The benefits may be intrinsic as well as instrumental, although Hirschman tends to focus on the latter.

is more likely to manifest itself in some form of *effective* pressure for recuperative change, that is, constructively voiced opposition to the ways in which the organization is declining. Indeed, it is just because the imaginative and effective exercise of voice is likely to involve greater personal costs than exit that reform depends on the presence of people who have some loyalty to the institution.[17]

As should be clear, Hirschman's argument is not intended to support unlimited or absolute loyalty. Although loyalty is not tailored to narrow self-interest, it is tailored to the perceived value of the institution. To the extent that the institution is intrinsically as well as instrumentally valued, it will constitute a social context for flourishing. Should it no longer offer the possibility of that presumed value, loyalty may be withdrawn and exit viewed as the better option. Hirschman is as critical of those who do not know when to leave as he is of those who leave too quickly.

For Hirschman, then, loyalty is valuable as an institutional preservative and restorative. It involves an active disposition to stick with, sustain, and renovate valued institutions. It creates space for their regenerative criticism, enabling them to counteract or overcome their endemic tendency to deteriorate as sources of value and thus to realize the values that give them their raisons d'être. Hirschman does not give much consideration to the kinds of value that these institutions have for those who participate in them, though one gets the strong impression that there are institutional *tele* that give them their raisons d'être and for which they are the vehicles or means. To that extent, his account of the value of loyalty is primarily consequentialist.

This is a suggestive and plausible account of the social value of loyalty. We should expect some such argument: even if their goodness does not consist in their social value, the virtues are likely to possess some instrumental value. Hirschman goes a long way toward identifying that value. Nevertheless, I do not think that he gets to the heart of the case for loyalty, and even as an account of its social value, I would offer some modest amendments.

First, I would not yoke loyalty as closely to institutional *decline* as Hirschman. Just because expressions of loyalty are sensitive to the interests of associational partners and failures of loyalty are destructive of the interests of associational partners, loyalty protects vulnerable associations from decline or disintegration. Nevertheless, the value of loyalty does not reside primarily in its ability to halt the processes of endemic institutional decline. It may be the failure of loyalty itself that initiates (rather than fails to stem) the decline. Although some might want to argue that adultery reflects a marriage that is already in decline, it is as likely to be true that the disloyalty

---

[17] In his later article, Hirschman qualifies some of his claims about the high cost of voice. For some people, he suggests, voice may have an intrinsic as well as merely instrumental value.

of adultery initiates a decline. The disloyal executive who leaves for what he sees as greener pastures may set in motion a decline that did not preexist his departure.

Loyalty may be the central (though not exclusive) virtue of associative relations, by "keeping us keeping on" in regard to what are for us intrinsically valued associations—relationships and institutions to which we are committed. It does so especially in bad times—as Hirschman notes—as a sustaining influence. But loyalty may also operate in good times—to foster or advance the interests of the institution: the loyal alumnus may make a large contribution to the university's endowment fund. What makes such an act an expression of loyalty is the fact that it represents a curb on what I have broadly characterized as narrow self-interest—self-interest that is inclined to trump the values of a certain kind of associative connection with others. In the face of possibilities that express some merely private vision, the lethargy of free ridership, or mere personal advantage, the loyalist chooses to devote her resources, energies, or whatever to secure or advance the interests of the relationship or institution in question. There may, of course, be a concurrence of self-interest (at least in some broader sense) with institutional interest, but in the loyalist's case, the costly furtherance of the interests of the associative object is an important part of what motivates the act.[18]

It does not follow from its institutional function that the cultivation of particular loyalties is always justified. Not every kind of institution expresses or serves values worth preserving. Indeed, the loyalty of a Klansman or Mafia soldier or Nazi may be socially detrimental. Loyalty per se is not enough: it needs to be associated with institutions that are sufficiently worth having and maintaining if it is to be justified.

Although Hirschman recognizes the value that loyalty may have as an institutional preservative, his account tends to be too instrumentalist. There are many institutions that we might value but have no particular loyalty to. It does not account for the particularity of loyalties—our loyalty being to those with whom we associate as our own. It is association with the institution and not merely it and its fruits that is valued and that loyalty preserves.

LOYALTY AND SELF-IDENTITY

The gap in Hirschman's account may suggest an alternative justification, one framed in terms of self-identity. Many of the social institutions that loyalty helps to sustain have attained core significance for us, mostly as elements of our self-identity. They

---

[18] That said, I suspect that some of the motivation behind what may be termed "conspiratorial" or "corruptive" loyalties may be pretty self-serving—a belief that if we stick together, we'll cover our criminality and secure ourselves against judgment (consider Watergate loyalties or the blue wall of silence).

have value both as formative influences for the particular selves we are and as vehicles for our flourishing—our self-expression and self-realization. It might be argued that part of the root significance of loyalty is to be found in its connection with our identity and integrity as particular individuals. Developing loyalties is partly a matter of developing a social self and ipso facto a self, and maintaining the loyalties we have formed is (in part) a matter of our being true to our selves, of holding on to what has made us the individuals we are. So conceived, the justification (not motive) for loyalty can be construed as self-regarding—on the one hand, of having a *particular* identity and, on the other, of *securing* that identity and integrity in the face of potentially derailing temptations or pressures of the moment. Loyalty acknowledges the critical place of sociality in our identity and protects our settled identity from the erosions of short-term advantage. As a matter of our self-respect and integrity—in both structural and evaluative senses of the latter—we remain loyal to what have become the objects of our loyalty.[19] More than gratitude or support for beneficial institutions, our loyalties register and affirm our personal integrity and self-esteem.

Construing the justification of loyalty as fundamentally self-regarding might also be understood to have important other-regarding implications. Not only do our loyalties sustain the elements of our self-identity but also they affirm our indebtedness to others and help to maintain the social fabric of trust within which human personality—others' as well as our own—may flourish. Disloyalty not only diminishes us but also weakens that fabric. In addition, particularly in cases in which other persons are intimately involved, disloyalty may constitute a very grave harm. A person betrayed is likely to be a person violated.[20]

This need not be viewed statically. In liberal democratic societies, for example, the loyal selves that acknowledge the obligations they have to their roots become self-conscious and deliberative selves, capable of reflecting upon and assessing their identities and thus their loyalties. That which holds our loyalty at one point may no longer sustain it at another. Generally, though, evolutions of loyalty will be gradual rather than cataclysmic and will not involve the self-servingness and contingency/ expediency that is usually associated with disloyalty. As noted earlier, the refitting of Theseus's ship must be undertaken while it is on the high seas.

If we connect loyalty to self-identity as suggested, it is to be expected that we will develop loyalties. Unless we acquire and maintain some loyalties, it is unlikely that we will constitute identifiable social selves or that there will exist a society that is

---

[19] See, for example, Fletcher, *Loyalty*, 16.

[20] Indeed, one might want to argue that disloyalty is one of the most serious ways in which we can violate another. The stands traditionally taken against betrayal, adultery, treason, and idolatry are consistent with this. See, in particular, Judith Shklar, *Ordinary Vices* (Cambridge, MA: Belknap/Harvard University Press, 1984).

safe for such selves. As Royce expresses it, you can "cut loose from all loyalty if you will. . . . [But] if you do so, if you wholly decline to devote yourself to any cause whatever, your assertion of moral independence will remain but an empty proclaiming of a moral sovereignty over your life, without any definite life over which to be sovereign."[21] Our loyalties help to constitute us as persons of substance, of character, and society as worthy of membership, albeit sometimes misguided and in some instances even fanatical. Even in the fanatical loyalist, the zealot, we may see some value that is lacking in both the moral chameleon, for whom expediency is the determinative impulse, and the extreme individualist, who rejects all deep commitments.

Is this a moral argument for loyalty? It is one thing to say that the formation of loyalties is a socially and psychologically necessary feature of human life; isn't it something else to argue that loyalty is a good and is to be encouraged, that it is a genuine virtue? Only the former has been shown; the latter remains to be established. Does the present argument, if successful, show more than the former?

It is arguable that the connection between psychic and moral integrity, and between integrity and the objects of our loyalty, is a close one. This is because our concept of distinctively human life is not neutral, but comprehends a certain normative formation. We conceive of and indeed value ourselves as subjects having valuational and relational capacities—as sensitive, deliberating, appraising, and choosing and as friends, colleagues, lovers, citizens, and believers. And, it may be claimed, we can become these things only if we are loyally grafted into an ongoing social life. To the central players in that social life, we owe our loyalty by virtue of what they are to us.

It might further be argued that loyalty, like conscientiousness and sincerity, is one of those virtues that constitute us as persons of character. To show that loyalties may be misplaced, like showing that conscientiousness or sincerity may be misguided, is not to show that they are not in themselves admirable and worth possessing. It is just that other things are important, too, and loyalty, like conscientiousness and sincerity, is not enough. We may be committed to the objects of our loyalty, conscientiousness, and sincerity without being blind to them. That is not all we should be committed to, but we cannot do without them.

But even with this support, I consider the argument that loyalty is a self-regarding obligation, rooted in our connections with the various associations that are core values for us or that enter into our identity, excessively egoistic. The tail—the important identity-conferring value of our loyalties—has come to wag the dog. This account fails to give adequate weight to the fact that our primary loyalties are always to others or, to put it more accurately, to others as our associative objects. Even if those others have become significant for our sense of self, our loyalties are to them and not

---

[21] Royce, *The Philosophy of Loyalty,* 93.

primarily to our selves. Disloyalty to them will also compromise us, but the primary wrong is done to them, even if our own integrity has also been sacrificed. Somehow we need to steer a course between a merely instrumentalist view of loyalty and one in which it is seen as primarily self-serving.

LOYALTY AS PROTECTIVE OF THE OBJECTS OF INTRINSICALLY VALUED ASSOCIATIONS

It should now be fairly clear that the importance of loyalty does not lie primarily in the way that it preserves instrumentally valuable institutions and relations or in the way that it secures our integrity in the face of self-serving challenges. It does these things, of course. More important, however, it secures the objects of associations that are or have become intrinsically valuable for us against what are primarily self-serving challenges, whether those challenges have arisen from competitors or from internal temptations and weaknesses.

Our lives are not solitary, not only because we are not eremites but also because our engagements with others are relational and not simply external or contractual. We connect with others in ways that come to have associative significance. Some of the objects of those associations we value for their own sake, even if the associations were initiated by what we thought their objects might provide for us by way of benefits. What began as instrumental has become intrinsically valuable to us. The organization we joined to advance our career has become valuable to us for its own sake, and we make our association with it a part of ourselves. To the extent that a relationship or association remains instrumental, it will garner no loyalty from us. And even if—in Hirschman's vision—we remain with an ailing association out of a belief that it would be strategically better for the production of some good were the association to be reformed, and that this is most likely to be achieved if we remain with it, our staying will not be expressive of loyalty unless the object has acquired an intrinsic value for us.

The value of loyalty is seen most dramatically in the case of friendship. It is, of course, possible to live a life without friends. Some may actually choose to live a life of that kind and, for a few of those, it may even constitute a way to live a good life. The contemplative life of a philosophical hermit, alone in the universe without even the friendship of God, is a possibility that I do not want to reject out of hand.[22] For the vast majority of us, however, a good life will almost certainly involve friendships with others. Our lives are enlarged and enriched by friendship, not just in the

---

[22] Though such a choice is itself likely to have been made possible only because of various preexisting associational ties.

consequentialist sense that through our friendships we are benefited in certain ways (as we might through networking), but because friendships with others have intrinsic value for us; they are relationships that give meaning and significance to our lives.

To anticipate the argument of chapter 8, loyalty is integral to friendship. Friends behave toward each other in ways that protect or serve the interests of each other. They are obligated to each other in the ways that are constitutive of loyalty. Not only will this associative bond generally find some emotional expression, a pleasure in the connection, but also there will be an (often) unspoken understanding that friends look out for and are sensitive to the other's interests. Although it is possible to commence a form of friendship for instrumental reasons—to commence, that is, a means-friendship—and for that friendship subsequently to become an end-friendship, friendships most often develop in a less calculating fashion. We find ourselves in contact with someone, recognize some commonality of interests and shared values, are perhaps attracted by certain features of the other's personality, gradually find a certain satisfaction and delight in the other's company, and after a while realize that the furtherance of this person's interests has become a significant interest of our own. The other has become our end-friend.

Some of our other relationships may also begin instrumentally, though not necessarily in a conscious way. So far as our families are concerned, we begin as vulnerable infants, initially dependent on parents for the wherewithal of survival, eventually recognizing not only them but also an extended family as providing an emotional and social milieu for our personal growth. But the relationships initially forged out of need often come to be enjoyed for their own sake. We experience a connectedness with those who are members of our family—a connectedness that sometimes extends beyond its immediate members to remoter relations whom we may not have met and even to our line or lineage. The genealogical interest that many of us acquire has little to offer by way of instrumental advantage. It is the connection with family that we value, a sense of belonging, of being part of a larger whole in which we are linked with those who have gone before.

Other relationships begin with a much more instrumental focus. We join a club to engage in a certain kind of activity with others, or we find employment in some organization. Our membership in the club or organization may impose certain obligations on us. We may be required to pay dues and contribute a certain amount of time and energy to its activities; we may be expected to conduct ourselves in certain ways—be punctual, give notice of absences, participate in certain assemblies or activities, observe a dress and behavior code, not make personal use of certain facilities, and so on. We may do all these things, and the club or organization may remain simply instrumental for us. We play the sport we want to or get paid a living wage. If we lose interest in the activity that defines it or we find some other place that offers opportunities for the same activity but is more attractive in certain respects, we will let our membership lapse and maybe go elsewhere. In such cases, no loyalty has been formed, and no obligations of loyalty qua obligations of loyalty (as distinct from membership) have been observed or, in withdrawal, betrayed. Of course, the club or organization may have wanted more from us. For the kinds of reasons that we observed when discussing Hirschman, it would probably have been to the club's or organization's benefit had we developed a degree of loyalty to it. But that was not a concomitant of membership. Loyalty cannot be imposed in quite that way, even though it may come about through a gradual process of identification.

In some cases of club membership and organizational employment, we will come to value our connections more than instrumentally. The associations will acquire a significance for us that goes beyond the instrumental values that first drew us to them. We see them not as external to us, as social instruments to be used or even manipulated to purposes we have, but as sources of satisfaction, valuable in their own right, and the interests of the club or organization will become interests whose protection or furtherance now become interests of our own. The well-being of the club or organization becomes—to some extent—part of our own well-being. The association becomes part of our identity, not in the sense that we become identified with the association, or that we lose our identity and separateness, but in the sense that we acquire a high-priority intrinsic interest in its well-being or flourishing.

In affirming the value of loyalty, then, we affirm the value of the objects that certain associations have for us. That does not, of course, amount to a validation of the object of every association for which we may develop loyalty, nor does it relieve us of the burden to form our loyalties carefully. The issue of what associative objects we should recognize as worthy of loyalty is a question that we will address in part II.

POSTSCRIPT ON THE SOCIOBIOLOGICAL CHALLENGE

Let me conclude this discussion with a brief excursus on what may be viewed as the sociobiological challenge to the foregoing account. In certain circles, sociobiological explanations are taken to reduce arguments such as the foregoing to epiphenomenal rationalizations of what can and should be given some form of broadly scientific explanation.

Certainly since Darwin, but with increasing frequency as evolutionary biology and psychology have developed, reductivist accounts of the virtues as adaptive mechanisms have emerged. On the view that distinctive or distinctively human traits have their origins in animal behavior and can have survived only because they contribute in some way to the evolutionary success of their bearers, the virtues (or, more generally, morality itself) have been seen primarily as instruments of environmental robustness. As James Q. Wilson expressed it, "the moral sense must have had adaptive value; if it did not, natural selection would have worked against people who had such useless traits as sympathy, self-control, or a desire for fairness and in favor of those with opposite tendencies."[23] How one takes such remarks is a matter of some contention even within the circles in which such views are espoused. Do such traits favor the individuals who possess them, or are they traits that contribute to the survival of populations? Does their value lie primarily in their contribution to reproductive success or rather in enabling the successful negotiation of local environmental challenges and opportunities? Even if they had (or have) survival value, did their value consist only in that?

Not surprisingly, loyalty is accorded its adaptive place. Though accounts vary, Ranyard West's early conjecture that "loyalty is grounded biologically in the need for unity, and for personal sacrifice for the sake of the 'herd' "[24] is reasonably representative. Such an account coheres with ideas of loyal wartime sacrifice, though it does not have much to contribute to arguments about limits—whether the "herd" *warrants* loyalty and, if it does, whether personal sacrifice of the kind envisaged is justified.

But leaving these latter questions aside, it might appear that on West's account loyalty—along with other virtuous traits—stands more in need of explanation than of justification. Even though the two need not be incompatible, it is often thought— mistakenly—that once something has been explained, the question of its justification has been made redundant.[25] Given a naturalistic explanation of the kind that West advances, is it for others to argue that the traits in question have some noninstrumental normative grounding?

There is, however, a fundamental flaw involved in dispensing with justificatory accounts in favor of explanatory ones. We can identify this flaw without focusing on the specific account that an evolutionary psychologist might give of a trait such as loyalty. Whatever else might be said of us as humans, we are—as we now find ourselves—reason-giving creatures, concerned not merely with achieving ends by whatever means work but with evaluating both means and ends. We hold ourselves and each other to account for what we do, demanding that what is done be accounted for not simply in terms of what might constitute a sociobiological background of the

---

[23] James Q. Wilson, *The Moral Sense* (New York: Free Press, 1993), 23.

[24] Ranyard West, *Conscience and Society* (New York: Emerson, 1945), 218.

[25] Explaining how John Stuart Mill came to be a utilitarian (his upbringing by James Mill in a household that had Jeremy Bentham as a frequent guest, etc.) does not render unnecessary a discussion of its justification. As we are creatures with histories, biological and social explanations of how we came to hold what we hold will always be possible; as we are rational agents, what we hold may also be subject to a different form of scrutiny. See, in general, Tziporah Kasachkoff, "Explaining and Justifying," *Informal Logic* 10, no. 1 (1988): 21–30.

conduct but in terms of the kinds of relations that we consider ought to exist among those who have the capacity to determine their goals and conduct for themselves.

And so, should it be discovered (as some have suggested) that forcible sexual intercourse has its roots in certain behavior that the human animal has adopted, it does not follow that if *A* rapes *B*, he can give an adequate accounting for what he has done in terms of that explanation, *even were it to account for* the origins of that form of conduct. If the enslavement of others is seen as an important factor in the origins and development of a particular form of civilization, it does not follow from that that it was or is justified or that justificatory questions have no place. They may have no place in the methodologies of those who wish to provide a certain kind of naturalistic account of human behavior—of human behavior as essentially continuous with animal and other nonhuman behavior. But that is not all that is to be said about the matter, just as one does not say all that is to be said about a novel when one has talked about the content of the ink and paper or the sentence structure or the language in which it is written. There may be a legitimate place for such inquiries, but qua novel it is not exhausted by such things.[26]

Whatever the scientific gaps, we should not eschew sociobiological accounts of the genesis of virtues. Nevertheless, such accounts do not render superfluous the normative discussions we undertake on account of what we have now become.

CONCLUSION

The obligations of loyalty are not a species of formal membership obligation, even if those who determine the obligations of membership seek to incorporate loyalty as a membership obligation. That is why many traditional arguments for political loyalty fail to work. The obligations that express loyalty arise out of a relationship with the object of loyalty in which an identification with the object of loyalty has taken place and it has come to be valued for its own sake. Loyalty to the object of that relationship or association is shown by sustaining it when it will be costly to do so. In the next chapter, we look more closely at the problem posed by particularistic relations such as loyalty when they confront the universalizing tendencies of what are often spoken of as ordinarily morality.

---

[26] I have expressed my general concerns about such projects in "Conceptual Cannibalism: The Social Scientific Appropriation of Ordinary Discourse," *International Journal of Applied Philosophy* 6, no. 2 (Winter 1991): 1–12.

5

PARTICULARITY

It is the most common thing in the world for a person to decide that he should (or should not) do so-and-so on grounds of loyalty to his friend, family, organization, community, country, or species. Indeed, it is likely that loyalties ground more of the principled, self-sacrificing, and other kinds of nonselfish behavior in which people engage than do moral principles and ideals.[1]

What magic is there in the pronoun "my," that should justify us in overturning the decisions of impartial truth?[2]

Andrew Oldenquist juxtaposes the partial obligations of loyalty with a universalized morality of principles and ideals and argues for the moral primacy of the former. That is a minority view. But it raises questions about the nature of partial or—as I will characterize them—particularistic obligations and their relations to general moral obligations. It has always been seen as a problem for loyalty and the obligations associated with it that they are particularistic and therefore appear to be in tension with what are often claimed to be the properly universalizable demands of morality. How genuine or serious is this problem?

In this chapter, I begin with an examination of Godwin's epigraphical challenge to the kind of partiality that loyalty expresses before reviewing several attempts to come to terms with the tension. In the end, I suggest that our moral world is a pluralist one and needs to accommodate both universalistic and particularistic expectations. Because of that, we are sometimes forced to make *judgments* about which should have priority.

[1] Andrew Oldenquist, "Loyalties," *Journal of Philosophy* 79, no. 4 (April 1982): 173.
[2] William Godwin, *Enquiry Concerning Political Justice and Its Influence on Morals and Happiness*, photographic facsimile, ed. F. E. L. Priestley (3rd ed., 1798, Toronto: Toronto University Press, 1946), vol. I. The quotations that follow are taken from 125–129.

GODWIN'S CHALLENGE

In his *Enquiry Concerning Political Justice*, William Godwin posits "justice as a general appellation for all moral duty." By justice, he understands "impartial treatment of every man in matters that relate to his happiness, which is measured solely by a consideration of the properties of the receiver, and the capacity of him that bestows." Such justice is "'no respecter of persons.'" Via this blend of distributive and aggregative ideas, Godwin asserts that even though humans qua humans are entitled to equal attention, some are "of more worth and importance" than others because "capable of a more refined and genuine happiness." Thus,

> the illustrious archbishop of Cambray was of more worth than his valet, and there are few of us that would hesitate to pronounce, if his palace were in flames, and the life of only one of them could be preserved, which of the two ought to be preferred.

It is not simply that Archbishop Fénelon was himself capable of a more refined happiness than his valet, but that he also had the inclination and greater capacity to contribute to the happiness of others:

> In saving the life of Fenelon, suppose at the moment he conceived the project of his immortal Telemachus, I should have been promoting the benefit of thousands, who have been cured by the perusal of that work, of some error, vice and consequent unhappiness. Nay, my benefit would extend further than this; for every individual thus cured, has become a better member of society, and has contributed in his turn to the happiness, information and improvement of others.

Having got his moral foot in the door, Godwin now confronts the partialities to which Oldenquist affirmatively adverts:

> Suppose the valet had been my brother, my father or my benefactor. This would not alter the truth of the proposition. The life of Fenelon would still be more valuable than that of the valet; and justice, pure, unadulterated justice would still have preferred that which was most valuable. Justice would have taught me to save the life of Fenelon at the expense of the other.[3]

---

[3] In the first edition of 1793, before Godwin became something of a political outcast, it was a "chambermaid," "mother," and "benefactor" who figured in his example; however, in response to public sentiment, Godwin thought it politic to change the gender of the actors. Mothers, especially, excited a strongly protective response. By the third edition of 1798, Godwin had

The brother or father, he notes, "may be a fool or a profligate, malicious, lying or dishonest." Even so, in and of itself their connection with one is of no moral consequence: "What magic is there in the pronoun 'my,' that should justify us in overturning the decisions of impartial truth?"[4]

Godwin is not so alienated from ordinary affections to think that relationships are irrelevant. But such relevance as they have is at best *instrumental*. He goes on to acknowledge the "indebtedness" a person generally has to his father for "existence" and support "in the helplessness of infancy" and the obligation of gratitude that is therefore owed. But, he observes, this is to concede no special status to one's father qua *one's father*. I owe gratitude to my father not because "he bestowed a benefit on me, but because he bestowed it upon a human being."

There is a stark double-fistedness about Godwin's position that almost succeeds in placing the burden of moral argument on the defender of particularist obligations. It is stark because his rhetorical challenge catches us off guard: as Oldenquist recognizes, "it is the most common thing in the world" to favor one's own, and we are therefore taken aback by Godwin's challenge to this commonplace. Do we need to defend such obligations any more than we need to defend obligations of justice and beneficence?[5] His position is double-fisted because, although Godwin is unashamedly an aggregative utilitarian, the marriage of his utilitarianism to a distributive impartialism is equally challenging. Why should the fact that someone is *my* friend, *my* sister, *my* parent, or *my* countryman carry any normative weight if impartial justice is best served by giving preference to others?

Responses to Godwin's challenge have come from both camps. Impartialists of both consequentialist and deontological stripes have sought to resist his rejection of the particularist obligations conventionally associated with friends, family, and fellow citizens. Their problem has been to show how—if at all—these special obligations might be accommodated within the larger framework of an impartial moral concern.

---

married and suffered the loss of Mary Wollstonecraft; in 1799, however, in the preface to his novel *St Leon*, he acknowledged the modification that his relationship with her had wrought in his views. There, writing specifically apropos of the position he had espoused in the *Enquiry*, he observed: "I apprehend domestic and private affections inseparable from the nature of man, and from what may be styled the culture of the heart, and am fully persuaded that they are not incompatible with a profound and active sense of justice in the mind of him that cherishes them." See *St Leon; A Tale of the Sixteenth Century* (1799), viii–ix.

[4] It is not absolutely clear what kind of point Godwin is making here. Is it a logical point about the *coherence* of discriminating on the basis of relational characteristics or an ethical point about the *morality* of so doing? His form of words might suggest the former (as though some logical sleight of hand is involved), but it is probably the latter that he intends.

[5] As I noted earlier (ch. 1, n. 28), the person who ponders which of two to save—his wife or a stranger—has "one thought too many." Godwin seems to have one thought too few.

In assessing the following attempts to accommodate particularist obligations, I focus especially on obligations that are expressive of loyalty. In the next section, I briefly recap the kinds of obligations that are usually said to be expressive of loyalty and place loyalty's partiality in the context of other partialities. In the section that follows, I review the claims of impartialism. Then I consider some attempts to reconcile particularism with impartialism. Finally, I offer an argument that seeks to provide an independent basis for the special obligations of particularism in general and of loyalty in particular.

LOYALTY'S PARTIALITY

Although the partiality of loyalty may sometimes be discretionary,[6] certain kinds of partiality are believed to be defeasibly obligatory. The specific content of the loyalty's obligations will depend on the association in question—in both its general aspects and its concrete particulars. These particularized obligations will reflect the conditions for sustaining what are or have become intrinsically valued associational ties. If the conditions become too demanding on one or both sides, the association may collapse. In the event of a collapse, whether one or the other party has been disloyal will depend on some judgment about the reasonableness of the conditions and the reasons the conditions were not fulfilled.[7]

Loyalty to another is not the exclusive vehicle of sustainable obligations of partiality. Partiality may be grounded in recompensive considerations, such as the need to compensate or express gratitude or in certain voluntaristic acts such as promises.

THE CLAIMS OF IMPARTIALITY

What is termed the Enlightenment Project has various facets, often including freeing human decision making from appeals to religious authority. More positively, however, there is a belief in the unity of knowledge, human progress, and the scientific method. With respect to moral matters, it includes attempts to subsume all morality under a unified universal rational principle—or, if not some unitary substantive principle, then some single principle that would function as umpire in the event of

---

[6] If I have a spare theater ticket and offer it first to my friend or lover because she or he is my friend or lover, this would probably be an unexceptionable exercise of discretionary partiality. But I might equally and unexceptionably have offered it to another person who had expressed an interest in going.

[7] It is for this reason that I would not regard Godwin's preference for the archbishop, however problematic, as an act of disloyalty. The parent or valet is not abandoned for self-serving reasons, but supposedly for high-minded consequentialist ones.

conflicts.[8] Both Kantian and utilitarian ethical theory reflect this project in the status they accord, respectively, to the categorical imperative and principle of utility. They offer a rational, universalistic, and impartial approach to ethical decision making. Even Hume, whose sentimentalism might seem to relativize and derationalize moral judgments, nevertheless identifies moral sentiments with those that are universally shared.[9]

Godwin accepts the project's major premises. As he sees it, moral rightness is constituted by doing that which maximizes happiness or good. The moral agent is to see each person, himself included, as a potential object and source of happiness and, in determining what ought to be done, is to calculate the course of action that will conduce to the greatest overall good. Although Godwin's impartialism is made starker by its association with a maximizing utilitarianism, the two are, as we have noted, only contingently connected.[10] Whatever the criterion of moral oughtness, it can be applied impartially.

On this account, there are a number of more or less radical ways of interpreting the agent's situation. The most radical version would require that the agent view each occasion for acting as presenting a matrix of options in which his task is to effect the response that will realize the relevant moral maxim without in any way privileging his own commitments. In theory, such decision making would require revision or reconsideration each time something in the objective situation changed, just in case a different realization strategy would be called for.[11] An agent faced with Godwin's dilemma would calculate which of the available options would be likely to maximize overall good and then seek to effect that outcome. Ceteris paribus, were the agent the valet, he would accept that saving the archbishop offered greater prospects for social good, and he would therefore sacrifice himself to that outcome. Were he a potential rescuer and the valet happened to be his brother or father, the decision to give priority to the archbishop would be the same. There would be no privileging of the agent's standpoint or perspective or associations. The view, if from anywhere, would be from above—that of an ideal or neutral observer.

---

[8] For the latter, see John Stuart Mill, *Utilitarianism* (1863), ch. 1; Henry Sidgwick, *The Methods of Ethics* (New York: Macmillan, 1901), 421.

[9] David Hume, *An Enquiry Concerning the Principles of Morals* (1751).

[10] Marcia Baron argues that the intuitive outrageousness of Godwin's position is due solely to his brand of utilitarianism and not at all to his doctrine of the impartiality of moral judgments: "Impartiality and Friendship," *Ethics* 101 (1991): 839–842. Certainly the counterintuitiveness of Godwin's position is exacerbated by his utilitarianism, but I do not think it is solely a product of it.

[11] In practice, one would have to factor in the transactional costs involved in decision making, and this would probably limit the kinds of changes in the objective situation that would trigger the recalculation.

Godwin may not have had in mind such a radical and strenuous view. On a more charitable reading, the calculus functions as a tiebreaker in cases in which an agent is faced with more demands than can be satisfied and a choice needs to be made. He may not envisage a "selfless self" with no projects or commitments of its own, but an ongoing, committed self faced with a conflict between some of its commitments and the demands of a moral maxim that does not privilege such commitments.

Yet the charitable reading seems to break down as the exposition unfolds, for the partiality a person might show to his father he shows to someone who was a benefactor to another qua human being, not qua *his child*. And others have not shied away from espousing such radical impartialism.[12]

It is against this radical understanding that Bernard Williams famously inveighed. Williams's attack, however, was not limited to the kind of utilitarianism to which Godwin and John Grote are committed, but was intended to apply with equal force to all radical forms of impartialism, including what he interpreted as its Kantian version. His challenge was to the Enlightenment Project itself. Indeed, because he saw *morality* as being inherently impartialist, Williams sometimes took his argument to challenge the common view that moral considerations have (if not by definition, then by virtue of their content) overriding significance.

Williams's contention was that if humans are to retain their integrity as agents, they must not place their "ground projects" and "deepest personal attachments" (which may be particular relationships, including loyalties) at the mercy of some impersonal and impartial moral demand or calculus. Such ground projects, commitments, and attachments, as constituents of the self, are not factors to be put in the balance with other considerations. Rather, they provide the very context within which any moral decision making must take place: "unless such things [for example, ground projects and deep attachments to others] exist, there will not be enough substance or conviction in a man's life to compel his allegiance to life itself."[13] If a person gives others' interests the same weight as his own, this will serve to

> alienate him in a real sense from his actions and the source of his action in his own consciousness[,] . . . to neglect the extent to which his actions and his decisions have to be seen as the actions and decisions which flow from the projects

---

[12] See, for example, John Grote, *An Examination of the Utilitarian Philosophy*, ed. Joseph Bickersteth Mayor (Cambridge: Deighton, 1870), 94; cf. David Hume, *Treatise of Human Nature*, ed. L. A. Selby Bigge (Oxford: Clarendon, 1888), 582.

[13] Bernard Williams, "Persons, Character and Morality," in *Moral Luck: Philosophical Papers 1973–80* (Cambridge: Cambridge University Press, 1981), 18.

and attitudes with which he is most closely identified. It is thus in the most literal sense an attack on his integrity.[14]

Whether it is one's own ground projects or one's deep attachments to others that one treats as nonprivileged, the effect is the same. Both are constitutive of the self that one is and the self that one has to be if one's decision making is to have any point.

We can accept Williams's thesis about the importance of "integrity" and the attachments that tend to be integral to it without accepting the further point that such ground projects and attachments are invulnerable to moral scrutiny or even unconflicted. It is surely possible for people to acquire deep commitments and to enter into attachments that are evil and should not be respected—either by themselves or others—in the name of some integrity. True, the person who possesses an essentially evil ground project might find it psychologically self-destructive to give it up in the name of some impartialist principle, but that need not count decisively in favor of respecting it.[15]

It might seem possible to ease the burden of impartialism by arguing that a rational, ethically sensitive person will—*or at least should*—incorporate into his ground projects the general principles that substantively characterize impartialism. That is certainly a reasonable expectation of the negative principles that populate the impartialist moral pantheon: one ought not to inflict force, fraud, and theft on others. It becomes more problematic when positive requirements such as helping those in need are involved. Such requirements have an almost limitless potential to engage one's efforts, and it might be thought that they would undermine our integrity from within—or at least the rich diversity of attachments that currently characterize our lives. This, however, does not strictly follow: just as our various attachments—to family, hobbies, and work—might come into conflict and require some modification and prioritization, so, too, might we need to decide how much of ourselves we will devote to aid as against the pursuit of other interests to which we are deeply attached.[16]

---

[14] Bernard Williams, in J. J. C. Smart and Bernard Williams, *Utilitarianism: For and Against* (Cambridge: Cambridge University Press, 1973), 116.

[15] Williams shows some recognition of this in "Persons, Character and Morality," 17. Also, some deep attachments—to family or country—may be sources of considerable internal conflict, and, over time, it may be the case that giving them up (perhaps for moral reasons) will be personally freeing. For a defense of the more radical thesis, see Susan Wolf, "'One Thought Too Many': Love, Morality, and the Ordering of Commitment," in *Luck, Value, and Commitment: Themes from the Ethics of Bernard Williams*, ed. Ulrike Heuer and Gerald Lang (New York: Oxford University Press, 2012), ch. 3.

[16] That decision might be influenced not only by our own internal metaprocesses but also by the arguments of others who may feel that we are too focused or not sufficiently focused on aiding others. To the extent that these are decisions that we can deliberate and decide on, no undermining of our integrity will be involved.

Impartialism becomes impossibly burdensome only when it is expressed in terms of a categorical general maxim, such as "one ought to do that which maximizes overall happiness," not when it is couched as a concrete imperfect duty, such as "one should assist the needy." In the former case, it would be impossibly burdensome even for someone who adopted it as a personal project. The flux of external circumstances would constantly challenge prior maximizing decisions.

A critique of radical impartialism does not require the equally radical prioritization of the self's existing projects and attachments. We can allow that those attachments have priority without absolutizing them. The difficult task will then be to determine when impartialist claims should trump—or, more reasonably, lead to a revision of—the self's projects. To such issues we will later return.

ATTEMPTS AT RECONCILIATION

Radical forms of impartialism tend to be destructive of particularist values—including the associative bonds that give rise to preferential obligations. Does this signal a significant weakness in the Enlightenment Project? Not necessarily. Various efforts have been made to reconcile the two.

(1) A facially seductive option is to universalize particularist obligations, thus bringing them into formal conformity with impartialism. Thus, although I have obligations to *my* parents and friends that you do not have, and others have obligations to *their* parents and friends that I do not have, we can universalize this by requiring all to fulfill their preferential obligations to their parents and friends. Thus "honor your father and mother" has the same universalistic form as "thou shalt not kill," impartially expected of all.[17]

However, this formalistic conceit confuses universalizability with impartiality. Even though "everyone ought to care for his own mother" is a universal principle, it does not follow (as it would for an impartialist principle) from "I ought to care for my mother" that "I ought to care for anyone who is relevantly similar to my mother" (except for the fact of being *mine*). The problematic issue for impartialism is to explain how something's being *mine* can give rise to preferential obligations. It is not resolved by claiming that everyone is preferentially obligated to *theirs*. The point is not to deny that an impartialist of this kind may have strong obligations to her mother, but only that they are the same as those advocated by particularism.

(2) The very strenuousness of the radical position might lead one to adopt some version of an intermediate, two-tiered position. Such approaches, often maximizing,

---

[17] For an appeal of this kind, see Marcia Baron, *The Moral Status of Loyalty* (Dubuque, IA: Kendall/Hunt, 1984), 26–27.

mediate their ultimate commitment with action-guiding principles that, if followed, would satisfy the demands of maximization without a maximizing calculus being invoked on every occasion. Only in cases in which conflicts of action-guiding principles arose would it be necessary to appeal directly to the ultimate principle.

The two-tiered position has a prominent representative in R. M. Hare.[18] Even though Godwin seems to be prepared to allow that one might owe one's relatives a debt of gratitude that would mark them out from others, Hare endeavors to impart some provisional magic to the "my" of association. Hare believes that special obligations can be justified by the way in which they contribute to well-being. Familial and other associative commitments, along with the obligations integral to them, can be seen to contribute more effectively to overall well-being (or social good) than would be the case were they not fostered. If we ask why mothers ought to favor or be loyal to their children,

> the answer is fairly obvious. If mothers had the propensity to care equally for all the children in the world, it is unlikely that children would be as well provided for even as they are. The dilution of the responsibility would weaken it out of existence.[19]

This is not a particularly persuasive reason for mothers to give preferential treatment to their own children. Hare elevates what might be seen as a natural disposition ("propensity") into a moral principle. But awareness of what he posits as the underlying rationale of such parental partiality and loyalty would tend to diminish its claim on us. Even if it has been found in the past that giving principled preference to members of one's own family has maximized social good, *we* might wish to rethink it in the face of manifest global suffering. Indeed, if it is an optimizing maxim, it should surely be rethought, given the evident imbalances that it and other time-honored partialities have either produced or sustained.[20] Even if a complete egalitarianism of concern would be impracticable or counterproductive, some intermediate communal arrangement might be thought to do better than what we have.

Not only will awareness of the underlying rationale tend to diminish attachment but also, even if what Hare says about its utility is correct, it mislocates the rationale. The reason mothers attend to their children is not a simple recognition of their needs

---

[18] See, particularly, R. M. Hare, *Moral Thinking: Its Levels, Method and Point* (Oxford: Clarendon, 1981). A similar approach is taken by Terrence McConnell, *Gratitude* (Philadelphia: Temple University Press, 1993), ch. 4.

[19] Hare, *Moral Thinking*, 137.

[20] Cf. Samuel Scheffler, "Individual Responsibility in a Global Age," *Social Philosophy and Policy* 12(1995): 222.

(as humans) or even a recognition that those needs will be served best by those who are biologically most closely related to them. The reason is that it is *their* children who are in need. It is the particularity of the children, the associative bond they have with *them*, that figures in the justification for parental obligations, and not simply a universal recognition of their need and of how it might best be met.

It could, of course, be argued that the underlying rationale for preferential treatment should—if the preferential treatment is to be truly maximizing—remain opaque to its adherents. That is, special obligations should be *viewed* as sui generis rather than as (even though they are) specifications of a maximizing principle. It would be a condition of their being maximizing that they were so viewed. The particularist, it might be argued, confuses a distinction between motivation and justification. But this seems disingenuous. The particularist sees his or her association with the other not only as *motivating* the special favor but also as *grounding* it. The distinction is put to illegitimate work.

Furthermore, in the cases at issue, separating motivation from justification in the way suggested will significantly compromise the utilitarianism that supposedly informs the special treatment. Instead of providing a coherent theory of right action, there will be a dislocation between theory and practice, what Williams spoke of as a "willed forgetting . . . to keep the committed dispositions from being unnerved by instrumental reflection when they are under pressure."[21]

(3) One need not be a consequentialist to adopt a two-tiered position. Many writers have sought to provide nonconsequentialist impartialist justifications for special responsibilities. Alan Gewirth is representative. For Gewirth, a prime motivating factor is avoidance of the moral pluralism that he associates with Michael Walzer, Isaiah Berlin, Thomas Nagel, and Charles Taylor. His own ideological roots are in the Enlightenment, and his resistance to moral pluralism not only expresses a desire for theoretical simplicity but, more important, also purports to provide a unified standard of morality against which other contenders for our allegiance can be measured. He believes that having such a standard will secure us against opacity with respect to our most stringent moral convictions.

As Gewirth recognizes, to start where he does—from a commitment to impartialism (or, as he calls it, ethical universalism)—is already to prompt the question: Why there? His answer is that the impartialist position is coherent, central, and justifiable—assertions that he seeks to establish in other writings.[22] His fundamental ethical contention is that, as necessary conditions for human agency, all people have

---

[21] See Bernard Williams, *Ethics and the Limits of Philosophy* (London: Fontana, 1985), 108–110.
[22] See, in particular, Alan Gewirth, *Reason and Morality* (Chicago: University of Chicago Press, 1978).

equal rights to freedom and well-being. The same fundamental commitment, he believes, will also ground the special obligations that find expression in personal, familial, and national loyalties.

How so? The general principle, by virtue of its commitment to individual freedom, permits the formation of voluntary associations, including exclusive ones, *as long as they do not interfere with others' basic freedom*. To further the purposes of freedom and well-being, we can envisage the formation of various groupings such as families, friendship circles, and political structures, each contributing in its distinctive way to our individual freedom and well-being. Along with membership or participation in such groups will go obligations that are particular to their members.

But Gewirth wishes to see his justification as intrinsic and not merely instrumental. That is, the formation of these various associations does not merely contribute to our freedom but is expressive of it, and our purposes in entering into such associations are themselves partially constitutive of our well-being.[23] On such an account, loyalties are not shortchanged.

What, then, are we to say about clashes between the special obligations that arise out of our participation in voluntary associations and more general obligations that might emanate directly from the general principle? Gewirth answers that priority does not entail exclusivity, and attention to the one does not require a neglect of the other. That being the case, one important problem will be to determine *how* the competing obligations should be played off against each other—obligations that I have to my family and obligations that I have to the needy stranger, or obligations that I have to the needy of my own society and obligations I have to the Third World needy. I am sympathetic to that position, but, unless Gewirth can show how such trade-offs are to be undertaken, it is not easy to see how his two-tiered impartialism succeeds where he thinks pluralism fails.

PLURALIST OPTIONS

(1) Although Gewirth eschews pluralism, he does not avoid the difficulty constituted by conflicts of obligations. Some pluralists, however, have endeavored to go where Gewirth does not, by positing a clear strategy for handling such conflicts—that is, giving priority to general impartialist obligations whenever they conflict with special obligations.

Here it is useful and salient to consider Stephen Nathanson's defense of "moderate patriotism." For Nathanson, patriotic loyalty involves, inter alia, a special affection

---

[23] Alan Gewirth, "Ethical Universalism and Particularism," *Journal of Philosophy* 85, no. 6 (1998): 295.

for and sense of identification with one's country, a particular concern for its well-being, and willingness to make sacrifices in its behalf.[24] From this account, it would appear that the particularist commitment to (patriotic) loyalty is essentially an affective one that manifests itself in supportive behavior. It is a deep attachment in something like Williams's sense. As such, it has a special place in a person's sense of self.

Unlike Williams, however, Nathanson wants to argue that loyalties and other deep attachments should be given free rein only to the extent that they do not conflict with the demands of impartial morality. Should the latter occur, they ought to give way. This somewhat unexpected conclusion can be partially explained by the very different conceptions of morality with which Nathanson and Williams operate. For Williams, many of the demands of impartial morality are positive in nature—whether conceived as utilitarian or Kantian requirements. The effort required to fulfill them poses a threat to an agent's integrity. Nathanson, on the other hand, along with Bernard Gert,[25] whom he follows, works with a conception of impartial morality that is mostly negative. That is, it is not the task of morality to *set* goals but to provide *side constraints* on an individual's pursuit of diverse goals. Among those expectations, however, will be the requirement that one does one's duty, a demand that encompasses a set of secondary moral rules in which there are positive as well as negative obligations. These are acquired as a result of promises made, contracts signed, social roles entered into, or statuses possessed and include not only general social roles, such as those of parent or citizen, but also the specialized roles of lawyer, teacher, waiter, or club member.[26]

Although Nathanson believes that patriotism's affective and psychic dimensions acquire moral import, he does not make it clear how they do so. Even if we assume that the duties of citizenship possess moral weight, one may be a dutiful citizen without being a patriot. Perhaps his point is this: the affective attitudes that distinguish patriotism supervene upon the role of citizen, giving the patriot a heightened sense of the duties associated with citizenship.[27] The patriot is thus a specially dutiful citizen. However the connection is made, it is Nathanson's contention that where the duties associated with patriotic devotion conflict with the demands of impartial morality, the former should give way: "The constraints of morality apply to the pursuit of all other goals and to the carrying out of our special duties toward other individuals and groups."[28]

---

[24] Stephen Nathanson, *Patriotism, Morality, and Peace* (Lanham, MD: Rowman & Littlefield, 1993), 34–35.

[25] Bernard Gert, *Morality: A New Justification of the Moral Rules* (New York: Oxford University Press, 1988).

[26] Nathanson, *Patriotism, Morality, and Peace*, 41–42.

[27] Communication with Stephen Nathanson, November 23, 1998.

[28] Nathanson, *Patriotism, Morality, and Peace*, 46.

To Nathanson's credit, he recognizes that there is something troubling about the simplicity of this formula. Although it allows for the psychological anguish of opposing that to which one is patriotically drawn, it does not present itself as a clash between competing moral demands. He recognizes that on his account patriotism is a morally permissible ideal rather than a specific duty[29] and that this falls short of what others—such as Alasdair MacIntyre and Andrew Oldenquist—have claimed. It may hurt to moderate one's patriotism, but the moral priorities are clear enough.

As far as MacIntyre is concerned, Nathanson "emasculates" loyalty because he takes the moral ideals for which the object of loyalty supposedly stands rather than the object itself as the primary object of loyalty. Although the "moderate patriot" has a deep affection for his country, that affection is primarily to his country's ideals, whereas, as MacIntyre sees it, the genuine patriot is committed to his country (in part) because it is *his* country and not just because it happens to support those ideals.[30] The regard that one has for specific objects of loyalty is "founded upon a particular historical relationship of association between the person exhibiting the regard and the relevant person, institution or group."[31]

Oldenquist makes a somewhat similar point to MacIntyre when he distinguishes the "loyal patriot" from an "impartial patriot."[32] Whereas the former's judgment about what he should do "is partly determined by the fact that the good of his country is at stake," the latter does not give the thought "P is my country" any role in his determinations. No genuine loyalty is involved in impartial patriotism because it contains no "uneliminable singular terms." Indeed, Oldenquist speculates that impartial patriots are generally self-deceived. Although they feel personally connected to their country because it is *theirs*, they want to believe that their commitment conforms to impartial and universal moral standards and so ground such feelings in their country's commitment to such standards.[33]

How telling are these criticisms? Nathanson might reply that there is no emasculation, no elimination of singular terms, because the affective attitudes and dispositions associated with patriotism are married to roles—to one's being a citizen of *this* country rather than of some other—and therefore that there will be for the moderate

---

[29] Ibid., 48, though Nathanson is not always clear about this. See Igor Primoratz's comment in "Patriotism—Morally Allowed, Required, or Valuable?" originally published in *Nationalism and Ethnic Conflict: Philosophical Perspectives*, ed. N. Miscevic (Chicago: Open Court, 2000), 101–113, and reprinted in *Patriotism*, ed. Igor Primoratz (Amherst, NY: Humanity Books, 2002), 198, note 6.

[30] Alasdair MacIntyre, *Is Patriotism a Virtue?* (Lawrence: University of Kansas Press, 1984), 4.

[31] Ibid.

[32] Oldenquist, "Loyalties," 184.

[33] We will return to this view in chapter 13, when we discuss Keller's critique of patriotism.

patriot a partiality about the commitment *even if* that commitment is subject to over-riding by impartial morality.

There is, I believe, something else going on here that helps to account for the sense that each side to this dispute has something to be said for it. It is encapsulated in the differentiation between loyalty and loyalties and in the recognition that even though loyalty may be an important virtue to acquire, the objects of loyalty—loyalties—may sometimes be morally problematic. Nathanson's moderate patriot may seem to have too much of an eye on his country's conformity with impartial morality; MacIntyre's and Oldenquist's patriots may seem to have too little. Whereas the latter sometimes seem committed to "our country, right or wrong," Nathanson seems to say only "our country, when it is right." But something more is needed—hinted at in Carl Schurz's memorable retort to Stephen Decatur: "our country, right or wrong; when right to be kept right; when wrong to be put right."[34]

The point, I think, is this. The associative bond that carries loyalty does not merely intensify the obligations that go with the assumption of a role but creates obliga-tions of its own—associational, and not merely role obligations. The former seem to be missing from Nathanson's account but are overly protected in MacIntyre's and Oldenquist's accounts. In assessing something such as patriotism, we must consider not only loyalty in the abstract but also the particular association that loyalty helps to secure. We return to these issues later and in part II.

In the end, the pluralism against which Gewirth argues may not be unaccept-ably messy. Although the pluralist claims that special obligations cannot be reduced to or subsumed under obligations of an impartialist variety, this may result in no more problematic trade-offs than are ordinarily involved in conflicts of, say, utility and rights.[35] Thus, the fact that one's brother or mother (or even one's own self)[36] is at risk and is accorded an independent weight in the situation, one that is not obvi-ously counterbalanced by the archbishop's potential for social good, may be just an-other example of the multiple considerations that legitimately come into play when moral decision making is involved, and the reason that, in the end, moral decision making is a matter of judgment rather than of algorithmic calculation. Although this independent—or, if you like, foundational—weight is something that the monistic

---

[34] Carl Schurz, remarks in the Senate, February 29, 1872, *Congressional Globe* 45 (1872): 1287: http://en.wikisource.org/wiki/U._S._Senate_Speeches_and_Remarks_of_Carl_Schurz/Sales_of_Arms_to_French_Agents_6.

[35] But that, the Enlightenment theorist might argue, is just the rub. If there is no principle that arbitrates between aggregative and distributive principles, then decisions in the event of conflicts between them will be arbitrary.

[36] Though here the situation is a little different. See, for example, Joseph Beatty, "Him or Me?" *American Philosophical Quarterly* 23, no. 3 (July 1986): 231–241; John Cottingham, "Ethics and Impartiality," *Philosophical Studies* 43, no. 1 (1983): 83–99.

tendencies of the Enlightenment Project cannot easily accommodate, that may be so much the worse for the Enlightenment Project.

(2) As I have already noted, Oldenquist's pluralism is specifically oriented to the particularism of loyalties. Not only can the "uneliminable egocentric particulars" that are embedded in loyalty-based judgments not be accommodated within the impartialist model[37] but also, Oldenquist claims, loyalty-based judgments are morally more fundamental than the judgments of impartial morality: "Loyalties are norms that define the domains within which we accept the moral machinery of universalizable reasons and relevant differences."[38] He claims that we are essentially tribal—that "all morality is tribal morality"—and that "our wide and narrow loyalties define moral communities or domains within which we are willing to universalize moral judgments, treat equals equally, protect the common good, and in other ways adopt the familiar machinery of impersonal morality."[39] In other words, universalizability is a feature of the moral discourse that governs the various moral communities—or tribes—within which our lives are lived. It is not appropriate to the relations between those communities, for these are communities of loyalty.

For Oldenquist, a moral community is constituted by the existence of a shared good to which its members are severally committed. But there are diverse goods to which we are committed and therefore diverse moral communities to which we belong—not just families, but professional, political, and ethnic collectivities. Even humankind may constitute such a community (giving rise to species loyalty). Particular loyalties and their partisan distributions will find acceptance within particular moral communities, although those outside will be able to appreciate them only insofar as they have analogous attachments of their own.

An account such as this attracts the following objection: Why should we not set these shared goods—goods about which the various moral communities are said to form—beside the demands of a universal (impartialist) morality and even in some cases subject them to such a universal morality? Allow that the flourishing of these various communities is associated with their fostering of goods to which we are committed: Why should the preferential loyalties toward their members not exist alongside, and even sometimes be accountable to, a universal impartialist moral standard?

Oldenquist's most radical response is that there is no such thing as nontribal morality. Whether it is Kantian rationalism or utilitarian happiness, either it will be

[37] Oldenquist, "Loyalties," 175. See also his *The Non-Suicidal Society* (Bloomington: Indiana University Press, 1986), ch. 8–10; and "The Ethics of Parts and Wholes," *Criminal Justice Ethics* 12, no. 1 (Winter–Spring, 1993): 43–47.

[38] Oldenquist, "Loyalties," 182–183.

[39] Ibid., 178, 177.

tribally constrained (confined to rational human beings or human happiness) or it will be counterintuitively broadened.

He considers the possibility that humankind itself might constitute a community within which the claims of impartiality will operate and that this accommodates all that needs to be accommodated. But it does not. The general obligations that will be required as part of species loyalty, even if they are impartially fulfilled, will not be identical with—or substitute for—the requirements of impartial morality. As Oldenquist notes, the requirements of species loyalty will demand that we give preference to humans, should it be necessary to make a choice between humans and, say, Andromedans. But the requirements of impartial morality would be equally applicable to Andromedans, should they share the characteristics that make such requirements applicable to humans. Impartial morality is not tribal, even if we expand the tribe to include all humankind.[40]

In the case of a utilitarian account of loyalty, he claims that the maximizing calculus of utilitarianism wrongly "assumes that species loyalty is always the most demanding one"[41] and, further, that its focus on the greater good of the greater number (that is, wider loyalty) leads to counterintuitive conclusions. I think this latter claim misrepresents both loyalty and utilitarianism. Even though utilitarians may have a limited place for loyalty, I doubt whether their commitment to the greater number—even when restricted to humans—is seen in terms of loyalty.

SPECIAL OBLIGATIONS AS SUI GENERIS

It is not necessary to see the relation between impartial and particular obligations as Oldenquist does. Each may be seen as having a particular force and, on occasions, as needing to be traded off against the other.

To round out the foregoing discussion, I want to offer three observations—first, on the way in which obligations may arise from a variety of associative connections; second, on the conditions under which these obligations will constitute obligations of loyalty; and third, on the kinds of associations that generate the special obligations of loyalty. To some extent, these observations pick up on earlier points I have argued.

(1) As mentioned earlier, various nonexclusive sources of particularistic associative obligations can be identified—some voluntaristic and others recompensive. But

---

[40] Oldenquist tries to avoid the Kantian turn by claiming—implausibly, I think—that if confronted by rational civilizations beyond our own, the Kantian "would come to think in terms of *our* rational beings and *their* rational beings" (ibid., 179). I see no reason a Kantian should do this. What we see as the requirements of impartial morality apply to all rational beings and not just those in our own (human) tribe. The class of rational beings does not constitute a tribe.

[41] Ibid., 180–182.

these do not exhaust the sources of particularistic obligations. Nor, for the most part, do they explain the special obligations most commonly considered to be obligations of loyalty.

To understand the latter, we need to appreciate two things—first, the value that certain kinds of associative relations have (or come to have) for us and, second, the central and identity-conferring character that these associative relations may have.

Serious friendships (end-friendships) provide the easiest starting point.[42] As social creatures, we do not usually exist comfortably in social and comradely isolation but value for itself association with particular others, especially in friendship. In serious friendships, we value for themselves the others with whom we are in association and not merely for other values—pleasure or benefits—that may be realized through or satisfied by the friendship. True, if the other values that are often realized in and through the friendship cease to be realized in and through it, the friendship may wither and, with it, what we intrinsically value. But that does not reduce one to the other.

Intrinsic to friendship are certain preferential obligations. If another is my close friend, I will see myself as specially obligated to that other and, because such friendships are generally mutual, the other will see himself or herself as specially obligated to me. Such obligations are integral to the relationship and not simply contingent on other dimensions of the relationship, such as the instrumental benefits it brings or specific acts of reliance-creation that it involves. As Samuel Scheffler puts it:

> To attach noninstrumental value to my relationship with a particular person just is, in part, to see that person as a source of special claims in virtue of the relationship between us. It is, in other words, to be disposed, in contexts which vary depending on the nature of the relationship, to see that person's needs, interests, and desires as, in themselves, providing me with presumptively decisive reasons for action, reasons that I would not have had in the absence of the relationship.[43]

There is nothing especially mysterious about this. There are various ways in which others may constitute sources of reasons for our action toward them. If I am traveling on a road and someone steps into the path of my vehicle, I have a reason to change my trajectory. Should I fail to do so, I will fail in an obligation that I have to that particular other.[44] True, it is not the same as that which arises out of a relationship that I have formed with another, but it is generated by the specific relation in which I have found myself. If I am walking to my office and pass an injured person on the sidewalk, her

---

[42] I discuss friendship at greater length in chapter 8.

[43] Samuel Scheffler, "Relationships and Responsibilities," *Philosophy & Public Affairs* 26, no. 3 (Summer 1997): 196.

[44] Of course, if I am unable to avoid him, I will have an excuse.

need generates a reason for my providing assistance. It is part of our recognition of others as fellow human beings, as vulnerable or suffering, that their being present to us in certain ways will generate a reason for action—specifically, an obligation to contribute to their well-being. So, too, when I enter into a special relationship with another, say, one of close friendship, that relationship will generate certain obligations as surely as any need, promise, or debt of gratitude.

The obligations generated by such specific relationships are powerful but not necessarily overriding. They are defeasibly sufficient for action.[45] Usually the obligations of friendship will override general imperfect duties. If a charitable organization and a friend both seek my assistance, and I can help only one, the obligation to my friend will generally take precedence—though if the disparity in need is great enough, the scale may tip in favor of the charity.

The strength of obligations generated by specific relationships will depend on the relationship. Some relationships are pathological or corruptive, and we may indeed wonder whether there is anything more than a *perceived* obligation to the other. Just as there is a problem about the obligation to fulfill promises to do what is wrong, so, sometimes, there will be a problem about the status of obligations generated by corruptive friendships. The parties to the friendship will see themselves as obligated to each other, but others—standing outside the relationship and drawing on the resources of impartial morality—may reasonably consider such obligations to be illusory, of minimal (discounted) significance, or overridden by more important considerations.

Role obligations provide another context in which the obligations associated with particular relationships may have to give way to other kinds of considerations. It will often be improper if the discharge of role responsibilities is influenced by the particular obligations associated with friendship or family connectedness. Often, but not always. Not every occasion on which institutional and associative obligations come into conflict will require that the latter yield to the former. It may be acceptable if I cancel a lecture to tend to the pressing needs of an ailing parent.

The general point, however, is that there is no simple formula—even if there are sometimes well-established conventions—for determining the priority of particularistic and universalistic obligations. We need to look at the details. I shall have more to say about this in chapter 7.

(2) What distinguishes loyalty-based obligations? As we have already noted, obligations of loyalty are not merely contractual but arise in contexts in which the

---

[45] Scheffler speaks of the reasons generated by special relationships as "presumptively decisive": "reasons which, although they are capable in principle of being outweighed or overridden, nevertheless present themselves as considerations upon which I must act" ("Relationships and Responsibilities," 196).

relationship in question is *personal* in a special sense. This is the sense in which the object of the relationship is or has become constitutively *mine* or *ours*. In such cases, obligations to the other *that sustain the relationship* with the other will be those constitutive of loyalty to that other. What sustains the relationship will vary with both the object and the relationship. Relationship-sustaining obligations in the case of family relations will not be the same as those for an organization with which one has identified oneself. And different families will generate different associative ties, even though there may be some widely shared conventional ones. What unifies these obligations is an understanding that the parties will conduct themselves in ways that do not harm the relevant interests of the associational other and particularly resist the temptations of narrow self-interest. This does not require that the loyal person adopt the interests of another. Even in the case of friendship, valuing the friend for her own sake does not require a commonality of interests, only an interest in the protection and satisfaction of the friend's interests.

Something like this will hold for other associations of a loyalty-generating kind. I will have an interest in serving (at least some of) the interests of the other, and though I will not lose myself in the other or come to see myself as mirrored in the other, I will nevertheless see my relationship to the other as constituting a core value or as an important facet of my own identity.[46] But though the association is partially constitutive of my identity, it does not exhaust it, and other temptations, pressures, and desires may put me at odds with the conditions for that association. When I am loyal, I accept a cost that will preserve my connection to the associative other.

There is no deep difference between obligations of loyalty and other obligations of membership, apart from the fact that the former bear a special relation to the conditions for associative flourishing in those cases in which the object and association have come to have value in their own right for those who are party to the association. Although efforts are sometimes made to incorporate such obligations into the conditions for membership, they are not usually activated unless and until those to whom they are applied come to value the associational object for its own sake. In cases in which that does not occur but in which it is said that the person ought to be loyal, it will be because the association is considered important to the human flourishing of those otherwise engaged by it.

(3) What associations may *properly* generate the special obligations of loyalty? This is a highly controversial question, for what is intrinsically valued may not be deemed valuable. Friendship constitutes the easiest case: even if particular friendships are seen as problematic by those outside them, most of us have little difficulty in seeing

---

[46] As I noted earlier, this identification with the other may be quite conflicted. An abusive father or wayward country may still evoke one's loyalty, even as they act in ways that threaten it.

close friendships as constituting forms of relationship that are partly constitutive of a good life and in including obligations of loyalty among those arising out of such friendships. Spousal relationships will tend to function in much the same way as friendships, though it is arguable that intimate relationships of that kind need not be important to a good life. Filial, parental, and some other familial relationships are also likely to be seen as identity-conferring and important to flourishing. Although there are (usually) biological dimensions to such relationships, and important instrumental values are served by them, they are likely to be deeply dysfunctional if they are viewed as merely biological and/or instrumental. Because of the role that families play in intergenerational development, there is a case for seeing them as sites for both significant interpersonal trust and social good.[47]

More problematic will be various other associations into which I enter. Professional, team, and organizational associations will impose obligations on me. My membership in an ethnic group, my citizenship, or residency in a certain place will also bring obligations with them. Should I see such associations as requiring the additional or enhanced obligations that we associate with loyalty?

We will pursue these questions further in part II. A few preliminary remarks may, however, be appropriate. Initially, many of these other associations will have only an instrumental value for us. Indeed, the very raison d'être of such associations may be instrumental. But what starts off as instrumental may come to have intrinsic value. There is nothing particularly surprising about that. It can also happen in the case of friendship: what starts off as an essentially instrumental relationship then comes to acquire intrinsic value for the parties as the association evolves from one of means-friendship to one of end-friendship. The same may be true of team and organizational membership, one's ethnic associations, and citizenship. Over time, the association becomes integral to one's being.

Whether an association has become identity-conferring can often be discovered by the sorts of emotions experienced when the associative other succeeds or fails—if, for example, there is a team or organizational triumph that brings it glory or scandal that brings it disgrace. If one's reaction to such circumstances is one of pride or shame, respectively, then the chances are that one's relationship to the team, organization, or whatever is not merely one of instrumental connectedness but has become identity-conferring.

But to return to the initial question, should I develop an identity-conferring connectedness to such collectivities? The temptation to say no mainly arises from the perversions to which certain identity-conferring associations are prone: various kinds of

---

[47] See, for example, Jonathan Lear, *Love and Its Place in Nature*, 2nd ed. (New Haven, CT: Yale University Press, 1998).

chauvinism and jingoism; the bigotry of racism, sexism, and certain kinds of elitism; cover-ups and codes of silence; hubris and contempt. Nevertheless, we are beings for whom particularistic associations are important—our individuality is significantly bound up with the pluralism of our associations. Moreover, these associations don't just happen: they are fostered and sustained by certain kinds of social environments. Our valuing of our country or culture or ethnic heritage may be both instrumental, because it allows us to sustain other associations that are rich and intrinsically satisfying, and intrinsic, because being so identified is itself a source of personal flourishing. Provided that such loyalties do not become blind or absolute, there may be good reason to foster them. Again, these are issues that we explore in part II.

CONCLUSION

It is, as we noted at the outset, a problem for loyalty that it obligates particularistically in the face of what are sometimes deemed to be the universal claims of humanity. Our task in this chapter has not been to erase that problem, even though we have explored attempts to rationalize it. We are complex beings, obligated to others not only by virtue of our common humanity but also by virtue of associative relations that are integral to our flourishing. Tensions will sometimes arise, and though it is tempting to find some relatively simple algorithm to deal with them, judgment is ultimately called for.

Nevertheless, there is still more to be said about the way we negotiate conflicts among values and why associations for which loyalty-related obligations would be appropriate are so. Are there some kinds of association into which we *ought* to enter in a loyalty-generating way and others into which we might (merely) *permissibly* enter in a loyalty-generating way? And if we do enter into such associative relations, do we sacrifice our individuality? These questions will continue to occupy us.

6

OPPOSITIONS

Our country! In her intercourse with foreign nations may she always be in the right; but our country, right or wrong.[1]

Our country, right or wrong; when right to be kept right; when wrong to be put right.[2]

LOYALTY AND DISSENT

It is frequently complained that loyalty involves at least complaisance but more commonly a blind devotion to its object. Loyalty asks no questions; it is a pledge to stand by another no matter what.

There is some historical support for this complaint. Those who demand the loyalty of their subordinates often brook no dissent. Loyalists are often yes-men (and women), and they are frequently passionately critical of those who remain uncommitted or questioning. For a time, the surge of patriotic loyalty that followed the events of 9/11 left little room for a serious questioning of American policies or values, and the plaintive "why do they hate us?" reflected bewilderment more than sober self-reflection.[3] It was not simply that thoughtful questioning displayed insensitivity toward those who were grieving (like delivering a critical eulogy at a funeral), but that it was considered unpatriotic to do so: this was a time for national unity, for supporting the country's leadership no matter what that leadership was saying, planning, or doing. At one point, Attorney General John Ashcroft accused of siding with terrorism those

[1] Stephen Decatur, "Toast Given at Norfolk" (April 1816).
[2] Carl Schurz, remarks in the Senate, February 29, 1872, *Congressional Globe*, 45 (1872): 1287: http://en.wikisource.org/wiki/U._S._Senate_Speeches_and_Remarks_of_Carl_Schurz/Sales_of_Arms_to_French_Agents_6.
[3] See Richard Reeves, "Patriotism Calls Out the Censor," *New York Times*, October 1, 2001, A23.

who raised questions about American policies. Even when those who raised questions indicated that their concern was to explain rather than justify what had happened, their inquiries were seen as evidence of a failure to pull together at a time when pulling together was paramount. The garrison was being attacked; it was time for a garrison ethic; there was no room for questioning, let alone dissent. If there is a critical problem for loyalty, particularly within a framework of liberal thinking, this surely is it.

How critical? The present chapter is intended to address that question. I begin by gathering together some strands from my earlier discussion that indicate a view of loyalty more open to critical reflection than the foregoing complaint suggests. As a strategy for reinforcing that, I turn to a political tradition that is usually underplayed in discussions of loyalty—that of a loyal opposition. As something of a case study, I trace its rather different articulations in England and the United States and conclude by asking whether appeal to the idea of a loyal opposition is sufficient to rescue loyalty from its detractors.

QUESTIONING LOYALTIES

First, let us grant that demands for loyalty often discourage questioning and dissent. They discourage it either by seeing dissent as disloyal or by fostering a self-deceptively unquestioning attitude. Even though a virtue, it can be and often is manipulated and/or exploited. Not that it is completely alone in its susceptibility to manipulation: kindness and generosity may also be exploited. Nevertheless, kindness and generosity have not suffered the same backlash, and this obviously calls for explanation. My initial response is that the social damage threatened or caused by the manipulation or exploitation of loyalties tends to be much greater than that threatened or caused by the manipulation or exploitation of kindness and generosity. Because it is an associative virtue, when loyalty is exploited, the effects are compounded: we may be dealing with whole countries and not just independent individuals, and the collective power of loyalty may be humanly destructive.

Although any loyalty can be manipulated, loyalties are more likely to be exploited in cases in which they are cultivated and demanded than in cases in which they are the natural outgrowth of a relationship.[4] Loyalty is most likely to be expected in situations in which instrumentally defined institutions are deemed to be under threat and need loyal support for the protection or optimization of that for which they exist. Paradigmatic will be countries under attack and profit-making enterprises in a competitive market situation. Because loyal citizens and employees are likely to be more

---

[4] I am, however, conscious that converts are often more militant than those whose loyalties are inherited.

productive than a-loyal ones, they will be more willing to risk themselves or put out for the institution or organization. That may be said to involve a willingness to do whatever it takes to secure the collective against external challenges.

Rogues and extremists may count on us acquiring particular loyalties and then seek to exact from us extensions that we may not be well prepared to resist or to which resistance will be costly. Like the seducer who says, "If you really love me, you'll go to bed with me," the exploiter of loyalty trades on our insecurities, fears, and uncertainties about what, precisely, the relationship may reasonably require of us.

Our vulnerability to the exploitation of loyalty is exacerbated by at least four factors that we have previously noted:

1. When excessive loyalty is demanded of us, we may not feel that demand as a demand for loyalty instead of integrity, but as a demand that exploits our integrity by playing off one element against another. The demand thus threatens disintegration—and, if acceded to, will result in reintegration with a somewhat different identity. Dealing with the initial demand may therefore be extremely stressful.
2. The boundaries of the "natural" virtues are indeterminate. Unlike the so-called artificial virtues, which correlate with perfect, strictly determinable duties, imperfect duties—the complement of the natural virtues—do not mandate specific courses of action.
3. Acceptance of the fiction that nonloyalty is disloyalty. And disloyalty is viewed as a primal sin—a betrayal of deeply tribal values with which we have been inculcated.
4. The demands of personal loyalty will have much greater *psychological* force for us than the seemingly impersonal abstractions of universal morality.

And so, when loyalty is *demanded* of us—as most extremist and roguish loyalties are—we may not find it easy to resist their force. We are made to feel not merely nonconforming but traitors to a cause that we should be upholding. Such loyalties, as we have often seen in religion and politics, may be played upon with devastating social effects.[5]

But as I have argued repeatedly, not every call to show loyalty is exploitative (any more than I would want to say it of calls to show gratitude). Sometimes such calls

---

[5] Consider, for example, the McCarthy-era anti-Communist witch-hunts in the United States, the police code of silence, Robert McNamara's loyalty to the U.S. president during the Vietnam years, the rushes into Afghanistan and Iraq, and similar excesses. Other societies probably fare no better, and sometimes worse. However, contrary to some critics of loyalty, I do not think that these abuses of loyalty provide a sufficient argument against political (and other) loyalties but for a more nuanced discussion.

may function simply as *reminders* of obligations we have to another, whether they are obligations of association (as in loyalty) or of benefaction (as in gratitude).

Nor is loyalty congenitally blind—that is, an attachment from which all critical reflection has been excluded. Unquestioning compliance represents a defect of loyalty rather than its modus operandi. Even if loyalties can be manipulated, there are usually deliberative presumptions in their development and exercise. Loyalties may be earned, owed, deserved, and forfeited, and, as I want to argue here, expressions of loyalty may not only be compatible with dissent, criticism, and even opposition, but be manifested best through them. That is one of the enduring lessons of Hirschman's *Exit, Voice, and Loyalty.*

In addition, and in anticipation of what I will argue in the next chapter, implicit in obligations of loyalty is the idea of *contextualized proportionality.* The legitimate expectations we will have of loyal friends, citizens, spouses, club members, and employees will be both *varied* and *limited.* We expect that loyal friends, when faced with competing attractions, say, attending a movie or party, will forgo them to be with us if we need them. We expect that if loyal friends hear us being bad-mouthed by others, they will at least not join in and, if appropriate, will speak in our behalf, even if this exposes them to criticism or ridicule. Loyal citizens might be expected to volunteer for, or at least not shirk the expectation of, service if their country is under threat. We may even expect that their doing so will subject their lives and well-being to grave risk. From a loyal spouse, we may expect sexual fidelity and a refusal to engage in certain forms of public disclosure or criticism. And so on. Such obligations are, for the most part, limited in the cost they exact or sacrifice they require. Even if I may be expected to lay my life on the line for my country, it would be unreasonable for my football club to expect the same. Leaving my wife for another woman may constitute disloyalty; leaving my university for another is less likely to do so.

Not only are the obligations of loyalty varied and limited but also they—or at least their performance—may be qualified even further by the exigencies of life. If my college seeks loyal financial support at a time when I have overwhelming domestic commitments, it will constitute no disloyalty if I regretfully decline to assist. My friend might normally expect me to visit when she is feeling depressed, but it would probably not be a breach of loyalty if instead I visit my equally needful mother. Obligations of loyalty, like other obligations, have a ceteris paribus or other qualifying phrase attached to them. What cannot legitimately qualify them are self-serving considerations.

This brings me to the idea of a loyal opposition, an idea that has its origins in the development of parliamentary democracy but has gained much wider significance for understanding the nature and limits of loyalty. Given that it remains unexplored in most philosophical discussions of loyalty, I give it more detailed and contextualized attention than it would otherwise get.

THE IDEA OF A LOYAL OPPOSITION

To point out that there exists room for the idea of (a) loyal opposition is not quite the same as showing its importance. It could be argued that the notion of a loyal opposition is of only marginal significance—a kind of limiting case—and that the idea of quiescence or ready, compliant support is much more central.

My contention, however, will be that a quiescent loyalty is corrupting. It is *only* as we provide ample space for the idea of opposition—albeit a loyal one—that loyalty can be rescued from some of the distortions that have made it such a problematic virtue. It will not, however, be my intention to argue that the only acceptable form of opposition is a loyal one. If loyalty is not—or no longer—owed or has been forfeited, then even loyal opposition may be inappropriate. Such opposition, however, will not ipso facto be disloyal. This does not mean that it will not be asserted to be disloyal. As noted earlier, loyalty is often manipulated: it is said to be owed even if it is not, or even if it is, it is claimed to be owed in certain ways even if it is not.

Critics may see talk of "(a) loyal opposition" as oxymoronic. Though this does not amount to saying that contradiction is involved, it suggests a way of talking that sits uncomfortably with the common presumption that loyalty requires an active support for and even devotion to its object. When the president of the United States gathers around him a group of loyal aides, he does not expect to get people who will criticize or oppose him. What he looks for are people who will help him to implement his policies and who, even if they have reservations about them and their implementation, will nevertheless support him. The support that is commonly assumed to flow from that loyalty is resolute—even absolute. As Edward Weisband and Thomas Franck put it:

> In America, every political appointee who joins the executive branch by fiat of the President is expected to remember that he owes his leader total public loyalty. [The appointee] must constantly bear in mind that his power is the President's revocable gift. . . . Presidents of the United States deliberately exclude from the executive branch the kind who resign and go public or, indeed, anyone who is likely to stand up, particularly in public, against Presidential will. . . . Loyalty to the President has become the overriding ethic[6]

When Ray Whitrod, a former Queensland Police Commissioner, arrived in Brisbane to take up his position, he was told that "the over-riding ethic in the Queensland

---

[6] Edward Weisband and Thomas M. Franck, *Resignation in Protest: Political and Ethical Choices between Loyalty to Team and Loyalty to Conscience in American Public Life* (New York: Grossman, 1975), 121, 123, 131. Note, though, the reference to "public" loyalty in excluding opposition. Such public loyalty is consistent with behind-the-scenes disagreement.

Government was loyalty. When I [Whitrod] asked what that meant in practice, I was told: 'The Minister always gets what he wants.'"[7] As we noted in an earlier chapter, Ewin treats this as integral to loyalty: loyalty involves "a willingness on the part of the loyal person to subordinate his or her interests to those of the object of loyalty,"[8] even to the point of "setting aside . . . good judgement."[9] And Royce's much-quoted definition of loyalty as "the willing and practical and thoroughgoing devotion of a person to a cause"[10] does not seem to leave much room for any opposition, let alone a loyal one.

AN EVOLUTIONARY HISTORY

The idea of a loyal opposition has struggled to gain a respectable foothold, but now both the phrase and idea have gained traction and respectability in politics and more widely. It is useful to track its evolution in British parliamentary politics and US White House politics. Rather than undermining the growth of liberalism, for the most part it has accompanied and reinforced that growth.

Archibald S. Foord dates the phrase "His Majesty's Opposition" to an intentionally humorous remark by Sir John Hobhouse in an 1826 parliamentary debate.[11] The

---

[7] Ray Whitrod, at a conference in Canberra, as reported in *The Age*, May 13, 1988. Whitrod's tenure as police commissioner was relatively short-lived. He resigned after egregious ministerial interference. Many years later, he was a potent witness for the Fitzgerald Royal Commission into the Queensland Police Service, an investigation that also brought down the long-serving Queensland government. Whitrod's experience of realpolitik is not unusual. In an article profiling Rudolph Giuliani, later to become a controversial but successful New York mayor, Connie Bruck quoted a former assistant on Giuliani's personnel appointments: "Rudy values loyalty above all." Bruck went on to claim that although some believed that "Giuliani liked being challenged and was open to persuasion," others saw him as choosing people who would go along with whatever he wanted. As another former assistant put it: "Rudy surrounded himself with people who are not exercising independent judgment, and because Rudy is such a gung-ho prosecutor, the easiest thing for those under him to do is not to make decisions for clemency—because those will be criticized—but to be gung-ho cowboys." "Rudolph Giuliani," *American Lawyer* 3 (March 1989). In his book, *Leadership* (with Ken Kurson), Giuliani also made it clear that loyalty is "the vital virtue" (New York: Miramax Books/Hyperion, 2002), ch. 10.

[8] R. E. Ewin, "Loyalty: The Police," *Criminal Justice Ethics* 9, no. 2 (Summer–Fall 1990): 4.

[9] R. E. Ewin, "Loyalty and Virtues,"*Philosophical Quarterly* 42, no. 169 (October 1992): 411.

[10] Josiah Royce, *The Philosophy of Loyalty* (New York: Macmillan, 1908), 16–17. In fairness to Royce, however, he allows that events may appropriately lead one to call into question the object of one's loyalty.

[11] Speech, *Hansard, House of Commons* 15 (April 10, 1826), 135. Quoted in Archibald Smith Foord, *His Majesty's Opposition 1714-1830* (Oxford: Clarendon, 1964). As for "His/Her Majesty's (Most) *Loyal* Opposition," it is unclear when the phrase was coined, though the idea of loyalty was probably intended in characterizing the opposition as "His Majesty's." Perhaps to

idea, however, has historical antecedents, traceable in the gradual erosion of absolute monarchical power and its replacement by a constitutional monarchy ruling by means of an increasingly independent parliamentary democracy. Its key points have been the Magna Carta of 1215, the Revolution Settlement of 1688–1689, and the emergence of political parties in the late eighteenth century. Absolute monarchies had little space for opposition: opposition was, if not treasonous or subversive, then disruptive. But the ceding (or loss) of monarchical powers to parliamentary rule created an institutional environment characterized by multiple voices, some of which were oppositional. Parties, initially seen as disruptive factions, eventually became the medium through which both parliamentary life and parliamentary opposition were regulated. With the formation of political parties, most particularly with the formation of a primarily two-party system, the institutional framework for "His Majesty's Loyal Opposition" was created.

Thomas Hockin provides a conceptual structure for this development via three successive historical models of loyal opposition:[12]

(1) The Old Tory Model (exemplified during the reigns of Elizabeth I and James I). During this period, a right of individual members of Parliament to register their opposition on local and private matters was recognized but did not extend to any "Great Matters of State." Excluded from challenge were issues relating to royal succession, the church, and foreign policy. These remained royal prerogatives. Members of Parliament were bound to make only those judgments that were suited to their authority and, it was claimed, the Great Matters of State did not lie within their sphere of competence. "The Crown represented the national interest and Parliament special and local interest."[13] Members were not bound to a party but to their local constituencies. Any member who chose to oppose the monarch on matters of state would constitute an opposition, but he would not constitute a loyal one.

Within the Old Tory Model, there was at best a minimal loyal opposition. Except for its toleration on local and private matters, opposition had no formal recognition. There was no recognition of the need for parliamentary watchdogs except, perhaps, in the matter of public bills. And to be characterized as a party man was stigmatizing: it was to be labeled as factional, lacking in public spiritedness, and narrow.

---

reinforce its essentially liberal democratic character, it was later felt necessary to make the implication explicit. The long version is often (incorrectly) dated from the same event. On its later import, cf. W. Ivor Jennings: "If there be no Opposition, there is no democracy. 'Her Majesty's Opposition' is no idle phrase. Her Majesty needs an Opposition as well as a Government." *Cabinet Government* (Cambridge: Cambridge University Press, 1936), 16. In what follows, I have made substantial use of Foord.

[12] Thomas A. Hockin, "The Roles of the Loyal Opposition in Britain's House of Commons: Three Historical Paradigms," *Parliamentary Affairs* 25, no. 1 (1971): 50–68.

[13] Ibid., 56.

(2) The Model of a "Balanced Constitution." In this postrevolutionary period (mid-eighteenth century), the national interest was no longer seen as the exclusive prerogative of the Crown but as one shared by the king, Lords, and Commons. With the advent of the Hanoverians, opposition in matters of national as well as local policy achieved some kind of constitutional basis. Here "the Opposition [is] an Opposition not only to a bad administration of public affairs, but to an administration that supports itself by means, establishes principles, introduces customs, repugnant to the constitution of our Government and destructive of all liberty."[14] If any one of the three sources of authority overstepped its powers, the other two would (in theory, at least) combine to restrain it.

On this model, there was still no idea of a disciplined, organized opposition. That would have smelled of disloyalty. Opposition was seen as issue-based and grounded in concern for the public interest rather than factional dominance.

(3) The Parliamentary Party Model. This contemporary model considers opposition to be vested in parties rather than individuals. The member of parliament is a party man, pledged to carry out the party program if his party is in power or, if in opposition, to criticize the ruling party's program—in the short run, to have it amended or withdrawn but in the long run to persuade Parliament or the electorate of a need for change so that the opposition's program may be instated as the program of government. In either case, failure to vote with the party may be seen as betrayal.

The theory behind this view is that only parties, and not individuals, offer the prospect of stable and coherent government. Because of this, it is seen as loyal to oppose the government in a systematic and continuing fashion, for the opposition represents a viable alternative government, sharing the same constitutional commitments as the party in power. One of the virtues of this form of opposition is said to be its openness—it is no longer necessary to engage in intrigue or backstairs negotiation if opposition is to be registered. Potentially, it also opens opposition to the public, since the public may actively involve itself in party matters.

As we now understand it, several ideas underpin that of a parliamentary loyal opposition:

(1) It refers specifically to elected representatives of the nongoverning major party (or coalition), whichever party that happens to be.
(2) Its central role is to critique the policies and practices of the governing party. There is some disagreement as to how relentless that criticism should be. Certainly, it is there to represent minority viewpoints, so that those in power do not neglect

---

[14] Viscount Bolingbroke, *Letter on the Spirit of Patriotism*, quoted in Foord, *His Majesty's Opposition 1714–1830*, 147.

the diversity that is found in the electorate. But should it also be with an eye to the instatement of alternative policies of its own if and when it comes into power? Or should its task be more resolutely oppositional, the purpose being to effect a change of power?[15]

(3) Whatever one's answer to the questions posed in (2), the loyal opposition is expected to be prepared to assume the responsibilities of political power if elected. It is dedicated to the seamless or at least peaceful transfer of power, either through shifts that occur in parliamentary opinion or as the result of a general election. In preparation for this, a loyal opposition is likely to develop alternative policies, a shadow ministry, and to practice political discipline of the kind that might be expected were it to be in government. In doing so, it may seem to provide a solution to the problem of political stability in a democratic environment.

The second and third ideas are often stated in the one breath, as though they are mutually reinforcing and compatible: "the Opposition is at once the alternative to the Government and a focus for the discontent of the people."[16] Bernard Crick, however, argues that if they are both kept as conscious goals, they may be in serious tension. He argues strongly for the second, claiming that if the opposition comes to power, its leader will be able to harness the disparate voices into a unified and workable government.[17]

(4) The tactics employed by the loyal opposition are expected to be consistent with the laws and conventions of the state. It is "a responsible body, obliged not to take any action calculated to drive the country into chaos."[18] Dictatorial regimes choose to ignore this underlying commitment of a loyal opposition, preferring instead to characterize it as destabilizing. What for the most part is ignored (or feared) is the accountability that is implicit in the idea—a loyal opposition forces those in power to answer for their conduct.

How liberal and democratic a loyal opposition is will depend on the way in which it is ritualized within a particular political order. Even a two-party system will provide only limited accountability if the representable range of options is too narrow, if the parties are too unevenly balanced, if party machines are not open to public

---

[15] See Bernard Crick, "Two Theories of Opposition," *New Statesman*, June 18, 1960, 882–883.

[16] Jennings, *Cabinet Government*, 15.

[17] For Crick, the opposition's task is nothing more and nothing less than to unseat the government, to attack it by every legitimate means available to it, whether or not it expresses a coherent alternative position: "an opposition is irresponsible if it pictures itself as an alternative, 'responsible' government; the public is then robbed of the constant root-and-branch criticism of government to which it is entitled." "Two Theories of Opposition," 882.

[18] Foord, *His Majesty's Opposition 1714–1830*, 2.

involvement, if the media are weak, and so on. Thus, to rectify some of the failures in democratic politics, Philip Pettit suggests "contestatory democratization," in which individuals have access to a variety of fora within which their voice can be heard, and governmental structures and procedures are designed to ensure that voices will be acknowledged and responded to.[19]

Although British parliamentary politics has evolved a stable form of loyal opposition, it sustains this by means of a fairly rigid party system. Even though the party in opposition is loyal, members who cross the floor on matters that are believed to express party policy do so at their peril. A member who does this is likely to be charged with disloyalty. The reason for this can be discerned in Benjamin Disraeli's criticism of Sir Robert Peel: He "seems never to have been conscious that the first duty of an English Minister is to be faithful to his party, and that good and honourable government is not only consistent with that tie, but is in reality mainly dependent on its sacred observance."[20] Fidelity to the party is important because, in English politics, the party system is believed to provide an effective forum for the interplay of diverse viewpoints and, since political candidates are voted for primarily by virtue of their party membership, a member of Parliament's failure to vote with the party is seen as a betrayal of the trust that has been put in him or her. If the people do not like what the party is doing, they can make their disapproval clear next time they vote.[21] It is complicated, of course, when a member represents a constituency that is likely to be adversely affected by the legislation in question. Here, what might express party policy comes into conflict with what many of the member's constituency perceive as good for them (for example, termination of rural subsidies).

The situation tends to be different, however, if, in opposition to his party's position, a member resigns, or if, in opposition to a cabinet decision, a minister resigns from his or her ministerial position. Then a public declaration of opposition is generally seen as legitimate (because principled and not self-serving).

The English tradition offers a number of fruitful contrasts with US executive branch politics. When the US Constitution was formulated, checks and balances were incorporated to prevent an overreaching of governmental power. Presidential power could be checked by Congress and the courts, and Congress and the courts each had its own internal balance. What was not envisaged was the need for a

---

[19] Philip Pettit, "Republican Freedom and Contestatory Democratization," in *Democracy's Value*, ed. Ian Shapiro and Casiano Hacker-Cordón (Cambridge: Cambridge University Press, 1999), 163–190.

[20] Benjamin Disraeli, *Lord George Bentinck: A Political Biography*, new ed. (London: Routledge, 1858), 282, quoted in Jennings, *Cabinet Government*, 15.

[21] It is, of course, far more complicated than this. Party policy is not nearly as seamless as it is sometimes made out to be.

balancing mechanism *within* the executive branch. Weisband and Franck explain the absence by reference to Madison's confident belief that "in republican government, the legislative authority necessarily predominates."[22] It was not envisaged that formally unchecked presidential power would expand to the degree that it did during the Bush administration. What is more, until Lincoln, those who were appointed to the executive branch were major political leaders such as Hamilton and Jefferson, and, like British cabinet ministers, they brought with them the traditions of political office.

However, from the beginning of the twentieth century, presidential power to influence both foreign and domestic policy increased enormously, and presidents gathered around them people who were not career politicians but bankers, industrialists, and corporate lawyers, seconded for a few years before returning (most likely) to something like the world from which they came. Furthermore, the ruling concept of presidential management came to be that of a team whose captain and coach is the president. Members of the team are expected to view their task as one of articulating and implementing the president's vision in a coordinated fashion. The premise has been that there is weakness, even paralysis, in individual assertion; only in teamwork is there strength. Team members have but one loyalty: the president. He is the people's elected representative, and any alternative views that members personally hold must take a back seat to those of the president.

Within this operating framework, there is little room for opposition, not even a loyal one. Nor is there much likelihood of opposition. (There may be disagreement and even disapproval but not opposition—not, that is, active steps to prevent the implementation or perpetuation of a particular course of action.) Presidential appointments are favors dispensed to people whose credentials are likely to include a history of nonpolitical service in which the same kind of resolute loyalty that the president wants is expected and likely to have been already demonstrated. Some of these presidential appointments, moreover, may be freighted with a personal dimension approaching that of friendship. Loyalties, then, will be personal rather than to Constitution or people: "To a public official with a taste for service but none for politics, maintaining a civilized standard of personal decency to the President tends to loom larger than any abstract duty to 'the public' or 'the system.'"[23]

If any member of the executive branch is unable to give his or her full support to the president, the only decent thing to do is resign. And the only decent way to resign is quietly, advancing reasons that deflect attention from possible conflict.

---

[22] *The Federalist*, No. 51, quoted in Weisband and Franck, *Resignation in Protest*, 124, from which I have shamelessly drawn.

[23] Weisband and Franck, *Resignation in Protest*, 85.

Loyalty is to be shown in disengagement as well as engagement, and a quiet resignation ("personal reasons") is the only form of loyal resignation. Protest resignations
are rarities.

If opposition is publicly expressed on the job or in leaving it, it will be seen not
merely as unforgivably disloyal but as also as punishable: the public-protest resigner
is likely to be seen as ineligible for any future public office (whichever party is in
power), her reputation is likely to be permanently besmirched, and even her return
to the world from which she came may be troubled.[24] Few want to deal with trouble-
makers who cannot be trusted. The quiet resigner, on the other hand—or even the
convicted loyal rogue—will retain her eligibility for a position of trust in which confidences will need to be kept and the boat will not be rocked.

The disincentives of public opposition (even if associated with assertions of continued loyalty) are such as to deter the public-protest resignation of all but the most
courageous or obsessive. What this punitiveness toward public-protest resignation
results in—and what Weisband and Franck claim it causes—is the subversion or dramatic constriction of individual ethical autonomy, the charge leveled by Agassi and
others against all loyalty. The president's men (and women) must be(come) yes-men,
unable to say no (except via a conspiratorially quiet resignation). Not only so, but
democratic values are also undermined because the official's concerns are not carried
to the people—or at least not carried to them by the person who is probably in the
best position to present them. Beyond that, some principled and competent people
are denied a continuing role in (a certain kind of) public life, other principled and
competent people will be deterred from entering it, and the likelihood increases that
those who respond to the presidential call will not be those in whom the public trust
should be vested.

Weisband and Franck note this difference between US presidential appointees
and British cabinet ministers. The latter are career politicians with constituencies,
and executive decisions are cabinet decisions rather than prime ministerial ones.
The prime minister is simply primus inter pares, and responsibility for decisions
is shared. Because this is so, debate over matters of policy is likely to be vigorous, with room not only for opposition to the prime minister but also for overrul-
ing him or her. If, after expressing opposition in the cabinet room, decisions are
made that sit too uncomfortably with a minister, she or he may not only resign,
but resign in protest. The latter, indeed, is expected, though there is a ritual aspect
to the resignation-protest process, lest the resignation cause damage that goes too
much beyond the issue in contention. (It is both a conscientious act and a political

---

[24] This is probably not true of academics, though they do not generally comprise a large proportion of those who are called into presidential service.

maneuver.) Provided that appropriate procedures are followed, such opposition will not be viewed as an act of disloyalty. Such members will return to their position on the backbench and will be eligible for promotion at some later time, particularly if events prove them right.

For the US presidential appointee, however, being right is no defense: "being right is no excuse for disloyalty to the team."[25] An appointee who, in resigning, focuses on the issues and the correctness of his perceptions will find that those who respond will "tackle his etiquette rather than his cause."[26]

As Weisband and Franck see it, the toleration and even encouragement of loyal opposition within the British cabinet structure constitutes a major advantage. Not only does it uphold the importance of moral autonomy and moral integrity within a vital public sphere but it also enables areas of significant disagreement to become issues of informed public debate. Moreover, British cabinet ministers, unlike their American counterparts, are "permitted" to draw on inside information to explain their reasons for resignation[27] and, if their claims gain enough public support, what was seen (by the ex-minister) as unconscionable policy may be reversed. This is hardly a travesty of democratic process: to the contrary, it makes the people the jury, all the more important on an issue that is deemed contentious and significant enough to generate a resignation.[28]

Charles Fried has endeavored to meet the charge that executive branch loyalty is incompatible with moral autonomy. In his memoir of the years he spent as President Reagan's solicitor general, he draws a distinction between (what he calls) "political-science" or "mandate" or (what I would call) "complaisance" and (what I will call) "commitment" conceptions of loyalty. Adherents of the complaisance view will take it as their task to discern and implement their chief's wishes. As Fried sees it, proponents of the commitment conception will not see themselves quite so instrumentally. Rather, they understand that it is as *persons* that they have their appointment, and that though this requires "congruence" between themselves and their chief, it is a congruence born of autonomous commitment rather than of self-interest or blind

---

[25] Weisband and Franck, *Resignation in Protest*, 62.

[26] Ibid., 65.

[27] Weisband and Franck point to the irony of the fact that whereas British disclosures formally violate the terms of the Official Secrets Act (1911) and American disclosures are permitted, the British make an informal exception of ministerial disclosures and Americans react toward the same in a socially punitive manner (*Resignation in Protest*, 118–119).

[28] The relative openness of British ministerial politics to dissent is counterbalanced by the greater controls on parliamentary voting. Whereas it is not uncommon for American politicians to cross the floor, even on matters that are important to the White House or the party in opposition, it is much rarer for members of the British House of Commons to vote against a party position. When it occurs, such dissent is likely to be considered betrayal.

devotion. This allows them to have some independence in determining what loyalty requires of them:

> [The commitment view] means that the President not merely deserves to be, but can only be effectively served by officers whose minds . . . "go along together" with his. That can only mean that what the officer conceives in his particular domain, as a result of his own independent judgment, extends and enlarges and conforms to the President's will. It is not at all a matter of guessing the President's mind— for he is unlikely to have one on the matter—but of constructing his leader's mind in a way that he will later embrace as his own.[29]

Although Fried's commitment view is clearly preferable to the strict complaisance view, it is easy to understand "congruence" too narrowly. There is no special reason why the congruence has to be thought of merely as "enlarging and conforming to the President's will" or, in the absence of an expressed will, of "constructing his leader's mind in a way that he will later embrace as his own." This is too submissive. There must be some room for disagreement, even opposition—that is, for attempts to change the president's mind, for showing the president that in terms of broader values that he affirms, and that one shares, a particular course of action would be better than one he is proposing or currently supporting. To be fair to Fried, his extended text supports the more expansive notion, for he illustrates his position by describing a decision he took that went against the will of his "political superiors" in the White House (albeit not an explicit directive from the president). Nevertheless, in saying that he "had been appointed to exercise [his] judgment," Fried understates the problematic character of his position: he was appointed to exercise his judgment by those who believed that he was in tune with the president, would conform his judgment to that of the president, and would not, as he reported, anger him.[30]

It is understandable, of course, that a president would want to gather around him aides sympathetic to and even supportive of his general vision. A president can be hands-on only to a certain degree and must rely on the hands of others. But there is arrogance involved in thinking that that vision cannot be enlarged and even amended in the course of governing. Although it is unreasonable to expect the president to be under constant challenge from those who have been appointed to implement his general policies, there is surely room for a more extensive autonomy than the one

---

[29] Charles Fried, *Order and Law: Arguing the Reagan Revolution—A Firsthand Account* (New York: Simon & Schuster, 1991), 195 (from ch. 6, "Loyalty").

[30] The moral hazards were seen in the use of Colin Powell to argue for the invasion of Iraq before the UN Security Council on February 5, 2003.

to which Fried adverts. Or, to put it in somewhat different terms: if the structure of presidential authority is such that there is very limited room for loyal opposition within the executive branch (because the president alone has a public mandate and appointees are the beneficiaries of his favor alone), then a genuine regard for autonomy should not make the costs of public-protest resignation as prohibitive as they currently appear to be. During the Bush administration, what one saw in presidential politics was a drift back into monarchical or even feudal notions of fealty and away from the robust debate and collective decision making that is intended to characterize democratic politics.[31]

BALANCING LOYALTY AND OPPOSITION

The foregoing narrative of some of the vicissitudes of political loyal opposition strongly suggests that even though loyalty need not be incompatible with some forms of opposition, the latter's place within a framework of loyalty is unclear and sometimes contentious. A more theoretical representation of this is found in Hirschman's *Exit, Voice, and Loyalty*,[32] where, as we have already noted, he argues for the importance of a "voiced" loyal opposition as a means whereby those who value an association can try to counteract institutional decline. A loyal opposition enables its recuperative return to the values that have underlain its associational commitments. Not only do loyalists give an ailing organization more breathing space and an increased opportunity for reform but—at least in theory—more *effective* pressure for recuperative change. Indeed, it is just because the imaginative ("socially inventive") exercise of voice may exact greater individual costs than exit that an effective use of voice can depend on the presence of people who have some loyalty to the institution.

Although he does not specifically intend it, Hirschman provides a structure for understanding the social place of a loyal opposition. Loyalty resists endemic institutional decline and empowers individuals to commit to an institution's recuperation. There is no paradox involved in being both loyal and critical, for what the loyal critic opposes are not the foundations but the superstructure. The loyal opponent operates within a framework of essential support for or agreement with the institutional raison d'être. Although it is true that the grounds for opposition may eventually reveal that something more basic is in contention, necessitating and justifying exit, at the point at which opposition remains loyal, there will nevertheless be shared

---

[31] Initially, of course, there was a complaisant opposition, but after a time the Supreme Court acted as an oppositional check.

[32] Albert O. Hirschman, *Exit, Voice, and Loyalty: Response to Decline in Firms, Organizations and States* (Cambridge, MA: Harvard University Press, 1970).

values, concerns, or ends that may be assumed to provide a basis for dealing with the issues that are in contention.

Loyalty to an institution, then, need not and should not involve passive acceptance of its activities. It involves, rather, a recognition that the institution is there to realize certain ends that are valued—whether products, social goods, intrinsic personal satisfactions, or moral ends. In this context, a loyal opposition does not represent the abandonment of loyalty so much as an expression of it. It seeks to ensure that those values are realized and enhanced, not diminished. Usually, it will attempt to do this through the exercise of voice, though if voice fails, the more radical response of exit with voice may be necessary. Even exit with voice can sometimes constitute an act of loyal opposition.

Although I have approached the idea of loyal opposition via its institutionalized and, particularly, political expressions, we can see it at work—albeit not under that rubric—in the more intimate context of friendship. We expect that our friends will be supportive of us, yet our "real" friends are usually those who call us out when we act stupidly or in ways that are erosive of the friendship. Although such opposition can sometimes be problematic—when, for example, it is expressed paternalistically— sometimes even that may be properly expressive of a legitimate ongoing loyalty.[33] As there are certain established rituals of loyal opposition in institutionalized contexts, so there are likely to be less formal rituals of loyal opposition in the intimate contexts of private relationships—taking someone aside, reaffirming commitment, and so on.

THE LIMITS OF OPPOSITION

Although we will return to the following two questions in the next chapter, it is appropriate that we raise them now, for they point to what might, by its critics, be seen as the soft underbelly of loyal opposition. First, what kinds of opposition are compatible with loyalty? And second, at what point is loyal opposition no longer appropriate?

A short answer to the first question is that when opposition is motivated directly by self-interest or disregards or seeks to undermine the interests of the associational object, it no longer operates as *loyal* opposition.

A requirement of loyalty, as of other virtues, is that it be appropriately motivated. The loyal person needs to have some concern that the interests of the relational object will be accommodated. They need to be accommodated for their own sake and not

---

[33] Thus a friend may be able to get away with taking away your car keys and ordering a taxi if he judges that you have had too much to drink. Occasionally, I guess, a friend's concern for another's interests may actually jeopardize the friendship. If that happens, it will be seen as a great loss.

merely as self-interested means. A person who unflinchingly serves his unpopular country may appear to show great loyalty, but our assessment may change if we discover that his primary concern is a knighthood or other display of social recognition. A person who criticizes the organization to which he belongs simply because it fails to do things the way he wants, or who criticizes it without regard to the consequences of those criticisms, no longer expresses loyal opposition.

Motivation is not the whole of it, however, for even a well-motivated person may fall short of acting loyally. That is likely to be the case if the effect of opposition is to undermine the interests of the object of loyalty.[34] I may think that I am helping my friend if I speak plainly to her. But if I thereby destroy her fragile self-confidence, it is unlikely that we will want to deem what I did an expression of loyal friendship. Not that it will be disloyal either. But loyal support requires some achievement on the part of the loyal person as well as his effort.

Whether the interests of an association are undermined by opposition can be a tricky question. In Canadian electoral debates during the mid-1990s, the secessionist Bloc Québécois, supported by the Liberals, presented themselves as "Her Majesty's Loyal Opposition." Bill Gilmour, a Reform Party MP, was skeptical. In a statement in the Canadian House of Commons, he remarked:

> According to the Oxford Dictionary, loyal means faithful, trustworthy, true, steadfast in allegiance, and devoted to the sovereign or government of one's country.
>
> In this House, the Bloc is certainly not loyal to her majesty or to Canada, and is in fact openly plotting against the government to set up a separate Quebec.
>
> Turning to the word opposition, according to Beauchesne, the Official Opposition is the largest minority group which is prepared, in the event of the resignation of the Government, to assume office. How can we have an opposition party who has no intention of becoming government, at least not in Canada, and is attempting to set up a separate independent state?
>
> Clearly, Mr Speaker, her majesty's Loyal Opposition in this 35th Parliament is neither loyal to Canada, nor is it prepared to fulfil the role of Official Opposition.[35]

---

[34] Looking ahead, this may need some explication. I may oppose my country's trade policy, even though it is economically beneficial to it, on the ground that it is exploitative of another country. Such opposition may be loyal, even if it works against my country's economic interests, if I think of my country as a project rather than as the status quo. See chapter 13.

[35] Bill Gilmour, MP (Comox-Alberni), Press Release: "Her Majesty's Loyal Opposition," http://www.parl.gc.ca/HousePublications/Publication.aspx?DocId=2332524&Language=E&Mode=1#16829.

Here, of course, there is a certain naked politicking. Formally, the Bloc constituted the loyal opposition, and there was little Mr. Gilmour could do about that. But his question, whatever its intent, raises the larger issue of how far an opposition may go before it loses its claim to being loyal. In this case, I suspect that it may have remained loyal. The aspirations of the Bloc Québécois were hardly secret (as Gilmour acknowledges). And the party believed that it spoke for a significant number of Canadians. It sought, if brought into a power-sharing arrangement, to initiate a process that would enable Quebec to secede in an orderly manner. Its methods for bringing about change were intended to be democratic. No doubt defenders of the status quo would oppose it. But that was not enough to make the Bloc Québécois other than a loyal opposition. Of course, secession is more serious than most political maneuvers, certainly not to be taken lightly or even encouraged. Nevertheless, it was not inherently unconstitutional or antidemocratic, and those who complained that it was so needed first to consider the sources of Francophone disaffection.

It is also worth reflecting on the McCarthy years. Did those who sympathized with or joined the Communist Party of America constitute a disloyal opposition? It depends on the story one tells. If it takes the form of a claim that members were seeking to bring the United States under the domination of a foreign power (in contrast to eighteenth-century revolutionaries who were seeking to free the people from what had in effect become a foreign power), then it is not hard to run a story about disloyalty. If the story is one about an unrepresentative group of people seeking to impose their private vision (ideology) on the mass of others, a similar charge might reasonably be made. But if the argument was that the existing political structure (the status quo) failed to express the founding ideals and that there needed to be a major political reconfiguration of the kind sanctioned by the Declaration of Independence, it is much harder to make out a case for disloyalty. A great deal depends on one's capacity to tell a particular story convincingly.[36]

The status of tattling and whistle-blowing might also be noted here, though whistle-blowing will be taken up again in chapter 10. Tattletales and whistle-blowers are often charged with disloyalty because their opposition is made known to a superior or to someone outside the association or organization.

Tattling, often seen as a childhood phenomenon in which a complaint is made to some higher authority (such as a parent), is often seen as a sign of moral immaturity—either based on a need to ingratiate oneself with authority or as expressive of a

---

[36] And, of course, there is a question of means, as the famous Dewey-Trotsky debate made clear. See Leon Trotsky, John Dewey, and George Novak, *Their Means and Ours: Marxist versus Liberal Views on Morality*, 5th ed. (New York: Pathfinder, 1973).

holier-than-thou attitude. To the extent that this is so, it may be seen as a type of disloyalty, a way of responding to some cause of complaint that undermines what should have been handled by the associational parties in question. Whistle-blowing, if motivated by a concern for a public interest that is being jeopardized by the organization against which it is directed, may constitute neither loyal opposition nor disloyalty. It will not be an instance of loyal opposition, because it will manifest only an indirect interest in the organization and its recuperation. But neither need it constitute disloyalty, for if the whistle-blower has followed what are generally thought to be reasonable internal procedures for rectifying the situation (and which might well constitute expressions of loyal opposition), the organization might be said to have forfeited its claims to the employee's loyalty.

Nevertheless, there are circumstances in which whistle-blowing may be thought to constitute a fairly radical form of loyal opposition. Frank Serpico thought of policing as a noble occupation, and he believed—even as a whistle-blower—that there was hope for the New York City Police Department. In blowing the whistle, he did not seek to bring it down or damage it but to provoke a major review of its structures, practices, and personnel.[37] He wanted to remain inside, but inside an institution that realized what he viewed as its social raison d'être. Of course, many did not see it that way, especially those others inside who *demanded* loyalty. They were the rogues and scoundrels who give loyalty its bad name.

A short answer to the second question is that when an association is no longer capable of recuperation—when it can no longer be expected to realize the values that are needed to sustain loyalty—then continued loyalty, even if expressed in oppositional terms, is not ordinarily justified.[38] Perhaps this is stated too strongly. It is not necessary that the association fail altogether to realize what made it worth belonging to. However, if its realization of what is valued in being identified with it is too compromised, its claims to loyalty may be undermined by its failures.

More tellingly, there is a conservatism about loyal oppositions that is sometimes noted in the political sphere but might also be observed in other contexts. It is sometimes argued that loyal oppositions are not questioning enough. *Just because* a loyal opposition accepts the basic framework of its opponents, it makes assumptions about that framework's acceptability that might be questioned. A traditional anarchist is not likely to be moved by talk of political reform. If any centralized governmental agency inevitably comes to focus on the requisites of its own power to the detriment of what it is intended to achieve, then loyal opposition is misplaced. It needs to be opposed root and branch. Less radically but also pointedly, the institutionalized

---

[37] See Frank Maas, *Serpico* (New York: Viking, 1973).
[38] A criminal operation—I shall assume—deserves opposition, but not a loyal one.

provisions for a loyal opposition may themselves be tamed to ineffectiveness—what Herbert Marcuse complained of as "repressive tolerance."[39]

This is the soft underbelly of loyal opposition—the opposition in question is not radical but reformist. Sometimes what is needed is radical opposition. Loyalty will not provide that. But as long as we do not see loyalty as absolute—as having limits—and as well that the withdrawal of loyalty need not constitute disloyalty, this supposedly soft underbelly should not cast loyalty into disrepute. Like any virtue, it has its limits.

CONCLUSION

Against its critics, I have argued that loyalty is not complaisance; it is compatible with and might reasonably expect forms of critique and opposition. Yet there is a presumption in loyal opposition that the associational bonds that link the loyal parties are worthy of preservation, indeed, of repair and rebuilding. There are nevertheless limits to loyalty, limits to associational bonds. Loyalty may not be enough, and opposition may not need to be restricted to that of the loyal sort. In the next chapter, I chart those limits.

[39] Herbert Marcuse, "Repressive Tolerance," in *A Critique of Pure Tolerance*, ed. Robert Paul Wolff, Barrington Moore Jr., and Herbert Marcuse (Boston: Beacon, 1969), 95–137.

7

LIMITS

Loyalty above all else except honor.[1]

Even among those who acknowledge the virtuous status of loyalty, the limits of loyalty constitute an ongoing challenge. The possibility of excess may infect every virtue, but in the case of loyalty, it seems to plague it. So badly does it affect some loyalties that Simon Keller is inclined to see the virtuousness or value of loyalty as a simple function of the type of association in which it is found. Filial loyalties are good, and, to a point, so are the loyalties of friendship. But Keller thinks there is little to be said for national or patriotic loyalties. And though he thinks it problematic if a person possesses no loyalties, he is troubled at the idea of teaching children the importance of loyalty. It is therefore particularly incumbent on those who argue for the importance of loyalty to provide some accounting of its limits.

Although loyalty is sometimes demanded as though the obligations associated with it were absolute, most of us recognize that particular loyalties may conflict, that loyalty may compete with other virtues and norms, and that there may be limits to the costs a loyalist may reasonably be expected to bear. Unfortunately, there is no simple algorithm to tell us when loyalty is required or what limits should attach to a show of loyalty. Although that is, I believe, true of every other virtue, in the case of loyalty the absence of a normative measure seems particularly problematic.

But we are not reduced to silence. Even though, as will become apparent in part II, there are contextual and circumstantial considerations that bear on the issue of limits, we can identify some of the broad contexts in which the issue of limits arises and identify some of the factors that will enable them to be resolved. As in almost every case involving ethical calculations, judgment is called for rather than computation.

[1] Lt. Vincent Hardy, in *Striking Distance*, dir. Rowdy Herrington (Columbia Pictures, 1993).

I begin with a discussion of loyalty among the virtues—in particular, what I have spoken of as the complementarity of the virtues.[2] Then I briefly review Josiah Royce's tiebreaking "loyalty to loyalty" before considering the limits placed on loyalties by corrupt associations, associational decline, proportionality, and competing values.

COMPLEMENTARITY OF THE VIRTUES

According to some versions of the ancient doctrine of the unity (or singularity) of *virtue*, there are no separate virtues but only virtue, and the virtuous person will be characterizable at one and the same time as courageous, loyal, temperate, just, and so on. Although the doctrine has undergone a revival in recent virtue theory, I will focus instead on a related view sometimes referred to as the doctrine of the unity of *the virtues*. According to this view, a person who is courageous will also be loyal, temperate, just, and so on.[3] The individual virtues have distinctive roles to play but are structured to take account of the demands of other virtues. If, for example, loyalty to a friend seemingly comes into conflict with justice to someone else, such that the loyalty "takes precedence," then the doctrine claims that in such a case the scope of justice is properly constrained by the demands of loyalty. Take an equally possible example in which dealing justly with someone seemingly comes into conflict with loyalty to a friend and in which justice takes precedence; in such a case, the doctrine claims, the demands of loyalty are properly constrained by the demands of justice. A person who, in one of these cases, appears to give justice or loyalty precedence when it is *not* justified, fails to display the virtues of justice or loyalty. If this is true, then the question of loyalty's limits will be theoretically clear—loyalty will be shown to the extent that some other applicable virtue is not compromised. The problem will be to determine the relevant boundaries. No trade-off will be involved.

Seductive though this view is, I think that a more plausible approach is what I dubbed the complementarity of the virtues. On this account, should the claims of loyalty and justice come into conflict, it is not the case that if the claims of loyalty are given unjustified precedence that what is given precedence cannot be considered loyalty, but that the loyalty has exceeded its appropriate bounds. There can be virtuous excess. As with the doctrine of the unity of the virtues, the problem of determining relevant boundaries will remain. It is to be resolved through an exercise of judgment, in which the reasons for favoring the precedence of one or the other will be juxtaposed and then, by means of a process of argument—the exercise of practical wisdom

---

[2] See chapter 3, note 25.
[3] For a helpful overview, see John M. Cooper, "The Unity of Virtue," *Social Philosophy & Policy* 15, no. 1 (1998): 233–274.

or *phronesis*—a conclusion is drawn as to which has the best claim. As in real-life situations, such a process may be quite lengthy, and even anguished, as the reasons introduced into the argument may themselves generate a further series of argumentative confrontations. But that is the nature of moral disagreement and resolution, not something peculiar to either the virtues or loyalty.

The virtues should not be possessed singly or viewed in isolation, but their multiple development should be seen as becoming a person of a certain kind, in which one virtue moderates or complements the other. This has special significance in the case of loyalty because of the tendency to manipulate and absolutize it: "if you are *really* loyal to me, *nothing* can or should come between us." I do not deny that in some circumstances loyalty may make high demands of one; nevertheless, the demands that it legitimately makes will depend on the circumstances of the case and what other legitimate demands there may be.

My suggestion that the virtues complement each other is not intended to deny that there may be some general hierarchy of virtues or even that in certain spheres some virtues may generally take precedence over others. We may well wish to rank justice over modesty or honor/integrity over loyalty in some general sense. If we are police officers, perhaps we should rate "courtesy, professionalism, and respect" more highly than loyalty. Some virtues possess much greater significance for the quality of our social intercourse and association, and others, such as discretion and wisdom, have a much greater regulative significance. And some, such as courage, might have a greater role to play in the military than in academic research (which is not to deny it a role in the latter). In the complex particularities of decision making, how one virtue relates to others will depend very much on the story we tell about the circumstances. The general ranking of a virtue may not be reflected in the place it should have in some concrete situation. "Let justice be done, though the heavens fall" is really a *reductio* despite the intentions of those who promulgated it. And though being killed with kindness has its lighter meaning, it does allow for a situational possibility that should be avoided.

Consider a common situation in which the virtue of truthfulness seems to conflict with the virtue of kindness. If I am truthful about my student's failings, I am likely to wound her deeply. One suggestion here might be that I should withhold the truth in order to be kind—that is, that there is a limit to the demand for truthfulness that, in a particular situation, is dictated by the need for kindness. But another and perhaps better way of approaching the situation is to draw on a further virtue—diplomacy— that will allow me to be both truthful and kind. In this way, the various virtues may complement and support each other. A virtuous person will be one who possesses a large range of virtues that will be called forth and exercised as a particular situation demands.

In some cases, the pairings of moderating virtues have been domesticated, if not institutionalized. So we temper justice with mercy, courage with discretion, truthfulness with kindness, and loyalty with honor/integrity. Such pairings remind us of ways in which a virtue may get out of hand or overreach itself. But there may be other ways in which these particular virtues need to moderate each other. Truthfulness may need to be paired with courage as well as kindness, lest kindness lead one to avoid being truthful, albeit being truthful with diplomacy. And loyalty may need to be paired with both forthrightness and open-mindedness, lest it become complaisant.

As we noted in chapter 3, I am begging the question about what virtues a virtuous person should have—whether a particular catalogue of virtues will allow them to complement each other or whether what we consider to be a virtuous person's complement of virtues begs much deeper questions about human nature and flourishing. We may find ourselves comparing inter alia Greek, Christian, Buddhist, and Nietzschean virtues and thus find ourselves in the grip of Gallie's "essential contestability." But this is not the place for that discussion.

My own view of the complementarity of the virtues differs from a broadly Aristotelian doctrine in more than one way. First, I think that people may sometimes have particular virtues without others. It is possible, for example, to be loyal without being modest or clever. True, it might be a slightly defective loyalty in a situation that calls for loyalty to be moderated by modesty or cleverness, but insofar as expressions of loyalty will not, for the most part, need to be moderated by these other virtues, a person may usually be genuinely and appropriately loyal without being modest or clever. Further, as I've already noted, I take it to be the case that the virtues, though complementary, sometimes come into serious conflict. Thus we may occasionally find ourselves in situations in which one virtue, say, truthfulness, must give way to another, such as responsibility, in a way that leaves us morally stained. This is well captured by Max Weber's classic discussion of the political leader whose concern for the well-being of a populace requires the sacrifice of her integrity. She finds herself in a practical dilemma in which one virtue is not merely moderated by but must also be sacrificed to another.[4] She does what she should, but the cost is a compromised integrity. And finally, I do not think that, despite their importance, the virtues exhaust morality. Though it is important to our interactions with each other that we develop appropriate virtues, there are also various principles, rules, and values to which we should conform our conduct. Although we seek some sort of normative harmony among the different elements to which we appeal in moral decision making, we probably ought not to reductively reduce morality to

[4] Max Weber, "Politics as a Vocation," in *From Max Weber: Essays in Sociology*, eds. H. H. Gerth and C. Wright Mills (New York: Oxford University Press, 1946), 77–128.

the expression of virtue, the adoption of principles, the following of rules, or the realization of values.

Given its place in associative contexts and the importance of such contexts to human flourishing, loyalty should rate fairly high as a virtue. Unfortunately, that high rating has enabled its exploitation by associative others—political, religious, and organizational leaders, parents, and friends—and may even constitute a temptation for us as we seek to deal with situations that will work out badly for us if others do not remain "loyal." That is a serious problem for loyalty, if not in theory, then in practice. It may no longer function as the virtue it is. It will be blind, unthinking, or exploitative loyalty, qualifications intended to negate or at least temper its virtuousness in much the same way as calling a lie "white" is intended to qualify its viciousness. It is also a major reason that loyalty has been brought into disrepute and regarded, as it is by Blamires, as a "sham virtue."

And so, although it may be true that in an ideal world our loyalties will be crafted to accommodate the rest of the virtues, the world as we must live in it is rather messier, and though a loyal person may also be just and caring and forthright and self-controlled and diplomatic and truthful, a person can still be genuinely loyal without these other virtues. One can understand the motivation behind the Aristotelian doctrine without taking it completely on board.

LOYALTY TO LOYALTY

Almost uniquely, Josiah Royce sought to free loyalty of limitations by advocating the principle of "loyalty to loyalty" as the centerpiece of his moral theory. Although there remains a devoted if sometimes critical coterie of Roycean disciples, his central claim has fallen into desuetude.[5] Nevertheless, given Royce's singular contribution to the study of loyalty, it is worth seeing how Royce sought to understand and implement this principle. Even though the principle is unbounded, it offers a formula for limiting particular loyalties.

What Royce means by "loyalty to loyalty" is that we should choose associational objects or causes that will maximize (or at least not detract from) others' possibilities for loyal commitment: the causes we choose should result in "more loyalty in the world rather than less."[6] It is an aggregative principle that limits or constrains the causes that a person might choose. Loyalties that threaten others' capacity for or exercise of loyalty, or expressions of loyalty that threaten such capacities or exercises

---

[5] Though see Mathew A. Foust, *Loyalty to Loyalty: Josiah Royce and the Genuine Moral Life* (New York: Fordham University Press, 2012).

[6] Royce, *The Philosophy of Loyalty* (New York: Macmillan, 1908), 121; cf. 138.

by others, should therefore be avoided. Loyalty to loyalty thus offers a possible solution to conflicts of loyalty.

For Royce, as we have noted, loyalty is critical to identity. It is by virtue of our commitment to "causes"—unified communities—that our lives have character, focus, and stability. Given this, it is not transparent what "loyalty to loyalty" amounts to. We do best if we track Royce's own argument. Having claimed the importance of loyalty to cause(s), Royce confronts the problem of diverse and competing loyalties. It is not good enough to have loyalties, for some are mutually incompatible and others are destructive. So Royce proposes that we seek to minimize conflicts of loyalty and the formation of destructive loyalties by assessing our concrete loyalties in terms of their contribution to the maximization of loyalties. This amounts to a commitment to the maximization of the social conditions under which people may pursue their various loyalties, hence our primary loyalty to loyalty. The formula, however, represents a framework for ethics rather than a generative maxim. We do not begin explicitly with "loyalty to loyalty" but with potential causes that suit our temperaments. We then legitimately ask of them whether their pursuit will impair others' capacity to pursue their own loyalties. If so, they should be revised. It is Royce's contention that over time our loyalties will expand and evolve and that they will increasingly embrace others' capacity to pursue their own loyalties. He anticipates that the discrete causes to which loyalty will be given will eventually be united in "one system of causes and so to one cause."[7] Indeed, in responding to a young critic who sees narrow and chauvinistic partialities in the development of loyalties, Royce seeks to turn the tables by praising his "loyalty to humanity."[8]

We can see, then, that for Royce loyalty to loyalty is not commitment to an abstraction or to a free-floating virtue, but commitment to choosing associational objects ("causes") that are likely to maximize the possibility of others' pursuit of their own causes. As with other general principles such as "the greatest happiness of the greatest number," which need not be directly consulted in deciding what to do, but function as ways of assessing particular decisional options, loyalty to loyalty works in the background, enabling us to refine or develop our loyalties or even giving us reason to abandon some of them.

There is no guarantee that the causes we choose, even on the assumption that they display loyalty to loyalty, will in fact further the cause of loyalty. Later experience—either changes in the associational object or better knowledge of the effects of pursuing a particular cause—may lead us to revise our loyalties. We may make

---

[7] Ibid., 133. Such unification of loyalties is, he notes, only an ideal, though sufficiently visible to constitute a practical guide (181).
[8] Ibid., 61.

bad decisions or find ourselves with ineradicable and unmeliorable conflicts. In the case of the latter, Royce advises decisiveness and fidelity. He instances Robert E. Lee, who, presumably, comes out better for have chosen decisively and having pursued his cause faithfully, even though he chose badly. Better to be decisive and faithful than indecisive and unreliable. Our only reason for abandoning a cause is when "growth in knowledge makes manifest that further service of that special cause would henceforth involve unquestionable disloyalty to universal loyalty."[9]

Royce makes even bolder claims for loyalty to loyalty. He writes that *"all the commonplace virtues, in so far as they are indeed defensible and effective, are special forms of loyalty to loyalty."*[10] How so? Our loyalties will, first of all, reflect our "natural temperament" and "social opportunities." Insofar as our choice of causes is then "controlled and unified" by the cause of universal loyalty, we will take care to develop virtues that will foster its cause. Thus truthfulness can be seen as "an act of loyalty to the personal tie which then and there binds me to the man to whom I consent to speak."[11] Well, yes, if I am loyally bound to this person. But what if the person is a stranger? Royce's strategy, so far as I can understand it, is to relativize strangerhood. By consenting to speak with another, I am linked with that person "in a certain unity,—the unity of some transaction which involves our speech one to another." Loyalty to loyalty is here working overtime, not simply as an ideal to be aspired to but as expressive of an existing compact with whomever I choose to speak. Honesty in business dealings gets much the same treatment. A "single act of business fidelity is an act of loyalty to that general confidence of man in man upon which the whole fabric of business rests."[12] Loyalty to loyalty is now no longer functioning as a second-order principle but operating directly on decision making. The cause is "owed to mankind at large."

How helpful is Royce's maxim to establishing appropriate constraints on particular loyalties? This is not the place for an extended treatment of Royce's philosophy of loyalty.[13] At first blush, there is an appealingly tolerationist simplicity to Royce's formula: it fosters joint endeavor (causes), and it fosters endeavors that leave others free to foster theirs. For tribalistic accounts of morality such as Oldenquist's and MacIntyre's, the Roycean formula appears to offer a valuable corrective to what may be viewed as their jingoistic tendencies. But that appearance may evaporate, for the maxim tends to detach the value of loyalty from the particular associational contexts in which it is embedded. This allows us to imagine—in *Brave New World* fashion—an

---

[9] Ibid., 190–191.
[10] Ibid., 129–130 (Royce's emphasis).
[11] Ibid., 140.
[12] Ibid., 141.
[13] For that, see Foust.

attempt to coalesce all loyalties round some person or social order (Royce's "great community"?), thus maximizing the amount of loyalty in the world. What may appear to save Royce from this possibility is his constant claim that loyalties are the products of "autonomous choice." A problem, however, is that many of our most significant loyalties do not start off as products of autonomous choice, even though they may eventually come to be. Are those loyalties less loyalties for that reason? If they are not, might making them autonomous be seen as a luxury that should be forgone for the sake of unified and universal loyalty? Would they ipso facto lack moral worth?

A final worry about loyalty to loyalty is that it does not appear to be sufficiently sensitive to the identity-conferring dimensions of loyalty and the tragedy created by certain conflicts of loyalty. Royce instances the case of a young woman, professionally trained and embarked on what is almost certain to be a very successful professional life. But an illness in her family now confronts her with a conflicting loyalty that would expect her to take care of the ailing family member. What should she do?[14] "Loyalty to loyalty" offers too rationalistic a solution. Royce says that if she is committed to loyalty to loyalty, she will make her best judgment as to which of the two loyalties most nearly exemplifies it and then "*decide, and have no fear.*"[15] Although he recognizes that the decision may have to be made in ignorance of which option will more satisfactorily fulfill the maxim, decisiveness without regrets is called for. This is too easy, even if, as he says, "loyalty to loyalty . . . is personal devotion."[16] It is an ideal, not an associative commitment, and, like much aggregative thinking, it fails to capture the tragic and wrenching quality of the decision that has to be made. It provides a solution, but not one that is congruent with the situation.

We now move to several morally relevant considerations that may function to limit loyalties—either their formation, scope, or continuation. Some associative arrangements are too deeply flawed to sustain acceptable loyalties, and legitimate loyalties may be limited by competing moral values, proportionality considerations, or possibilities for institutional renewal.

IMPERMISSIBLE LOYALTIES

One way of approaching the limits of loyalty is via its legitimate objects. If a possible object of loyalty is morally suspect, then loyalty to it (at least qua an object of that kind) will also be suspect. I distinguish this limit from another in which a legitimate object may subsequently forfeit its claim to loyalty.

---

[14] Ibid., 183–184.
[15] Ibid., 189.
[16] Ibid., 185.

As we have already had occasion to observe, such illegitimate objects may exist. Whatever may be the value *to one* of a particular association, it may nevertheless be the kind of association that one ought not to value and therefore that ought not to be an object of one's loyalty. The loyal Nazi and Klansman do not owe or warrant loyalty qua Nazi and Klansman.

The legitimacy of associative objects is not always easy to determine. Many associations have multiple ends, some of which may be legitimate and others illegitimate, and an association that once had high-minded ends may—by the time one becomes involved—have degenerated into a largely illegitimate one. That may have been the case with the Mafia, a group that began as an alternative to a corrupt administration but in later years focused heavily on organized crime.

And what if an organization is devoted to high-minded ends but uses problematic means? How are we to determine that the means are, in relation to the ends, unacceptable to the point of rendering any loyal association impermissible? When, in the 1970s, the Symbionese Liberation Army fought against poverty, racism, and sexism and for the improvement of public schooling, it fought for important social ends but used means that alienated most from its loyal membership. In the more recent war on terrorism, the battle has included a fight for ownership of a label—not just over whether those belonging to a particular group should be seen as freedom fighters rather than terrorists but also over the identification of a group as one organized for illegitimate purposes. If, for example, a Palestinian shows loyalty to his people by donating to a charitable cause, this may be interpreted as giving aid and comfort to the enemy, should some recipients of the charity be deemed to have terrorist connections. Admittedly, there is some sort of continuum here, because charities may serve political as well as welfare functions. Nevertheless, it is regrettable when lines are drawn in a way that makes almost any tangible support for one's people impermissible.

OVERRIDDEN LOYALTIES

Leaving aside the rare, even if possible, case of absolute loyalty, any loyalty can expect to encounter circumstantial demands that outweigh its moral claims. Although loyalties are often advanced as though they are overriding demands, this is almost certainly an exploitative ploy. The psychological power of loyalties is invoked to overwhelm the moral authority they rightly possess. A person who resists is threatened with a fractured identity that requires reconfiguration.

It is not easy to determine the conditions under which a loyalty may be overridden. There is no formula. A police officer who is challenged by the code of silence when a handcuffed prisoner is brutalized may not find it morally, let alone psychologically, easy to know what to do. On the one hand, there are the original determinants of the loyalty—the dangers associated with police work that make sticking together an important cultural value. And if the prisoner has given the officers a hard time, hindering the capacity of the police to do a job that they are under public pressure to complete successfully, it may be rationalized that he had it coming to him. There will also be the moral challenge constituted by whether a transgression is best responded to internally and informally or externally and formally (whistle-blowing). This latter choice may be made harder by the belief that going outside would expose officers to a system that is politicized and unfair. On the other hand, and no less important, there is the fact that the primary loyalty of police officers should be to a "sustaining" public that they serve.[17]

As I've said repeatedly, decisions of this kind cannot be made algorithmically, but require judgment as reasons for and against particular options are traded off. The challenges vary.

Conflicts between Role Obligations and Obligations of Loyalty

Consider the situation in which one's loyalty to ensure that one's daughter's interests are protected and advanced come into conflict with certain role obligations one has. Perhaps she is an applicant for a job for which one has some decision-making authority. Perhaps one is a police officer and has some reason to believe that she has committed a criminal offense. There a conflict of interest. In many such cases, the most appropriate response would be recusal.

But conflicts of interest cannot always be circumvented, and decisions have to be made. If Alan, a store's security manager, observes on a monitor that his son is engaging in shoplifting despite clear warning signs in the shop indicating that shoplifters will be prosecuted to the full extent of the law, he will face a hard choice. If Alan turns a blind eye, that will involve not only partiality to his child but also a serious breach of his role obligations. Alan might ignore the fact that the shoplifter is his child and take the same action as he would in another case: set in motion the enforcement process. That would satisfy the role obligation but could jeopardize the loyal bond between parent and child. Indeed, it may suggest that loyalty has no moral traction in such cases. A possible solution would be for Alan to confront his son and impose informal costs that would both register the offense's seriousness and be likely to deter his son in the future. There would be an attempt to satisfy the point of the role obligation without sacrificing the expectations of familial

---

[17] For an extended discussion, see John Kleinig, "The Blue Wall of Silence: An Ethical Analysis," *International Journal of Applied Philosophy* 15, no. 1 (Spring 2001): 1–23.

loyalty.[18] What might work for shoplifting, however, would not work with a more serious offense—if, for example, a police officer observed his son shoot someone else. Here, no discretionary application of rules will do. The son must be arrested and processed as anyone else. What happens to the loyalty? It need not be extinguished, though it may have to take a different form. The parent might continue to express loyalty by retaining contact, visiting the child in prison, and otherwise seeking to encourage the child's moral redemption.

Sometimes, though, one's loyalties may override one's role obligations—as when I choose to cancel a lecture to attend a close relative's funeral. The judgment will take into account the importance of the loyalty (one reason that spouses may not be required to testify against each other), the importance of the countervailing reason (say, saving a life or helping to convict someone guilty of a serious offense), the social importance of the role, alternative possibilities, and so on.

Conflicts among Loyalties

Most of us have multiple loyalties. We form numerous friendships; we relate variously to members of our families; we may be connected to a number of ethnic, tribal, or racial groups; we acquire nuanced cultural and religious identities; we enter into work-related and professional organizations; we become members of clubs, recreational groups, and other social organizations; and so on. The control we have over our entry into or continued participation in these various associative arrangements generally ensures that conflicts will be minimal.

It is not always so. I may marry someone who cannot get along with my parents, and, because of the conflict of loyalties that is generated, I may have to make some hard choices. In the worst case, I may have to sacrifice loyalty to one, or, not as radically, I may have to give one loyalty priority over the other. It was possibly some such conflict—and ordering—that the writer of Genesis had in mind in speaking about the way in which, when a man and a woman enter into a relationship, "the man leaves his father and mother and joins himself to his wife, and they become one body."[19] The new relationship that is entered into creates a new ordering of loyalties. In Sophocles's *Antigone*, there is a clash between familial and civic loyalties: if Antigone buries her brother, Polyneices, she violates a regal prohibition. Robert E. Lee must choose between loyalty to Abraham Lincoln and the Union, on the one hand, and the loyalty he owes to kith and kin in Virginia, on the other.

---

[18] A similar conflict of role and loyalty arises when police pull over fellow police officers for speeding or driving under the influence. For a discussion, see John Kleinig and Albert J. Gorman, "Professional Courtesies: To Ticket or Not to Ticket?" in *Handbook of Police Administration*, ed. James Ruiz and Don Hummer (New York: Taylor & Francis, 2007), 193–205.

[19] Genesis 2:24.

Our judgments in such cases will have to accommodate various considerations:

1. Our identities are likely to be more deeply bound up with some objects than others. Should we sacrifice a more central object of loyalty to a less central object, we sacrifice more of what we stand for. But it does not follow that we should sacrifice the lesser object of loyalty, if what we stand for is unacceptable. Going with the more central loyalty will show us to be conscientious rather than correct. Nevertheless, the change of priorities is likely to be wrenching.

2. Sometimes a less central but legitimate loyalty may take precedence over a more central and no less legitimate one. Familial loyalty may call for my presence at my mother's ninetieth birthday celebration. I would be willing to make the arduous journey to Western Australia for the occasion. If, however, a moderately good but not intimate friend is dying of AIDS in a New York hospital, rejected by his family and without others who will stay with him during his final days or, perhaps, weeks, his greater needs, albeit more easily responded to, may take precedence. I judge that it would be worse to abandon him to visit my mother, even though the rest of the family will be there for this milestone birthday. I may need to explain the situation to her and apologize for having to make such a decision. I trust she will understand but realize that it may not be easy for her see the situation as I do.

3. Conflicting loyalties need not be unrelievedly tragic. They may sometimes assist one in sorting out priorities, and though that can be stressful, it may not be fragmenting. One may be led to see that one loyalty takes priority over another, such that loyalty to the first does not constitute disloyalty to the second. That, of course, will not be the case if the second prevails. This is a common issue in work-family conflicts of loyalty.

Conflicts between Loyalty-Based Obligations and General or Universal Human Obligations

As we noted in chapter 5, several writers who discuss relations between particularist and universal obligations take the view that, in the event of a clash, particularist obligations should give way to universal ones. But that does not seem to be obviously correct. Whatever I invest as part of the bond I have with my family might have been used to relieve poverty, disease, and so forth elsewhere. And maybe there is a point at which I ought, all things considered, to shift resources from my family to others (do my children really need a pool room and heated swimming pool?). But there is also a level at which the preoccupation with universal obligations will represent a violation of legitimately demanding particularistic bonds.

The "telescopic philanthropy" of Charles Dickens's Mrs. Jellyby exemplifies this failure:

> [Mrs. Jellyby] was a pretty, very diminutive, plump woman of from forty to fifty, with handsome eyes, though they had a curious habit of seeming to look a long way off. As if . . . they could see nothing nearer than Africa![20]

As with many other conflicts between loyalty-based obligations and universal ones, circumstances and context will be critical. A good friend may be right to tell someone I am not available when I am (but have reason not to be disturbed) but not justified in providing a false alibi in the event that I am reasonably suspected of committing a serious offense.

Although the expectations of a loyal bond may not override a universal obligation, the latter will sometimes transform it. Return to the shoplifting case discussed earlier. This time, however, Alan is not the security manager; nevertheless, he spots his child stealing from the shop. Had it been another child, Alan might have considered reporting the incident to the shop's security manager. But it is not, and, in the circumstances, it is understandable that Alan does not report his child. The bond, however, does not nullify or override the prohibition against stealing, and Alan should take steps to ensure that his child does not get away with what he has done or attempted to do. Were Alan to have treated his child no differently from any other child in these circumstances, it would not only have reflected the importance of the universal prohibition against stealing but also have suggested that his child bore no different relation to him than any other child, and that would have threatened the relation. A child caught shoplifting might be expected to feel guilt; if the child Alan catches is his own, the child might also be expected to feel shame. The terms under which he relates to Alan will be exposed as deceptive and potentially undermining of the trust that informs their loyal bond.

Nevertheless, when Alan punishes his child privately the bond is perpetuated despite the strain. By not taking him to the manager where his guilt will be made public, but by punishing him privately, Alan indicates that the child still has a special place in his life.

* * *

Should we worry that, in many of the cases in which the obligations of loyalty come into conflict with other moral claims, there is no formula or algorithm for resolving them? I doubt it. A simple strategy for moral problem solving has its attractions. It was the hope of many Enlightenment theorists that a singular rational strategy could

---

[20] Charles Dickens, *Bleak House* (1852–1853), esp. ch. 4, www.gutenberg.org/ebooks/1023.

be articulated and then applied—if not directly, then via mediating and compatible duties. This hope—sometimes expressed as a demand of rationality—was used to advocate the necessity of a unified moral theory. In a famous review of what he called intuitive and inductive approaches to ethics, with their catalogues of principles, John Stuart Mill wrote that they

> rarely . . . make any effort to reduce those various principles to one first principle, or common ground of obligation. . . . Yet to support their pretensions there ought either to be some one fundamental principle or law, at the root of all morality, or if there be several, there should be a determinate order or precedence among them; and the one principle, or the rule for deciding between the various principles when they conflict, ought to be self-evident.[21]

Would that it were so. When such writers came to offer their own first or tie-breaking principles, they found themselves burdened with either counterintuitive consequences or the need to build into their theories—as Mill himself did—complications that compromised the theory's singularity.[22]

Although Fletcher sees us as "doom[ed] . . . to a mixed system of independent but compelling systems of thought,"[23] we should not think of this negatively but rather as a way of ensuring that moral reflection remains a matter of authentic judgment rather than a sphere for authoritative expertise. Deciding how important the demands of a particularist obligation should be in the face of some competing claim should be a matter in which we engage with others (or even oneself) in a dialectic of reasons. This dialectic reaches its natural but not necessarily final end when the interlocutors have satisfied each other (or, perhaps, have not but have agreed to differ). This is what justification is, and it is in this kind of engagement (not a Sartrean leap) that we express our humanity most authentically.

PROPORTIONALITY AND LOYALTIES

We should say more about the onerousness of the obligations associated with legitimate loyalties. Obviously, loyalties will differ in their demandingness. One may risk

---

[21] John Stuart Mill, *Utilitarianism*, 1863, ch. 1. A similar position was taken by Henry Sidgwick: "we require some higher principle to decide the issue" (*The Methods of Ethics*, 1874). Sidgwick used the utilitarian principle as a tiebreaker.

[22] Most notoriously, Mill's distinction between qualities and quantities of pleasure, *Utilitarianism*, ch. 2. In *On Liberty*, Mill's recourse to "man as a progressive being" serves a similar complicating function.

[23] George Fletcher, *Loyalty: An Essay on the Morality of Relationships* (New York: Oxford University Press, 1993), 172.

one's life for one's friend or country; it is unlikely that one would (or might be expected to) risk it for one's football team or job. Of course, if one is a police officer, then risking one's life may be part of the job, though it is not the job one risks it for, but the public or community one serves. There is a proportionality between the associative object and the obligations it appropriately garners. The legitimate costs associated with a particular loyalty must be proportionate to its importance.

But how are we to understand "importance" here? Subjectively or objectively? Subjectively, what might reasonably be expected of us will be a function of the importance *we* place on the associational object. I might be prepared to make great sacrifices for one friend but only modest sacrifices for another because the first friendship has much greater importance for me. Or I might be prepared to risk my life if my (beloved) country is attacked but take fewer risks if my company is the object of a hostile takeover. Or I may be prepared to make considerable sacrifices to secure my occupational union against an employer's attack but risk much less for my favorite but struggling basketball team. Here, what I will accept as a legitimate cost will reflect the value of the associational object to me—how important it is to my identity, my sense of who I am and wish to be.

Objectively, we may think of the legitimacy of loyal obligations by reference to certain conventionalized understandings of the importance of their associational objects.[24] We would ordinarily expect someone to bear greater costs for a spouse than for a sporting club. And though we might expect that a child will make sacrifices for an aged and ailing parent, we would not demand that he abandon his spouse and children for that parent.

I do not know that we need to choose between these accounts. Each generalized associative arrangement is likely to be compatible with a range of commitments, and what Alan is prepared to sacrifice for his friend Colin might be different from what Brian is prepared to sacrifice for Colin, even though Colin is also a friend of Brian's. If Alan and Colin are better friends than Brian and Colin, what Alan is subjectively prepared to do for Colin might be thought quite reasonable. Thus, it may be appropriate for Alan to look after Colin's children for several months while he cares for his dying wife, even if Brian would not. Brian, however, may be willing to lend his car or even some money to Colin. Of course, Brian may be willing to take in Colin's children. Then, given that the friendship is not so close (though it would undoubtedly become closer), we might see it as supererogatory—admirable, though not called for. In other circumstances, however, even though the associative relationship is legitimate, we might consider that an expression of loyalty oversteps acceptable

---

[24] Acknowledging that different reference groups may recognize different conventions leaves us with a much less tractable situation.

boundaries. One may not be justified in taking the rap for an old friend or covering for one's criminally involved child.

Whether we approach via the subjective or objective value of their friendships, what might be reasonably owed to Colin by Alan or Brian is not determined simply as a matter of proportionality. There may be different filial expectations of two children, brought up by loving parents. One child may have resources that the other lacks, and it will be no failure of loyalty if the one lacking in resources is not able to assist to the extent that a situation may need.

ASSOCIATIONAL DECLINE

On several occasions, we have referred to Albert Hirschman's theory of institutional decline and recuperation and have noted the importance he gives to the voice-exit options. I will not repeat that here, except to note the relevance of voice and exit to the question of limits. At some point, the loyal voice should give way to exit. The determination of that point will take into account:

1. the social importance of the institution. Social importance can be viewed both abstractly and concretely—abstractly, in the value of institutional continuity (and the various transaction costs that may be involved in developing a substitute institution, if that is called for), and concretely, in the social value of what the institution provides. Hirschman views a nakedly market view of society and its institutions with some consternation. In such a society, self-interested individuals would associate themselves with institutions only to the extent that they could directly benefit from them. They would look for a new host at the first signs of institutional distress. But this, Hirschman believes, would breed major social angst, even if, foreseeing the disruption caused by institutional collapse, such self-interested individuals would (self-interestedly) stick with the distressed institution for longer than they might otherwise do. Thus we should recognize the value of institutional continuity, both socially and for the specific values that the institution realizes, and not keep a constant eye out for better hosts for our self-interest. There is a defeasible presumption in favor of institutions and other associations that have established their social place.

2. the point of associational identification/involvement. When we become loyally attached to an institution, it is usually because it fits with who we are and what we want to be. Even if its social purposes are limited, our association will be contingent on a wider set of considerations than those purposes. If I accept a job as manager of a button factory, I should—at the very least—believe in the social acceptability of button making. But I may also want to be sure that the factory

does not rely on indentured labor, that it observes appropriate safety standards, that it pays fair wages, that it does not use illegal accounting practices, that it has an efficient administrative structure, and so on. Probably it need not optimally satisfy these other considerations. Indeed, I may have been brought in to turn around what has become an ailing institution. Nevertheless, these, in addition to button production and my salary, are likely to be important if I am to identify myself with the institution.

Depending in part on the nature of the failures and the importance of the institution to who I am, I may persevere in my loyalty to it in the hope that—as a result of my interventions—recuperation will be possible.

3. the seriousness of the decline and remediability of the institution. If institutional failure is judged too serious or turnaround seems unlikely, continued loyalty may be inappropriate. Loyalty has been forfeited and exit is called for.

CONCLUSION

Judging the limits of loyalty can pose a difficult challenge, though probably no more difficult than the challenge inherent in any morally fraught situation. Multiple considerations must be brought to bear on the conflict. They must first establish their relevance, and then their relative claims must be scrutinized and juxtaposed. Over time, the outcomes of some of these juxtapositions have been conventionalized. Nevertheless, the process can be frustrating: the relevant considerations might not be commensurable, and the reasons we advance for preferring one set over another may be essentially contestable. What it is important to recognize, however, is that this can be a reasoned—if prolonged—engagement and, moreover, that the claims of loyalty, though often strong, do not automatically override those of other relevant considerations.

PART II

Although we have spoken generally about loyalty and tried to address some of its problematic features, loyalty is not a free-floating virtue to be acquired and exercised in some general way, but one that is developed and manifested within certain relationships and associations. It is clear from our earlier discussion that some of loyalty's problems arise from or are exacerbated by the character of these relationships and associations. The next seven chapters look at loyalty in context—they explore the ways in which different associational arrangements generate their own challenges for the loyalties they engender and seek to show how those problematic features might be met within them.

Although the chapters that follow try to offer a reasonably rich account of the associational contexts within which loyalties most commonly figure—friendships, familial relations, professional and organizational relations, tribal–ethnic–national and state memberships, and religious affiliations—they do not seek to be comprehensive. Their intention, rather, is to provide sufficient depth for considering the problems of loyalty as they arise within them. The key questions are, first: Are they appropriate sites for loyalty? Second: What is the character of the loyalties these sites engender? And, third: What are the limits of such loyalties?

8

FRIENDS

A good friend will help you move house, but a really good friend will help you move a body.[1]

As the epigraph hints, even friendship, the quintessential locus for loyalty, can render loyalty problematic.

The paucity of philosophical writing on loyalty has, until recently, been accompanied by a paucity of philosophical writing on friendship. By way of contrast, the pervasive literary interest in issues of loyalty has been accompanied by a similarly pervasive interest in issues of friendship. The nexus is unsurprising. Loyalty and friendship are deeply intertwined, and it is difficult to write about the latter without considering the former. Although loyalty is shown—and often expected—in other associative relationships, in no other (with the possible exception of intimate or marital relationships) is it as integrally involved as in friendship. A friendship without loyalty barely qualifies as serious friendship, and nothing is more calculated to destroy friendship than disloyalty.[2] In addition, moral philosophers have neglected loyalty and friendship for some of the same reasons. Whereas morality is often thought to be focused on the universal, friendship and loyalty are both concerned with the particular, and both are criticized as being partisan. Also, although some see friendship as a product of choice, others see both it and loyalty as natural and sentimental bonds, growing out of our sociability, likes, and needs

---

[1] Origins unknown.
[2] Disloyalty can, of course, be as fatal to other relationships and associations, such as marriages and political connections. However, it gets close to oxymoronic to speak of a "disloyal friend" (except as a way of saying that the person was but is no longer a friend), whereas we can refer much more easily to a disloyal spouse or citizen.

and formed without any regard to ethical considerations.[3] Added to this is the fact that the motivations of friendship are often viewed as divergent from traditional moral motivations, such as a sense of duty or desire to serve the common good.[4] To the extent that universalizing moral philosophers such as Kant carved out a place for friendship, it was as a prudent bulwark against the distrust of one's fellows. Nevertheless, Kant cautions us to "so conduct ourselves towards a friend that there is no harm done if he should turn into an enemy. We must give him no handle against us."[5]

In what follows, I explore several aspects of friendship, focusing especially on the relationship of friendship to morality and the intertwining of loyalty with friendship. My intention is not to offer a comprehensive account, but the narrower one of identifying what it is about friendship that engages loyalty and to examine the moral dangers embedded in that association.

Because most discussions of friendship have taken Aristotle's discussion in the *Nicomachean Ethics* as seminal, I will outline that account and indicate some of the challenges confronting it before moving to some of the ethical problems that are raised by the bond between friendship and loyalty.

---

[3] See Søren Kierkegaard, *Works of Love*, trans. H. Hong and E. Hong (New York: Harper & Row, 1962), 64. However, it needs to be said that our "natural" affections are unlikely to be natural in the empiricist's sense; they will be expressive of our normative selves.

[4] Cf. John Cooper, drawing on Michael Stocker's important discussion: "There seems no doubt that one grossly betrays one's friendship if one visits a friend in hospital out of a general duty to succor those in distress, or for the sake of giving the greatest pleasure to the greatest number of sentient beings possible. Friendship requires that one act out of sentiments of love and personal attachment to this specific individual, not for any such universalistic considerations. It may be replied that these theories do permit the formation of true friendships—relationships of which such motivations and actions are important constituents. They only require that acting out of motives specific to friendship should be approvable from some universal point of view; and there is good reason to think most friendships, and most acts of friendship, would pass this test. No doubt some acts of friendship (and so, some friendships) would not pass it (. . . acts involving . . . lying and other immoralities . . .) but it is doubtful whether any true friendship should (or can) ever require them." See "Friendship," in *Encyclopedia of Ethics*, ed. L. Becker (New York: Garland, 1991), vol. 1, 390.

[5] "Lecture on Friendship," 208. Although Kant's views on friendship have garnered many critics, and my selection reflects one of the sources for that criticism, other writers have come to Kant's defense. For a comparison of Aristotle and Kant, see Nancy Sherman, *Making a Necessity of Virtue: Aristotle and Kant on Virtue* (Cambridge: Cambridge University Press, 1997), chapter 5. But even if friendship suffered neglect in much post-Enlightenment philosophy, the ancients viewed it as a serious philosophical topic. See, for example, Plato, *Lysis, Symposium*, and *Phaedrus*; Aristotle, *Nicomachean Ethics*, bks 8 and 9; *Eudemian Ethics*, bk. 7; *Magna Moralia*, bk. 2, 11–17; and *Rhetoric*, bk. 4; Cicero, *Laelius de Amicitia*; Plutarch, *Moralia*, 48E–78E; 86B–92F; 93A–97B.

TYPES OF FRIENDSHIP: THE ARISTOTELIAN CONTRIBUTION

In Aristotle's rich but somewhat freewheeling discussion, the friendship relation (*philia*) is characterized very broadly, more broadly than the English term *friendship*. It is also central to his idea of what contributes to a flourishing life. At its heart is a reciprocated well-wishing and concern, though this core is differentiated into three main types of friendship that he distinguishes primarily by the qualities that form the basis for mutual attraction.[6] Briefly, these types of friendship are:

1. *Instrumental friendship*, which is friendship grounded in the utility and assistance that people can provide each other. Such friendship is based on accidental or contingent features of the friend and is motivated "primarily by each friend's independently defined goals"[7]—whatever those goals may be (and whether worthy or unworthy). When the other ceases to be useful to the achievement of those goals, the friendship will also end. An important (but nonindividual) subcategory of instrumental friendship is what Aristotle refers to as "civic friendship"—the interest that citizens take in each other's qualities of mind and character, an interest based on the experience or expectation of mutual benefit from the activities in which it is expressed.[8]

2. *Companion friendship* is a type of friendship grounded in the mutual pleasure that people take in each other's company. Neera Kapur Badhwar speaks of this as "a practical and emotional relationship of mutual and reciprocal goodwill, trust, respect, and love or affection between people who enjoy spending time together."[9] In companion friendship, one cares for the other as an essential part of one's own ends. In that caring for others, friends recognize each other for the particular persons that they are—that is, as having their own varied character traits and perspectives.

---

[6] In what follows I lean heavily on John Cooper's excellent contributions to Aristotelian scholarship on friendship, particularly "Aristotle on the Forms of Friendship," *Review of Metaphysics* 30, no. 4 (1977): 619–648; "Friendship and the Good in Aristotle," *Philosophical Review* 86, no. 3 (1977): 290–315; "Political Animals and Civic Friendship," reprinted in *Friendship: A Philosophical Reader*, ed. Neera Kapur Badhwar (Ithaca, NY: Cornell University Press, 1993), 303–326. All are reprinted with minor changes in John Cooper, *Reason and Emotion: Essays on Moral Psychology and Ethical Theory* (Princeton, NJ: Princeton University Press, 1999).

[7] Badhwar, ed., *Friendship*, 3.

[8] See esp. Cooper, "Political Animals and Civic Friendship." That Aristotle should construe civic relations in these terms indicates the importance he ascribes to the *polis* in human flourishing and, we might add, the importance that he would accord to collective or communal loyalty.

[9] Badhwar, "Introduction: The Nature and Significance of Friendship," in *Friendship*, 2–3.

As Aristotle presents them, although both instrumental and companion friendship are means-oriented friendships, they also involve wishing the other well for the other's sake. He considers some form of this un-self-interested well-wishing to be a minimum requirement of friendship even though, in the case of instrumental companion friendship, such well-wishing will be framed and constrained by the usefulness or pleasurability associated with the other. Because instrumental and companion friendships are contingent on the other's usefulness to one's ends or provision of some kind of pleasure, if the friends change significantly in these respects, the friendship will most likely dissolve. Aristotle calls such friendships "imperfect"—as not quite fully friendships—though he persists in using that appellation because, as he somewhat implausibly puts it, genuine, complete, or "perfect" friendship—character friendship—will also have utility and give pleasure to those involved in them. As much to the point, I suspect, is the fact that some type of companion friendship is what we most commonly have in mind when we speak of friendship.

3. *Character friendship*—Aristotle's ideal of friendship—is friendship based on or at least grounded in an appreciation that people have of each other's good qualities of character. Such friends not only wish each other well for the other's sake, enjoy each other's company, and confer benefits on each other but, because they are attracted by the good character of the other, they achieve good that is not available in other friendships. By virtue of each person's engagement with the other's good qualities, character friends will participate in each other's goodness. John Cooper notes that they do this in two ways:

> First, one expresses one's own personal virtues in doing one's part in [the common activities that manifest the friendship], and that is intrinsically good. Second, because the activities are shared, one also shares in the additional goodness that derives from the friend's virtues that are equally expressed in them. [But] in addition, the friend's appreciation of one's own good qualities provides valuable confirmation of the correctness of one's own views about what is worthwhile in human life, and strengthens one's capacity to express them in action.[10]

At first blush, Aristotle's account of true friendship appears excessively idealistic, purchased at the expense of genuine friendships that seem to be grounded in much less. But as Cooper points out, when defining something, Aristotle tends to look for the best and most fully realized instance of the definiendum. Moreover, his idealism is underscored by strong ties to a conception of what is grounded in reality. There are two points to be made here. First, as is the case with the other two forms of friendship,

[10] Cooper, "Friendship," 389.

in which the pleasurability or usefulness of the other need not extend across the whole range of activities but may be limited to a few, so, too, in the case of character friendship, the engaging virtue of the other may be limited: I may warm to the other's generosity and tolerance as a key to our relationship while recognizing that he is somewhat lazy and spendthrift. Second, and no less important, the significance for Aristotle in grounding true friendship in another's character traits is that these are what belong to the other *as a human being*—they are intrinsic to his nature—and, unlike the other's ability to please or be useful, are not merely incidental to him. Character friends are friends "without qualification" and not just "incidentally." And so, even though character friendship may for Aristotle be the highest form of friendship, indeed, the only true friendship, it is not undifferentiated, and some of its expressions will be less ideal than others. Aristotle allows that even these friendships may cease if one of the friends changes significantly for the worse, but he believes that a friendship based on character possesses internal incentives for stability.

RETHINKING ARISTOTLE

With the recent revival of interest in friendship, there has been a return to what are proffered as Aristotelian accounts of friendship and, in particular, to attempts to see friendship as not only undergirded by moral values but also a vehicle for moral improvement.

And yet, whatever attractions it has, an overly moralized account appears to elevate what may be an important value and role of friendship into a defining feature. Or to put it in somewhat different terms, Aristotle takes what is often a feature undergirding companion friendship and elevates it into a criterion of true friendship—character friendship—that, in the end, may even threaten the viability of much that reasonably passes for friendship. Less tendentiously, Aristotle works with a broader understanding of character and the virtues that may inform it than is encompassed by many contemporary accounts of morality, and so the platform for deep and lasting friendship appears too narrow.[11]

Let me develop these claims in more detail. As we encounter the social phenomenon of friendship—generally, some version of companion friendship—it will involve inter alia a noninstrumental concern for the well-being of the other. By virtue of the relationship and emotional bond that is established between them, friends care for each other for their own sakes, and this leads them to take each other's perspectives

---

[11] I also note here a motivational problem embedded in Aristotle's account. We might wonder whether, if what motivates character friendship is the character of the friend, we fall short of caring *for the friend* as our motivation. Aristotle, too, may fall foul of the schizophrenia that Michael Stocker associates with modern ethical theories. See "The Schizophrenia of Modern Ethical Theories," *Journal of Philosophy* 73, no. 14 (1976): 453–466.

into account in considering their own well-being. Such caring will, moreover, generally reflect a positive appraisal of the friend.

Nevertheless, except perhaps as idealized examples of friendship, we should be cautious about yoking that appraisal too deeply or narrowly to judgments of moral virtue or worth, for it would appear that deep and genuine friendships may be built upon or, more likely, incorporate shared perversity rather than expectations of the other's good character. What a person values in a friend for whom he cares may even be evidence of moral corruption. Think of Thelma and Louise, Bonnie and Clyde, Mickey and Mallory Knox (of *Natural Born Killers*), or, more recently, the close friendship of two New York detectives, Louis Eppolito and Stephen Caracappa, who worked both sides of the street before retiring with their families to comfortable lives in Las Vegas.[12] They would never have cheated on each other, but others were fair game. Their good times together were significantly centered on their secret bond and on what each brought to bear on a vulnerable society.

The positive appraisal that friendship usually involves also has a further feature that should inhibit the temptation to overmoralize it. The mutuality of friendship has an interactive dimension—a give and take—that can lead to our appraisal of a friend being influenced by the relationship as well as functioning independently of it. And so a friendship can either enhance or cloud our objectivity; it may raise or lower our moral sights. As well as being based on corrupt values, it may itself corrupt.

Aristotle may be correct in thinking that stable friendships are most likely to be grounded in the kinds of virtues that ordinarily sustain good relations between human beings. He may also be correct to believe that friends for whom moral values are important will likely make a greater contribution to the flourishing of each than will friendships that place greater store on other considerations. What is less clear is whether such friendships will be more *real* or complete as friendships than those that place greater weight on friendship's companionate dimensions, or even whether such character friendships should be seen to represent an ideal of friendship to which we should aspire.

BEYOND ARISTOTLE

In their perceptive contributions to our understanding of friendship, Dean Cocking and Jeanette Kennett give extended expression to some of these doubts.[13] They

---

[12] See Guy Lawson and William Oldham, *The Brotherhoods: The True Story of Two Cops Who Murdered for the Mafia* (New York: Scribner, 2006).

[13] Dean Cocking and Jeanette Kennett, "Friendship and Moral Danger," *Journal of Philosophy* 97 (2000): 278–296. See also Dean Cocking and Jeanette Kennett, "Friendship and the Self," *Ethics* 108, no. 4 (1998): 502–527; and Dean Cocking and Justin Oakley, "Indirect Consequentialism, Friendship, and the Problem of Alienation," *Ethics* 106 (1995): 86–111.

provide a number of examples of the ways in which genuine friendships may generate and accommodate moral compromise. One of their key examples is the following: Carl, in an unfortunate turn of events, accidentally kills someone for whose death he believes he will be held responsible.[14] In a panic, he calls his best friend, Dave, to help him deal with the situation, and they decide that the best option—or at least the "best friend" option—is for them to dispose of the body. This they are jointly able to do. The victim's disappearance remains a mystery to others. Dave, on Cocking and Kennett's account, shows himself to be a good and loyal friend even though significant moral wrongdoing has been perpetrated, including the deception of others and additional heartache for the victim's family. Dave shows himself to be willing to help move not only house but also a body.

It is not a completely unproblematic example, and Cocking and Kennett review a range of alternative ways of reading it. But the plausible upshot of their discussion is that there are ways of characterizing the case that allow the description "good and loyal friend" to be reasonably given to a person whose expression of friendship is morally transgressive. Even though the ideal of character friendship would bar Dave from being considered a real friend, good friendship, as we generally understand and value it, is not so constrictive. A really good friend may be prepared to act immorally for one, and, by contrast, a moral saint may not have made such a good friend.

The lesson that Cocking and Kennett wish us to take from this and other cases they provide is that what they call "the highly moralized account of friendship" is not only excessively demanding but also probably not the only ideal of friendship. One may most need a friend when some (im)moral cover is required—someone who will lie *for you*. It does not follow from that, of course, that friendship is not a human good, that it does not (in general) contribute to a morally good life, or even that it would not have been morally better had a particular friendship been less morally transgressive. But to have at least an important part of the value they do, friendships need not be free of moral compromise. As I argued in an earlier chapter, human flourishing is not ordinarily achieved or sustained in isolation. As social beings, a great deal of our worthwhile activity—including the realization of our persons—is expressed in and accomplished through our associations with others. And friendship constitutes one of the most potent and valued sites for our self-development, self-expression, and personal accomplishment. That much Aristotle has exactly right.

Cocking and Kennett go beyond critiquing the moralized ideal of friendship. Someone might accept their critique but argue that friendship still expresses a fundamental moral concern. That is, by virtue of their caring for each other, friends

---

[14] Their example, spelled out at greater length, is based on the 1991 Australian film, *Death in Brunswick* (dir. John Ruane).

manifest a type of moral regard, and we may have to weigh the moral value of that mutual care against the moral disvalue of the transgressive ways in which it may otherwise manifest itself. This view, which Cocking and Kennett dub the "plural moral values" account, is exemplified in Larry Blum's assertion that

> friendship is an expression of moral activity on our part—of a type of regard for another person, a giving of oneself and a caring for another for his own sake. . . . It is genuine care for another person which constitutes a moral activity of the self.[15]

Thus we might argue that even though Dave has expressed his friendship for Carl in a morally transgressive way—by helping him to dispose of the body—his friendship nevertheless constitutes a moralized relation by virtue of his seeking to do what will contribute to Carl's well-being. Even this more modest position is disputable, though Cocking and Kennett acknowledge that "all accounts of the nature of close friendships agree that such things as mutual affection, the disposition to promote the other's serious interests and well-being, and the desire for shared experiences are necessary constituents of the relationship." They dispute it by eliciting a further feature of friendship, namely, that friends are "characteristically receptive to being directed and interpreted and so in these ways being drawn by each other."[16] That is, friends' interests have action-guiding force for each other independent of any moral scrutiny to which they could be subject. Moreover, by contributing to each other's self-conception, friends shape each other. The salient point is that one way or another, the interests of *the other* shape one's own, and in that mutual drawing and influencing, room is created for the other's less morally desirable characteristics being reasons for each one's support of the other. In some cases, the support may be given *because* the interests are less morally desirable. They thus try to show how a genuinely good friendship "might embrace the moral vices of a friend, such as his recklessness or cruel wit."[17]

---

[15] Cocking and Kennett, "Friendship and Moral Danger," 282, quoting Lawrence Blum, "Friendship as a Moral Phenomenon," in *Friendship*, ed. Badhwar, 198–199.

[16] Cocking and Kennett, "Friendship and Moral Danger," 284.

[17] Ibid., 287. The examples are a little tricky, partly because the intimacy and responsiveness of genuine friendship is not shown in complaisance or an unthinking devotion to another's interests. It expresses a concern for another's well-being, a desire that the other flourish, and though that may be construed in ways that are morally transgressive—as when Dave agrees to help Carl dispose of the body—nevertheless, it is done under the description of doing what is best for Carl. I doubt whether embracing a friend's recklessness or cruel wit can always be so characterized, and it seems to me that insofar as a friend supports such things, that friend might fail as a friend.

I do not want to argue that a good friend could never embrace another's reckless-ness. What a good friend will want to do is determine how important the reckless behavior is to the other's flourishing. If the friend is Evel Knievel and the reckless activity is that of being a motorcycle daredevil, then some form of support for controlled recklessness might well be part of the relationship. In that case, the embrace of another's recklessness may be part of a morally admirable care for that other as the other sees himself or herself. I distinguish this from the kind of random reckless-ness in which a person may wish to indulge—a game of Russian roulette or joyriding while under the influence, for example—that a friend might be called to witness or participate in. It is the former that Cocking and Kennett see as a genuine expression of friendship. In the latter cases, in which the person seriously wishes to engage in reckless behavior, a genuine friend will seek to discourage it, even, perhaps, to the point of acting paternalistically. There it is not simply a moral failure in the friend that leads him to embrace the friend's recklessness, but a failure in friendship. I would sometimes be willing to hazard much the same criticism of support for another's cruel wit. To the extent that we see constraints of morality as the glue that holds human social life together, the person who displays a cruel wit engages in conduct that is humanly alienating, and a real friend will be aware of that and seek to curb it, albeit in ways that are compatible with the friendship. The cruelly witty friend may garner laughs and even a certain social cachet for his savage displays, but it is a cachet likely to be obtained at significant social cost. The good friend will seek to moderate and defang the wit.[18]

That said, a friendship in which part of the attraction includes some of the other's moral failings is not out of the question, and just as a thriving friendship may be morally elevating, it may also be morally corrupting, not only in what it demands of one but also in the values that help hold it together.

THE VALUE OF FRIENDSHIP

How, then, are we to view companion friendship as a form of human association? Is it, as some of its more transgressive examples may suggest, a corrupting or deeply corruptive relation? Is it, perhaps, a morally neutral form of association, sometimes morally valuable but at other times morally perverse? Or is it, rather, an essentially valuable form of human relationship that can be corrupted in various ways? Each possibility has something to be said for it, though I shall argue for the last of these as a prelude to saying more about the reasons for associating it so closely with loyalty.

---

[18] Perhaps one of the lessons to be taken from Bonnie and Clyde or Thelma and Louise is that such friendships may easily end badly for the friends, even if they remain good friends.

(1) Although there are few who go so far as to argue that friendship as such is immoral, there are resources for such a claim that are similar to the resources used to show that there is something gravely deficient about loyalty.

Consider some of the following. Our friendships with others may require that we sometimes are willing to lie, cheat, or otherwise act wrongly for them. Or even if our friendships do not require it, they might at times place us under strong pressure or temptation to lie, cheat, or otherwise act wrongly. More generally, the particularism of friendship's obligations may stand in tension with the universalism that "morality" expects of us. And finally, it is arguable that because what a friend asks of us constitutes a reason for our doing it, this registers, if not a temporary suspension of our autonomy with respect to another, at least a strong reason to give up our independence.

These are, however, not persuasive reasons for thinking that there is something fundamentally problematic in friendship (and hence, of course, with the loyalty that is integral to it). On the one hand, the objection misleadingly characterizes the ways in which friends ordinarily influence each other; on the other hand, there is a questionable inference from what friendship may sometimes be used to require of one to a general conclusion about the character of friendship. Even if friendship sometimes sanctions lies, it will not sanction any and all lies. And as for the view that friendship is flawed because of its particularism, the argument might just as easily be seen as manifesting a flawed moral universalism, for the latter has usually acknowledged some forms of particularism, such as special obligations to parents and children. An argument that seeks to undermine the general value of friendship needs to show that there is something inherently problematic about it such that a general obligation to give special attention to the well-being of friends would be inappropriate. I know of no such argument.

(2) What about the view that friendship is a nonmoral sentiment or tie and that any assessment of its moral worth—as good or bad—depends on what this bond leads to or makes possible?

Such neutrality could be seen as an alternative inference from Cocking and Kennett's treatment of friendship. As they point out, friendships are sometimes uplifting and ennobling, sites of moral triumph, whereas at other times they become sources of and resources for moral evil. Might friendship's value lie exclusively in the ways in which it expresses human goodness or depravity, rather than in some inherent value?

Tempting though such a position may be, it fails to give sufficient weight to the ways in which friendships—and acting out of friendship—are woven into human flourishing. Michael Stocker, for example, uses acts of friendship to challenge the ability of traditional moral theories to provide an account of motivation. Appeals to moral duty or optimal good to justify acts of friendship fail miserably. And even

Peter Railton, in his attempt to defend a form of consequentialism against Stocker's critique, nevertheless concedes that

> we must recognize that . . . friendships . . . are among the most important contributors to whatever it is that makes life worthwhile; any moral theory deserving serious consideration must itself give them serious consideration. . . . If we were to find that adopting a particular kind of morality led to irreconcilable conflict with certain types of human well-being . . . then this surely would give us reason to doubt its claims.[19]

Whatever we might want to say about the moral status of particular friendships, it is odd to view friendship in general as evaluatively neutral.

Larry Blum also seeks to counter the view that friendship is no more than a natural attraction of no particular moral significance by showing how much of friendship is the product of thought and effort. He argues that the caring for another that is integral to friendship is as morally significant as the caring for another that arises out of unconditional love (*agapē*).[20]

(3) Although it is common to think of the third option in strictly moralistic terms, we have already suggested that will not do. Friendship—even a good friendship—need not be a vehicle for virtue: people may be bound in friendship by forms of immorality or banality. What, then, might we see as the good of friendship? More than one possibility presents itself, and each may capture some element of the good that friendship may be and have for us without committing us to Aristotelian character friendship.

Consider what our lives would be like were friendship not an option. We are not social beings only in the sense that our flourishing is ordinarily manifested as well as nurtured and aided by activity with others, but also beings whose flourishing is fostered and importantly expressed in the context of intimate relationships. No intimate relationship is better fitted to our self-realization than friendship. We need not deny that other relationships, such as familial or mentoring ones, may also play a role, but there are forms of mutuality and equality in friendship that make it a peculiarly and especially important site for personal flourishing.[21]

---

[19] Peter Railton, "Alienation, Consequentialism, and the Demands of Morality," *Philosophy & Public Affairs* 13, no. 2 (1984): 139.

[20] Lawrence Blum, "Friendship as a Moral Phenomenon" (from *Friendship, Altruism, and Morality*, Routledge, 1980), in *Friendship*, ed. Badhwar, 192–210.

[21] As we have noted, Aristotle saw that in terms of the development of our essential nature as tending toward virtue. Hence his focus on character friendship—though, once we grant that Aristotle is working with a much broader conception of virtue than is readily captured by our contemporary understanding of "morality," this may not be too different from what I have in mind here.

To some extent, the value we accord friendship is shown in the time and effort we devote to its fostering and expression. Many of us invest a significant proportion of our social and personal resources in friendships, particularly close friendships: this is one of the reasons Aristotle suggests that we should not have too many friends.[22] The expectations—or, if you like, demands—of friendship frequently take precedence over other obligations. And, as we have seen, those calls upon us are sometimes given precedence over what we would ordinarily see as the demands of morality. It is not that friendship is completely disconnected from or more important than morality, for though we may be prepared to justify, excuse, or mitigate some moral breaches that occur because of the expectations of friendship, we may and ought to be quite critical of friendships that become a cloak for major moral wrongdoing. The joke about a good friend helping you to move a body is two-edged precisely because it draws attention to the borderline between what is and what is not permissible in friendship. It gestures at what Cocking and Kennett refer to as friendship's moral dangerousness. Although Dave shows himself to be a really good friend to Carl, we may be less certain about the justifiability of his expression of friendship.

Simply being with a friend can be a source of great satisfaction. The other's presence can be enjoyed for its own sake, or there may be the simple mutual satisfaction of passively enjoying the setting sun or the waves rolling in, the friend's presence heightening one's enjoyment just because it is being shared with that person. But friends also constitute very active participants in our self-expression and self-realization. It is through our friends that we see ourselves, not in the sense that they are alter egos—though that can be the case—but rather in the sense that they help us see who we are. We are often too close to ourselves to have a good sense of what is important to us, what our values are, and what we are able to accomplish.[23] Others in society are often too distant from us in too many ways to provide an accurate appreciation of who and what we are. Friends, however—at least really good friends—are usually able to see our distinctive qualities, our strengths and weaknesses, and can draw attention to them and thus foster a form of self-reflection that is conducive to our self-understanding and growth—our *eudaimonia*. Unlike many others, friends can tell us like it is in the firm yet kind and constructive way that enables us to hear what is said and benefit from it. Thus they may provide an important form of access to ourselves as well as a stimulus to inner growth or flourishing that we would otherwise find it difficult to achieve.

---

[22] *Nicomachean Ethics*, bk. IX, ch 11, §1171a.

[23] Although Aristotle uses the metaphor of a mirror—friends as alter egos in whom we see ourselves—this does not seem generally right: the point is rather that our friends are able to see us more objectively than we can manage on our own. See *Magna Moralia* 1213a10–26; and Cooper, "Friendship and the Good in Aristotle,"295–299.

Others, such as parents and teachers, can also foster self-awareness and personal growth. Nevertheless, close friends, by virtue of the special form of intimacy they provide, can usually be relied on for support when parents and mentors cannot— unless, of course, the latter have also become friends to us. Because of this, it is not always easy to separate the intrinsic from the instrumental value that friends have for us. Their support and encouragement often enables us to be what we would be unlikely to be without them. Nevertheless, such instrumental value as they have is embedded in the intrinsic value that particular friendship relationships have for us.

Although this account of some of the values inherent in friendship is not strongly moralized, nevertheless, just because friendship is so closely involved with our flourishing, it has, on the one hand, a privileged position in the realm of human relations and, on the other hand, its particular expressions are generally quite sensitive to moral criticism. Friendships that are perverse and self-destructive may be notorious but are not generally admired. As well, because friendships may demand much of us, we are often sensitive to the ways in which they can become exploitative. Does Carl go too far in his expectations of Dave? How reasonable is it to ask one's friends to bail us out when we have repeatedly created the messes in which we find ourselves? Although friendship may sometimes anticipate that friends will lie for each other, occasions on which they do so will be susceptible to moral scrutiny—not directly, perhaps, but via the particular contribution that friendship makes to the lives of each.

FRIENDSHIP AND LOYALTY

Close friendships represent forms of association that are not only intrinsically important to us but also important resources as we engage in the business of living—of creating flourishing lives for ourselves. Friendships are naturally geared to loyalty. Because of the mutual care that friendship involves, friends are responsive to us when we need them. What would be characterized by others only as an inconvenience or sacrifice is for friends also an expression of their relationship. It is just that kind of costly commitment to the relationship that constitutes loyalty to the other. When Carl calls Dave, Dave is seriously inconvenienced, not only by being called in the middle of the night but also by the demands that the situation makes of him. As a loyal friend, however, he allows himself to be inconvenienced and even placed at risk by Carl. The risk is moral as well as legal, social, and physical. He does for Carl what he would ordinarily resist.

Whether Dave is morally *justified* in doing what he does is something about which I have so far remained fairly noncommittal. Dave has been a good and loyal friend, but was it good that he was so? Even though friendship may not be an essentially moralized relation, our friendships are nevertheless open to moral scrutiny.

Moreover, given friendship's close connection to our flourishing as persons, it is important that friendships be scrutinized. Cocking and Kennett put it thus: "I might be a perfectly good friend. I might just not be a perfectly moral one."[24] Although that could be taken—and I think Cocking and Kennett intend it to be taken—as a gentle rebuke to the idea of moral overridingness, my own view is that no form of association, even friendship, is exempt from moral scrutiny and possible criticism. True, friendship may morally permit acts that would be impermissible were they to occur outside the friendship. But in this respect, friendship is similar to other social relations or professional roles. Just as police, by virtue of their professional role, may be permitted to engage in forms of deception morally barred to others, friends may do things for each other that would not be sanctioned outside that relationship. There are obviously limits to this, as indeed there are limits to the kinds of deception that should be permitted to police. What we as moral critics need to do—as indeed we need to do in the case of police—is ask, first, whether the seemingly immoral conduct that is perpetrated—say, Dave's helping Carl dispose of the body—is a best friend response to Carl's situation; second, whether the particular friendship is ethically acceptable;[25] and, third, whether friendship as a form of association is one that we are willing to support.

As to whether Dave's helping Carl dispose of the body is a best friend response, I am somewhat agnostic—mainly because there are details about the situation that are left unstated. If Dave is—as he seems to be—really concerned about Carl's well-being and not simply as Carl sees it (albeit not dismissive of how Carl sees it), and if the situation is one in which Carl's well-being is best served by disposing of the body, then it may indeed be a best friend response. We need then to ask about the friendship itself—whether the particular friendship that Dave and Carl have formed is one that serves their flourishing in ways that we have previously outlined, or whether it is ultimately self-destructive, exploitative, or something of that sort.[26] Finally, we need to provide an overall justification for the friendship relation or be prepared to state why friendship should have no special claim on us. That it should have *some* claim on us is an issue to which we gave our attention in the last section.

Dave's loyalty to Carl will be judged in the same way that we judge his act of friendship. We may see it as admirable, misguided, or blind, basing our determination on

---

[24] Cocking and Kennett, "Friendship and Moral Danger," 287.

[25] I take it that what may constitute a best friend response in a Mafia context (whacking someone who insulted your buddy) would fail at this stage because the friendship was grounded in perverse commitments.

[26] That is not an easy question to answer. We may need to distinguish the question: Is it best for Carl and Dave to enter into the friendship they have? from the question: Given their friendship, is it best for Dave to act as he does?

a consideration of whether, for example, the friendship with Carl was worth having or continuing, whether what Dave did for Carl had Carl's best interests at heart, and whether he correctly discerned and wisely engaged them. Although we value friendship as a virtue, we will think loyalty in friendship as admirable only insofar as we see the particular friendship as a good one and the particular expression of loyalty within that friendship as well conceived. Whether it is well conceived may be determined by how well it actually serves the interests and well-being of the other, but it may also be subject to a wider moral determination. As we have already noted, just because loyalty to the friend may justify deception, it does not follow that it justifies any deception. If, for example, Dave had good reason to believe that Carl had *murdered* his victim, then, though it may have been an expression of loyal friendship to help Carl dispose of the body, doing so would *not* have been a morally acceptable expression of loyalty. In such a case, Dave might have decided either that what Carl did forfeited his claims to Dave's friendship or that, because there was so much else to the friendship, his loyalty would be best expressed by encouraging Carl to face up to the consequences of what he had done, while promising to stay by Carl's side no matter what the outcome. Even if Carl thought that his interests would be best served by disposing of the body, Dave—here as a loyal opponent—might have judged that Carl's overall well-being, as well as overriding moral demands, would be best served by Carl giving himself up. Of course, though Dave may see this and his remaining by Carl's side as the best he can do as a loyal friend, Carl himself might demand more and thus seek to sever their relationship should more support not be forthcoming. Carl and Dave may disagree about what friendship may reasonably demand and what would be an appropriate expression of friendship loyalty.

LOYALTY AND FRIENDSHIP

Although I have tried to give a "healthy" account of friendship, in which those who constitute friends serve to advance each others' serious interests and to foster each other's well being, it has also been suggested that friendship, because of the loyalty integral to it, poses unacceptable risks to autonomy and objectivity, two important human values. On the first count, it has been argued that, by virtue of their receptivity to each other, loyal friends sometimes or temporarily cede their autonomy to the other: the fact that one party wants something functions as a compelling reason for the other to seek to satisfy that want. On the second count, it is claimed that friends become mutual admiration societies and that "friendship closes the eyes."[27] Friends say what they think will please the other and thus fail to constitute for that other a vehicle for self-understanding.

[27] Quoted in Badhwar, *Friendship*, 7.

A version of this latter criticism runs through Simon Keller's discussion of friendship and loyalty. Indeed, he uses the criticism to cast doubt on the virtuousness of loyalty. Keller thinks of loyalty as a vice because, as he puts it, the identification that goes with loyalty leads to bad faith. In the case of friendship, Keller holds that the bad faith of loyalty is generally harmless and that the overall good of friendship is such that bad faith loyalty will constitute a permissible vice. By contrast, he considers patriotic loyalty to be not only a vice but also a dangerous one.

For Keller, the close connection between friendship and loyalty is partially expressed by what he calls "loyalty in belief"—that is, a "tendency to form certain beliefs and resist others, independently of the evidence."[28] A good or loyal friend will be inclined to believe the best of one—even if the evidence suggests otherwise—and will also tend to be less than truthful if what is felt to be correct would be hurtful to one. Loyalty in belief, he maintains, conflicts with the virtue of "epistemic integrity"—the commitment to grounding beliefs on sufficient evidence.

Although Keller carefully crafts his theoretical discussion in terms of "tendencies" and "inclinations," he has little doubt that appropriate expressions of loyal friendship will sometimes require acts of epistemic *ir*responsibility. His central case concerns Eric, who, because of his friendship with Rebecca, agrees to attend a poetry reading she has arranged at which she hopes to catch the attention of a visiting literary critic. As a good and loyal friend, Eric agrees to provide moral support, despite his strong but unexpressed belief that poetry read at the venue is always mediocre. Nevertheless, even though he is unfamiliar with it, he will give Rebecca's poetry a sympathetic and supportive hearing. He will listen for its strengths and perhaps overlook its weaknesses and not let her know that he believes the visiting critic will be unimpressed by what he hears.

Despite its nuance, Keller's account of the epistemic shortcomings of loyalty in friendship—and, with that, certain *moral* shortcomings of loyalty in friendship—is unconvincing. We may, for starters, question the stringency of his principle of epistemic responsibility. Rigidly interpreting the Socratic commitment to following the argument where it leads is unreasonable; at least, for a time it is often advisable to resist "the force of evidence," especially if the consequences of accepting it would be too radical.[29]

---

[28] Keller, *The Limits of Loyalty*, 25.

[29] One of the important lessons that every first-year philosophy student has to confront is the skeptical challenge of Descartes's First Meditation. For a wider discussion, see Tziporah Kasachkoff and Isaac Nevo, "Is It Wise to Teach Our Students to Follow the Argument Wherever It Leads?" *Teaching Philosophy* 29, no. 2 (2006): 157–172; and Thomas Kelly, "Following the Argument Where It Leads," *Philosophical Studies* 154, no. 1 (2011): 105–124.

Moreover, Keller's example allows for a much more flexible position than he concedes. Eric has never heard Rebecca's poetry, and his only reason for thinking that her poetry will be mediocre is a fairly weak inductive one—namely, that others who read their poetry at that café are mediocre. But perhaps the critic has heard something about Rebecca's poetry, and that is why he is attending. Eric has good reason for not voicing weakly supported suspicions before he has seen or heard Rebecca's poetry.

Another reason for resisting Keller's skepticism has to do with his somewhat narrow understanding of how to be truthful with others. One can tell the truth in a number of ways, and those who take the view that truth telling is only telling it like it is, as though truth telling cannot be done in a diplomatic or sensitive or timely fashion, fail to appreciate the social nature of discourse. If Eric's friendship with Rebecca gives him reason to save Rebecca from humiliation or disappointment, he has reason to let her know the truth but also reason to let her know it in a kind and considerate way.

There is, of course, also an important place in friendship for telling it like it is, even if it hurts. Sometimes that is what friends are for—to keep each other from stupidity and other behavior that will later come to be regretted. But if Eric has strong enough reason to believe not only that the reading will provide Rebecca with little satisfaction and probably humiliation but also that telling her outright will be painful and alienating, his concerns ought to be aired gently and diplomatically.

Finally and most critically, Keller's understanding of "loyalty in belief" as a tendency to form beliefs independently of the evidence that bears on them, and to resist challenges to those beliefs, arises out of a narrowly focused understanding of loyalty that gives inadequate attention to the factors that (ideally) go into both its formation and retention. Presumably, Keller is inclined to give some preference to a friend's word against a stranger's *on matters on which each may be thought to have equal access.* One reason for this will surely be an assessment that he has made of his friend's trustworthiness and competence as part of the process leading to and informing their close friendship. There may, of course, be exceptions to this. We sometimes form and retain friendships with those we consider unreliable in certain respects, albeit compensated for by other things they bring to the relationship. In such cases, we may not be inclined to take their word—we may indeed joke about their promises to come on time or their poor sense of direction or color sense, while trusting them in other respects. Thus, loyalty is not a blank check for the friend. To be sure, we take the word of friends because we believe we can trust their honesty, and we generally become friends with those whom we believe we can trust—but that is trust in their honesty *with us*, not necessarily trust with respect to every matter on which they pronounce. Trust is not credulity. And just as trust should not be construed as blind faith, we may expect the loyalty of belief in friendship to be erected on some prior evidence of reliability (albeit on a limited range of matters). Such trust will be confirmed by our subsequent experience or, in some cases, eroded or modified by that experience. Generally speaking, loyalty does not start as blind commitment, and it need not become blind. What Keller interprets as a tendency to disregard evidence is, I believe, often an enhanced principle of charity that, drawing on its earlier relational roots, looks positively on the object of trust and loyalty.[30]

Of course, one could claim (as indeed Keller does) that the problem with loyalty in friendship is not that it always leads to bad faith but that it draws us in that direction and that the tendency toward epistemic irresponsibility casts a shadow over the virtuousness of loyalty. If this is true, then a similar shadow is cast over the virtues of faith, hope, trust, and love, all of which involve certain positive attitudes toward their objects and thus may incline one toward epistemic irresponsibility. Arguing that loyalty is deleterious to epistemic integrity has many ripples.

One other matter calls for comment. It has been argued that, because friendship may sometimes require that one behave in ways that, outside of that context, would invite moral censure, the loyalty associated with it predisposes one to act more generally in morally questionable ways: a person who is willing to lie *for* a friend is also likely to be willing to lie *to* a friend. Cocking and Kennett reject this argument for the reason that we contextualize and compartmentalize our behavior: what we consider appropriate in one sphere we may consider inappropriate in a different sphere. The fact that Dave is prepared to lie for Carl does not show that he is likely to be willing to lie to Carl. Others, however, Keller among them, maintain that once bonds of loyalty loosen the grip that moral constraints have on behavior, it is likely to stay loose: if loyalty requires that one lie for a friend, it will too easily require that, out of loyalty, one will think it appropriate to lie to a friend. This a problematic inference. If Eric is really convinced that Rebecca's poetry reading will result in sad disappointment for her, his loyal support will no doubt require diplomacy. But this need not involve

---

[30] To look ahead to chapter 13, Keller's view that patriotic loyalty is a vice draws attention to important differences between friendship and patriotism that give some credibility to his concerns about the latter. Patriotic loyalty is frequently indoctrinated from a young age, before we have an opportunity to ask appropriate questions about it, and by the time we are able to ask those questions, our reasons and emotions may have been skewed to the acceptance of what we have been brought up to believe. Once in the patriotic box, we may be neither emotionally nor rationally equipped to think outside it. Friendships, on the other hand, are usually chosen, and our close friendships often take a long period of time to develop, as we come to acquaint ourselves with the other to whom we find ourselves drawn. No doubt our friendships and the loyalty that accompanies them can also be—and too often are—corrupted, and maybe loyalty is more easily manipulated and corrupted than other virtues, but this is not sufficient to sustain a generally dismal view of loyalty.

untruthfulness. A wise and caring friend will know the difference between gently conveying strong doubts and concealing them.

CONCLUSION

The connection between friendship and loyalty is peculiarly and particularly close—so close that one can hardly understand the notion of serious friendship without reference to loyalty. Loyalty may be shown and is often expected in other associational relationships, but in friendship, it is an internal expectation. Friendship without loyalty is dead.

This becomes understandable when we appreciate the close tie between human flourishing and friendship. Our intrinsic sociality finds some of its deepest expressions in friendship. Not only are friends sources of great satisfaction, but the emotional and epistemic bond that friendship involves is also critical to our self-understanding and growth.

Nevertheless, although loyalty is deeply implicated in friendship, and lack of loyalty will kill a friendship, it does not follow that every loyal act of friendship will pass ethical muster. Acts of genuine friendship are not restricted to narrow moral boundaries, and loyal friends may express their friendship unwisely and immorally. Although some writers (such as Keller) see the problematic character of loyalty in friendship as stemming from the nature of loyalty rather than that of particular friendships, I have argued that the opposite is more likely the case. A deep friendship may form around problematic values and goals, and the loyalty it engenders may be corruptive. Although loyalty can go wrong in various ways—as indeed can other virtues—this should not incline us to doubt its status as a virtue. Too often it goes wrong because of failures in its associational object.

9

FAMILY

The one thing I can pass along with some degree of certainty is that family loyalty is the highest form of loyalty that human beings can give to each other in everyday life.[1]

Filial piety is the source of all human virtues and the most important principle in human relations.[2] *Loyalty is the application of filial piety to serve the ruler.*[3]

Although loyalty is not as integral to other relationships and associations as it is to friendship, James Carville is not alone in giving preeminence to familial loyalty. And Confucian thought, as the quotation from Nakae Tōju indicates, sees familial loyalty as the root of all virtue. Perhaps there are causal reasons for thinking this way. We are—and here we can speak with some universality—members of families first, and our experience as family members may determine our capacity for friendship as well as the kinds of friendships we will later develop. That said, it does not follow that familial bonds and the loyalty that often goes with them should be accorded the status that Carville or Confucian scholars wish. Moreover, despite its social role and apparent "naturalness," the family has often been subject to radical criticism. In addition, there is an instrumentality to the family that, even if it impacts on the possibility and kinds of friendship we may have, may render it a problematic candidate for our deepest, most fulfilling and demanding loyalties.

---

[1] James Carville, *Stickin': The Case for Loyalty* (New York: Simon & Schuster, 2000), 85.

[2] Nakae Tōju, *Okina mondō*, in *Nihon shisō taikei* (Tokyo: Iwanami Shoten, 1974), vol. 29, 33.

[3] Nakae Tōju, *Kōkyō keimō*, in *Nihon shisō taikei*, vol. 29, 197. Both quotations reflect his reading of the Confucian *Xiaojing* (*Classic of Filial Piety*), available at www.chinapage.com/confucius/xiaojing-be.html. Although a distinction is drawn here between loyalty (*zhong*) and filial piety (*xiao*), reserving the former for political loyalty, the two virtues appear to be distinguished by context rather than content.

Along with these concerns, we need to accommodate a complexity in familial relations that permits a variety of familial loyalties—loyalties that, even if often coordinated, may also exist in tension. The loyalty that parents may have for each other is not identical to the loyalty that they may have for their children or vice versa or that siblings may have for each other, and these loyalties may also differ from the loyalty that is often found within an extended family or even a lineage. In itself, conflicts among these loyalties should not count decisively against the preeminence of "family loyalty," for what may be viewed as preeminent is a diverse package of loyalties that collectively make a distinctive contribution to human flourishing. So, to what extent should we see families as appropriate associational objects of loyalty, and with what problems must familial loyalties grapple?

We should first say more about what is meant by *family*. As is common with every other social institution—such as those of marriage, friendship, the firm, state, or tribe—the family is not amenable to a single or simple characterization, even though there is probably enough cohesion and coherence to the idea to distinguish those who defend the institution of the family from those who oppose it. Leaving aside the universalistic idea of "the family of man," *family* is generally used to characterize the primary sociobiological site for human nurture—and therefore usually includes as its central members parents and their offspring. Insofar as we tend to think of humankind historically and normatively—especially as the vehicle for a moral order—a family represents the unit most deeply involved in its perpetuation. New members of the "human family" are first and foremost members of human families, ordinarily though not necessarily the product of sexual relations between a couple committed not only to the generation of a new human being but also to its formation as a moral agent. Moral agents (persons) are the outcome of an extended period of nurture, and families are the institution most intimately involved in that process.

Of course, considerable debate surrounds not only the foregoing sketch but also the conditions under which the nurturing task of the family can be successfully prosecuted. No doubt because of its human and social importance, the family has been the object not only of ongoing moralization but also of unrelenting political, religious, economic, sociological, and psychological scrutiny. Debates concerning in vitro fertilization, surrogacy, single and same-sex parenting, nuclear and extended families, kibbutzim, and family-state, family-school, and family-church relations, to name just a few, have all focused on how to "best" or "appropriately" nurture new generations of human beings. These debates all impact on the kinds and claims of familial loyalties, their strengths as well as their weaknesses.

It will provide a useful transition from the last chapter's focus on friendship to the present chapter's concern with familial relationships to review some points of contrast as well as of convergence. Following that, I will also provide a brief historical review of the family as an institution to indicate some of the ways in which this ubiquitous institution evolved, with consequences for the loyalty it often engenders.

FRIENDSHIP AND FAMILY RELATIONSHIPS

Laurence Thomas's attempt to distinguish friendship and familial relations provides a helpful peg for considering their differences, as well an illustration of the issues to be confronted in giving a broadly functional characterization of the family.[4] Thomas suggests that three distinguishing features—choice, authority, and dependency— differentiate familial from friendship relations and point to the distinctively nurturing role that families have.

He notes, first, that whereas friendships are grounded in choice, we do not ordinarily choose our families. This, of course, reflects the perspective of those who are born into families rather than those who choose to "start a family" and focuses particularly on the family as a generative and nurturing institution. Although there are sometimes provisions for severing those ties or even—in the case of an adoptive family—of reestablishing links with a biological family, family membership remains one of the most enduring of our social connections. Even those who choose to start a new family do not generally sever their ties with the families into which they were born. We can often forsake our religion or citizenship more easily than we can break free of our family.

One might wonder whether friendship should be seen as the natural outgrowth of familial relations. If, as the outcome of our family experience, we are helped to be those who choose our associates and particularly those who will be our friends, might we expect familial relationships to develop into friendship relationships? The *if* that opens the last sentence hints at the fact that the experience of family might not always be as helpful as the question suggests. For many, the experience of growing up is a mixed blessing. Yet even if the process is relatively untroubled, there may be no special reason for such relations to transform themselves into friendships. If they do, this may serve to perpetuate such connections beyond the point at which we can expect the nurturing task to be completed. Although family life seems to be concentrated on nurture, we often consider that familial obligations will continue into later years and that now-emancipated children have ongoing loyalties to their parents and even to the larger family circle: obligations to siblings, to grandparents, and maybe

---

[4] Laurence Thomas, "Friendship and Other Loves" (from *Living Morally: A Psychology of Character*, Philadelphia: Temple University Press, 1990), in *Friendship: A Philosophical Reader*, ed. Neera Kapur Badhwar (Ithaca, NY: Cornell University Press, 1993), 48–64; cf. also his "Friendship," *Synthese* 72, no. 2 (1987): 217–236; and Joseph Kupfer, "Can Parents and Children Be Friends?" *American Philosophical Quarterly* 27, no. 1 (1990): 15–26.

to uncles and aunts (should there not be others for whom those obligations are more immediate). If friendship develops within the family circle, the obligations of friendship will likely manifest themselves when relationships and associations become amenable to responsible choice.

As we will argue later, however, ongoing familial obligations are more likely to be grounded in other factors—such as indebtedness, gratitude, the recognition of vulnerability, and other specifics of familial life.

Thomas's second distinguishing feature highlights the absence of authority that usually characterizes friendship relations but which is—at least during the period of nurture—central to parent-child relations. To the extent that we think of familial relationships as complex and differentiated, the relation between younger children and parents at least is one in which parents are regarded as having authority over their children, and children are seen as having obligations of obedience or deference to their parents.[5] That is not ordinarily the case with friends (at least insofar as they are friends).

Parental authority is often considered quite extensive. Although this authority is by no means unlimited, even in liberal societies parents are permitted considerable latitude in determining their children's future—encompassing schooling, moral values, religious participation, friendships, and other social relations. Viewed in a certain way, the authority accorded to parents creates acute tensions for liberalism and its desire to foster commitment to autonomous personhood. Parents may seek to bring up their children to be (as liberals would see it) intolerant bigots and relatively doctrinaire ideologues. They are given significant rein to determine what is "good" for their children and to impose it—and though liberals are likely to characterize such paternalism as "soft," the imposition will often go contrary to the respectful concern for wishes that generally characterizes friendship.[6]

The soft paternalism associated with parenting will generally cease when children reach adulthood or the age of majority (or, less artificially, when children gain the ability to make wise decisions of their own). Ironically, to the extent that strong or autonomy-infringing paternalism is considered justifiable, it is most likely to be thought justifiable as part of a friendship. Friends, by virtue of sharing core values and sympathizing with each other's aspirations, are sometimes thought justified in intervening when one of them foolishly places his or her well-being at

---

[5] The obligation to obey is not unqualified, though; to the extent that it carries moral weight, it is grounded primarily in the presumption of parental wisdom and youthful ignorance.

[6] There may be some exceptions to this, for friends, too, may act paternalistically toward each other, but when such occurs, it is not usually grounded—as it is in the case of parents—in the paternalist's independent determination of what will be for the other's good. But see the next note.

risk.[7] Though we may hope for a similar identification by parents with their adult children, it is less likely to be the case.

Can people of unequal authority be friends?[8] Although some consider that because of their differential authority minor children cannot be friends with their parents, I disagree. An adolescent child may think of one or both parents as his or her best friend(s) or as no friend, though the dual role that friend-parents have with respect to their minor children is a possible source of tension. What the authority relationship may demand and what might be expected as part of the friendship can create role conflict, and a parent who is too much a friend to the child may fall short as a parent.

The unequal authority may manifest itself in other cases besides those of parent and child. The roles of teacher and student, employer and employee, or, more generally, supervisor and supervisee may also generate tensions if close friendships develop. In some circumstances, no doubt, those in dual relationships will develop formal or informal strategies for avoiding or handling the conflicts that are likely to arise. Still, the potential for conflict remains.

Thomas's third contention is that whereas friendships are characterized by mutual trust (resulting, critically, in mutual self-disclosure), parent-child relations will be characterized by the trust of dependency (thus excluding *mutual* self-disclosure). At younger ages, if the trust of dependency is coupled with mutual self-disclosure, the emotional burden may be too heavy for the dependent child. No doubt, if mutual trust, and the self-disclosure that goes with it, eventually develops, then parent and child can become friends as well as remaining parent and child. Often, however, even after the child has outgrown dependency and the obligations of obedience, mutuality will remain partial.

Although Thomas's account of the differences between familial and friendship relations focuses fairly narrowly on parent-child relations and not parent-parent

[7] We might consider the case of after-party driving, in which one's friends call a taxi rather than permit one to drive home. Even this, however, is sometimes thought to be controversial. See, for example, Norvin Richards, "Paternalism toward Friends," in *Person to Person*, ed. George Graham and Hugh LaFollette (Philadelphia: Temple University Press, 1989), 235–244; Debra Shogan, "Trusting Paternalism? Trust as a Condition for Paternalistic Decisions,"*Journal of the Philosophy of Sport* 18 (1991): 49–58; Ellen L. Fox, "Paternalism and Friendship," *Canadian Journal of Philosophy* 23, no. 4 (1993): 575–594; Sin Yee Chan, "Paternalistic Wife? Paternalistic Stranger?" *Social Theory and Practice* 26 (2000): 85–101.

[8] Thomas's claim may be at variance with an earlier tradition about friendship in which differential authority in friendship relations was frequently understood. Cf. Jesus' remark: "You are my friends if you do what I command you" (John 15:14); also E. A. Judge, "St Paul as a Radical Critic of Society," *Interchange* (Australia)16 (1974): 191–203; and John T. Fitzgerald, ed., *Friendship, Flattery and Frankness of Speech: Studies on Friendship in the New Testament World* (Leiden: E. J. Brill, 1996).

relations, sibling relations, or even on parent-child relations after the age of majority, this is not an unreasonable way of making such differentiations, given the deep connection between the idea of family and the creation and nurture of new generations.

EVOLVING IDEAS OF THE FAMILY

Determining the status of familial loyalties requires that we investigate the family's associative structure. As with other long-standing institutions, familial relations have evolved over time, and, depending on the social standing that the family has been accorded, internal family loyalties have been given greater or lesser significance. Although the selective and potted "evolution" that follows provides some sort of progress in such relations, at any point of history each of the views represented has had its advocates, even if one argues that intellectually dominant representations of the family have shifted in roughly the manner suggested.[9]

One important reason for that scrutiny has concerned relations between families and the political and social order. Within Confucian thought, this tends to be conceived fairly simply, even if controversially. The family is viewed as the preeminent social grouping, and the political order is construed as the family writ large. That of course does not exclude tensions between the two, as members of individual families will also be members of the larger political family, and sometimes their demands may come into conflict. Although there is considerable discussion in Confucian thought about such tensions, it generally emphasizes the centrality and priority of the microfamily. Family loyalties come first. In a well-known passage in the *Analects*, it is reported:

> The Duke of Yeh said to Confucius, "In our community a man who behaves with honesty would testify against his own father for stealing a goat." Confucius said, "In our community an honest man is different. A father would shield his son and a son would shield his father. And there is honesty."[10]

---

[9] It might, for example, be reasonably complained that I have largely ignored accounts of the family that can be extracted from early Jewish and Christian, not to mention other major non-Western traditions. That is a fair criticism, though I am not entirely convinced that a less stylized history would alter the conclusions I reach about family loyalties.

[10] *Analects* (Lún Yǔ) 13.18, available at www.confucius.org/lunyu/lange.htm. This incident and other similar incidents have given rise to much discussion by Confucian scholars. See, for example, Greg Whitlock, "Concealing the Misconduct of One's Own Father: Confucius and Plato on a Question of Filial Piety," *Journal of Chinese Philosophy* 21, no. 2 (1994): 113–137; Li Chenyang, "Shifting Perspectives: Filial Morality Revisited," *Philosophy East and West* 47, no. 2 (1997): 211–232. I am grateful to Xuetai Qi for references and discussion.

Within Western thought, however, the direction of thinking has just as often moved in the opposite direction. Both Plato and Aristotle are concerned about the challenge that the family (or household: *oikonomia*) presents to the city-state or *polis*. Although keenly aware of the nurturing role of the family, institutionally conceived, they are exercised by the way in which the family can either undermine or promote the larger—and for them more central—purposes of the polis.[11] For Plato, the family, conceived of as a relatively autonomous child-rearing institution, is a threat to the res publica, and he advocates its elimination in favor of state-run child-rearing institutions.[12] Familial loyalties challenge political ones. Plato resolves the challenge by conceiving of the polis as the true family, the ruler being thought of as the manager of a household. By the time of the *Laws*, however, Plato has acquiesced in the family's perpetuation, though it is to be regulated in such a way that the larger social order is not threatened.[13] Aristotle, on the other hand, tends to be more positive about the family's place in the polis, seeing it as a venue for preparation of a new generation's participation in political life. He does not, moreover, approve of using the familial metaphor to characterize the polis, which he views as a community of equals.[14]

As with Plato, Aristotle does not see family relations as intrinsically valuable or making their own distinctive contribution to human flourishing. The closest he comes is his acknowledgment that "parents love their children as being a part of themselves, and children their parents as being something originating from them."[15] Essentially, though, the relation is one of benefactor to beneficiary, and what children owe their parents is based in gratitude, albeit gratitude that is unlikely to be fully repaid. "Benefactors are thought to love those they have benefited more than those who have been well treated love those who have treated them well."[16] The love of parents for children, however, will be more significant, for it is parents who have

---

[11] According to Philippe Ariès, the idea of the family as—centrally—a private child-oriented institution comes much later, in the sixteenth century. See Philippe Ariès, *Centuries of Childhood* (London: Cape, 1962).

[12] "Plato does not merely believe that the private family is one focal point of loyalty alongside the state or that, in deciding to retain the private family, we merely tolerate the possibility of occasional conflict between private and public interests. Rather, he is convinced that when familial claims are recognized and admitted into social life, they draw off energies and affections from the common purpose of the larger community and detract from the patriotism demanded of the true citizen." Jeffrey Blustein, *Parents and Children: The Ethics of the Family* (New York: Oxford University Press, 1982), 32. I have made liberal use of Blustein's discussion.

[13] *Laws*, 788–790.

[14] Aristotle, *Politics*, 1255b. Although Aristotle thinks that the relationship between husband and wife is one of essential inequality, the inequality between father and son is contingent. A son will eventually outgrow his dependence to become his father's equal in virtue.

[15] *Nicomachean Ethics*, 1161b17.

[16] Ibid., 1167b17.

bestowed life and provided nourishment and nurture, and they "can get no honor which will balance their services."[17]

A social revaluation of the family emerged with the rise of Christendom and its focus on individual salvation. Augustine, in particular, sees the family as a redemptive opportunity for people whose sexuality was (inevitably) tainted with moral fallenness. He writes:

> Marriage has also this good, that carnal or youthful incontinence, even if it is bad, is turned to the honorable task of begetting children, so that marital intercourse makes something good out of the evil of lust. . . . [A] kind of dignity prevails when, as husband and wife they unite in the marriage act, they think of themselves as mother and father.[18]

Yet with the begetting of children, there also goes a solemn responsibility. Because conception takes place in sin and their offspring inherit the sin of Adam, parents have a special obligation to curb the willful self-centeredness through which such taint is expressed, and children themselves have a corresponding obligation to accept the authority of their parents.

There is a further shift in Thomas Aquinas, who sees families as the vehicles through which God's creation mandate to "be fruitful and multiply" is appropriately realized. Children are not mere extensions of their parents but individuals in their own right, with rights as well as obligations. They are "objects of justice in some manner,"[19] and parents are charged with providing them various material, educational, psychological, and moral as well as religious benefits. For their part, children have two kinds of duties to their parents—duties of obedience (which last until they come into maturity) and duties of piety (which remain throughout their lives). The former include not only obedience to parents but also respect (acknowledgment of their rightful authority) and reverence (regard for their superior qualities). In a turn that has Confucian parallels, Aquinas thinks that the reverence owed to parents ought to exceed that owed to the state, because parents originate the benefits that are later expressed in the political realm.

Duties of piety are initially expressed in the honoring of father and mother and later displayed in forms of assistance as parents come to need it, especially in old age.[20] Aquinas identifies three possible sources for such duties—commutative justice,

---

[17] Ibid., 1164b5.

[18] Augustine, *The Good of Marriage*, trans. C. T. Wilcox (New York: Fathers of the Church, 1955), 13.

[19] *Summa Theologica*, 2a2ae, q. 57, art. 4

[20] Ibid., 2a2ae, q. 101, art. 2.

friendship, and gratitude.[21] He rejects the first two. We do not have a business re-lationship with our parents such that they do things for us in return for benefits. Indeed, following Aristotle, Aquinas does not believe that we can repay what our parents have given us. Friendship works no better, not because it does not have obli-gations of its own, but because duties of piety exist independently of any friendship that may come to exist between children and their parents. Gratitude remains, and it seems to be Aquinas's favored rationale, though, since we commanded to honor our parents, it may also be seen as an aspect of our worship of and obedience to God.[22] But even if this provides space for a duty of piety as part of our loyalty *to God*, it does not yet provide for the kind of associational connection that would mandate *loyalty to parents*. Familial associations are not characterized in a way that indicates why they should be valued for their own sakes.

With the Enlightenment, there was a further revaluation of the family. Some treatises—Robert Filmer's *Patriarcha* being a notable example—clung to the family as a model for the political order.[23] Others, however, located the family in a private domain, radically distinguishing its relations from those in the political sphere. Locke thought that the political order, unlike the family, was constituted by equality, not hierarchy. Political authority required the consent of the governed. Although both groups accorded parents considerable authority over their children, the former group viewed that authority as an opportunity to develop habits of obedience that would be replicated in civil society (under a monarch), whereas the latter group saw it as pro-viding an environment in which children could develop into political equals. They differed, too, in the extent of parental authority. Whereas some of the former group saw parental authority, such as that of monarchs, as absolute, extending to power over life and death, those in the latter group were more conscious of the extent to which parental authority no less than political authority, could overreach and there-fore sought to produce arguments for its more limited role. Children were owned by God, not their parents, and the latter—especially their mothers—were entrusted with their children's care. The father shared a "joynt Dominion with the Mother."[24]

Locke distinguishes two kinds of duties that bear on parent-child relationships—the duty of parents to educate their children and the duty of children to honor their parents. Duties of the first kind terminate when children reach adulthood ("when the

---

[21] Ibid., 2a2ae, q. 106, art. 5.

[22] Ibid., 2a2ae, q. 106, art. 1.

[23] Blustein suggests that some traditionalists, such as Jean Bodin, do "not offer a familial model for the political order so much as a political model for the familial order" (64).

[24] John Locke, *Two Treatises of Civil Government* (1689), *First Treatise*, §55. Locke suggests that by virtue of her gestational role, the mother might even be considered to have greater authority—though only over her children. She remains subordinate to her husband.

business of Education is over") and constitute the main ground for parental authority: "This *power* so little belongs to the *Father* by any peculiar right of Nature, but
only as he is Guardian of his Children, that when he quits his Care of them, he loses
his power over them, which goes along with their Nourishment and Education, to
which it is inseparably annexed."[25] The latter duties are contingent on the fulfillment
of the former. Unlike political authority, which is based on consent, parental authority is sustained by trust. If trust is extinguished, so is authority.

Increasingly, as Enlightenment values prevailed, family life came to have a value of
its own and, within that framework, loyalty to the members of such associational ties
became not only a realistic option but also one to be fostered for reasons other than
gratitude. There are particular forms of intimacy characteristic of family life that are
not otherwise realizable, and these are valued for their own sake.[26] It should be noted,
however, that at the same time as the family was coming to be perceived as a site
for intrinsically valued relationships, there was also a move to outsource some of its
educative responsibilities to tutors and private (and later public) schools. Some of the
roots for this could be found in the Kantian (and Hegelian) perception that domestic
education has particularistic "drawbacks" that compromise the Enlightenment ideal
of autonomous individuality coupled with a universalist morality. Kant observed:

> In general, it appears that public education is more advantageous than domestic,
> not only from the point of view of skillfulness, but also as regards the character
> of a citizen. Domestic education not only brings out family faults, but also fos-
> ters them. . . . Here public education has the most evident advantage, since in it
> one learns to measure his powers and the limitations which the rights of others
> impose upon him. In this form of education no one has prerogatives, since op-
> position is felt everywhere, and merit becomes the only standard of preferment.[27]

With these remarks, we see the emergence of a liberal concern about the family's
place in a liberal democratic order. If that order is marked by certain social values
such as equality of opportunity as well as moral values such as tolerance, is there
any place for a strong view of family independence and, correspondingly, of familial
loyalty?

---

[25] *Second Treatise*, §65. Locke believes that the duty to educate can be alienated to tutors,
though he points out that parents lose thereby some claim to their children's obedience.
[26] See Jean-Jacques Rousseau, *Émile*, trans. B. Foxley (London: J. M. Dent, 1974), 13, 16. Even
so, Rousseau thinks that families are steeped in conformist prejudices and that parental education needs emancipation, so that children can develop self-sufficiency or autonomy (36).
[27] *Lecture-Notes on Pedagogy*, §§25, 30. Cf. also G. W. F. Hegel, *Philosophy of Right*, trans. T. M.
Knox (Oxford: Oxford University Press, 1967), ¶158 and addition.

Without responding at this point to these reemerging caveats about the family, what might lead us to consider familial associations worthy and even demanding of our loyalty? Because of the central role that family has as a site for the nurturing of future generations, I focus initially on parent-child relations and then discuss parent-parent relations more briefly. Along the way, I will say a few things about sibling relations. Not only is the discussion that follows not intended to be exhaustive but also its relational divisions are not intended to be construed as discrete associational ties but rather as focusing on aspects of a complex whole—*family*, and not simply parents and children, children and parents, adult partners, and siblings with each other.

THE VALUE OF FAMILIAL RELATIONS

Some of the foregoing discussion might well tempt us to think that familial relations are (or at least ought to be) driven by the welfare interest that children have in being prepared for adult social life—centrally, though not exclusively, for their participation in a moral order. Such interests, it might be thought, give the family its special social place and justify the privileged position that we accord it. As securer and protector of children's interests, the family is best suited to shoulder the important task of nurturing future generations.

There is, no doubt, a good deal to be said for this view—the appeal to children's interests can ground important social constraints on familial relations. But the argument from children's interests provides at best a contingent case for privileging family life.[28] Because of its contingency, others have been able to argue for Platonic-style nurseries or traditional kibbutzim as alternative nurturing options. And even if families would generally do better than the latter, it would not prevent removing at least *some* children from their natural families in order to improve their lot.[29] But even if such outsourcing and trading up sometimes seem reasonable (though more often it goes badly wrong),[30] it is unwise—even in a liberal society—to remove children from their natural families in order that their best interests can be addressed. Why?

Harry Brighouse and Adam Swift offer a perceptive response. They articulate four kinds of associational or "relationship goods" that family life—particularly the

[28] See Harry Brighouse and Adam Swift, "Parents' Rights and the Value of the Family," *Ethics* 117 (October 2006): 86.
[29] No doubt there is a case for this where there is manifest abuse or neglect, but the argument is not limited to "prevention of serious harm" cases.
[30] The Australian tragedies of "the stolen generation," in which Indigenous children were removed from their families, and the "orphanages" in Australia to which (often nonorphaned) British children were sometimes sent represent the outworkings of a view in which it was thought "better" for the children that they be removed from their primary families.

parent-child relationship—is distinctively able to realize.[31] Such relational experiences are not simply available and instrumentally valuable within the context of a family but are apprehended as valuable in themselves. True, not every family will realize them, but familial relationships provide an opportunity for the realization of these goods that is unlikely to be replicated in alternative settings.[32]

One such relationship good is constituted by the bond that is created between a child and a particular adult or adults, a bond that, although often important to emotional and social development, also has an intrinsically satisfying character. Another is the satisfying sense of having a personal history to which one belongs by virtue of one's membership in a family. A third relationship good is the sense of security that a child is given by someone who has a special duty of care for its well-being. Although security is instrumentally valuable and valued, the sense of security constitutes a good of its own. And finally, parents are able to experience the distinctive pleasures of intimacy with their offspring. This experience is one in which mutuality and intimacy are involved, and in which the parent has a fiduciary relationship that embraces the child's physical, emotional, moral, and cognitive development so that, inter alia, the child can become an autonomous being. There are peculiar satisfactions to participation in the project of enabling one's child to develop into a responsible adult.

Granting their legitimacy, how important are such goods? What moral and social weight do they carry? Paradoxically, perhaps, in most liberal-democratic societies, we grant them considerable weight. Not only do we tolerate conduct within the family that we would be loath to tolerate in other social settings, but to a considerable degree we also allow families to conduct themselves in a way that fosters values inimical to the values of autonomy and tolerance that we expect to characterize liberal societies.

As Brighouse and Swift point out, and as we have noted in the historical excursus, there is an inherent tension between the microrelations that generally exist within the family and the macrorelations that are usually fostered and supported within the wider society. For one thing, familial relations are generally unequal in the sense that some members of the family are accorded unconsented-to authority over others. Children are not normally at liberty to disobey their parents' judgment about what it would be good for them to do. Admittedly, this is soft rather than hard paternalism, because children are not yet considered autonomous. Nevertheless, parental authority does not extend only to protecting children from manifest harms but also to exposing them to goals and values of the parents' own choosing and, more generally,

---

[31] Brighouse and Swift, "Parents' Rights and the Value of the Family," 80–108; Harry Brighouse and Adam Swift, "Legitimate Parental Partiality," *Philosophy & Public Affairs* 37, no. 1 (2009): 43–80. Although I have taken over much from their discussions, I do not claim to have represented their points in exactly the way that they do.

[32] See Brighouse and Swift, "Legitimate Parental Partiality," 53.

controlling the direction their lives will take. This may well imbue illiberal and non-democratic values in their children.

Are we justified in giving such liberty to parents in the name of the relational goods available through family life, or should we give priority to liberal democratic values? I am inclined to agree with Brighouse and Swift that the relationship goods made possible by family life are sufficiently important not to be derivative of or secondary to liberal values but accorded some independence of them. They constitute a cluster of fundamental moral rights or liberties. On the one hand, they permit parents to give priority to their own interests with respect to those of their children; on the other hand, they permit them "to do [things] to, for, and with their children that it is not permissible for anyone else to do."[33] Such rights are fundamental in the sense that they do not derive from the rights of children, as would be the case were we to argue (as we might) that the legitimate interests of children would be best served if those most closely related to them were given a free hand in their upbringing.[34] They are, rather, based in the interests of the parents themselves—their interest in having a particular relationship with their children that realizes the aforementioned relationship goods. It does not, of course, follow from their being fundamental that they are absolute. Some parents act so egregiously that their parental rights ought to be suspended, overridden, or even forfeited. Nevertheless, this is best seen as a last resort.

What, then, do such rights amount to? As noted, they are not unlimited. We do not permit parents to kill their children, allow them to die, or treat them cruelly or inhumanely, though they may be permitted to treat their children quite harshly and manipulatively. Admittedly, as Brighouse and Swift point out, some of what we permit parents to do or allow happen to their children as the parents pursue their own interests may not be permissible as of right but only because any mechanisms for intervention would be too problematic to manage. Nevertheless, parents are permitted to act toward their children in ways that need not reflect or straightforwardly serve liberal democratic purposes. Children may be raised in ways that inhibit their capacity for liberal autonomy. We permit parents to expose their children to their own restricted and restrictive religious beliefs, to forms of intolerance and discriminatory attitudes that they themselves possess, and to authoritarian or class-related attitudes that ill fit those underpinning a liberal society. As regrettable as such outcomes are, we generally tolerate them as a cost of recognizing the more important values embedded in family life. The values realizable through family life are special to it and would not be realizable were parents not permitted a fair degree of social autonomy.

[33] "Parents' Rights," 81.
[34] Ibid., 81, n. 2.

Parental rights are first and foremost rights to forms of intimacy with their children that would be compromised or impossible in the absence of such rights.[35] Were parents forbidden to expose their children to their own narrow political or religious beliefs, it would be crippling to the relationship that they wished to have with their children. Although children are not necessary to the possibility of intimate relationships, the form that intimacy takes with respect to *one's own* children is distinctive and contributes in a unique manner to their parents' sense of well-being.

Brighouse and Swift detail four features of parent-child relationships that inform the distinctive good of family relationships in which fundamental rights are recognized. The first is the vulnerability of children to their carers. Their well-being is integrally connected to the relationship they have with their parents, and this asymmetrical relationship gives a distinctive quality to the relationship. Second, it is not usually within the child's power to leave the relationship. Although the power to exit is a matter of degree—and may also be quite difficult in some other intimate relationships—it is much more difficult in the case of children, who generally lack physical as well as other resources to exit. Third, one may anticipate a distinctive form of trust as part of the parent-child relationship. Because of their vulnerability and the parents' role as caretaker, children tend to develop an unconditional trust in and love for their parents, giving the relationship a quality that is generally absent from other relationships. Not only is the bond of trust a distinctively valuable experience but also it can foster in parents other qualities that contribute to their own flourishing. Distinctively, and finally, the relationship is a fiduciary one. The parent has a responsibility not only to keep the child safe during a period of physical vulnerability but also and especially to oversee the child's psychological, cognitive, and moral development so that it becomes capable of functioning on its own initiative within the larger decisional contexts within which it will exist—friendships, career choices, political participation, and religious communities. This may involve significant exercises of coercive power and require considerable investments of effort by parents. If they fail to exercise such power in behalf of their children's development, they fail *as parents*. In addition, it is likely to signal a failure for the parents as well—failure with respect to an ingredient of their own well-being.[36]

---

[35] The intimacy that exists between parents, in cases in which two parents are involved, would also be compromised were similar liberty not given to parents themselves.

[36] A clarificatory point needs to be made. Even though many parents see the experience of having and raising children as contributory to their own flourishing—an experience whose absence is often regretted by those who do not have children—it may not be true of every adult person that having children and raising them is essential to their flourishing. Human lives can flourish in different ways, and although the experience of having and bringing up children offers distinctive forms of human satisfaction, it need not be the sine qua non of a good life. See further, Brighouse and Swift, "Parents' Rights," 98–100.

Although the right of parents to have a self-chosen intimacy with their own children allows for relationships to develop that may be inimical in the long run to their children's well-being, such developments may be internally constrained by the fact that the relationship will break down if it departs too far from what is broadly consistent with the child's well-being. It is, after all, a fiduciary relationship, and parents are committed to bringing up their children in ways that are not destructive of the child's welfare interests. There are, as we have noted, controversial limits to this as we consider possible societal constraints on those who are deemed to have abused their children. Even the religious scruples and desires of a parent with respect to the child may be overridden if the child is likely to be placed in serious harm's way.[37] Because the relationship is a fiduciary one, it does not disregard the interests of children, even though the parents' rights are not derived from the interests of their children. The point is not that parents lack an interest in doing what they see as best for their children, but that the latter is subordinated to their desire for a certain kind of intimate relationship with their children—intimacy that may well be shown in their doing, as they see it—the best that they can for their children.

LOYALTY BETWEEN PARENTS AND CHILDREN

Because the relationship between parents and children is forged round its distinctively valued intimacy, familial relationships become a natural site for the development of loyalties, and because the loyalties that develop in familial relationships are grounded in the experience of a form of intimacy that is unlikely to be replicated in other contexts, there is good reason to think that those who experience family relationships are not only likely but ought to forge loyal bonds to other members of their families—in particular, to their parents and/or children.

The loyalty that arises out of the intimate bond that develops between parents and children will carry—as bonds of loyalty ordinarily do—a minimum commitment on the part of both parents and children not to act in ways that damage the familial bond. It may often involve rather more than this, as a parent or child puts itself out for the other to advance, not merely not jeopardize, the other's interests. This can be very costly to one or other or both. For example, children may be born with or come to have serious disabilities that challenge the expectations and resources of parents, and parents may age in ways that challenge the expectations and resources of their children.

---

[37] Notable have been cases in which Jehovah's Witnesses have not been permitted to deny their children blood transfusions and various "faith healing" parents have been prosecuted for denying their children appropriate medical attention.

Consider first the loyalty that parents should display toward their children. It involves the development of an intimacy with their children in which trust is created—trust that the parent is there for them in their vulnerability and dependence. The parent must be there for them in the sense of providing for not just their physical needs but also their other needs—cognitive, emotional, social, and moral. The parent does not do this only out of a concern that the child's interests will be served, but as an expression of the relation that the parent wishes to create and maintain with the child. A child who experiences profound abandonment by a parent is a child who may have been betrayed.[38] Sometimes, no doubt, the sense of abandonment can lack a significant factual basis, but it may arise in a range of cases in which the parents' pursuit of their own interests has resulted in an emotionless or uncommitted relationship. Parents whose career or social interests lead to the child being placed almost completely in the care of nannies might develop that sense of abandonment. By way of contrast (albeit a problematic one), a parent who travels to another country to earn enough money to send back home may—if there is emotionally freighted contact—preserve the familial bonds that (at some future time) will be displayed face to face.

There may be no greater betrayal of parental intimacy than exploitation of the child's vulnerability to engage in sexual relationships.[39] Given that awareness of one's sexuality is gradual and ordinarily expressed in a very different kind of relationship, parents who confront their young children with sexual expectations create deep confusion and distort the intimacy that underlies the parent-child bond. We may not cavil so deeply about incest between adults, though even here there is a clear transition from one kind of intimate bond to a very different one. It is not clear how well the two can coexist.

Loyalty might well extend to adult children, even though it may sometimes present difficult decisions. Consider a case in which parents become aware that their adult son is almost certainly guilty of the rape-murder of a woman he has picked up. They have seen blood-stained clothes in the laundry. If questioned about their son's activities, should they cover for their son and, if they do not, would they be disloyal (or at least less than loyal)? There is no reason to think that familial loyalties are absolute even if, in some cases, people would be willing to die for their parents,

[38] The experience of adoptive children can be illuminating. Such children often desire not only to reestablish contact with their biological parents but more especially to find out why they were given up. Was it that they were unloved and unwanted, or was the parent, though loving, convinced that the child would have an opportunity to flourish only if given up?

[39] Such is the familial bond, however, that incest cases often create serious family dilemmas when it comes to deciding how to respond to them. See Ann Wolbert Burgess, Lynda Lytle Holmstrom, and Maureen P. McCausland, "Divided Loyalty in Incest Cases," in *Sexual Assault of Children and Adolescents*, ed. Ann Wolbert Burgess, A. Nicholas Groth, Lynda Lytle Holmstrom, and Suzanne M. Sgroi (Lexington, MA: Lexington Books, 1978), 115–126.

children, or siblings. The demands of universal morality may sometimes override those of loyalty—or at least those demands of loyalty that might countenance a lie. In the case described, unless it is believed that what the child did constituted a betrayal of the parents, their ongoing loyalty might be shown in support while the child faced the courts and, in the event of conviction, in continuing to visit and otherwise sustain him as he serves his sentence. The point is not that the parents could not have expressed their loyalty by refusing to cooperate with the police, but that had they done so it would have expressed a misguided or even blind loyalty.

Now consider the loyalty of children toward their parents. Because familial loyalties are based on certain relationship goods, they are not restricted to the period during which children mature. Some of those goods continue throughout life. The familial bonds of childhood may be transformed by adulthood, but they are not extinguished, and associational obligations are likely to manifest themselves as parents age and become as vulnerable as the children were when young. Once we recognize this, we can see why many arguments about the obligations of children to their aged parents are misplaced. The loyal bonds developed in childhood are the primary bearers of the obligations, not debt, gratitude, friendship, contract, or some other consideration. Of course, gratitude may figure, along with friendship, and we may hope that they will, but they do not provide full accounts of filial obligations (and loyalty), and neither lies at the heart of the loyalty-based obligation that children have to their aging parents.

Thus Simon Keller articulates what he calls a "special goods theory" to account for the loyalty that children should display to their parents.[40] Like that developed by Brighouse and Swift, it is based on the singularity of the parent-child relationship and its differences from other relationships we have. The decision to start a family is a decision to shape one's life in a certain way—to have a child to whom one can relate as one relates to no other. And out of that relationship emerge distinctive goods for both parent and child. The relationship may shape itself differently at different stages of a life. The special goods of being a parent of a young and dependent child can then be succeeded by those of sharing in that child's growth, and then followed by pride as the child makes its way into the world, now perhaps to start its own family. Then may follow further intergenerational satisfactions as a grandparent. For the child, there is first the parent in whom one can place one's trust, who is there for one as one struggles to make one's way in the world, and then the parent who must stand on the sidelines as one makes one's own way in the world but who continues to take a close interest in one's life. Finally, there is the parent to whom one may now have to relate as infirm or vulnerable but precious nevertheless. Even if, as Keller suggests,

[40] Simon Keller, *The Limits of Loyalty* (Cambridge: Cambridge University Press, 2007), chap. 6.

the goods of this relationship do not necessarily make one a better person, they may contribute to one's well-being.

Keller distinguishes several special goods of the parent-child relationship—essentially, ways of articulating the distinctive intimacy that Brighouse and Swift identify, but here applied to relations between adult children and their parents.[41] First, there is the ongoingness of a relationship established in childhood. Parenting is not like a contract in which, once the work of childrearing is done, parents and children part ways. Although transformed, the intimacy established in childhood continues as parents and children maintain contact with each other. In some respects, this may be like an ongoing friendship (and may indeed involve friendship), but in other respects it has a very different quality and indeed can continue without the parents and children actually becoming friends. There can still be a special sadness when that connection is broken by death, for a part of one's personal history is gone, no longer to be recovered or revitalized. Second, for children, there is someone with whom they can share in an especially knowledgeable way—not quite or just in the manner of a friend or counselor, but with someone whose history encompasses their own and who therefore has a special and especially intimate understanding of one that others cannot have. Third, the ongoing bond with parents can be a unique source of self-understanding. As we reflect on our lives, on who and what and why we are, we are often illuminated by the ongoing interactions we have with our parents as we see where we got a particular trait, why we react in a particular way, and so on. Fourth, there is a sense that there is always someone there for you—someone to step in to help in certain kinds of emergencies and to provide things that you would not ask of your friends. Of course, friends no less than parents can be there for one at times of significant need, but, if the child-parent relationship is working as it should, the familial bond might be more reliable and available. If an adult child must go into a hospital for an operation, it may be more reasonable to expect a parent to step in and assist, look after grandchildren, or otherwise help out. Fifth, parents may gain a sense of their self-perpetuation, of a legacy that sustains them as they get older. Parents are not marooned but can end their days with a sense that what they have done will in some way continue through their children and grandchildren. There is often a wistfulness about the aged (and childless) person who says: "I am the last of my family."

Although such goods have instrumental value for those who possess them, they also have the intrinsic significance that makes loyalty between parents and children natural and desirable. With that loyalty come certain obligations—obligations to act with regard to the other in ways that will sustain the other in the relationship.

[41] Ibid., 124–127.

This account of family relationships is not intended to capture all family relationships as we actually encounter them or even as what they aspire to. Rather, it articulates associational features of family life that can make such relationships worth pursuing and worthy of loyalty when they can be realized. As we know too well, much of what passes for family life shows little of the idealized intimacy that I have been outlining, and even families that do much better may fall well short of the ideal. This is not surprising, not only because of the historical and immediate social pressures with which families have to cope but also and especially because of the difficult balance that needs to be maintained between essential parental authority and the interest that children have in becoming moral agents and autonomous beings. There is no simple formula for resolving this tension.

One important way in which family loyalty may often be shown is through the familial code of silence.[42] Within the intimate bonds of a family, children may learn things about their parents, and parents may come to know things about their children that, if made public, would be detrimental to the parents' or children's interests and to the family's cohesion. A child may learn of a difficult time in the parents' relationship, of some medical problem with which a parent has had to deal, or of a financial crisis that it would be deeply hurtful to the parent were others to be apprised of it. Parents may know of things done by their child when they were young or of failures they experienced that would be mortifying to their children, were they to become public knowledge. And so conventions develop about what goes on in the family staying in the family or even about the family washing its own dirty laundry.

The special intimacies or goods that family life makes available are socially vulnerable, and children learn early on that the family has an interest in sustaining itself as something of a cocoon in the face of various social threats or invasions. Its interest in doing this is not just because it may be harmed by those outside it but also because of what the family is to its members—a source of special intimacy or goods that can be sustained only if it is relatively secure and secured in its relationships.

The code of silence may also have internal dimensions. Things will pass between parents to which children are not made privy and, perhaps, to which they should not be made privy. "Not in front of the children" is often an understandable refusal to convey matters to children that, were they to know them, would disrupt the quality of relations and intimacy that parents wish to sustain with their children. Children,

[42] Although I here treat the code of silence as a manifestation of loyalty, codes of silence tend to be quite complex phenomena, often sustained by other factors as well, such as fear of ostracism, reciprocity, or even shame. See John Kleinig, "The Blue Wall of Silence: An Ethical Analysis," *International Journal of Applied Philosophy* 15, no. 1 (2001): 1–23.

too, may develop their own code of silence, learning early on to work out certain problems between or among themselves.[43]

As with other loyalties, the loyalty implicit in the code of silence will sometimes be justifiably breached. Although there are few who would advocate an absolute ban on lying, there are almost certainly limits on exceptions to it, even in the context of family relations.[44] We may differ about the point at which lies or other forms of deception might be legitimately employed in the interests of family relations, but there is—as there always is—a tipping point at which universalistic moral demands will take precedence over the heightened demands of the family.

MARITAL LOYALTY

As already noted, family may encompass inter alia relations between parents and among children, as well as those between parents and children. Here I focus only on the first.

The loyalty of (spousal) partners (whether heterosexual or single sex) to each other is often treated as of critical importance. Traditionally, probably because of its close connection with procreation and nurture, the loyalty of partners has been associated most visibly with sexual fidelity. Adultery is viewed as the archetypal form of marital disloyalty. Nevertheless, marital loyalty extends well beyond sexual fidelity, as even the traditional form of the marriage vow makes clear. The bond between spouses extends to loving, comforting, honoring, and protecting the other, and the partners pledge to "have and hold" each other "for better, for worse, for richer, for poorer, in sickness and in health, to love and to cherish, till death do [them] part."[45] Marital loyalty excludes abandonment, humiliation of the other in public, and otherwise working to undermine the partner's interests. So important is the marital bond that many jurisdictions privilege it in court, protecting confidential communications between partners and permitting a partner's refusal to testify against the other.[46]

---

[43] See chapter 6. In Carville's book, the editors report an incident in which Carville, caught smoking behind the shed by his sister, then gave her a puff so that she would be implicated and not tell on him (89).

[44] Here, at least for Western liberals, there is a problem with Confucian elevation of filial piety.

[45] This version is from the Church of England, *Book of Common Prayer*, available at www.cofe. anglican.org/worship/liturgy/commonworship/texts/marriage/marriage.html.

[46] This is something of an idealization. The history of the spousal privilege is more complex than this, and justifications often include appeals to consequentialist considerations in addition to (or instead of) those grounded in the marital bond. See, Note, "Developments in the Law–Privileged Communications: I: The Development of Evidentiary Privileges in American Law," *Harvard Law Review* 98, no. 7 (1985): 1450–1471; Pamela A. Haun, "The Marital Privilege in the Twenty-First Century," *University of Memphis Law Review* 32 (2001): 137–178. At present, the legal privilege does not generally extend to same-sex and unmarried couples.

Despite the traditional concern with sexual fidelity—albeit burdened with some-what double standards[47]–its rationale has of recent times been revisited, partly, though not exclusively, because of our increased ability to separate sexual activity from procreation. Some have advocated "open relationships" and, even if "a good (usually monogamous) marriage" is held to be some sort of ideal, love affairs are sometimes considered a legitimate second best.[48]

Apart from the potential procreative repercussions, is there any reason to take a strong view on adultery?[49] Prominent among the traditional reasons for marital fidelity have been that infidelity involves a breach of promise, deception and lies, hypocrisy, disregard of another's feelings, or unfairness, or threatens various social harms. Except for the last, these claims may or may not be true, depending on what the parties agreed to in marrying each other.[50] But even when they are involved and constitute wrongs to the partner, such reasons do not adequately explain why the breach is usually felt to be so serious. Other broken promises, deceptions, and lies that occur within a marriage do not usually have the same opprobrium attached to them. Breach of promise and deception do not by themselves constitute disloyalty, whereas adultery is seen as a betrayal.

If we are to regard sexual fidelity as a form of loyalty, it is because we have a par-ticular view about the significance of marital sexuality as an intimate bond between partners. If we see marital sexuality not as a vehicle for physical pleasure but as the expression of affection and exclusive commitment, then adultery will be seen as a relational breach, an undermining of what was understood to exist between the mar-ried couple. The *if* is important. How expressions of sexuality should be seen is a matter of considerable controversy. At one end of the spectrum, sexual expression is reserved for marriage and for circumstances in which the possibility for procreation is not artificially removed; at its other end, sexual activity is viewed simply as a plea-surable form of recreation that may, should those who engage in it wish, be used for other purposes as well. All it requires is that the participants understand for what purpose they are engaging in it. Between these two extremes lies a range of other

---

[47] See, for example, Keith Thomas, "The Double Standard," *Journal of the History of Ideas* 20, no. 2 (1959): 195–216.

[48] See Richard Taylor, *Love Affairs: Marriage and Infidelity*, rev. ed. (Buffalo, NY: Prometheus, 1997).

[49] Here understood narrowly as actual sexual involvement by a marital partner with another. I leave to one side the more expansive account implied in the Sermon on the Mount (Matt. 5:27–28). See David Carr, "Chastity and Adultery," *American Philosophical Quarterly* 23, no. 4 (1986): 363–371.

[50] The question of social harm is more difficult to gauge, relying not simply on contingencies such as the transmission of STDs but also on speculations about the social effects that uncon-demned adultery would have, as well as the significance of marriage to social cohesion.

possibilities, some of which detach sexual activity from its procreative possibilities, and others of which link it to varying degrees of affection but reject exclusivity as part of its meaning. An extended discussion of the significance of sexual activity would take us too far afield.

I shall, nevertheless, offer an argument for seeing sexual fidelity as a concomitant of the commitment that is sometimes formalized as marriage. It runs roughly as follows. Whatever position we take on sexual activity outside the marital bond, the commitment that two people make to each other in marriage or some nonformalized equivalent is a commitment to embody a particular type of love in their relationship. It is one that involves a cherishing and care for the other, a regard for the other that sets him or her apart from and in some sense before others.[51] The marital other is elevated to a special place in one's life, and this special place is generally symbolized in what usually becomes the most intimate of all acts, sexual sharing. The sex of marital sexuality is more than the pleasuring of bodies; it is, rather, an expression of one's oneness with the other. The point is not that sexual activity intrinsically expresses a deep intimacy with the other—for otherwise prostitution would not thrive—but that when two people enter into the kind of commitment that we identify with marriage, their sexual expressions generally take on a different significance. As part of that commitment to a shared life (at least in the case of heterosexual relationships), there may—though need not—be added the potential fruit of that sexual activity in which the couple become a family. In that case, couplehood becomes a major structural feature of life—family—through which the riches and vicissitudes of the respective lives are addressed. Hence we have the expectation that marriage will not only encounter but be sustained and will sustain the partners through poverty and wealth, health and sickness, good times and bad times. It may not, of course, for much over which one has little control can happen in and to a relationship. But the expectation—the commitment—when marriage (or its equivalent) occurs is that the relationship is not entered into in a conditional manner.

Why should sexual fidelity be seen as an (or most) apt expression of marital commitment, and adultery be seen as a particularly serious form of disloyalty? Insofar as it is, perhaps the key lies in the *capacity* for sexual sharing to express intimacy in a singular way. True, it need not actually do so. Sexual desire can be (more or less) satisfied through masturbation or using the services of a prostitute. But because sexual relations have the capacity for expressing great intimacy on the part of those involved in it, sexual sharing is a symbolically powerful way of affirming the specialness of the

---

[51] Of course, this does not come to terms with bigamous or polygamous traditions, though I suspect that resistance to what often continues to be their patriarchal environment draws on an inherent tendency toward exclusivity in this form of love.

other. For the same reason, there is always an implicit danger in affairs that they will derail a relationship and not merely supplement it. Where sexual "needs" are considered to be greater than a particular marital relationship can accommodate, resort to prostitutes is often seen as preferable to an affair, or even a mistress.

Of course, a couple may agree to an arrangement in which their commitment to each other does not imply sexual exclusivity. There is nothing incoherent to that. But for the reason just mentioned, it is likely to be an especially hazardous arrangement, as another object of what may be largely sexual desire may develop through the intimacy invited by sexual sharing into a rival for the partner's affections.

One might wonder, nevertheless, whether the socially developed capacity of sexual sharing reflects the traditional nexus of intercourse with pregnancy and therefore with some form of ongoing commitment to "family." With the loosening of that nexus, might one therefore anticipate a diminished significance of adultery as a form of disloyalty? That is quite possible, though one might also think that as long as it is through sexual intercourse that "families" are generally created, sexual intercourse will tend to have a privileged position as an expression of associative intimacy.

CONCLUSION

There is clearly much more to be said about the associative relations that are generally thought to comprise family experience. What I have indicated, however, is the potentially rich web of relationships that can be constitutive of such experience, relationships that can have intrinsic value for those involved in them and be generative of deep and ongoing loyalties. Even if such loyalties are sometimes forfeited or overridden by more compelling normative demands, they are sufficiently distinctive in their contribution to our human flourishing that we are legitimately concerned at efforts to diminish them either through their replacement or through overconcern with their instrumentalization.

10

ORGANIZATION

I look for two things in my people: loyalty and competence, and in that order.[1]

If an organization wants you to do right it asks for your integrity; if it wants you to do wrong, it demands your loyalty.[2]

It is one thing to suggest that the associative relations found in friendships and families are appropriate sites for the development of loyalties. They are sites for distinctive goods that are deeply implicated in our flourishing. But can we say the same of the more amorphous types of collectives that we refer to as organizations? Organizational loyalty is frequently sought, often demanded, and sometimes given. It can also be deeply problematic. As the epigraphs indicate, although organizational loyalty is strongly asserted, it may be the agent of serious moral compromise. Nevertheless, I shall indicate here how organizational loyalty may sometimes play an important role.

First, though, what are we to understand when referring to an organization? It is generally a collective, but beyond that it becomes harder to pin down. It will do for present purposes if we characterize organizations as independent, structured, and continuing social arrangements that pursue specifiable collective goals. Included will be firms, companies, corporations, church denominations, the military, law firms, manufacturers, supermarket chains, airline companies, nongovernmental organizations (NGOs), and universities.

The two main questions to be considered are, first, whether organizations are conceptually appropriate objects of loyalty and, second, whether organizational loyalty is desirable—or even obligatory—and if so, under what circumstances? If we answer

[1] Frank J. Macchiarola, speaking after his appointment as New York Schools Chancellor in 1976.
[2] I owe this to Aaron Rosenthal, a former Deputy Chief in the New York City Police Department.

either of the latter affirmatively, then how are we to construe it and link it to related loyalties—those to superiors or supervisors, to management, to peers, to the collective purpose, and so forth? And what constraints ought to be placed on organizational loyalties? For example, is whistle-blowing an option, and, if so, under what circumstances?

It might seem odd to ask whether an organization ought to be considered a *conceptually appropriate* object of loyalty. Organizational loyalty is sought and given and withdrawn all the time, and whistle-blowing is often viewed as the archetypal form of organizational disloyalty. The question is generated, however, by my general view that the primary context of loyalty is personal—hence loyalty to friends, one's parents, the king, one's team, and so forth. But there is an intelligible progression from loyalties to individuals and small groups to collectives such as organizations and ultimately countries. True, loyalties to organizations are not likely to be composites of loyalties to individuals—after all, organizations generally outlast the individuals who make them up at any point of time. Nevertheless, organizations, which are often referred to as artificial or legal persons, often function much like persons, and of course, if one does damage to an organization, one is also likely to damage many individuals who are employed by, members of, or dependent on it. This is not to say that organizations are natural persons writ large, but that for certain purposes they can be considered as such.[3] No less important, the agents of an organization are generally individual persons or people who act in some collective fashion (such as a board of directors). Perhaps it is best to think of an organization in terms of people structuring their activities in a coordinated way to achieve certain collective ends (even though the organization is likely to outlast those persons).

A graphic example of the demand for organizational loyalty is provided by Marcia Baron.[4] She cites a 1973 CBS documentary on Phillips Petroleum, Inc., in which one of its chief executives was asked about the qualities sought when making employment decisions. Loyalty, he said, was the most important quality. But he went further than that to detail what such loyalty would embrace. A loyal employee would, he said, always prefer a Phillips product over rivals, would vote for political candidates likely to be sympathetic to Phillips's interests, and would remain with the firm for the long haul. In relation to the last, wives of candidates were screened to ensure that they did not have career interests that would be incompatible with their husbands' long-term employment at Phillips. Despite its totalistic aspects, this is a relatively

---

[3] There is of course an intense debate surrounding this issue that we can leave to one side.
[4] Marcia Baron, *The Moral Status of Loyalty* (Dubuque, IA: Kendall/Hunt, 1984), 1, citing "The Corporation," *CBS Reports*, December 6, 1973.

benign statement of what might be—or at least was in the early 1970s—expected by way of employee loyalty. In some areas, and particularly in the realm of engineering, the demand for loyalty has often had a much more dangerous cast. Corporate loyalty has been demanded for the sake of profit and organizational advantage even when public safety has been put at risk, and many of those who were deemed disloyal suffered serious consequences.[5]

Although it is now less common for companies to express their employee expectations in such public and encompassing terms, we should notice the way in which (1) it erodes the distinction between private and public life[6] and (2) it removes from employees any independence of judgment or autonomy. In the executive's thinking, the obligations that derive from an employee's professional judgment, religious affiliations, domestic situation, or moral reflection must take a subordinate place.

The value of workplace loyalty and its capacity sometimes to override personal and other obligations cannot be presumed in advance, particularly when some of those obligations—such as professional obligations relating to workplace competence—might carry considerable, if not greater, weight.[7] It is for this reason that the membership of the National Society of Professional Engineers requires that "engineers, in the fulfillment of their duties, shall hold paramount the safety, health and welfare of the public."[8] If one's employing organization expects one to fudge test results or turn a blind eye to the risks in a product, this expectation should not take precedence. It may, indeed, provide grounds for blowing the whistle.

These problems may not have seemed compelling to executives of the companies in question. They may have believed that loyalty was owed because the company reciprocated it. Early in the 1970s, at least, large corporations that demanded great loyalty often offered a good deal in return. Along with a paycheck, companies also provided considerable benefits for their staff. American company towns (now mostly defunct)—and certainly many Japanese companies of the 1970s—provided housing, medical care, schooling, and entertainment for workers, along with job security and

---

[5] Baron provides many instances. See also Myron Peretz Glazer and Penina Migdal Glazer, *The Whistleblowers: Exposing Corruption in Government and Industry* (New York: Basic Books, 1989).

[6] In the 1960s, the Gillette Company forbade its employees to grow beards and required them to shave with Gillette blades. We might contrast these cases with some of the constraints sometimes placed on the private lives of police officers. What police do in private—such as engage in "inappropriate associations"—impacts negatively on the public confidence that people have in them.

[7] See, especially, Michael Davis, "Thinking Like an Engineer: The Place of a Code of Ethics in the Practice of a Profession," *Philosophy & Public Affairs* 20, no. 2 (1991): 150–167.

[8] NSPE Code of Ethics for Engineers, www.nspe.org/Ethics/CodeofEthics/index.html.

wages or salaries.[9] Executives of such companies considered that as far as company decisions were concerned, *they* were the appropriate judges of the wisdom of company policies and decisions and that lower-level employees or even professionals were not in a position to take adequate account of all the complexities involved ("the big picture"). They were often bitterly antiunion and would not have considered that the judgment of their executive officers might be improperly skewed by economic or more personal considerations.

In Western industrialized economies, the conditions that openly prevailed during the 1970s no longer do so to the same extent, albeit to the chagrin of some business executives. To a degree, this semidemise of employee loyalty followed the business downturns of the later 1970s, the layoff of many employees, and the outsourcing of work to foreign countries, even by companies with a reputation for carrying employees through temporary slowdowns. Loyalty is a two-way street. Employee advocates argued that because the companies showed scant loyalty toward those who had often served them long and faithfully, they had no right to expect more from employees than their contracts explicitly required of them. But even without the firings and closings of the 1970s and 1980s, many workers found their organizations caught up in mergers, acquisitions, and restructurings that left scant continuity between the company they joined and the company that now employed them. Although the 1990s saw a concerted effort by many businesspeople to regain a more nuanced loyalty from employees (one less focused on long-term commitments), the recent economic recession has once again loosened the bonds and modified such expectations. Understandable as this is, given the generally reciprocal character of nonpathological loyalties, it is nevertheless ironic that it is undermined just when employee loyalty might be needed most. It often looks more like a strategy of convenience than a serious relationship.

A further contributing factor to diminished employee loyalty has been greater public awareness of the abuses to which large organizations are prone, and greater willingness, if not to blow the whistle, then to leak critical information into the public domain. Much of the impetus for this came from Ralph Nader in the 1960s and 1970s, who called especially on professionals to make public any "employers' policies or practices that they consider[ed] harmful to public or consumer interests."[10]

---

[9] See, for example, Pullman, IL; Koehler, WI; Bethlehem, PA; Midland, MI; Scotia, CA; and Hershey, PA.

[10] John D. Morris, "New Nader Group Seeking Tipsters; Asks Professionals to 'Blow Whistle' on Employers," *New York Times*, January 27, 1971, 32. Nader subsequently broadened his call to all employees to determine whether their responsibility to society transcended their responsibility to their organization (*New York Times*, March 21, 1971, sect. 6, 16). Edward Snowden is the latest in a long line of such people.

THE NATURE OF ORGANIZATIONAL LOYALTY

Any person who voluntarily joins an organization assumes certain (role) obligations: membership has its responsibilities as well as its privileges. If it is an employing organization, such responsibilities include turning up for work, putting in a full day, and not stealing from the company or otherwise acting in a manner clearly detrimental to the company's interests (by being rude to customers, being inefficient, or performing incompetently). But these are not obligations of loyalty so much as general obligations of employment. Breaches are not ipso facto acts of disloyalty.

Loyalty obligations arise out of a further commitment that employees make (or, perhaps in some cases, should make) to the organization—a commitment that goes beyond the requirements of contract and in which employees come to identify with the organization, seeing it as relationally *theirs*. Accomplishment of the organization's collective goals comes to be seen as integral to the accomplishment of the members' own. Employees who come to see the organization in this way will probably see themselves as having further obligations to the organization—including, for example, obligations to put in extra hours, to work hard and well without supervision, to travel on behalf of the organization (despite inconvenience), to speak in defense of the organization if the need arises, to speak well of and defend the organization if it is criticized, to inform the company of matters that may be adverse to it,[11] and, perhaps, to stay with the organization even though equally or more attractive offers come along. The list is an indeterminate one, depending on the nature of the organization and the challenges it faces, and, even if taken at face value, will incorporate obligations that may be overridden by obligations associated with other loyalties (say, domestic ones) or by more general moral obligations. Of course, some companies—believing that employees ought to develop and display loyalty—may seek to build into their employment obligations what are just as, or even more, appropriately viewed as loyalty obligations.

Loyal employees will not necessarily fulfill such obligations *as a matter of obligation* or even *out of loyalty* (as an occurrent motive), but rather as part of their personal commitment to and identification with the organization and its collective goals. It is the associative bond that motivates. A conscious awareness of and responsiveness to the obligatoriness associated with loyalty is more likely to arise when the employee is seriously inconvenienced by what the organization needs or wants and when what would naturally motivate (the organization's being *one's own*) needs to be bolstered by a sense of the obligations that go with such commitment. From the perspective of the loyal employee, as Ewin writes, "that I do the work I am paid for ceases to be

[11] Richard T. DeGeorge, *Business Ethics*, 3rd ed. (New York: Macmillan, 1990), 351.

simply a matter of meeting externally imposed requirements in order to earn a living and becomes rather a matter of working out one of my own personal projects. If I am working out one of my personal projects, there is no question of simply watching the clock until it is time to go home."[12]

Loyalty obligations vary in stringency. Some we might expect to be perfect, or strict. That is, loyal employees or members will be strictly bound to observe them. These will usually be negative obligations—for example, those requiring them to refrain from actions or activities that would seriously undermine the interests of the organization. That is why whistle-blowing tends to be viewed so harshly by organizations. Positive obligations, on the other hand—those requiring that employees do certain things to advance the interests of the organization—will generally be imperfect.

As indicated earlier, it may not always be easy to tell the difference between role obligations and loyalty obligations. Although differently motivated, they can intersect in content. Moreover, organizations will differ in what they can reasonably expect of their members or employees, and we will be able to see what it is that should be categorized as a loyalty obligation only by taking account of the costs or sacrifices that are exacted in relation to the formal benefits of membership. Of course, for employees who have come to identify with the organization and its purposes, loyalty obligations will generally be viewed as reasonable expressions of a bond that has been forged with the organization. Although an organization may rely on its committed employees to sacrifice their family's well-being to the fulfillment of organizational goals—and, indeed, some employees may be willing to make that sacrifice—it is unlikely to be a reasonable expectation of loyalty, and employees who fulfill it are not thereby admirable for doing so. No doubt there may be difficult trade-offs as employees seek to negotiate the various commitments they have. Some other relationships may have to be renegotiated in the light of the pressures under which loyal employees find themselves.

Not only may it be difficult to distinguish between role and loyalty obligations but also the latter may change over time. Many commentators have noted that changes in the nature of the post-1970s workplace—particularly its insecurity and mobility— have led not so much to the death of workplace loyalty as to its reconfiguration. For example, loyalty may no longer be seen simply as complaisance but instead as accommodating a critical dimension ("I speak up because I care about what happens to this company"), and it is not so often construed to include long-term commitment ("I've always chosen a company where I could be loyal to my employer. I show my loyalty by working hard, being extremely dedicated and honest, and by contributing far beyond

---

[12] R. E. Ewin, "Corporate Loyalty: Its Objects and Grounds," *Journal of Business Ethics* 12, no. 5 (1993): 390.

my job description. It's just that I'm more interested in developing my abilities than I am in staying with one organization forever").[13]

Might one want to argue that by joining the particular organization individuals ought to not only accept its general membership obligations but also develop a loyalty to it? This is difficult to answer in the abstract. A lot would appear to depend on the kind of organization we are considering, its dependence on the loyalty of its members, and its ability to earn the employee's loyalty. Moreover, even if an organization justifiably earns the loyalty of Employee A, it would not follow that Employee B should also develop it. It depends on their respective places in the organization, what is attractive to them about their job, and so forth. Perhaps the organization in question would *like* more from B so that she would voluntarily work after hours and on weekends, arrange her holidays to suit her employer, and so forth. But apart from an employment contract, the organization may not provide anything for B that would warrant her loyal, as well as her dutiful, engagement.

That said, some measure of loyalty may be important to an organization—*any* organization. We have already had occasion to review Hirschman's contention that organizations are subject to market fluctuations and other vicissitudes and therefore probably need a core (or more) of loyal employees if they are to ride out ups and downs or to recuperate in the event of entropic decline. All that can be inferred from this, however, is that if the organization is to survive and thrive, it needs the loyalty of (some) employees. It does not follow that the organization is owed loyalty. Once again, we need to look at the details of the particular organization to determine (1) whether its social value makes it worth keeping and supporting and (2) whether it has earned the loyalty of its members (and clients). We will return to this issue.

POTENTIAL CHALLENGES TO ORGANIZATIONAL LOYALTY

As can be expected with any complex arrangement, loyalties, whether developed or fostered, may be variously directed. A person may be loyal to the organization's goals and values—to what it stands for, to superiors, to a division or group within the organization, to the union, to organizational peers, to a profession employed within the organization, or to the organization as a provider of goods or services. Whatever the moral status of organizational loyalty, these other intraorganizational loyalties may come into conflict with it, creating loyalty dilemmas. We review several of these,

---

[13] From Carol Kinsey Goman, *The Loyalty Factor: A Management Guide to the Changing Dynamics of Loyalty in the Workplace* (New York: Donald I. Fine, 1991), 5–6. Within the "new" workplace, what managers need to offer in place of "lifetime employment" is open communication (ibid., ch. 4).

specifically to assess the kinds of problems or challenges they pose for organizational loyalty. For present purposes, I make the defeasible assumption that the organization is morally defensible.

(1) A person whose loyalty is to the *organization* itself will be concerned to act in ways that protect or further its particular collective goals and values and to be responsive to the structure of policies and decision-making processes that are implemented to realize those goals. Most organizations are collective wholes in the sense that they have some overarching administrative structure (even if there are several semiautonomous substructures within it) and a limited and specifiable set of goals (a "mission"). Organizations also aspire to continuity, though in these days of mergers and acquisitions (or takeovers), a particular organization may have a relatively short life span, and its members may want to consider whether any loyalty they have to the organization they initially joined should be maintained as it is transformed or absorbed into a somewhat different one. Essentially, though, loyalty to the organization is likely to encompass not only what the organization seeks to accomplish but also its various administrative processes, ways of operating, work conditions, and other provisions that it makes for its employees. Especially in large organizations, such loyalty should not be incompatible with a critical view of some of its practices. An "organization man" need not be a yes-man. Within bounds, loyal employees ought to address deficiencies in its operations—say, a deficient approach to customer service, an overly bureaucratic structure, or a glass ceiling for women or minorities. An organization's response to such critiques by loyal critics may affect both the quality and persistence of the loyalty.

(2) Loyalty to the organization needs to be distinguished from loyalty to *management*—that is, to those responsible for ongoing organizational policy and for supervising its execution. An organization's management is often construed as a team, a coordinated group that plans, leads, and organizes the activities of an organization with a view to its achieving its goals. One might expect that a well-functioning organizational management would be synchronized with what the organization seeks to achieve and therefore that loyalty to management would be functionally equivalent to loyalty to the organization. But all too frequently that is not the case. The life of an organization ordinarily extends beyond that of its current management, and loyalty to the incumbent management may be incompatible with loyalty to the organization. In universities, for example, it is a common complaint that particular administrations often function as semi-independent structures within the organization, with functional goals that only partially mesh with those for which the institution stands. Academics who rise in the university hierarchy to take their place in a university administration sometimes fail because of this tension, as the goals of the management team may differ from those that constitute the university's success as an

academic institution.[14] One would ordinarily expect loyalty to an organization's mission to take precedence over loyalty to a particular management team, though there is nothing hard and fast about this—in changed social circumstances, a management might legitimately see itself as inaugurating a new vision for the organization.

(3) Loyalty is often expected by or developed toward *superiors or supervisors*. Within most organizations, a structure of authority or leadership will evolve as its modus operandi. It may be pyramidal or relatively flat. Higher level occupants of that structure may see themselves as exemplifying the objects of a person's organizational loyalty. Such loyalties are sometimes more easily developed and intense than an amorphous organization is able to attract and may even substitute for it.

It is sometimes important to develop such loyalties. Because supervisory roles are often highly demanding—requiring more than can be managed by a single person—those in leadership or managerial positions need to have in place those they can trust who can be entrusted with the responsibility to realize organizational goals. The loyalty of those one supervises may therefore be important, just because those who are bound to another by loyalty will seek to act in ways that will further—and certainly not subvert—the interests and expectations of the supervisor, even if they have not been explicitly stated. Recall Fried's distinction between political science and commitment conceptions of loyalty. Proponents of the former interpret the task of a loyal subordinate to discern and implement their supervisors' wishes, whereas the latter express their loyalty more creatively. Fried's role as Ronald Reagan's solicitor general went beyond guessing what the president thought—he assumed that the president had no thoughts on the matter—to "constructing his leader's mind in a way that he [would] later embrace as his own." This captures quite well the importance of loyalty to superiors within a large organization, even though it fails to make explicit the extent to which loyalty may be oppositional and thus require the loyal servant to seek to change the leader's mind.

At first blush, loyalty to supervisors might seem to mesh comfortably with loyalty to the organization, especially if we think of the structure and its supervisory personnel as advancing the organization's mission. However, there is no guarantee of this, for a distinction must be made between the office and the officeholder, and the personal ambitions of the superior (officeholder) may be in tension with the goals of the organization. Those in administrative or managerial positions may seek to create fiefdoms that detract from the fulfillment of organizational goals.[15] Such tensions

[14] For a provocative discussion, see Josef Martin (pseud.), *To Rise above Principle: Memoirs of an Unreconstructed Academic Dean* (Urbana: University of Illinois Press, 1988); http://henryhbauer.homestead.com/files/trapfull.pdf.

[15] See Sam S. Souryal and Brian W. McKay, "Personal Loyalty to Superiors in Public Service," *Criminal Justice Ethics* 15, no.2 (1996): 41–58.

need not be intended. A person in a leadership role may come to have a very personal (rather than team) view about how the organization's purposes should be realized, and, if the loyalty of subordinates is demanded, it may create serious ethical as well as operational difficulties. In theory, a loyal subordinate may be a loyal opponent, though opposition may also be viewed as insubordination, leaving the junior person with a difficult decision to make. There is no doubt that some of the bad press associated with loyalty arises because it has become detached from the larger structures within which it is fostered.

(4) What is true of loyalty to superiors is true also of *peer* loyalty. In many organizations, such as policing and the military, it may be important to develop peer loyalty. The work is inherently dangerous, and there is a need for teamwork and for reliance on others. Loyalty is critical to the confidence that individuals can have as they work. Someone is watching their back. Nevertheless, such loyalty frequently becomes a cover for laziness, inefficiency, incompetence, corruption, or worse. Even if the larger organizational goals of the organization are served—and served more effectively—they may be served in ways that undercut the larger ethical presumptions that underlie the organization. Police units may operate in ways that disrupt drug trafficking and organized crime rings but do so by violating civil liberties presumed to undergird the mission of the police organization and, of course, the liberal democratic ethos of the society.

Organizations should not have to tolerate peer loyalty that tolerates serious misconduct. Although a person's organizational loyalty might coexist with loyalty to a lazy and incompetent employee, it is unlikely to do so if one of the sources for (or undergirdings of) that organizational loyalty is a belief in the excellence of what the company does and how it achieves it. A bane of policing has been the propensity of police officers to have greater loyalty toward their peers than toward the profession or organization, leading to a "blue wall of silence" that protects corruption, misconduct, and incompetence and shields them from accountability for the public trust that is vested in them.

(5) *Professional* loyalties present a different challenge. It has become increasingly common for professionals to be employed by large organizations. Such organizations—say, medical centers or law firms—might seem to be committed to the same ends as the professions they represent. And for the most part, it will be important to their success that they are. Yet the commercialization of the professions has often resulted in distorted priorities and corruption, and economic considerations have compromised professional ones. An HMO or medical center might pressure doctors to see four patients or more an hour or to abandon appointments for walk-in medicine, even though this will lead to hurried and inadequate examinations.

The tension may be more explicit where professionals are employed in organizations whose ends do not claim to be compatible with the professions from which the professionals are drawn. Medical personnel and social workers in prisons or lawyers employed by large corporations are cases in point. The organizations for which they work may make demands of them that would compromise their professional loyalties, loyalties that theoretically should be accorded high standing within the respective organizations. In some cases, the tensions are written into the raisons d'être of the organizations, as is the case with prisons, where security considerations are usually given priority over welfare ones. In other cases, however, the tension is a temptation to moral line crossing, as when organizational lawyers or accountants are pressured into exploiting or fudging. Conflicts between professional and more general organizational loyalty may sometimes be grounds for whistle-blowing.

In themselves, such tensions do not constitute an argument for detaching professions or professionals from organizations or for giving either a free rein, but for developing decision-making strategies that will enable loyalties to be modified without being violated. Such tensions and decisions are not significantly different from those that arise in the ordinary course of life, when loyalty to one friend may conflict with loyalty to another friend, loyalty to a friend may conflict with loyalty to family, or a patriotic loyalty may conflict with a religious one. Conflicts of organizational and professional loyalties may, however, be more amenable to regularization. In the more personal cases, an individual will engage in an internal discourse that will result in a—sometimes anguished—prioritization of loyalties; in the case of professional-organizational conflicts, one of the important ethical questions will involve the identification of who should have responsibility for resolving it. A social worker in a prison situation or doctor in a hospital is not the only important stakeholder involved in making whatever trade-off decisions have to be made, but one of a number, and a major task in organizational ethics is to develop decision-making procedures that will acknowledge, identify, and accommodate the relevant stakeholders. There will often be a two-step process, one to develop policies—in which the different stakeholders should have a say—and the other to implement them. The former will not constitute an argumentative strategy able to ensure good decision making, but it may locate responsibility in the right place.[16]

(6) In reaction to the failures to which the foregoing loyalties are prone, Sam Souryal and others have sought to transform organizational or workplace loyalty into a loyalty to *principles or causes*. This is typified by Donald Schultz's dedication of his book on policing "to those Police Officers Whose first Loyalties are to Principles,

---

[16] See Dennis F. Thompson, "The Institutional Turn in Professional Ethics," *Ethics & Behavior* 9, no. 2 (1999): 109–118. For an example of this process in practice, see Eva C. Winkler, "The Ethics of Policy Writing: How Should Hospitals Deal with Moral Disagreement about Controversial Medical Practices?" *Journal of Medical Ethics* 31 (2005): 559–566.

not Men."[17] Such principles are taken to be the guiding values of the organization (as might be embodied in its code of ethics). As I have already argued, it is neither pragmatically nor analytically helpful to detach loyalties too radically from their broadly interpersonal associations and to extend them to principles. Sidney Axinn contends that even abstractions such as principles or causes have rarely gained people's allegiance apart from leaders in whom they were believed to be embodied: "Would the principles of Christianity have persisted through the centuries without the story of Christ? Would we have Mohammedanism without Mohammed, Confucianism without Confucius, Buddhism without Buddha?"[18] I am drawn in this direction. Analytically, we are better served by recognizing that our loyalties generally begin as personalized particularistic commitments and in recognizing that these particularistic commitments must also confront the demands of universalistic principles. Otherwise, we fail to see that loyalty to principles must itself respond to the demands of a critical universalistic morality. I do not prejudge whether a particular loyalty should prevail over some universalistic demand. That will depend on the loyalty, the demand, and the circumstances in which each is being asserted.

(7) To this point, the discussion of organizational loyalty has focused on the loyalty of members of the organization to it or to elements within it. But organizational loyalty sometimes refers to *client or consumer* loyalty. Organizations, especially competing ones, seek to cultivate the "loyalty" of clients to their "brand" and engage in various strategies to gain and retain it. "Loyalty programs" reflect this form of loyalty. It is, however, loyalty of a relatively thin kind, encouraged or bolstered by the inducement of rewards of various kinds—free flights, discounts, gifts, and so forth. Those who participate may feel (or have) little or no loyalty at all but simply treat the benefits as one might treat a discount voucher that comes one's way.[19] And the supposedly loyal consumer who instead opts for a cheaper product because it is cheaper is hardly to be considered disloyal. For the most part, it is loyalty without real cost.[20]

This not to reject all forms of consumer or client loyalty. If my favorite restaurant is struggling in an economic downturn I might go more often, distribute leaflets, or

[17] Donald O. Schultz, ed., *Critical Issues in Criminal Justice* (Springfield, IL: Charles C Thomas, 1975).

[18] Sidney Axinn, "Thoughts in Response to Fr. John C. Haughey on Loyalty in the Workplace," *Business Ethics Quarterly* 4, no. 3 (July 1994): 355.

[19] Marketers are sometimes aware of this and seek to add "cue-compatible" incentives. See Michelle L. Roehm, Ellen Bolman Pullins, and Harper A. Roehm Jr., "Designing Loyalty-Building Programs for Packaged Goods Brands," *Journal of Marketing Research* 39, no. 2 (2002): 202–213.

[20] The person who accrues loyalty points by traveling with Airline A, even when the fares are sometimes more expensive, expects to recoup with flights financed by frequent flyer miles—a "calculated loyalty."

encourage my friends to go so that it might ride out the recession. Or I may continue to send my child to the school I used to attend, even though it is currently doing rather poorly. Even in these cases, however, there may be no disloyalty if one does nothing to help. I may be enthusiastic about the restaurant or have had good memories of the school without having identified with either, and it is questionable whether one's loyalty was owed.

Ronald Duska has argued that organizational loyalties are chimerical. Unlike friendship and familial loyalties, which he takes to be paradigmatic, so-called organizational loyalties do not embody a trust that "depends upon ties that demand self-sacrifice with no expectation of reward, e.g., the ties of loyalty that bind a family together."[21] Rather, organizational (work) relationships are based on self-interest instead of a mutual willingness for self-sacrifice, thus negating any pretense of loyalty. But that, surely, goes too far. Both may coexist, though expectation of reward will not ground such loyalty. Other differences may be suggested. In Raymond Pfeiffer's more nuanced account, it is asserted that family loyalty is given without the expectation of something in return, whereas "when continued loyal performances go unrewarded by an employer, or at least unrecognized, the feeling of loyalty may fade, and even turn to bitterness."[22] Pfeiffer thinks that family and employee loyalty differ in their longevity—the former generally lasts a life time, whereas the latter begins and ends with the employment. It is "more conditional."[23] It is more plausible, however, to see their difference in the kind of good that each constitutes for the loyal individual. Generally, involvement in organizations does not offer important satisfactions that would otherwise be unavailable to their members, even though particular organizations may provide satisfactions for particular individuals that they would not otherwise experience. Families and friendships, however, as types of associations, do offer distinctive *human* satisfactions that are not, for the most part, individual in the way that organizational experiences are. That family and friendship relations often fail in this task is not due to some lack in the form of association they represent but because of some other factor, such as human failure or bad luck. And when they do, they, too, may result in faded loyalties and even bitterness.

THE MORAL STATUS OF ORGANIZATIONAL LOYALTY

For their own interests and even survival, organizations are likely to take steps to foster the loyalty of their employees (and, where appropriate, their clients or

[21] Ronald Duska, "Whistleblowing and Employee Loyalty," in *Contemporary Issues in Business Ethics*, ed. Joseph DesJardins and John McCall (Belmont, CA: Wadsworth, 1985), 297.
[22] Raymond S. Pfeiffer, "Owing Loyalty to One's Employer," *Journal of Business Ethics* 11, no. 7 (1992): 536. I am not so sure that this is foreign to families.
[23] Ibid.

consumers). Especially in competitive businesses, employees who are loyal are likely to be motivated to work harder and better than others. They are likely to be more willing to pitch in if the business is going through a difficult period. And loyal clients and consumers may also be inclined to stay when attractive rival opportunities appear or times are tough. Although it is easy to be cynical about the motives of organizations that encourage and even demand loyalty from their members, the desire for employee and other loyalty may not be crudely yoked to a bottom line of self-interest. Even organizations less interested in their own bottom line may seek and need the loyalty of those who work for them or benefit from what they do. As Hirschman has argued, few, if any, organizations can do without some degree of employee loyalty.[24] This is not just because many organizations have to compete with other providers of whatever product or service they offer but also because of the phenomenon of institutional entropy.

There are, it would appear, factors affecting most organizations that, unless countered, will lead over time to their decline. Some of these will be external. For example, the social interests that an organization was set up to address may evolve, and the organization will need to be flexible enough to adapt to changed circumstances. Or should the organization do well, it may—as organizations tend to—seek to add other socially desired or desirable products or services and, in the process, generate increasing bureaucracy, perhaps strain its resources, and lose its clarity of focus. Or there may be larger social changes that have nothing specifically to do with the organization but nevertheless diminish its capacity. Another set of entropic factors may be internal to the organization. If an organization becomes more bureaucratic, there will likely be fewer available opportunities for workers' personal satisfaction (along with greater frustrations for those who are its clients). Despite intentions, bureaucratization will also generate various inefficiencies. In addition, internal conflicts will often harden over time, and enthusiasms that were present at the organization's creation will dissipate, especially as new members come in who no longer share the founding vision or dedication of its creators. Finally, if the organization begins to decline, internal tensions that were contained during good times may now come to the surface.

As Hirschman points out, one thing that helps to counter organizational decline will be the loyalty of members and clients—the willingness of those for whom an organization has become something with which they identify to engage in "costly" activities on the organization's behalf. The loyal members of an organization will put out for it when it is not personally advantageous for them to do so, and what they see as their obligations of loyalty will be a function, first, of their judgment whether

[24] Albert O. Hirschman, *Exit, Voice and Loyalty: Responses to Decline in Firms, Organizations, and States* (Cambridge, MA: Harvard University Press, 1970). See also Brian Schrag, "The Moral Significance of Employee Loyalty," *Business Ethics Quarterly* 11, no. 1 (2001): 56–58.

the organization is capable of being turned around and, second, of their individual capacity to contribute to its turnaround.

Although this might be seen as an argument for every organization seeking the loyalty of those associated with it, it does not follow that organizational loyalty is always permissible or even obligatory or, if the latter, obligatory for all its members. As we have pointed out, criminal and racist organizations lack goals that warrant loyal attachment. And loyalty to one's football team may be for most only permissible. What Hirschman sees as the particular value of organizational loyalty requires only that a critical mass within an organization are loyally bound to it, and any general obligation to develop loyalty to it would, even in an organization devoted to good ends, probably amount to no more than an imperfect obligation.

Consider an organization such as Oxfam or a public interest law firm. Here it is arguable that loyalty to it would be entirely appropriate and desirable. In addition to membership obligations, a person who developed loyalty to it would ipso facto assume certain loyalty-related obligations to it (and presumably its mission). But would they be *moral* obligations? Probably, but not necessarily. If the amount of good that Oxfam or the public interest law firm is capable of doing would be significantly affected by whether one developed loyalty to it, it is at least arguable that failure to develop loyalty would represent some kind of moral failure. But if one could be easily replaced (as would be likely were one employed in a custodial role within the organization's offices), then doing no more than what one's contract required would probably be sufficient. One could take on the job simply as a way of earning enough money to put oneself through college, intending to leave as soon as one had finished.

There are also many morally acceptable organizations to which one could develop loyalty without the obligations attached thereto being seen as moral obligations. I might, for example, develop a deep loyalty to the shipping company that employs me because it satisfies my passion for the ocean and sailing vessels. But the obligations associated with this loyalty would not be exclusively moral in character any more than those associated with my loyalty to a particular football team. True, I might have a moral obligation not to transmit financial information about the shipping company to a rival shipping company, but that would be an employment obligation as much as a loyalty obligation, though such an obligation would be reinforced by my loyalty. My loyalty would commit me to preserving my association with the company and therefore not passing on the information, whereas my simple breach of the company's contractual expectations might lead to my being sacked, something that might not bother me were I intending to resign.

Still, we might recall a somewhat abstract argument for developing organizational loyalty. Given that what we require for our human flourishing is access to associations, it is arguable that, in an advanced and reasonably populous society, human well-being is dependent to some degree on the existence of organizations capable of providing needed goods or services.[25] Although we might make some sort of life for ourselves if left to our own devices, it would be far more restricted than possible with the assistance of supportive organizations. This is not an argument for whatever organizations we have or even an argument for everyone developing loyalty to whatever organizations he or she is associated with. But if what the organizations provide is something that contributes to human flourishing, then it is at least arguable that *some* within these organizations ought to develop a degree of loyalty to them. To the extent that loyalty is completely lacking, organizations become vulnerable to external and internal pressures that jeopardize the realization of their collective goals. No doubt it could be argued that a structure of incentives could produce the same outcomes. This, however, would not represent a very stable solution, and so, despite its manipulability, an appropriately reflective loyalty would do better at keeping an organization efficient and honest.

LIMITS TO ORGANIZATIONAL LOYALTY

Not surprisingly, given the great variety of organizations, both in scope and importance, organizational loyalty may often be deeply problematic, not only because it is given but also because of what it demands. How do we structure organizational loyalties to minimize the likelihood that they will be improperly given and unjustifiably manipulated? It may be possible to answer such questions only by considering *particular* organizations and the *place* that a particular person occupies within them. Nevertheless, a couple of general remarks can be proffered. Most organizations need some loyal members if they are to do well. From that, however, it does not follow that there is a moral obligation to keep the organization afloat. But if an organization provides a socially important product or service, then it is at least arguable that some of its members ought to be loyally committed to it. It might help us identify those members by means of an analogy with Good Samaritan situations in which a person is drowning and there is a crowd on the beach. Only one person needs to swim out to the distressed individual, but until that person does, all who can assist are obligated to do so. The analogy is more suggestive than exact, but it indicates how an organization's health may require its members to consider the impact of their role and actions on the organization's well-being.

The strength of any such loyalty obligation will presumably depend on what is at stake: the importance of the products or services that the organization provides. Are they as well or even better provided by other organizations? How much will this person's loyalty affect its capacity to provide them? If the sole power company in an

---

[25] This is not to prejudge the structure of such organizations—whether they function hierarchically or cooperatively, and so forth. That is a different issue.

area is in danger of failing, should some of its members allow their loyalty to it to be easily overridden by other loyalties they may have? May they argue that they are not contractually obligated to put themselves out in the way required by the situation? Here the obligation of loyalty to the power company is a strong one, as many will be seriously disadvantaged if the power cuts out. That may not be the case if the organization is only in the business of providing entertainment.

Consider what is at stake in the case of the military. Soldiers take it upon themselves to defend their country with their lives, a high price that is not likely to be paid absent a loyal commitment to the purposes of the collective—say, to protect the Constitution against its enemies. Because of the costs involved, the military requires the loyalty of its members and gives such loyalty considerable weight.[26] In past times, soldiers who deserted could be shot. Nevertheless, the expectations of loyal obedience are not absolute. The requirement to obey is a requirement to obey all *lawful* orders, and though there is a wrenching epistemological dispute about the identification of an unlawful order, the consequences of obedience to an unlawful order cannot be deflected simply by saying: "I was just following orders."[27] As stated in the instructions for the conduct of soldiers in the Civil War, "Men who take up arms against another in public war do not cease on this account to be moral beings responsible to one another and to God."[28] Military obedience ought not to be blind but reflective. Richard Gabriel distinguishes between *acts of obedience* ("sterile loyalty"), in which officers "execute the precepts of the code without knowing why," and *ethical action*, in which "the precepts are understood and its obligations are undertaken willingly." Ethical action involves "judgment, choice, and responsibility." In a crisis, the soldier must exercise his sense of loyalty as *fides* (faith), and this must always take precedence over any sense of *obsequium* (obedience). In fact, the complexities are even greater, given that wars may be unjust; in a deep moral crisis, the soldier may have to override his oath to the profession and to the Constitution in order to be loyal to humanity itself.[29]

The longevity or persistence of organizational loyalty is also a contentious issue.[30] Members of organizations are often made privy to information and occurrences that,

---

[26] See Alasdair MacIntyre, *Is Patriotism a Virtue?* (Lawrence: University of Kansas Press, 1984).

[27] See Richard A. Gabriel, *To Serve with Honor: A Treatise on Military Ethics and the Way of the Soldier* (Westport, CT: Greenwood, 1982).

[28] *Instructions for the Government of Armies of the United States in the Field* (1863), General Order No. 100, http://avalon.law.yale.edu/19th_century/lieber.asp.

[29] Gabriel, *To Serve with Honor*. It is, perhaps, not without significance that honor is usually placed before loyalty in military ethics.

[30] It can be a contentious issue in friendships and marriages as well. It is usually expected that if an intimate couple break up, they will keep to themselves various aspects of their intimate relationship and not think: now that the relationship is over, all constraints are off.

were they to be more widely known, could be very damaging to the organization. The genre of "tell all" memoirs from those who have served in (or those in) high offices trades on their privileged position. In a particularly strong reaction to Matt Latimer's exposé of White House goings-on after he left his job as special assistant for speechwriting to President George W. Bush,[31] the conservative commentator Bill Bennett caustically remarked: Latimer "needs to read his Dante. . . . The lowest circle of hell are for people who are disloyal in the way this guy is disloyal and [at] the very lowest point Satan chews on their bodies."[32] There is a lot that cannot be built into an employment contract without violating free speech rights (and destroying necessary trust). But just as there can be obligations to the dead because people have interests that survive their demise, there can also be obligations to organizations with which one has cut one's ties. The organization has a continuing interest in its behind-the-scene affairs being kept out of the spotlight. Nevertheless, the obligation is hardly absolute; there may be overriding public interest reasons for disclosing what went on while one was employed.[33] At some future point, moreover, there may be strong historical reasons for having access to such first-person behind-the-scenes accounts—one reason there is often a time limit on the secrecy of official documents. Nevertheless, where, as is sometimes the case, the tell-all account focuses on facts more likely to produce embarrassment than enlightenment or is substantially motivated by financial considerations, there is reason to think that a form of disloyalty has been perpetrated.

In sum, it does not follow from an organization's demand for loyalty that loyalty should be given. And when it is given, it does not follow from that that it cannot be overridden by other claims. Even a moral requirement to give some measure of loyalty to an organization will need to compete with other expectations. Nowhere is this clearer than in cases of whistle-blowing, to which we finally turn.

WHISTLE-BLOWING

Since the term was coined in the middle of the twentieth century, the literature on whistle-blowing has ballooned. The term's origins are somewhat unclear, some suggesting that it refers to the whistle that is sounded at an industrial site to warn of

[31] Matt Latimer, *Speech-less: Tales of a White House Survivor* (New York: Crown, 2009).

[32] Bill Bennett, commenting on CNN's *The Situation Room*, September 23, 2009, http://transcripts.cnn.com/TRANSCRIPTS/0909/23/sitroom.02.html.

[33] These will have to be weighed against some consequentialist reasons for nondisclosure—the chilling effect, increased secrecy, an atmosphere of suspicion, and so on. The issues have been sharpened by the advent of organizations such as Wikileaks and the disclosures of secret documents by Private Bradley Manning and Edward Snowden.

a hazardous condition, others claiming that it refers to a football umpire's whistle, blown to bring play to a sharp halt. In either case, it was employed to provide a more neutral or even affirmative characterization of the activity of an employee in an organization—private or public—who alerts a wider group to setbacks to their interests as a result of waste, corruption, fraud, profit seeking, or some violation of important rights.[34] Although the term was first used to refer to public servants who made known—"went public"—concerning governmental mismanagement, waste, or corruption, the term has now been extended to cover the activity of any employee or other officer of a legitimate public or private organization who alerts a wider (usually more powerful) group to setbacks to their interests as a result of waste, corruption, fraud, profit seeking, or rights violations. By those against whom they blew the whistle, such employees had previously been characterized as disloyal traitors, snitches, weasels, squealers, rats, or a host of other derogatory terms. Hence a term was needed that did not automatically beg the question against the practice.

Although the foregoing characterization of whistle-blowing is adequate for most practical purposes, several of its features have been subject to contention. Most whistle-blowers are current officers or employees of the organization against whom the whistle is blown, but some have contended that former officers or employees might sometimes qualify as whistle-blowers. Others have suggested that they could be subcontractors or even people who work in an honorary capacity for an organization. Connected with these issues is the question of whether obligations of loyalty might extend after formal associations have been severed. To the extent that we may sometimes wish to respond affirmatively to these questions, it would seem possible to recognize former employees and other associates as potential whistle-blowers.

There have also been disputes about the kinds of "setbacks to interests" for which whistle-blowing might be appropriate. Such setbacks usually involve significant wrongdoing by officers of the organization, often amounting to the violation of human or other important rights, particularly the rights of those catered to or served by the organization. The threat to a broader public makes more sense of a strategy of going public. However, even this condition has fuzzy edges. Sometimes the wrongdoing may affect those within the organization more immediately than those served by it—for example, exploitative and dangerous work conditions that are ignored by management. And what counts as going public may depend on the way in which an organization is structured. In police organizations, with their strong horizontal loyalties, even a person who reports wrongdoing to a supervisor or internal affairs is usually considered a whistle-blower (though some writers prefer to distinguish them as "internal witnesses").

[34] See further, William De Maria, "Whistleblowing—International Bibliography" (1995), University of Queensland, www.bmartin.cc/dissent/documents/DeMaria_bib.html.

The normative background to the debate about whistle-blowing is driven by two factors. First, there is an organizationally promulgated expectation that employees or members owe loyalty to their organization, requiring that they not jeopardize their organization's interests by revealing certain kinds of information to those outside it. If employees or members are unhappy about some aspect of what the organization does, it should be handled within the organization or group ("we wash our own laundry"). The ethical case for whistle-blowing is based on a recognition that internal mechanisms often fail to deal adequately with an organization's failures and, further, that because the interests jeopardized by those failures are generally wider than those of the organization, a wider group or public has a prima facie right to know what is behind the costs it faces or has incurred.

The second background factor is constituted by the negative cost that "disloyalty"—blowing the whistle—is likely to have for an organization. A frequent effect of blowing the whistle is significant disruption within the organization. It may lose control of its affairs as it is subjected to external inquiries and constraints, it may find itself crippled by costs or other restrictions, and many within it who are little more than innocent bystanders may suffer from the repercussions of an externally mounted investigation. As an act of putative disloyalty, its costs may be very significant. Although whistle-blowers are likely to argue that the organization has forfeited (or had overridden) any loyalty owed to it, it may be necessary to justify the significant costs that whistle-blowing risks or causes.

For these two reasons, it is arguable that whistle-blowing will be justified only if cognizance is taken of several considerations:

(1) Because of the threatened disruption, the whistle should be blown only as a matter of *last resort*—only if other less disruptive avenues for warning, protest, or rectification have proven ineffective. To the extent that whistle-blowing is a publicly supported practice, it generally needs to conform to the principle of the least restrictive alternative. That is, corrective actions should be no more intrusive than needed to achieve their goals. No doubt the risks that confront whistle-blowers may sometimes make less extreme forms of reporting impracticable (or risky). If, for example, an organization's management is deeply implicated in the wrongdoing, then the whistle-blower may well find his or her life at risk. Although whistle-blowers might be expected to demonstrate good faith, their martyrdom cannot be demanded.[35]

(2) The organizational wrongdoing should be sufficiently *serious*. As well as the magnitude of the setback to interests threatened or caused, an assessment of

---

[35] See Mike W. Martin, "Whistleblowing: Professionalism, Personal Life, and Shared Responsibility for Safety in Engineering," *Business and Professional Ethics Journal* 11, no. 2 (1992): 21–40; Richard L. Rashke, *The Killing of Karen Silkwood: The Story Behind the Kerr-McGee Plutonium Case*, 2nd ed. (Ithaca, NY: Cornell University Press, 2000).

seriousness will also include a consideration of the imminence of the setback and whether it is reversible. In many cases, responses to setbacks or wrongdoing should probably take other forms—confrontation, ostracism, transfer, and so on—in which costs to the organization are not likely to be disproportionate to the costs of the setback. The whistle-blower must be more than a tattletale. Administrative grievances, such as a bad-tempered supervisor or concerns about promotion fairness, do not justify whistle-blowing (though they may justify other forms of complaint).

(3) The public complaint should also be *well-grounded*. Once again, the costs for organizations against whom the whistle is blown require that whistle-blowers have good reasons for believing that their organizations are perpetrating the wrongs with which they are being accused. The evidence whistle-blowers possess should be strong enough to be defensible in a public forum—though not necessarily a court of law.

(4) A potential whistle-blower needs to consider whether he or she has a special *role-related obligation* to take action—for example, a supervisory role associated with the source of the wrongdoing. Although any member of an organization might bear some responsibility for what is done in its name, some members will have enhanced, role-related responsibilities for the way in which the organization conducts its activities and, perhaps by virtue of that, will also be better placed to make appropriate assessments of seriousness. As well, such people may or may not be complicit or be expected to be complicit in the matter to be reported.[36]

(5) Because the purpose of blowing the whistle is to bring about change—or at least a cessation of harmful activities and strategies for preventing their recurrence (including bringing perpetrators to account)—the likelihood of whistle-blowing being *effective* should also be factored in. If blowing the whistle is unlikely to accomplish any public good, and the damage it causes is likely to outweigh any other values it may have, it may be questioned why this particular strategy is being adopted. Sometimes, the best one can do is leave.

(6) It is sometimes argued that the act of whistle-blowing needs to be *appropriately motivated*—that is, it must manifest (at least) a concern for those whose interests are being jeopardized. This consideration, however, may bear on the whistle-blower's praiseworthiness rather than the justifiability of blowing the whistle. Whistle-blowing—even when justified by circumstances—may be and sometimes is motivated by revenge, the desire for promotion or ingratiation, self-protection, or as penance. Because this is so, it is common for those against whom the whistle is blown to attempt to undermine the whistle-blower's credibility. Although such attacks are, strictly speaking, beside the point, they may, like defense attorney attacks on the

---

[36] Michael Davis develops a complicity theory of responsibility for whistle-blowing in "Some Paradoxes of Whistleblowing," *Business and Professional Ethics Journal* 15 no. 1 (1996): 3–19.

credibility of witnesses, serve to cast doubt on the credibility of whistle-blowers without addressing the substance of their claims. The point, then, is not that the morally compromised are exempted from blowing the whistle but that (1) they may not garner moral praise for doing so and (2) doubt may be cast on their credibility (and hence on the effectiveness of their initiative).

Even if the foregoing considerations have been satisfactorily addressed, it might be wondered whether whistle-blowing is obligatory or merely permissible.[37] It may be argued that a person has an obligation to report such wrongdoing within the organization, but no obligation to blow the whistle in the event that internal reporting goes nowhere. Sometimes it may be merely permissible.

If failure to blow the whistle is seen as an *omission*, then we must engage with debates about the moral obligatoriness of our acting to prevent setbacks caused by others. Here—even if one is a member of the organization—there will be differences, depending on how practically involved one is in the wrongdoing in question. An engineer whose safety assessment is ignored is in a different position from someone in the organization who just stumbles across serious wrongdoing by others. However, even if blowing the whistle is seen as morally obligatory, the strength of that obligation may be contentious. Should it be made legally as well as morally obligatory? Might its obligatoriness in either case sometimes be overridden or excused by the costs that the whistle-blower will be made to bear? Although the doctrine of "employment at will" has been modified in recent years, it remains the case that whistle-blowers are generally regarded as traitors (or insubordinate) by their employing organizations and that they (and those closely associated with them) may be made to suffer dearly for their whistle-blowing. It might therefore be thought too burdensome to require a potential whistle-blower to sound it.[38]

Because whistle-blowers are likely to be victims of retaliatory behavior by the organizations on which they blow the whistle, many jurisdictions have promulgated whistle-blower protection acts.[39] Such is the organizational aversion to whistle-blowing, however, that these acts have generally provided inadequate protection. Either they are watered down in the process of securing legislative passage, or they are circumvented because retaliatory behavior may be successfully disguised as something else.[40] And those whistle-blowers who leave an organization by choice

[37] Richard De George, "Ethical Responsibilities of Engineers in Large Organizations: The Pinto Case," *Business & Professional Ethics Journal*, 1, no. 1 (1981): 1–14.

[38] See Glazer and Glazer, *The Whistleblowers*; Martin, "Whistleblowing."

[39] In the United States, Michigan introduced the first such act in 1981. A federal act was introduced in 1989.

[40] See, for example, Brian Martin, "Illusions of Whistleblower Protection," *UTS Law Review* 5 (2003): 119–130.

may, because they acquire a reputation as "untrustworthy," find it difficult to get work elsewhere. So, for many legitimate whistle-blowers, the law has proved an inadequate protective vehicle. Occasionally, within governmental organizations, whistle-blower protection programs have been developed, designed to offer the same personalized protection of whistle-blowers that witness protection programs have offered witnesses in court cases who are at risk of retaliatory action.[41]

The likely costs to whistle-blowers have sometimes generated a debate over the merits of anonymous whistle-blowing. Although the anonymous whistle-blower may be secured against retaliation, the strategy can open the door to whistle-blowing—or what poses as whistle-blowing—that is motivated by revenge, rivalry, or other unworthy motives or to whistle-blowing that reflects an irresponsible or careless investigation of what are interpreted as setbacks to the public interest. Even the anonymous whistle-blowers may suffer, especially if, subsequent to investigation, they are deemed to have been aware of the wrongdoing that has now come to light. In some police organizations, the latter possibility has been minimized by giving whistle-blowers a code number that can subsequently be used to clear whistle-blowers who might otherwise be tainted by a resultant investigation. Usually, though, except for a narrow range of cases, it is considered better that whistle-blowers identify themselves.

CONCLUSION

Although any generalizations about the value of organizational loyalty are likely to be overbroad—especially in view of the wide diversity of organizations—we have seen why it might be in the legitimate interests of most organizations to foster and even expect some loyalty from at least some of their members. Even without the presumptions of the market, the ordinary tendency of organizations to decline over time, absent mechanisms to sustain their missions, provides them with a rationale for fostering the loyalty of their members and perhaps their client base. There are clear dangers of self-servingness in this—the cultivation of undeserved and corrupted loyalties—and so forms of protest such as those indicated by whistle-blowing may be necessary to keep loyalty clean.

[41] See, for example that operating in the US Department of Labor, www.osha.gov/dep/oia/whistleblower/index.html.

11

PROFESSION

Professional loyalties derive solely from contract, from voluntary commitments, not from an historical self.[1]

In *Loyalty: An Essay on the Morality of Relationships*, George Fletcher marginalizes the idea of professional loyalty. He claims that in its core sense loyalty has to do with obligations that arise out of our "being historically rooted in a set of defining familial, institutional, and national relationships."[2] Loyalty involves a commitment to the constitutive sources of our historical being, to those relationships and communities that define us as the particular individuals we are—not just as *generic* persons, but as members of *particular* familial, ethnic, religious, and national groups. Such core loyalties, he says, are not to be confused with the secondary loyalties that lawyers owe their clients, that physicians owe their patients, or that corporate managers owe their firms. The latter, as he asserts in this chapter's epigraph, "derive solely from contract, from voluntary commitments, not from an historical self."

Fletcher runs together here what I have chosen to separate—professional and organizational loyalties. He runs them together because he sees each as arising out of a voluntary commitment rather than as expressing a history of which we find ourselves a part—as members of particular families, ethnic groups, religious and national communities. Perhaps, too, the fact that many professionals work in organizations might also lead us to run the two together. But there are often significant tensions between loyalties that arise out of one's professional community and those that may

---

[1] George Fletcher, *Loyalty: An Essay on the Morality of Relationships* (New York: Oxford University Press, 1993), 22.
[2] Ibid., 21.

arise out of one's organizational involvements,[3] and it seems better that we keep them conceptually distinct, even if they are often practically connected.

Are the loyalties that derive from voluntary commitments so different from those that are integral to the historical self? Do the latter have a centrality that the former do not? More particularly, how much weight should we accord to professional loyalties? Is there something about professions that secures loyalty against its problematic expressions?

TWO DIMENSIONS OF PROFESSIONAL LOYALTY

The literature on professional loyalties focuses mainly on the loyalty of lawyers to their clients and of medical personnel to their patients. For convenience, I will focus on these and especially on the former. We might, however, extend the discussion to teachers, architects, engineers, clergy, and accountants. The list is contested and somewhat open-ended, as different occupations seek to professionalize themselves.[4] But more on that later.

There are two ways to approach professional loyalty. One, the most common, sees it as loyalty to client or patient. The professions are seen as specialist providers of important socially valued services, and the professional loyalty called for is a loyalty to those who are the beneficiaries of those services. This is Fletcher's view: "professional loyalty is expressed in the intensity of care and attention [shown] to the client or patient."[5] So understood, loyalty is often said to be central to the lawyer-client or doctor-patient relationship. Geoffrey Hazard, for example, writes that "in the relationship with a client, the lawyer is required above all to demonstrate loyalty,"[6] a point in which he is followed—with somewhat greater cultural specificity—by Charles Wolfram: "Whatever may be the models that obtain in other legal cultures, the client-lawyer relationship in the United States is founded on the lawyer's virtually total loyalty to the client and the client's interests."[7]

---

[3] See Dennis F. Thompson, "The Institutional Turn in Professional Ethics," *Ethics & Behavior* 9, no. 2 (1999), 109–128. It may not be without significance that, in Harvard University's "Policies Relating to Research and Other Professional Activities Within and Outside the University," "every member is expected to accord the University his or her primary professional loyalty" (§1)—a position that organizationally constrains the professional loyalty. See www.fas.harvard.edu/~research/greybook/policies.html.

[4] Harold L. Wilensky, "The Professionalization of Everyone?" *American Journal of Sociology* 70, no. 2 (1964): 137–158.

[5] Fletcher, *Loyalty*, 23.

[6] Geoffrey C. Hazard Jr., "Triangular Lawyer Relationships: An Exploratory Analysis," *Georgetown Journal of Legal Ethics* 1, no. 1 (1987): 21.

[7] Charles W. Wolfram, *Modern Legal Ethics* (St. Paul, MN: West, 1986), 146.

In his classic work, *The Patient as Person*, Paul Ramsey self-consciously makes use of a quasi-religious covenantal metaphor in characterizing the relationship between doctor and patient. Central to that covenant are what he refers to as "canons of loyalty," chief of which is the existence, on the part of the patient, of a "reasonably free and adequately informed consent" to undergo certain medical procedures.[8] In this view, loyalty to patients makes their informed consent a prerequisite to any medical intervention.

So understood, professional loyalties are often held to be almost absolute. The legal locus classicus is Lord Brougham's defense of Queen Caroline against George IV's accusation of her adultery:

> An advocate, in the discharge of his duty, knows but one person in all the world, and that person is his client. To save that client by all means and expedients, and at all hazards and costs to other persons, and, amongst them, to himself, is his first and only duty; and in performing that duty he must not regard the alarm, the torments, the destruction which he may bring upon others. Separating the duty of a patriot from that of an advocate, he must go on reckless of the consequences, though it should be his unhappy fate to involve his country in confusion.[9]

The ominous last sentence was intended to be seen as a veiled threat that Brougham would reveal the king's secret "marriage" to a Catholic, an arrangement that would have required that he give up the crown, thus throwing the country into "confusion."[10]

In medical ethics, likewise, one frequently finds a preoccupation with the grammar of consent—whether actual, anticipated, prior, subsequent, hypothetical, substituted, or proxy—as an essential precondition for legitimate treatment. This ragbag of qualifying adjectives is expressive of the need to find some consent basis for medical interventions: volenti non fit injuria.

For most of those who defend it, what informs this account of professional loyalty as loyalty to clients or patients is recognition of the *dignity* of clients and patients. That includes, broadly, an acknowledgment that clients and patients are moral agents with a capacity to frame for themselves the choices they make, the paths they tread, and the goals they pursue, a capacity that they share with others, and which gives them an equality of standing with others as well as certain prerogatives and

[8] Paul Ramsey, *The Patient as Person: Explorations in Medical Ethics* (New Haven, CT: Yale University Press, 1970), 2–5.

[9] J. Nightingale, ed., *Trial of Queen Caroline* (London: J. Robins, 1820–1821), vol 2, 8. But see also n. 16.

[10] See David Luban, *Lawyers and Justice: An Ethical Study* (Princeton, NJ: Princeton University Press, 1988), 55.

responsibilities with respect to decisions that concern themselves. On such an account, the loyalty of lawyers and doctors to their clients and patients requires them to serve the interests of their clients and patients *as their clients and patients see those interests*: they are to maintain confidentiality as they do whatever they professionally can, at whatever cost they incur, for those whose agents they are.

If we account for professional loyalties as loyalty to clients, then it is not difficult to see how Fletcher is able to marginalize them. This object of loyalty does not seem to have the self-defining importance that Fletcher ascribes to other loyalties.

But there is another and often unspoken account of professional loyalties—one that sees such loyalties as holding between the members of a particular profession. Centrally, this loyalty to the profession has regard to the aspirations, standards, and values that bind the members together *as a profession*. It makes reference to the social goals of the profession, the competency standards that members can be expected to satisfy, and their commitment to the profession's ethical standards. Often all these will be institutionalized through some professional association such as the American Bar Association or the American Medical Association. Although loyalty to the profession may not require its members to belong to such associations, professional organizations tend to act as formal guardians of the professional community, and their standards are often used as benchmarks by the courts. Occasionally, as in other cases, "the profession" and its "organizational embodiment" may come into conflict.[11]

Lawyers and doctors are generally loyal to their professional communities. They constitute a filial *Bund* or collective whose members can be expected to support and, if necessary, favor each other professionally. Although that often involves a salutary commitment to what the profession stands for, it sometimes manifests itself in partisan services (professional courtesies) and, problematically, in the reluctance of doctors and lawyers to testify against each other.

Informing such loyalty to fellows is a sense of interdependent community, one that promotes a solidarity that is necessary and sometimes sufficient to shield its members against external threat and misunderstanding.

Contrary to what I see as the standard view, I wish to suggest that this second account is to be given priority. Professional loyalty is to be located first and foremost in the collective ideals and technical aspirations of the profession in question. These collectively defined norms and standards—the primary objects of professional

---

[11] This was graphically illustrated in the drawn-out dispute over the American Psychological Association's unwillingness to condemn interrogatory torture. See, for example, Sheri Fink, "Tortured Profession: Psychologists Warned of Abusive Interrogations, Then Helped Craft Them," *ProPublica*, May 5, 2009, www.propublica.org/article/tortured-profession-psychologists-warned-of-abusive-interrogations-505.

loyalties—are neither the constructs of an individual consciousness nor Platonic universals, but the shared values, aspirations, and expectations of a community of dedicated service providers. Other loyalties, such as those to clients and fellow professionals, are at best derivative, constrained by loyalty to what gives the profession its raison d'être. As I will indicate, however, this is not always an unproblematic position.

GROUNDING PROFESSIONAL LOYALTIES

The story has now been told quite often of events that took place on January 27, 1986, the day before the space shuttle *Challenger* disaster. Robert Lund, Vice-President for Engineering at Morton Thiokol, the firm that manufactured the O-ring seals located in the joints of the shuttle's solid rocket boosters, presided over a meeting of engineers at which they had unanimously recommended that the shuttle not be launched. In their professional judgment, the temperature at the launch site would be well below that of the known safety range for the seals and, because of known low-temperature corrosion, leaking followed by an explosion was a significant risk. As an engineer, and one of a group of concurring engineers, Lund felt that his loyalties should conform to professional standards. But there was strong resistence to refusal to approve the launch. The Space Center argued that launching the shuttle had some urgency about it. There had been significant delays in the space program, there were grumbles from Congress about the program's funding, and the president wished to mention the launch in his State of the Union message the following evening. So pressure was put on Lund's boss, Jerald Mason, a Senior Vice-President for Morton Thiokol, to get Lund to change his mind. He initially resisted, but then Mason is said to have told Lund: "Take off your engineering hat and put on your management hat." Lund did, and the rest is known and well-publicized history.[12]

Professional loyalties were sacrificed to organizational loyalties. The primary focus of loyalty—at least as it initially represented itself—appeared to be neither the client nor even (though they concurred) the particular group of engineers who met, but certain professional standards shared by the larger engineering community. They were not merely individual standards but communal ones, standards that married technical knowledge and expertise with larger social values and purposes, such as safety, health, and welfare—values and purposes to which engineers are expected to devote themselves.

---

[12] See the documents collected under "Challenger STS 51–L Accident" at http://history.nasa.gov/sts51l.html

Step back for a moment. Professions are privileged occupations. They generally serve broad and important social ends—such as health, public safety, education, justice, and general well-being. Serving those ends in the manner expected of the professions generally requires superior knowledge and skill, and members of the professions ordinarily undertake significant educational preparation. Very often there is considerable public investment in providing the infrastructure for professional education, certification, and updating.

Members of the professions generally have some kind of exclusivity with regard to the services they offer, and they probably exercise significant oversight over their provision of services. In many cases, they are well remunerated. But for the various privileges of professional life, there are also social expectations. It is expected that professionals will offer a consistently high level of service, that their motivation will include the good provided to others and not merely economic gain for themselves, that they will evolve and maintain high technical standards, and that appropriate ethical standards will be observed in service provision.

A professional ethic is central to the professions. It is necessitated by several factors, including the social importance of the service provided, the public trust that is placed in those who provide such services, the privilege of exclusive provision, and the social investment made in professional education. Such professional ethics are structured by the ends, purposes, or ideals that drive the profession and the technical and delivery standards that need to be observed if the public trust vested in the profession is to be sustained. Professional ethics are not simply ethics in general. As Lon Fuller puts it, a code of professional ethics "must contain a sense of mission, some feeling for the peculiar role of the profession it seeks to regulate. A code that takes the whole of right and wrong for its province breaks down inevitably into a mush of platitudes"[13] So, even though a professional ethic must find its ultimate justification in the broader arena of common morality, its own provisions will be governed by the narrower concerns of a particular role and service.[14]

Professional roles frequently become constitutive elements in a person's identity, and therefore the loyalties associated with them can qualify as elements within what Fletcher refers to as the historical self.

Becoming a professional has various dimensions. It involves more than taking on a particular job. It includes membership of a community of fellow professionals and socialization into a set of values and practices—ways of looking at and doing

---

[13] Lon L. Fuller, "The Philosophy of Codes of Ethics," in *Moral Responsibility and the Professions*, ed. Bernard Baumrin and Benjamin Freedman (New York: Haven, 1984), 83.

[14] This is developed at greater length in my *The Ethics of Policing* (Cambridge: Cambridge University Press, 1996), ch. 2.

things—that become significant for one's identity. And within these processes of membership and socialization, the loyalty that one generally acquires includes a commitment to the norms that the professional community embodies. Such loyalties are far more significant than those that Fletcher seeks to marginalize.[15] By focusing on what are in effect derivative or secondary loyalties, he makes professional loyalties appear more problematic and insubstantial than they are.

Although Fletcher does not espouse Brougham's view of loyalty to clients, he nevertheless accepts that a lawyer's professional loyalties are to clients, and his own point of departure is Charles Fried, who, with Brougham, adopts a "pure advocacy model" of legal representation, in which the lawyer's will is subordinated to client interests. This provides too one-sided an account of a lawyer's loyalties to clients, and it does so by mischaracterizing the primary focus of a lawyer's professional loyalties. On the one hand, it tends to ignore or minimize the very significant constraints that are imposed on the lawyer as *a servant of the court*. A lawyer's loyalty to clients cannot be seen as countenancing illegality on the part of the lawyer. It does not allow the lawyer to suborn the perjury of clients or witnesses, destroy incriminating documents, or threaten prosecution witnesses. And it does not require that the lawyer represent clients on matters unrelated to those initially agreed to. As Fletcher quite properly recognizes, a lawyer's loyalty to clients, though significant, is constrained.

On the other hand, and more important, proponents of the pure advocacy model (and Fletcher) fail to appreciate the significance of lawyering *as a profession* and the significance of the constraints on loyalty to clients as elements of a larger conception of the lawyer as a professional. A professionalized conception of lawyering views the legal system and its representatives as creatures of a public trust, designed to ensure or at least contribute to fairness and order in human affairs. The various factors that make up the system—rules of procedure, diversity of roles, qualifications for representation, and so on—are to be understood and judged as contributions to that larger design. To the extent that they fail to sustain an ordered fairness, they are subject to criticism and review. The lawyer is also a *servant of the public*.

Lord Brougham's unvarnished remark that the "advocate . . . knows . . . but one person in the world, [his] client and none other" has contributed to a fundamental

---

[15] Fletcher's distinction between the loyalties that derive from contract, from voluntary commitments, and those that derive from a historical self tends to break down here. Although we voluntarily commit ourselves to some profession, there are generally various rites of passage associated with the achievement of professional status. Had Fletcher focused more on friendships and loyalty in marital relations than on familial and national loyalties, the contrast would not have seemed so great.

misunderstanding of the *profession* of law. His view of client loyalty as that which "does not regard the alarm, the suffering, the torment, or the destruction which [the advocate] may bring on any other" makes hired guns of lawyers; it does not elevate the profession as much as diminish it and bring it into disrepute.[16]

I do not deny that there is a proper place for loyalty to clients within a larger conception of the lawyer's role. Indeed, it is part of the professionalism of a lawyer that clients' interest *are* zealously pursued. But that zealous loyalty to clients finds its primary justification *and boundaries* in loyalty to the wider norms and purposes of the legal community. It is to the latter (understood as an evolving collectivity) that one owes one's primary loyalty *as a professional*, and other loyalties need to be subsumed under or be moderated by that larger loyalty.

David Luban has done much to illuminate this connection between the lawyer's role, the legal system, and common morality in his detailing of what, following Schopenhauer, he calls a fourfold root of sufficient reasoning. By means of a progressive series of questions, this justificatory strategy is designed to show how the various practices of the profession—including the practice of client loyalty—need to be accounted for, justified, and, if necessary, limited.[17] Particular acts of advocacy need to be justified by appeal to larger role obligations, such as the duty to give zealous advocacy. In turn, the duty to be zealous has to be supported by appeal to the role that demands it. The advocate's role needs to be defended by its place within an adversarial system. And the adversarial system itself has to be justified by direct argument—that is, by reference to the larger social values that the adversarial system is intended to secure. This strategy does not rule out zealous advocacy, but the "zeal" cannot be construed and displayed as though it exists in a justificatory vacuum. Nor, if justified, should it be thought to be unconstrained. Whatever the merits of the final outcome of the O. J. Simpson trial, it was a memorable and expensive example of what happens when participants

---

[16] Lord Brougham's remarks did not go unqualified. At a dinner some time afterward, the Lord Chief Justice, Sir Alexander Cockburn remarked: "My noble and learned friend, Lord Brougham . . . said that an advocate should be fearless in carrying out the interests of his client; but I couple that with this qualification and this restriction—that the arms which he yields are to be the arms of the warrior and not of the assassin. It is his duty to strive to accomplish the interests of his clients *per fas*, not *per nefas*; it is his duty, to the utmost of his power, to seek to reconcile the interests he is bound to maintain, and the duty it is incumbent upon him to discharge, with the eternal and immutable interests of truth and justice." George P. Costigan Jr., "The Full Remarks on Advocacy of Lord Brougham and Lord Chief Justice Cockburn at the Dinner to M. Berryer on November 8, 1864," *California Law Review* 19, no. 5 (1931): 523. Lord Brougham, it is reported, assented to this qualification.

[17] Luban, *Lawyers and Justice*, 129–133.

in the system focus on tactical advantage rather than on the securing of just outcomes.[18]

A professional ethic of legal representation needs ultimately to appeal to the profession's overarching norms, and it is to these shared communal norms that the lawyer—as a professional—owes his or her primary loyalty. Loyalty to clients is subordinate to that more fundamental loyalty. Lawyers owe a loyalty to their clients, in part to advance the aims of fair and rational decision making, but also because they may be tempted to satisfy more self-regarding interests. Looking at professional loyalties in this way, we can see how they may represent something that is partially constitutive of the identity of the professional whose loyalties they are.

AN OBJECTION

I have linked professional loyalty to the shared values, aspirations, and expectations of the profession in question. But are there such? And what might they be? The questions are challenging ones, and it might be wondered whether they have as unambiguous an answer as my foregoing remarks have suggested. Some professions (say, engineering) have reasonably clear and broadly shared standards. But I have chosen here to focus largely on law. Can the same be said? Confronting that question, Michael McChrystal doubts whether there is a single uncontested answer.[19] "There may have been a time," he writes, when the community of legal professionals had a shared sense of the profession's norms and aspirations, but that time is gone. Corporate lawyers and those who represent individual clients have very different views of what they are about.[20] Added to that, the profession has diversified, not only in its inclusiveness but also in the development of niche lawyering. There is no shared conception and often a strident polarization, especially over the issue of zealous advocacy.[21]

---

[18] Of course, it might be argued that such tactical struggles are just the way in which we maximize the likelihood of just outcomes. I doubt it. The system is constantly manifesting inadequacies that need attention. And in response to some of those manifest inadequacies, changes are made. Tinkering with social practices is an ongoing affair. One can see this in the evolution of various legal codes of professional responsibility.

[19] I am grateful to Michael McChrystal for his robust and perceptive response to an early attempt to address this issue. See Michael K. McChrystal, "Professional Loyalties: A Response to John Kleinig's Account," *American Philosophical Association Newsletters*, Newsletter on Philosophy and Law, 98, no. 1 (1998): 83–90.

[20] See John H. Heinz and Edward O. Laumann, *Chicago Lawyers: The Social Structure of the Bar* (New York: Russell Sage Foundation, 1982).

[21] In what follows, I confine myself to criminal cases. Some have argued that in civil cases the adversarial system has a different rationale. See David Luban, "The Adversarial System Excuse," and Murray L. Schwartz, "The Zeal of the Civil Advocate," in *The Good Lawyer: Lawyers' Roles and Lawyers' Ethics*, ed. David Luban (Totowa, NJ: Rowman & Allanheld, 1984), chaps. 4 and 6.

At one extreme are those who see the adversary system as a vehicle for nonviolent combat—a process that has its own "laws of war" but depends in the end on who is the strongest in court. It satisfies the parties because their opportunity to have their day in court has been met. The system is seen in pragmatic terms as a way of bringing bloodless closure to social disputes of one kind or another. *In the middle* are those who take justice as their central legal norm and see the lawyer's role in larger social terms. On this view, there is a premium on truthfulness and rules that maximize its likelihood, and, even if they are legally permitted, lawyers are morally bound not to use tactics that would obscure the facts and skew the result away from a just one. *At the other extreme* are those who support a "client-centered" (or what was earlier referred to as a "pure advocacy") approach who, taking the Bill of Rights as their normative touchstone, focus almost exclusively on clients' rights or autonomy. Part of the background to this approach, as in the case of the Bill of Rights, is a belief that because the state (via the prosecution) has power and resources that are unavailable to an individual accused of crime, the individual needs protection against their overwhelming deployment. That protection is provided in large measure by the lawyer. To provide the needed counterweight, the lawyer owes the client "complete loyalty and service in good faith to the best of his ability."[22] Strict confidentiality is assured. Not only may the lawyer's zealous or vigorous advocacy allow the use of whatever tactics the law permits (such as trying to discredit weak but not venal witnesses) but to a degree it also enables the lawyer to be less than fully candid.

Given this division in the understanding of professional norms, how can an admonition to invoke shared norms help to resolve questions about the limits of lawyer-client loyalty? The challenge is a serious one but not necessarily fatal. One possibility is to argue that unanimity about ends is not necessary; all that is required is a dominant view about the profession's shared values. The gladiatorial approach first enunciated has a more limited following than the other two. But there is significant support for both the justice and client-centered approaches. The latter, in particular, has forceful representation in the work of Monroe Freedman,[23] and though his theoretical position is sometimes viewed as too extreme, it has a considerable support in legal practice. Luban robustly defends the former.[24] Assume a profession that is divided on how far a lawyer may go in defense of his client. The dispute is not about whether a lawyer should vigorously advocate for his client, but over the limits of that advocacy. Neither is it a dispute over whether justice should be served, but rather a dispute over

---

[22] *Johns v. Smyth*, 176 F. Supp. 949, 952 (1959).
[23] See Monroe Freedman, *Lawyers' Ethics in an Adversary System* (Indianapolis, IN: Bobbs Merrill, 1975); Monroe Freedman and Abbe Smith, *Understanding Lawyers' Ethics*, 3rd ed. (New York: Matthew Bender, 2004).
[24] Luban, *Lawyers and Justice.*

how justice is best served—whether the lawyer, in advocating for his client, should go in Freedman's direction or in Luban's. In many cases, both accounts will work in tandem. It is, for the most part, only in some hard cases that the two will diverge.

For this reason professional groups such as the American Bar Association, with its motto "Defending Liberty, Pursuing Justice," can nevertheless produce a *Model Rules of Professional Conduct* that is fairly closely followed by most state bar associations.[25] The current *Rules*, first published in 1983, undergoes regular review and revision, as one might hope and expect from a professional body not blessed with either omniscience or moral perfection. For the most part, the point of division comes in the interpretation of the *Rules*, and in particular the rule concerning vigorous advocacy. Although this rule has always been constrained by the requirement that such advocacy takes place within the bounds of the law, there is dispute about the way in which this should be understood. Some would see a firm distinction between what is legally permissible by way of advocacy and what is morally permissible; others take the view that just as the law itself answers to the somewhat anarchic morality of the state of nature, what the law allows is what a public morality allows. Although that may lead to revisions within the code—because the law itself is always open to critical moral review—at the level of a morality that is not beholden to the vagaries of individual judgment, what the law allows is what the lawyer is morally permitted to do.

As I indicated earlier, the challenge posed by McChrystal is serious without being fatal. There is enough cohesion in the legal professional community for considerable agreement about what the profession stands for, even though there are radical differences about what zealous or vigorous advocacy may permit. In a significant—though not crippling—range of cases, that division is of critical importance. That is something the legal community still has to work through. For the most part, however, such differences do not detract from a solid core of agreement about what professional loyalty requires.

A DEEPER ISSUE

I have been speaking as though the shared norms of a professional community obligate members of the profession to show loyalty to both the professional community and those it serves. I have assumed that what we speak of as a profession is a community that embodies norms that make professional loyalty justified and even obligatory. But why should we think that membership in a profession is a good thing?

Becoming a profession is largely a matter of acquiring a certain social status, one that carries various privileges (including financial ones) with it. Professional status

---

[25] Center for Professional Responsibility, ABA, *Model Rules of Professional Conduct* (Chicago: American Bar Association, 2007).

is highly desired, and over the past century—though especially after the increased division of labor that occurred during the twentieth century—a vast number of occupations have sought to professionalize themselves. Not that professionalization is a simple desire for self-aggrandizement. Other social inputs are also important. In societies that are becoming more complex and depersonalized, in which trust is easily betrayed and important interests are at stake in our dealings with service providers, it is important to develop a community of service providers who are sustained by a shared commitment to service excellence.

What this push for professionalization appropriately amounts to is strongly debated. But if one takes the traditional professions as one's template, one comes out with a picture that goes roughly as follows. A profession is characterized by:

1. The provision of a public service
2. A code of ethics
3. Special knowledge and expertise
4. Higher education by its practitioners
5. Broad practitioner autonomy and discretion
6. Self-regulation[26]

There is some wiggle room to or interpretive controversy about each of these items as more and more occupations have managed to edge their way under the professional umbrella. The possession of these six characteristics is believed to warrant professional status. But what moral claims follow from its acquisition (or even aspiration)?

Appeals to what professional loyalty requires will be no stronger than the values and technical expertise that give shape to the profession. Although we may believe that the traditional service professions have little to fear on this account, the movement toward professionalization that has occurred in many occupations should give us some pause. We should not assume that what has achieved, or is gaining in, professional prestige is ipso facto worthy of its pretensions. And this may apply to the classic professions as much as the more recent ones. Some, for example, may wish to argue that divinity has fallen into professional desuetude and the profession of arms should be subject to similar scrutiny.

As a graphic illustration of this need to look deeper, an illustration that is more powerful because of its remoteness, consider the case of Charles-Henri Sanson, the executioner of Paris from 1778 to 1795.[27] Sanson's tenure covered not only the French

---

[26] I have discussed these in much greater detail in *The Ethics of Policing*, ch. 2.

[27] My discussion draws heavily on Arthur Isak Applbaum, "Professional Detachment: The Executioner of Paris," *Harvard Law Review* 109, no. 2 (December 1995): 458–486.

Revolution but also the period known as the Terror. A noteworthy feature of his career was the fact that, despite the turnabouts of that turbulent period—turnabouts that had Sanson executing those for whom he had previously carried out executions—Sanson himself survived the upheavals virtually unscathed. A major factor seems to have been his complete and utter professionalism—his belief that the task of an executioner was a publicly responsible one that needed to be approached with dedication and a commitment to serving the cause of public order as efficiently as possible.[28] The record shows that Sanson took as much professional care and pride in his work as executioner as any surgeon.

Sanson viewed what he did in the larger context of social good. He saw himself as a servant of law and order, a dike against the pressures of the mob and other forces of social disruption. In every aspect of his work, Sanson was concerned to ensure that the due processes of the prevailing law were carried out in a manner compatible with the maintenance of political security and stability and the avowed purposes of public execution.

Yet we might reasonably ask whether the larger purposes he served were worth serving or, if so, were well served through the services rendered by his profession. Even if Sanson's role was sustained by an appeal to law and order, it does not follow that that appeal was appropriately and best served by activities of his kind. We need to ask whether the larger purposes of law and order justified execution and, if so, whether it was justified in the particular cases in which it was prescribed, or at least under the administration that would be making such determinations. Although he should have, Sanson did not address these questions. Even for a professional, concerned not to corrupt the implementation of social policy with idiosyncratic determinations, there must be a way of asking such questions and, even if not answering them, showing that they give one pause.

Arthur Applbaum, on whose account of Sanson I have relied, uses the example of Sanson to call into question the pure advocacy view of lawyering, the view that one must be loyal to clients no matter what.[29] But it may also be used more radically to call into question the rationale for whatever presents itself as a profession and claims the

---

[28] I note here an important distinction between professionalism and professionalization. The latter refers to the process of securing a certain social status for an occupation, whereas the former refers to the manner in which an occupational task is approached. We expect that those who have professional status will act professionally, though some who display professionalism will not have professional status. Professionalism is shown in one's commitment to the *tele* of an occupation, the competence one shows in carrying out its tasks, and in the desire to better oneself in their performance. A janitor no less than a doctor can display professionalism, even though few would consider the former as belonging to a profession. So also may a hitman display great professionalism in how he goes about his task. Sanson not only believed in acting professionally but also saw what he was doing as a profession.

[29] See also Arthur Isak Applbaum, "Are Lawyers Liars? The Argument of Redescription," *Legal Theory* 4, no. 1 (1998): 63–91.

loyalty of practitioners to its norms. No professional service that offers itself as contributory to the public good or seeks to provide that service in certain ways is immune to moral scrutiny. The established professions represent evolving communities that must engage in self-reflexive accountability and, even if they pass muster, cannot close themselves off to further scrutiny. That is one reason why professional self-regulation has proven so problematic. Occupations that have not acquired professional status but have room for and show a commitment to professionalism must likewise open themselves to justificatory questioning. The loyalty here may be to high expectations that have no moral credibility. A bomb maker may be known for his professionalism and loyalty both to those for whom he works and to such standards that may operate within the bomb-making community. But such professionalism, like that of the Nazi extermination program, may constitute the fruit of a poisonous tree.

My point is not to cast aspersions on the professions and professional loyalties or even on professionalism. Insofar as the traditional professions display some commitment to social well-being and professionalism involves a commitment to the standards upheld by an occupational community, we may hope that they can rise to the moral challenges that are put to them. But like friendships and familial and patriotic loyalties, they can also go badly wrong, and the cloak of professional status or professionalism should not be seen as a moral shield.

CONCLUSION

Professional loyalties, if understood as loyalties to a community that seeks to embody in its practices certain normative and social aspirations, may constitute a legitimate and important part of our self-identity. It is no accident that, in presenting ourselves to others, we frequently include our professional affiliations. Although these recitations may be social ploys to ingratiate ourselves, they may also manifest some of our deeper commitments.

How weighty are the loyalties that go with professional commitment? Leaving aside the deeper problem to which I adverted in the last section, we should generally expect professional loyalties to trump organizational ones. Physicians have every right to complain if their work in prison settings is severely hampered by the security or bureaucratic needs of the prison facility. Mason's admonition to Lund to take off his engineering hat and to put on his management hat was a particularly egregious example of asking someone to give organizational loyalties priority over professional ones. As well, there will often be cases in which professional loyalties should take precedence over more limited personal loyalties, such as those represented in friendships. However, once we take into consideration the deeper problem of the professions—their own susceptibility to moral scrutiny—it is less certain that professional loyalties will always take normative priority.

12

TRIBE/NATION

Born in iniquity and conceived in sin, the spirit of nationalism has never ceased to bend human institutions to the service of dissension and distress.[1]

It is in general a necessary condition of free institutions that the boundaries of governments should coincide in the main with those of nationalities.[2]

Nationalism gets a mixed press. Thorsten Veblen speaks for many who see in nationalism everything that is wrong with loyalty; it represents a discriminatory and divisive tribalism that undermines the universal values of humanity. Others, however, see it as essential to political order and stable institutions, and if they see any problems with it, they are deemed to be only contingent. Although Mill is usually thought to be the archetypal liberal, his views on nationalism are often considered a serious blind spot. Does nationalism represent a legitimate expression of loyalty, or does it manifest loyalty's clay feet? In what follows, I will offer a qualified defense.

INTRODUCTION

Nationalism has a checkered history. As recently as 1990, Eric Hobsbawm argued that nationalism was passé. Reflecting on burgeoning cross-cultural fertilization, migration, and globalization, he predicted increasing polyethnicity and a "supranational restructuring of the globe."[3] Maybe the emergence and growth of the European

---

[1] Thorsten Veblen, *Absentee Ownership and Business Enterprise in Recent Times: The Case of America* (New York: B. W. Huebsch, 1923), 38–39.
[2] John Stuart Mill, *Representative Government* (1861), www.constitution.org/jsm/rep_gov.htm.
[3] Eric Hobsbawm, *Nations and Nationalism since 1780: Programme, Myth, Reality* (Cambridge: Cambridge University Press, 1990). Hobsbawm was echoing Marx and Engels: "National differences and antagonism between people are daily more and more vanishing, owing

Union offered some evidence for such a position. But for the most part, Hobsbawm's prediction has been wide of the mark. The 1990s witnessed a surge of often bloody nationalistic fervor, particularly in some of the ex-colonial African states and in the wake of the Soviet and Yugoslavian collapses. Even in Europe, despite the expanding umbrella of the Union, nationalist sentiment and activity has not been absent. It has ranged from the terroristic efforts of Basque separatists to the relatively peaceful division of Czechoslovakia, the substantial devolution of Scotland, active nationalist movements in Galicia, Catalonia, the Flemish region of Belgium, and the reunification of Germany. We could go on.

This last example, however, might give us pause. What, exactly, are we talking about when we speak of a nation and its normative expression in nationalism? Did the reunification of Germany accomplish the unification of a divided *nation* or a divided *country*? How in any case do we distinguish one nation or nationality from another? How important, if at all, *should* national identity be to a person or group of people? Is the loyalty that is implicit in nationalism something to be fostered and maintained, or should it be assimilated to other territorial ideals? May nationalist aspirations be benign, or is there something about national loyalties that makes them inherently suspect, if not morally dangerous? In particular, does nationalism necessitate the formation (or preservation) of a nation-state? How, if at all, is nationalism to be distinguished from patriotism? And if they are to be distinguished, is one to be privileged over the other (presuming that there is something to be said for either)?

These are complex questions, and all controversial, even in their formulation. In the interests of procedural transparency, albeit in anticipation of a more detailed discussion to come, I want to highlight four terms that do a fair bit of conceptual legwork in the discussion that follows in this and the next chapter. They are *nationalism*, *patriotism*, *cosmopolitanism*, and *multiculturalism*. Like many isms, they are mostly creatures of the late eighteenth and early nineteenth centuries,[4] though I would argue that in some cases their roots and the ideas they represent have much longer histories. My purpose, however, is not to provide a history of their development so much as a heuristically helpful schema for assessing what are sometimes seen as competing and contentious loyalties.

I offer the following as a rough working characterization.[5] Although nationalism and patriotism often intersect and even converge, it is important that *in the first*

---

to . . . freedom of commerce, to the world market, to uniformity in the mode of production and in the conditions of life corresponding thereto," *The Communist Manifesto*, 1848, Part II, www.anu.edu.au/polsci/marx/classics/manifesto.html.

[4] See H. M. Höpfl, "Isms," *British Journal of Political Science* 13, no. 1 (January 1983): 1–17.

[5] My account is not only rough but also prescriptive. Each of the terms at issue is used in several senses, and I make no claim to cover whatever others have understood by any of them.

instance we clearly distinguish them.[6] Whereas patriotism is loyalty linked to a specific *polity*—in particular, a country—the loyalty of nationalism is connected primarily to a *people*, defined by other, mostly ethnic, cultural, historical, and symbolic considerations. Although nations generally have a territorial base (a homeland), they are groupings based on ethnic (or perhaps racial), religious, linguistic, folk, or other cultural factors, factors that may be invoked in support of patriotism but may also and often do exist independently of it. In nation-states, nation and *patria*—nationalism and patriotism—tend to converge, and this no doubt contributes to their frequent conflation and confusion. Part of the reason for this convergence, I shall suggest, is that nations usually need some form of autonomy if they are to maintain their integrity, and countries need some form of national identity if they are to inspire patriotic commitment. Cosmopolitanism, an umbrella term for a variety of positions, can be contrasted with either nationalism or patriotism. It can be construed either as an alternative to nationalism, in which a universalistic humanism is embraced that eschews the particularistic connections characteristic of nationalism, or it can be seen as an alternative to patriotism in which—most plausibly—separate self-determining polities have been incorporated into a federation of states bound by certain overarching identity-conferring institutional norms and procedures. I associate multiculturalism with a polity that in some sense embraces national diversity. Obviously, there is more that needs to be said about all these ideas, but some of that will come later.

What strikes one about nationalism and patriotism (as well as cosmopolitanism and multiculturalism) is the strongly normative investment in each. Some writers (often cosmopolitans) firmly reject both. Others support both, usually by conflating them. More often, at least in contemporary debates, nationalism is viewed as a corruption of what patriotism should be. "Patriotism," one of Richard Aldington's characters remarks, "is a lively sense of collective responsibility. Nationalism is a silly cock crowing on its own dunghill and calling for larger spurs and brighter beaks."[7] This differs from many other disparaging comparisons only in the colorfulness of its expression.

In what follows, I begin with a case study in which a benign nationalism calls into question Purfleet's unflattering characterization. This benign example enables me to provide the beginnings of a less toxic account of nationalism that then opens the

---

Insofar as my account of each is to be placed on a continuum of understandings—for each has something to be said for it—it constitutes a *moderate* version of the phenomenon in question.
[6] Stephen Nathanson, a major contributor to the discussion of patriotism, writes that "'patriotism' is simply another name for nationalism" ("Nationalism and the Limits of Global Humanism," in *The Morality of Nationalism*, ed. Robert McKim and Jeff McMahan (New York: Oxford University Press, 1997), 178). I do not think this a helpful starting point.
[7] Reginald Purfleet, in Richard Aldington, *The Colonel's Daughter: A Novel* (New York: Doubleday, 1931), pt. 1, ch. 6, 49.

door to varieties of nationalism that are more problematic. It also helps to provide a framework for asking whether national groupings are the kinds of associations that might or should lay a claim to our loyalty, and, if they do, what limits we should understand such loyalties to have.

CASE STUDY: SORBIAN NATIONALISM

Gerald Stone's *The Smallest Slavonic Nation*[8] offers a history of the Lusatian Sorbs (more commonly known in Germany as Wends), a small Slavic nation whose roots and settlement go back to the seventh century C.E. The Sorbs have never had, nor are they ever likely to have, a separate political identity.

Originally formed from the residues of two of many Slavic tribes, the Milceni and Luzici, the Sorbs once occupied a substantial region between the Rivers Elbe and Oder, but are now confined to a small area in eastern Germany, south of Berlin. Although united nationally, bound by similarities of culture, custom, and especially language (albeit with two extant dialects), the Sorbs are divided religiously and to some extent territorially. Their "Christianization" (a product of their subjugation to others) began in the eleventh century, but during the Reformation, most of the Sorbs of Lower Lusatia (centered in Cottbus/Chóśebuz) became Lutherans, whereas those in Upper Lusatia (in an area bounded by Bautzen/Budyšin, Kamenz/Kamjenc, and Hoyerswerda/Wojerecy) remained predominantly Catholic (although there is also a large Protestant community in and around Bautzen).

The history of the Sorbs is one in which they have vigorously but peacefully sought to retain tribal and later "national" identity in the face of persistent efforts to assimilate or even suppress them. The efforts have not been without effect, and their identity has been an evolving albeit continuous one. Modern-day Sorbs no longer seek to recover or preserve their once pagan heritage, though some elements remain embedded in their religious customs and other folkways. And although the differences in their latter-day religious identities—as Catholic or Lutheran—are visible and important, they are not considered determinative. Sorbian nationalism is stronger among Catholic Sorbs in the south than among the northern Lutheran Sorbs; this, however, may be mostly a function of their historically different political experiences within Saxony and Brandenburg. Sorbian national identity is thought of primarily in terms of an ethnically based folk and religious culture embedded in the language and literature of a Lusatian homeland.

As noted, there have been recurrent efforts to assimilate the Sorbs, and from the seventeenth century until quite recently, there were official policies to Germanize

---

[8] Gerald Stone, *The Smallest Slavonic Nation: The Sorbs of Lusatia* (London: Athlone, 1972).

them, effected largely though not exclusively through constraints on the use of their language. Over the seventeenth and eighteenth centuries, some 300 Lower Lusatian villages were successfully Germanized, and in the nineteenth century, significant numbers of Sorbs traveled to Australia and Texas, ostensibly with (rather than in) the hope of preserving their traditions in a more congenial environment.[9] However, the Australian Sorbs assimilated within a generation or two, intermarrying with their once-German competitors; the small Sorbian-speaking community in Lee County, Texas, persisted somewhat longer. Under National Socialism, Sorbian institutions in Germany were outlawed. But from 1945 to 1989, when the Lusatian region became part of East Germany, the East German authorities supported efforts to preserve Sorbian culture and institutions, albeit on the understanding that Sorbs would not challenge the prevailing regime.[10] One result of political complaisance was that East Germany's dependence on brown coal led to the destruction and "relocation" of 73 Sorbian villages. With German reunification, the Sorbs were granted constitutional protection within the *Länder* of Brandenburg and Saxony. Nevertheless, the forces of economic rationalism have not been quieted, and the Sorbs actively protest against what many of them see as ongoing efforts to destroy their nation.[11]

THE IDEA OF NATIONHOOD

Let us pause here to take stock. The first thing to note—at least in the case of the Sorbs—is that their national identity developed from a previous tribal identity, albeit not that of a single tribe. Although the terms *tribe* and *nation* are notoriously slippery and probably "essentially contestable," one senses that the idea of a nation (if not the word) began to get a grip only when a previously tribal society achieved a certain critical mass and level of complexity while still retaining a fairly high level of integration and self-consciousness. Not only did the intertwining of lineages and unity of language continue but as well a distinctive culture, a diversity of roles and activities, a developed and preserved aesthetic and literary tradition, and an enlarged public sphere were nurtured into existence, along with unifying institutions, such as (in

[9] See George R. Nielsen, *In Search of a Home: The Wends (Sorbs) on the Australian and Texas Frontiers* (1977; rev. ed., College Station: Texas A. & M. University Press, 1989). Economic factors figured significantly in the decision—a famine extending over four years—though, because of their refusal to assimilate, Sorbs were largely relegated to being peasants and small farmers.

[10] See Peter Barker, "From Wendish-Speaking Germans to Sorbian-Speaking Citizens of the GDR: Contradictions in the Language Policy of the SED," in *Finding a Voice: Problems of Language in East German Society and Culture*, ed. Graham Jackman and Ian F. Roe (Amsterdam: Rodopi, 2000), 39–54.

[11] Mostly because of commercial pressures to access the lignite on which their villages stand.

the Sorbs' case) the Domowina.[12] *National* self-identity is characterized by a certain completeness or comprehensiveness, as well as integration of human achievement.

This account of nationalism, though geographically specific and institutionally sustained, is mostly apolitical in the sense that it seeks accommodation and only a soft form of self-determination or autonomy rather than sovereignty. The concern is with national integrity, not with statehood. The Sorbs want a home rather than a country. Although I defend this somewhat heterodox position on nationhood in the next section, I do not wish to deny that its more political expressions have often been (or become) important—if not critical—to its cultural expression.

The latter has come to be true not only in a preservative sense. As Erica Benner notes, the causal connection between ethnic and political nationalism has not just been in one direction. The latter sometimes helps to define and develop the former.[13] Consider the following: (1) Although Jewish ethnicity (given its largely matrilineal perpetuation) might well have persisted in its dispersed form, there is little doubt that the formation of a Jewish state in Palestine has intensified Jewish nationalism. The diaspora may not have been the end of the Jewish people, but Jewish nationalism probably required a geographical center. Nevertheless, that nationalism may not have been as intense had Zionist aspirations been realized in Uganda or Australia (as was once seriously contemplated) rather than in Palestine, where the religious symbolism runs more deeply.

(2) More radically, a polity may sometimes provide the platform for developing a form of nationalism that has no clearly defined tribal roots, as previously discrete groupings come together and—over time—realize a new national identity. This is certainly true of some New World nations, which have forged a national identity from the experience of statehood, rather than vice versa. Australian national identity has been created almost wholly through (controlled) migration—those possessing somewhat diverse national identities having had them reconstituted as a new and evolving identity.[14] And maybe even certain Old World countries can claim their national identity as the product of political statehood. One is tempted to suggest this of the nineteenth-century Italian Risorgimento, though it is also arguable—as the label is intended to suggest—that the sense of nationality represented the restoration

[12] An umbrella organization formed in 1912. See "A Slav Nation in Germany: The Sorbs and Their Organisations," www.domowina.sorben.com/strony/kurzienglish.htm. However, the Sorbian flag was first raised in 1848.

[13] Erica Benner, "Is There a Core National Doctrine?" *Nations and Nationalism* 7, no. 2 (2001): 158–159.

[14] The evolution of a distinctive Australian identity has been most noticeable since 1970, with the abandonment of the White Australia Policy, the loosening of European ties, and Australia's partial reorientation to Southeast Asia.

of a lost national unity, if not in reality then as a national myth. If so, a national consciousness as well as a political unity needed to be re-created. Attempts to create a national identity are often fostered by imaginative re-creations of the past. Australia's largely convict past has provided one such touchstone for national consciousness. And "imaginings"[15] of Rome helped feed the unification of Italy.[16]

(3) Might a similar story be told about the United States—with its even greater diversity of origins and continuing diversity? Here I think one is more likely to speak of patriotism than of nationalism, though writers who make a distinction between ethnic and civic nationalism are inclined to characterize the United States as a case of the latter.[17] Such national identity as exists in the United States is crafted around an ideology and embodied in a polity rather than rooted in ethnicity, and its diversities are celebrated as elements within that ideology ("the melting pot"). In the American case, the greater achievement is the formation of a successful polity with a diversified national identity (hyphenated Americans). What in other contexts might have resulted in various nationalist movements has to a significant extent manifested itself as multiculturalism held together by a supervening national identity.

Whether naturally evolved or artificially constructed, nationalism conveys the idea that a group of people consciously stands for something, for identifiable cultural traditions and a communal style that are worth preserving beyond the wherewithal for their physical survival. Along with that there are symbolic and often revisionary traditions (such as Thanksgiving in the United States). At what point the Sorbs came to see themselves in "national" terms is unclear, though we have clear evidence of a growing national consciousness in the nineteenth century. For the Sorbs, it required the development of a small lay intelligentsia and the creation of a "national" literary tradition.[18] It was given clearer shape by an emergent pan-Slavism that enabled the Sorbs to articulate their distinctiveness in the face of German culture.

In addition—though some writers treat this as a separate and more authentic source of national identity—the forces of modernization that were sweeping through the Western world during the nineteenth century made a contribution of their own. The industrial revolution, the development of the market, and rising literacy actively

---

[15] The term is well-chosen: "to forget and . . . to get one's history wrong are essential factors in the making of a nation" (Ernest Renan, "What is a Nation?" first published in French in 1882, available in English, www.cooper.edu/humanities/core/hss3/e_renan.html).

[16] It is not irrelevant that in 1860 only 2.5 percent of Italians spoke Italian.

[17] The distinction between ethnic and civic nationalism has something to be said for it, though not necessarily as a way to distinguish "good" from "virulent" of nationalism. See Anthony D. Smith, *Nationalism* (Cambridge: Polity, 2001), 39–42.

[18] The fact that the Sorbs overlapped the boundaries of Prussia and Saxony may also have delayed the formation of a unified national identity.

and reactively accelerated nationalist consciousness. The need for markets to have a mobile workforce, a lingua franca, and some degree of regulatory uniformity encouraged hegemonization on the part of dominant ethnicities and the assimilation of minorities.[19] To the extent that bearers of the particularist traditions of a tribal culture wished to preserve them in the face of "modernization," they had to assert themselves in "nationalistic" terms. Although they were often no less nationalistic, those who had dominance did not usually need to have recourse to the language of nationalism. They could condemn nationalism simply as the desire to preserve partisan interest in the face of a common good.

NATIONALISM AND THE NATION-STATE

Many scholars would argue that the primarily ethnocultural account I have given of nationalism is seriously deficient because it includes no central reference to nationalistic strivings for statehood or at least some fairly strong form of political self-determination. Even writers who argue for an ethnocultural dimension to nationalism and resist the explanatory force of modernization usually include some reference to the political dimension or aspirations of nationalism. They would distinguish what I have so far characterized as nationalism as mere national sentiment or consciousness. Nationalism is taken to have a significant political component.

This is a powerful contention, one that is almost irresistible when one looks at nationalist movements. There are, moreover, reasons to accept it. And yet, with some qualifications, I want to offer modest resistance to it.

Certainly I resist the idea that nationalism must contain some conceptual reference to political self-determination, in the form of either sovereignty or some lesser mode of political self-determination. As with the Sorbs, it is altogether possible to have a genuine nationalism without building into it a separate political existence. It is more productive to ask whether a *viable* nationalism, conceived in the ethnocultural terms that I have outlined, can survive apart from demands for or possession of statehood.

In the case of the Sorbs, I think the answer is a qualified yes. Because the Sorbs were divided between Prussia and Saxony, political assertion was always problematic.[20] Even so, they have shown remarkably little passion for what others have deemed to be essential. For example, during the upheavals of 1848, at the very time

[19] See, for example, Ernest Gellner, *Nations and Nationalism* (Ithaca, NY: Cornell University Press, 1983). Although I think that the modern state may have catalyzed nationalist sentiment and aspirations, I am not convinced by Gellner's belief that it originated them.

[20] That, too, has been the fate of the Kurds, caught between Turkey, Syria, Iraq, and Iran, though the Kurds, understandably, have been more active in seeking a separate political identity.

they were designing their own flag, the Sorbs made it clear that their nationalism did not compromise their patriotism:

> Among the Sorbs there is peace, and peace will remain. The Sorbs have always been faithful to their kings and will continue to be faithful. We enjoy everywhere the reputation for the greatest loyalty.[21]

And so it has generally continued with the Sorbs, despite modest efforts to lobby for independence after World Wars I and II.[22] The point is this: if a national grouping is able to perpetuate itself and preserve the integrity of its culture and traditions within the ambit of another country, then it may well be content to do so. No doubt some form of soft political autonomy is required for that—as the Navajos have been able to recover in Arizona, Utah, and New Mexico—but it does not require anything as strong as political self-determination or statehood.

The real problem is that the sociocultural aspirations that are central to much national identity frequently find themselves frustrated by the political vicissitudes of the larger countries in which they are located. That has been the case with the Sorbs: their relatively apolitical traditions have led to dilution and will, perhaps, lead ultimately to their extinction as a distinctive nationality. The various sociocultural and other factors that are constitutive of national identity are vulnerable unless there is some way of securing them against corruption and destruction—even though that machinery need not be the nation's own.

Antagonistic state policies may not be the only or greatest threat to national identity, since some forms of state repression can serve to heighten the sense of national identification. In the Sorbs' case, the economic value of Sorbian lands for lignite strip mining, as well as the post–World War II resettlement of East Germans probably did more to erode the region's unity and change its urban culture than earlier deliberate efforts at Germanization.[23]

A major part of the problem, for the Sorbs as for many other cultural minorities, has been the association of national identity with a particular territory and the problems that arise when that territorial connection is challenged in the name of

---

[21] From a newspaper editorial in March 1848, quoted in Stone, *The Smallest Slavonic Nation*, 24.

[22] See Peter Barker, "Wends, Serbs or Sorbs? The British Foreign Office and the Sorbs Of Lusatia (1942–47)," *German Life and Letters* 48, no. 3 (1995): 362–370.

[23] Not that statehood would guarantee a significantly more secure national identity. Nation-states often exist in something like a Hobbesian tension, able to secure themselves only by entering alliances with others that risk compromising their cultural integrity and self-determination.

some more powerful entity—either a polity or commercial enterprise that wishes to encroach on that territory in the pursuit of some larger purpose (for example, lignite mining) or some other group that considers its ancestral claims to be stronger than those who currently occupy the territory (as has been the case for Israel's Arab-Palestinian population).

Peoples do not generally thrive apart from a particular territory.[24] A people's history, traditions, and symbols are often closely bound up with a physical homeland and particular sites within it. The Sorbs have lived in Lusatia for over a millennium, and some of their major complaints against the German states in which they are incorporated have been connected with land. Not land in the sense of mere earth, but in sites and locations as bearers of history and culture. Recent disputes in which the Sorbs of Lower Lusatia have been involved have concerned the formidable and ultimately successful efforts of a Swedish mining company to destroy and resettle Sorbian villages so that large open-cut lignite mines can be excavated. In the political battle surrounding the destruction of Horno/Rogow and the resettlement of its inhabitants approximately fifteen kilometers away, it was argued (by the mining company) that the Brandenburg constitution protected only the Sorb "settlement area," not its "settlements," and that, because the Sorbs in question would be rehoused within the settlement area, no constitutional violation would be involved. Not surprisingly, the Sorbs were unconvinced, even though they failed in their efforts to prevent it in the European Court of Human Rights. The villagers argued that even though the alternative site was historically Sorbian, it did not embody the long history of Horno.[25]

A sense of territorial connection via history and culture is surely a major factor in the fragility of nationality without statehood. Where more than one national group lays historic claim to the same piece of territory, deep and costly conflict is almost inevitable and seemingly intractable. In the case of the Sorbs, the battle has been with profit, and though they have generally failed in the courts, the conflict has not been a bloody one. In the case of places such as Israel, however, the conflict lies much deeper, and though one might wish for a diplomatic resolution (as may eventually succeed in Northern Ireland), the prospects are not good. Elsewhere, as in the break-up of Yugoslavia, we have seen the difficulties of resolving territorial claims through diplomatic means.

---

[24] Though the persistence of certain national diasporas suggests that territory may sometimes be secondary to social and religious factors.

[25] Details can be found in Michael Gromm, "The Battle of Horno," http://zb.eco.pl/zb/164/orginal/horno.htm. See also Catherine Hickley, "Germany's Sorb Minority Fights to Save Villages from Vattenfall," *Bloomberg.com*, December 18, 2007, www.bloomberg.com/apps/news?pid=20601088&sid=aCW1fh0XInBE&refer=muse.

To the extent that national sentiments translate themselves into ambitions for po-litical self-determination, there will often be competition—and possibly significant conflict—between nationalistic and patriotic loyalties. Those committed to the pres-ervation of an existing polity will see nationalist sentiment as a threat and thus seek to curb it. An illustration is provided by the growth of Québécois nationalist senti-ment in Canada. Although much early French-Canadian nationalism focused on the promotion of cultural and religious institutions, the rise of the Québécois in 1960 represented a major refocusing of that sentiment toward political separation. What it meant was that nationalism and patriotism came to be cast as alternative rather than compatible possibilities.[26]

Nevertheless, both quiescent Sorbian nationalism and predominantly democratic Québécois nationalism stand in contrast to the virulent nationalism that has contrib-uted so much to the backlash against the fostering of national identity. Indeed, they raise the question whether nationalism is a single phenomenon or whether, rather, there is a spectrum of nationalisms with varying roots and rationales, making it problematic to speak at all of nationalism and of the value of national loyalties. I am tempted to concede the latter. It does not, however, relieve us of the task of determin-ing whether, even in its more benign cases, we ought to foster or even acquiesce in a sense of nationalist identity and loyalty.

Before I focus more specifically on the value that national loyalty may have, let me again presage my ultimate conclusion, namely, the gradual convergence (even if not a coalescence) of nationalism and patriotism. Just as national identity and aspirations will, given the exigencies of human social existence, most likely move in the direc-tion of some form of political autonomy, so constitutionally constructed countries, in order to generate and retain the allegiance of their citizens, will seek to create something like a national identity for themselves. This will occur either de novo (as in the United States and Switzerland) or be constructed out of preexisting ethnocultural materials (allowing that these do not represent exclusive alternatives).

THE VALUE OF NATIONALISM

Let us begin again with the Sorbs. What value might there be to Sorbian national iden-tity and the kind of loyalty to it that would seek its perpetuation and advancement?

---

[26] One can imagine a situation in which a national group might consider that its future se-curity would be most likely ensured by incorporation into a larger whole in which it would constitute a small (protected) minority. Thus it has been argued that Singapore—which, for partially nationalistic (ethnic, social, and cultural, as well as economic) reasons, separated itself from Malaysia—should attach itself to the United States. See Pang He How, *Singapore: From Hope to Certainty* (Maroubra, NSW, Australia: Privately Published, 2003).

First of all, the value possessed by Sorbian national identity need not be something that attaches to it qua Sorbian rather than as qua German or Japanese. Indeed, to think of its value in that way may be to encourage what is often seen as the toxic character of nationalism. It is not that what Sorbian culture has to contribute to human advancement and well-being is something in which other national identities are deficient, or even that what it offers is superior to that available through surrounding or other groupings. The Sorbs have been content to leave (other) Germans to their ways and even to learn the German language. Their contention has been—in effect—that their Sorbian traditions and culture are part of who *they* are and of what *they* value as an element in *their* human experience. No doubt there is also a belief that Sorbian traditions and culture are good things for people to have and that there is therefore value to Sorbs preserving, developing, and passing on their culture. But this recognition is not incompatible with the view that other cultural traditions might also be good things to have and to be worth preserving and that it would be good for (most) other people to preserve their own cultural traditions.

The point is that these traditions are *theirs* and that, by virtue of that association—that connection, that identification—there is reason *for them* to preserve their national identity that others may not have (though, of course, others may have a similar reason for preserving their own). As long as there are no overriding reasons for seeking to destroy a particular cultural tradition, those who are brought up in it may see that particular tradition as something they value for its own sake and to which they have some loyal obligations. Their national identity gives shape to a form of life, it provides a sense of belonging or home, and it connects them with a community in whose challenges and achievements they willingly share, all things that will be intrinsically valuable to them.[27]

Nevertheless, it does not follow from the argument that some form of nationalism is valuable to those who are committed to it that one *ought* to have a sense of *national* connectedness with others. It is entirely possible that a person could live happily and well within the confines of a much more narrowly circumscribed grouping (as do many of the Amish of Lancaster County), as members of an eclectic social culture (as do some devotees of large urban centers such as New York), or even as a cosmopolitan citizen of the world. Yet, for a significant number of people, only something as broad (or narrow) as a national culture will provide the scale needed for their sense of identification and their flourishing—or at least for their flourishing in ways that would generally be recognized as *flourishing*. Admittedly, the argument becomes quite tendentious at this point. We do not have a very clear or fixed idea of what the

---

[27] See Avishai Margalit, "The Moral Psychology of Nationalism," in *The Morality of Nationalism*, ed. McKim and McMahan, 84–85. This need not be seen as an argument for stagnation.

constitutive ingredients of our human and individual flourishing are, and so, even if it is important for our own flourishing, it is difficult to generalize the argument that a national identity is essential to human flourishing.[28]

Second, the foregoing prompts an additional—external—argument for preserving and fostering national identities, arising from the fact that identity as a Sorb, German, or Japanese is valuable to Sorbs, Germans, and Japanese, respectively. This is the liberal view that there is a value to there being a diversity of cultures.[29] This can be parsed in more than one way. It may be interpreted as an argument for the intrinsic value of diversity. If that is so, however, it will not work well on its own. There is probably no value to diversity as such without it being presupposed that the diverse objects have some identifiable value: on the one hand, little is added to the value of sand by the diversity of shapes possessed by individual grains; on the other hand, the world is unlikely to be poorer for the virtual disappearance of the smallpox virus, and, notwithstanding our delight in natural diversity, we might well applaud efforts to rid the world of certain species of virus-carrying mosquitoes.[30]

But other ways of thinking about diversity might be expected to appeal to those for whom cosmopolitan or multicultural options are likely to be appealing. Those who are strongly averse to restrictive and exclusive political nationalism often proclaim the virtues of ethnocultural eclecticism. Their personal horizons are not limited by a single cultural experience, however coherent and rich it may be, but encompass other national traditions—Japanese aesthetics, Russian literature, Italian theater, French cuisine, American traditions of liberty, Australian-style mateship, and so on. An important thing to note about this way of valuing diversity, however, is that it would probably not be available were it not for the persistence of strong ethnocultural national traditions. The continuing development of Frenchness would not have arrived at a Japanese-style aesthetic any more than Greek ethnocultural traditions would have evolved into Russian literature. This is not an argument for national diversity

---

[28] The difficulty we confront in identifying the ingredients for human flourishing are probably a good thing for, as is the case with most salvationist traditions, there would otherwise be a strong temptation to impose such a conception on others. Whatever the deficiencies of a liberal social order, with its acceptance of diverse ways of flourishing, it is often rooted in the acknowledgment of our epistemic shortcomings. For further reflections on this, see John Kleinig and Nicholas G. Evans, "Human Flourishing, Human Dignity, and Human Rights." *Law and Philosophy* 32, no. 5 (September 2013): 539–564.

[29] See, for example, C. L. Ten, "Multiculturalism and the Value of Diversity," in *Multicultural Citizens: The Philosophy and Politics of Identity*, ed. Chandran Kukathas (St. Leonards, NSW, Australia: Centre for Independent Studies, 1993), 7–16; also C. L. Ten, ed., *Multiculturalism and the Value of Diversity* (Singapore: Marshall Cavendish, 2004).

[30] For some preliminary discussions, see Mathieu Bouville, "Is Diversity Good? Six Possible Conceptions of Diversity and Six Possible Answers," *Science and Engineering Ethics* 14, no. 1 (2008): 51–63.

for its own sake, simply because it requires that the national traditions need to meet some ethically acceptable threshold. But given that we—here a broadly liberal we—often come to value a diversity of cultural artifacts, we need to acknowledge the conditions under which those artifacts are likely to emerge and remain available.[31]

And third, insofar as it is common for people to be raised within a particular ethnocultural tradition, albeit not that of the Sorbs, we may also have reasons of reciprocity for recognizing and appreciating national cultures other than our own. We have reason to acknowledge the integrity of their commitment as we may recognize its importance in our own case.[32] This may be so with respect to other particularistic associations. One reason for your recognizing the integrity of my family relations and friendships is that you have family relations and friendships of your own that you value as I value my own. Even if I think that my national traditions are better than yours—a hazardous judgment, given the ways in which our judgments are likely to be colored by our own traditions—that will not generally provide a sufficient reason for my seeking to interfere with yours. Unless there is something about your tradition that makes it manifestly evil, there are at the very least strong reasons of reciprocity to tolerate yours.

The situation is altered somewhat—though not entirely—should one choose or even need to relocate to the domain of another national grouping. Although one might anticipate that the national group into whose domain one goes will accept one for what one is, it can become a problem if the migrant group begins to make serious inroads on the national identity of the group that has accommodated them. That often occurs if the migrant group becomes economically or politically dominant. Thus the presence of large numbers of people of Indian background in Fiji and the economic dominance of Chinese in Malaysia have at times been sources of serious tension. In the case of the Sorbs, although East German transfers into Sorbian areas after World War II did not lead to civil strife, there were deleterious social and cultural consequences.

What migration generates—though we shall leave the argument for it until the next chapter—is the need, politically, to foster some measure of multiculturalism, that is, the need to provide opportunities within polities for multicultural recognition. As I wish to understand it, multiculturalism involves an acceptance that

---

[31] See, for example, Margalit, "The Moral Psychology of Nationalism," 79. We also need to recognize that eclecticism has some hazards associated with it—the likelihood that in cherry-picking cultural traditions we may dilute and even distort them (yoga without the metaphysics), even though in doing so we may also develop them in new and sometimes worthwhile directions.

[32] The sense of obligation may be muted if the tradition is robust and little would be lost were A or B or C to "convert" to another tradition.

national identities are significant for those who possess them, that national identities offer frameworks for personal development that are important to the flourishing of those who have them, and that for all of us, there is—within certain bounds—a value to there being a diversity of national cultures.[33]

Such an argument need not deny but rather embrace the idea that nationality is an evolving social phenomenon, to be preserved but not frozen, and permitted to develop in ways that enable people to take stock and accommodate change. The reason for considering this in the next chapter is that countries structured by liberal polities will provide a better framework for national diversity than simple national groupings.

Even though the foregoing is intended to provide a case for the development and perpetuation of national loyalties, it does not provide an argument for requiring those who are part of a national group to develop loyalty to it or remain within it. No doubt parents who are members of a national group and who wish their children to become and remain loyal to it will have familial reasons for nurturing their children in its ways. They will have that right as a result of their position as parents, not because the "guardians" of a national culture are justified in requiring it. If children brought up within a national culture are no longer under familial tutelage and become disenchanted with it or feel too confined by it, they may seek to abandon it.

That a national identity is important to those who have one goes only to the permissibility of their retaining and fostering it and to a prima facie obligation on the part of others to tolerate and even support it, but not for requiring it of those adults who may not wish to keep it. Although national diversity may be a liberal good to be welcomed, no particular *nation* qua *nation* has any claim to require the loyalty of its members, except in the negative sense that those who may be disaffected ought not to subvert the national aspirations of those for whom it remains a value. That, of course, is not the same as refusing to challenge the status quo.

THE PERILS OF NATIONALISM

As we currently find them, humans usually have fairly strong tribal inclinations. That is, even if they have been born into a particular polity, their lives tend to be strongly influenced—often through their own families—by what I have referred to as a national culture. It may be Greek or Chinese or Jewish/Israeli. And that may be the case

---

[33] We encounter significant challenges when we confront deeply racist or sexist national cultures, in which, for example, there may be deeply rooted practices such as slavery, female genital cutting, or child marriage. Even here, though, it is arguably better to try to bring about cultural change from within rather than seeking to impose it from without. However, migrant groups who wish to continue in such practices have a more difficult argument to make.

whether they are brought up in Greece, China, or Israel, respectively, or the United States.[34]

It is easy to understand how nationality may be a formative influence in a homeland. The more interesting cases are those in which the national identity is acquired outside the homeland or—perhaps just as accurately—within a new homeland. The hyphenated American will often feel a dual identity—on the one hand, as ethnically Greek or Chinese and, on the other, as American. This is likely where the culture is both diverse and open.[35] Here, a multiculturalism may exist that is broadly welcoming of the different nationalities within its midst. Over time, no doubt, and especially if the new homeland is congenial, significant accommodation is likely to occur, resulting either in the formation of a dual identity or in almost complete assimilation. Thus, for Greek Americans, Thanksgiving, July 4, the Civil War, and the bombing of Pearl Harbor will eventually become events with which transplanted nationals (or at least their children and children's children) will identify, even though these events were not part of their own historical experience.

My argument for the generally enriching experience of national identity needs to be qualified by what may also be its cloying and repressive effects. Although (in *Representative Government*) Mill argues somewhat awkwardly for the importance of "nationality" to the existence of free institutions, he is no less insistent (in *On Liberty*) that a strongly homogeneous culture may be oppressive. His paean to individuality is a warning against treating cultural norms as firmly constraining boundaries. Thus, he writes:

> It is not by wearing down into uniformity all that is individual in themselves, but by cultivating it and calling it forth, within the limits imposed by the rights and interests of others, that human beings become a noble and beautiful object of contemplation; and as the works partake the character of those who do them, by the same process human life also becomes rich, diversified, and animating, furnishing more abundant aliment to high thoughts and elevating feelings, and strengthening the tie which binds every individual to the race, by making the race infinitely better worth belonging to.[36]

---

[34] I shall suggest in the next chapter that countries, as well as national groups, will tend to develop a national culture of their own—that is, the Italian, Irish, German, and African-slave identities that went to America will be subsumed under and within an evolving secondary national culture that is distinctively American.

[35] If the national culture is not open or is aggressively assimilationist, quite opposite effects are possible. Either the familial national identity will predominate as the group seeks to secure itself against an alternative identity that is either not available to it or threatening it, or the familial national identity will be given up. I am not sure what conditions must hold for one or the other of these directions to be taken.

[36] John Stuart Mill, *On Liberty*, ch. 3.

No doubt what are construed as the "rights and interests of others" and even Mill's own expressed commitment to the idea of "man as a progressive being" can be heavily influenced by narrowly ethnocultural values, traps into which he himself falls when comparing national cultures.[37] Nevertheless, the central impetus in his support for nationalism is on the capacity of particular national traditions to create and sustain "free institutions." Individuality is fostered only within a society that supports free institutions, and—he thinks—free institutions are possible only when there is a broadly shared sense of national identity.

There is no necessary tension here, for what Mill views as important to the development of individuality—a rich diversity of cultural possibilities—is likely to be available only if a society is willing to embrace some degree of national diversity—some measure of multiculturalism.

There remains, nevertheless, a tension. Every national culture, insofar as it is directed toward its own perpetuation, will place certain constraints on its members by supporting some forms of flourishing to the exclusion of others. And in some cases those may be constricting and discriminatory. My response to that, though, is not to reject the fostering of national cultures, but to reinforce the need to recognize all cultures as evolving, not fixed, and therefore as needing some degree of openness to such developments. Provided that the members of a national culture have the opportunity and ability to offer culturally sensitive responses to alternative ways of thinking and being, there should not be any reason to respond in garrison-like fashion.

The pressures that tend to transform national consciousness into a political project—the nation-state—not only secure nations against the threat of destructive interference but often transform a national identity that can be personally and socially enriching from being benign into something oppressively malign. National consciousness can become aggressively exclusionary—ethnically, racially, or religiously. It need not do so (as in the case of the Québécois or Czechs), but the capacity to exclude and the desire to secure one's identity against perceived threats to it often lead, on the one hand, to a denigration or even demonization of the other and, on the other hand, to terroristic or autocratic uses of power. No doubt some form of "liberal nationalism" is possible, but even in what might be seen as a paradigmatic instance of liberal nationalism, albeit of a civic rather than ethnic kind, centered on the so-called American way of life, the United States has sometimes expressed itself in exceptionalist terms. Those who wish to make the world "safe for freedom" have been guilty of seeking to force others to be free. And so, what might appear as

[37] See, for example, Michael Levin, *J. S. Mill on Civilization and Barbarism* (London: Routledge, 2004); Beate Jahn, "Barbarian Thoughts: Imperialism in the Philosophy of John Stuart Mill," *Review of International Studies* 31, no. 3 (July 2005): 599–618.

the most benign form of nationalism—gradually constructed not out of an ethnic or racial identity or religious tradition, but out of liberal ideals—can come to express itself oppressively, as was the case during the McCarthy years and has more recently occurred in the invasion of Iraq.[38]

LIMITS TO NATIONALISM

It has always been a challenge for certain kinds of cosmopolitanism to represent themselves in such a way that the so-called family of man is more than a hollow phrase. We are more easily drawn to particularistic associational connections than to humanity as such. Particularistic associations need not exclude but can help us ground ourselves manageably within the larger framework of humankind. And nationalism constitutes a particularistic connection of a fairly broad kind, among the broadest on offer now that the sun appears to have set (for a time) on empire.

Many varieties of cosmopolitanism offer themselves as antidotes to the chauvinism that often accompanies nationalistic identification. They summon us to look beyond the attachments of place and culture to recognize our common humanity. Moreover, at least for those of us who have been the beneficiaries of a broadly liberal democratic experience, it seems entirely reasonable that, over a period of time, some who have been brought up with a fairly narrow national identity should detach themselves from many of the particularities of that identity and either adopt another one or, more likely, develop an identity that is a creative amalgam of several. Increasing migration and travel have impacted both national cultures and those who have been reared within them in ways that need not be seen as detrimental to either. National cultures were never fixed; at most, one could expect that the pace at which they changed would not be too disruptive to their adherents. And many individuals who leave behind the trappings of their national backgrounds do so by degrees— adding other cultural interests here, leaving old traditions there. There need be no disloyalty about it, for it may not represent a selfish attempt to deny or disparage the traditions of one's youth, but instead a desirable expression of human growth and flourishing.

We should be concerned about cultural homogenization and with it the potential for cultural flattening. The McDonaldization of the world, whatever may be said for it, along with the export of a pervasively Western youth culture, has not been an unmixed benefit, especially as its corporatization has frequently been disruptive of local and, for those locals, intrinsically valuable ways of being. At the same time, the

---

[38] The Iraq war was allegedly initiated as a preemptive strike against threatening weapons of mass destruction. But the absence of the latter popularized "Operation Iraqi Freedom."

hardening of national arteries has also brought with it a crushing of individuality. Mill strove for balance when he wrote:

> Whatever really tends to the admixture of nationalities, and the blending of their attributes and peculiarities in a common union, is a benefit to the human race. Not by extinguishing types, of which, in these cases, sufficient examples are sure to remain, but by softening their extreme forms, and filling up the intervals between them.[39]

But Mill's sentiments are more acceptable than his way of expressing them. We want to encourage and preserve within certain broad moral boundaries the diversity of human types and ways of living. At the same time, we want to enrich existing ways of living through the cross-pollination of ethnicities and cultures. And we want to do the latter without destroying the former. How to do that is the challenge.

CONCLUSION

At an individual level, nationality need not be eschewed, but neither need it be seen as obligatory. A nonexclusionary nationalism can provide a rich framework for personal development, a sense of belonging that has historical and ideological depth. At the same time, though, there are dangers to making one's heritage a central source of identity. At a collective level, too, a national identity may contribute significantly to our understanding of human possibilities and diversity. Yet it, too, especially if it seeks to secure itself through political means, may endanger that which makes it valuable.

In the next chapter, I suggest that much of what is valuable in nationalism can be retained through the cultivation of a responsible patriotism. Patriotic loyalties can be defended most plausibly, and are likely to survive most acceptably, when informed by a variety of national loyalties—commitment to a polity and broad traditions that reflect and enable a multicultural or multiethnic society.

[39] *Representative Government*, ch. 16, http://philosophy.eserver.org/mill-representative-govt. txt.

13

COUNTRY

No matter that patriotism is too often the refuge of scoundrels. Dissent, rebellion, and all-around hell-raising remain the true duty of patriots[1].

"My country, right or wrong," is a thing that no patriot would think of saying except in a desperate case. It is like saying, "My mother, drunk or sober."[2]

Barbara Ehrenreich's and G. K. Chesterton's contrary riffing on Samuel Johnson and Stephen Decatur capture much of what has bothered many about patriotism. It has offered a cover for excess and absolutism. Although Decatur aspired to his country always being in the right, it claimed his fealty whether or not it was. Chesterton was less than persuaded. Johnson, on the other hand, saw in patriotism a refuge for scoundrels—the exploitation of a noble name by rogues and villains. Without exactly denying it, Ehrenreich sees better possibilities for patriotism—the dissent that goes with being a loyal opposition. Our purpose in this chapter is to offer a way through these disparate accounts and to link patriotism more precisely to the nationalism already discussed.[3]

SOME DEFINITIONAL PRELIMINARIES

Dictionaries—and most commentators—are inclined to characterize patriotism as "love of one's country." Each of the major terms presents its own challenge.

---

[1] Barbara Ehrenreich, "Family Values," in *The Worst Years of Our Lives: Irreverent Notes from a Decade of Greed* (New York: Harper Collins, 1991).

[2] G. K. Chesterton, "A Defence of Patriotism," in *The Defendant* (1901), www.cse.dmu.ac.uk/~mward/gkc/books/The_Defendant.html.

[3] Some of the material in this chapter is extended and defended in a forthcoming volume, John Kleinig, Simon Keller, and Igor Primoratz, *The Ethics of Patriotism: A Debate* (Malden, MA: WileyBlackwell, 2014).

Although I have no strongly principled objection to the favored representation, it is more helpful to see patriotism as loyalty to one's country.[4] Loyalty is inherently particularistic in a way that love is not. I happen to love New Zealand, though it is not my country. And I also love my apartment in New York, though it is not mine in the sense that my country is mine. I identify with my country in a way that I do not with my apartment. Further, although *love* captures a passion that many patriots feel for their country, such passion is not required for patriotic commitments to be genuine. Of course, one might not wish to deny that a patriot who answered the call to serve also loved his country, but it may be the kind of love more closely associated with service to or concern for another than that characterized by passion. Part of the problem is that the English word *love* covers too much. As Eamonn Callan observes, it is broad enough to cover a fickle love, whereas patriotism must be construed in terms of constancy.[5] Not that I deny the passion that is often associated with patriotism. Just because patriots identify with the country they willingly serve, we should expect there to be an emotional component to their patriotism, even though it may also be muted and mixed with apprehension and even some upset, because they have been called on to serve in a particular way. We do not have similar problems with loyalty, even though loyalty itself is generally infused with feeling.

The other definitional concern is with the object of patriotic loyalty—the *patria* or country. One's country is not to be identified with either a state or government, although a country will almost always include a polity. Mark Twain's remark that his "kind of loyalty was loyalty to one's country, not its institutions or office holders," draws on the point.[6] We need to think of a country in more holistic terms, generally as comprising a land, a terrain, a people, a culture, a history, a collective self-understanding, and a network of social institutions and traditions framed and bound together by the juridical structure of a governing order.[7] A country is a narrative entity that reaches

---

[4] See also Alasdair MacIntyre, *Is Patriotism a Virtue?* Lindley Lecture, 1984 (Lawrence: University of Kansas Press, 1984), 4; Simon Keller, *The Limits of Loyalty* (Cambridge: Cambridge University Press, 2007), ch. 3.

[5] Eamonn Callan, "The Better Angels of Our Nature: Patriotism and Dirty Hands," *Journal of Political Philosophy* 18, no. 3 (2010): 249–270. Cf. also Eamonn Callan, "Love, Idolatry, and Patriotism," *Social Theory and Practice* 32, no. 4 (October 2006): esp. 527.

[6] Mark Twain, *A Connecticut Yankee in King Arthur's Court* (1889; London: Penguin, 1971), ch. 13.

[7] Whether all of these are necessary and jointly sufficient is a question I leave aside. As with most complex concepts, there is a tendency for somewhat divergent conceptualizations to develop from core features, and, as is common with social concepts, competing normative considerations are also likely to be at work. Wittgenstein's analogical use of a rope when explicating social concepts has a parallel in George Orwell's characterization of England as "an everlasting animal stretching into the future and the past, and, like all living things, having the power to change out of recognition and yet remain the same," in "England Your England"

backward and forward and embodies distinctive (though not uniform) forms of life. Real patriotism, like loyalty in general, is not free-floating—one does not start off as patriotic and then look for a country to be patriotic to. One's patriotism is always developed—if it develops at all—in the context of some particular country, whether it is Australia or the United States or Ecuador. Certainly it can change, but it is always particularized. The person who wishes that there were a country about which he could feel patriotic is not patriotic, even though he would like to be.

There is clearly more to be said about what a country is and what it is about a country that inspires or grounds patriotism, but some of that will emerge later. It should, however, be noted that the idea of a country already carries within it the seeds of a cultural nationalism. Those who seek to defend their country are interested not only in its acreage or government but also in its cultural character and political traditions, its freedom from domination by subversive ways as well as powers. The questions we need to consider are whether "a country" constitutes the kind of associational entity that warrants and even requires our loyalty and, if so, the character and demandingness of that loyalty. Each of those questions harbors certain problems for patriotic loyalty.

I begin by briefly revisiting what I have already said about the associational dimensions of human flourishing and then consider the conditions under which that flourishing is likely to take place. That will draw attention to the political dimensions of patriotism and lead to a discussion of the relation between a polity and a country and, further, to what it is about a country that evokes (or should evoke) patriotic attachments. I consider the moral status of such attachments before turning to some of the moral constraints that patriotic loyalties ought to observe and, finally, the convergence of nationalism and patriotism.

HUMAN FLOURISHING AND HUMAN ASSOCIATION

It has been an underlying assumption of this study that human beings are essentially social. As we earlier observed, our flourishing is enabled and to some extent constituted by various associational connections and ties—families, friends, schools, and a range of other relations and institutions through which we learn to be autonomous, sensitive, morally discerning, and competent beings, able to craft, within broader or narrower limits, decent lives for ourselves. We have also noted that some of our associational connections will come to be valued for their own sake. They become sources

(1941), part 1 of *The Lion and the Unicorn*, www.netcharles.com/orwell/essays/lion-and-unicorn1.htm. Add to this the challenges posed by "essential contestability," and attempts to delineate the idea can become highly nuanced.

of satisfaction and meaning to us. This is almost certainly true of good friendships, but it will often be or become true of other relations and associations. In such cases, in which we identify with the associative others as "ours," we will also develop bonds of loyalty.

Again, to recapitulate, associative connections may be either self-chosen or given, allowing that there may be degrees to which we can exercise control over them. We have little choice about our family or ethnicity. We generally have considerable choice over those who will be our friends and marriage partners. Patriotic ties, or the citizenships in which such ties are usually grounded, tend to be unchosen, a fact that can have some relevance to the acceptability of a person's patriotism. Although we may have some choice about whether to be patriotic (or to give up our patriotism), patriotism is usually inculcated, and we have even less choice about the object of our patriotism.

For those of us privileged to live in liberal democratic societies, flourishing generally occurs through multiple associational involvements—a significant number of friends, different family groupings, and various educational, cultural, vocational, religious, sporting, occupational, and professional involvements. Even though it is appreciated that disruptive conflicts will occasionally occur, these involvements work for the most part in manageable concert. In the event that tensions arise, there are recognized prioritizations What is of critical importance, however, is that many of these associational groupings and connections, along with the people who populate them, require substantial infrastructure and mediating structures if they are to be sustained. That is, our flourishing presupposes a stable and functional network of supporting institutional structures and processes.

It is at this point that the issue of a polity (or, more accurately, polities) arises—though not de novo, because the cluster of associations that are important to our flourishing would not have developed to the point at which they could help us were it not for the prior existence of a (local, regional, and national) political order. Let me now attempt to develop this.

FLOURISHING AND CIVIC ORDER

The ultimate question here is whether a person's country or *patria* is the kind of associative arrangement that it would be good or even obligatory to value for its own sake, as one's own, thus involving loyal commitments and obligations. It is by no means self-evident that it is. Paul Gomberg, for example, argues that patriotism is on a par with racism.[8] Simon Keller has forcefully argued that patriotism almost inevitably

---

[8] Paul Gomberg, "Patriotism Is Like Racism," *Ethics* 101 (1990): 144–150.

engenders bad faith.[9] And Igor Primoratz concludes that unless one construes patriotism as ethical patriotism—something of a revisionist claim—patriotism is morally neutral: "morally speaking, it has nothing to be said for it."[10] So it is incumbent on me to offer an argument for seeing what Primoratz dubs "worldly patriotism" as something to be morally anticipated in the ordinary course of events. I then attempt to meet Keller's charge, which is grounded in a critique of loyalty more than of country.

There is heuristic value in working with a variant of a familiar though admittedly controversial argument in political philosophy—that of the social contract. For present purposes, its more controversial aspects can be harmlessly bracketed.

As I wish to exploit it, the argument starts with an assumption that, *as we encounter them*, humans are agents whose relations with each other are, at their deepest level, appropriately governed by moral considerations. The point is not that all human conduct is morally motivated and justified, but that in determining how to live, humans give a notional preeminence to moral considerations.[11] This is not to dispute Bernard Williams's arguments about the importance of personal projects, but to recognize that our deepest projects also need to pass some form of moral muster if the claim that without them we would not have a life worth living is to bear the argumentative weight it is given.[12]

The capacity to determine our conduct by means of normative judgments of appropriateness and inappropriateness, as well as the exercise of this capacity, is what for Kant constitutes our dignity as humans: "the dignity of man consists precisely in his capacity to make universal law, although only on condition of being himself also subject to the laws he makes."[13] Classical social contractarians such as Locke spoke instead of a "natural law," discernible by all rational beings as properly mediating the relations of right holders. However we formulate the argument—and there are many ways of making it—the fundamental point is that we accord moral considerations a distinctive and authoritative place in human associational life.

---

[9] Simon Keller, "Patriotism as Bad Faith," *Ethics* 115 (April 2005): 563–592.

[10] Igor Primoratz, "Patriotism: A Deflationary View," *Philosophical Forum* 23, no. 4 (Winter 2002): 456.

[11] Cf. Joseph Butler: "Had it [conscience] strength as it has right; had it power, as it has manifest authority, it would absolutely rule the world" (*Fifteen Sermons*, http://anglicanhistory.org/butler/rolls/, II.14). Of course, and here is a point that I am already bracketing, there is debate about this supposed "overridingness" of moral considerations.

[12] Bernard Williams, "Persons, Character and Morality," reprinted in *Moral Luck* (Cambridge: Cambridge University Press, 1981), 14, 18, and esp. 17; but cf. Williams, in J. J. C. Smart and Bernard Williams, *Utilitarianism: For and Against* (Cambridge: Cambridge University Press, 1973), 116.

[13] *Groundwork of the Metaphysic of Morals*, trans H. J. Paton (New York: Harper & Row, 1956), sect. II, Akad. 440.

Taken together with my earlier remarks about the essential sociality of humans, morality (not to be identified with a particular moral theory) thus assumes a fundamental importance for human flourishing.[14] Add to this the point made at the end of the last section, namely, that for those whose conception of human flourishing has been nurtured by liberal values, there will be a great diversity and complexity to associative involvements. Two further features of this are worth noting. First, our flexibility, or even malleability. There may be no one fixed way in which we can individually flourish, and our ways of flourishing may develop and change over time. Second, the diversity of our associational involvements tends to function as a kind of check-and-balance mechanism that keeps us individually from monomaniacal passions and socially from megalomaniacal institutions.

My contention is that the complexity and diversity of our associational involvements are practically manageable only if there is some form of morally responsive social order that both provides for their coordination and support and responds in situations in which moral boundaries have been breached. Although, as the old social contractarians saw it, the ideal situation would be for the morality that undergirds our individual relations to mediate our various associative involvements as well, that is not how it goes for people as we find them.[15] Therefore, we need some form of social organization that will both regulate our individual relations and oversee our various associative involvements so that we can mediate their interactions and secure them against invasion. For classical liberals, this form of social organization was centrally represented by the system of lawmaking, adjudication, and enforcement that is at the heart of the juridical order we refer to as a polity or state. And the state—or a statelike formation—ordinarily constitutes the administrative core of a country or *patria*. Note, however, that such a regulatory order was not intended to constitute an abandonment of morality so much as an articulation of it for a complex social environment, and the various dimensions of that order are themselves susceptible to and in need of moral scrutiny and criticism. There is nothing sacrosanct about a state or the state.

States are not themselves countries or *patriae* and, as Mark Twain observes in the earlier quote, one may oppose a particular state formation in the name of the country. Nevertheless, it is almost always the case that some state formation (or interlocking series of formations) will constitute a critical juridical structure within a country or *patria*. For the—or a—state will bind together, moderate, imprint itself upon, and help to secure the people, land, terrain, culture, history, and network of social institutions

---

[14] See further John Kleinig and Nicholas G. Evans, "Human Flourishing, Human Dignity, and Human Rights," *Law and Philosophy* 32, no. 5 (2013): 539–564.

[15] See John Locke, *Second Treatise of Government*, http://oll.libertyfund.org/?option=com_staticxt&staticfile=show.php%3Ftitle=222, ch. 9.

that comprise a country. Patriotism, conceived of as a loyalty that has regard to this complex whole, encompasses or is at least linked with a governed social order that reaches backward and forward and embodies a distinctive and roughly characterizable (though not uniform) form of life. As noted earlier, any actual patriotism will not be free-floating; it will always be particularized. Thus, a patriot will be Australian, American, Italian, or Ecuadorian, and it should be possible to provide some broad and recognizable, even if contestable, specification of what it is to be each of these.

Although this account of a *patria* may appear instrumental—and indeed has an important instrumental dimension to it—we can also see how a country can come to be valued not merely instrumentally but also for its own sake as an aspect of what one perceives oneself to be. Not only does a country enable the protection of rights and mediation among potentially conflicting groupings but also this complex becomes integral to the *distinctive forms of life* that its citizens will value for their own sake and with which they identify. Thus Australians will develop a loyalty to Australia—to forms of life that are constituted not only by social, cultural, and political institutions but also by the land and environment represented in the unity that is a country— *their* country—because their identities are, in part, created by and expressed through that complex of institutional and cultural forms that constitute it as what it is. And so also will it be for Americans to the United States and Germans to Germany. Australians will not value Germany in this way, and Germans will not value Australia in that way. Nevertheless, Americans, Germans, and Australians may each acknowledge the legitimacy of and even admire others' distinctive patriotisms. In multicultural societies—such as the United States—that have been consciously constructed via broad immigration policies combined with liberal social ideals, there may even be celebrations of hyphenated patriots: Irish Americans, Chinese Americans, and even Newyoricans—people who blend forms of life in distinctive ways. Although it is assumed that there will be some compromise and even subordination of traditions and loyalties in such blendings, they need not be seen as inimical to American patriotism but as partially constitutive of it.

It is not easy to pin down what is distinctive about each country and therefore not easy to give precise content to, say, Australian or American patriotism. Probably there is no unitary set of patriotically relevant characteristics but rather overlapping clusters of factors that articulate a broadly recognizable representation of the country. We should probably think in terms of a mostly shared commitment to basic institutions (as enshrined in founding documents or a constitution),[16] a mostly shared

---

[16] Though maybe not even that. Bernard Boxill suggests that Frederick Douglass's patriotism was anchored in the Declaration of Independence rather than in the Constitution (which for a time he saw as sanctioning slavery). See Bernard R. Boxill, "Frederick Douglass's Patriotism," *Journal of Ethics* 13, no. 4 (2009): 301–317.

primary language, a symbolically recounted history, widely shared social rituals, a distinctive territory, and beyond that a large number of characteristics (with relations among them), some of which will engage some citizens more than others but that are nevertheless held together by structural bonds and institutional and cultural overlaps. Sport, for example, may serve to bind people with very diverse political and religious backgrounds.

Just because of the integrative and formative role that a country is likely to play in the lives of its citizens, especially those who have been born in it, loyalty to it is likely to develop. That is, a country's citizens are likely to develop a commitment to it in the sense that they will be prepared to put out for *their* country in the event that it is threatened or falls short of how they conceive it to be. Patriots will (ordinarily) fight for their country's security and may well support a coherent though somewhat restrictive immigration policy. This, however, does not require that patriots be committed to a rigid cultural, ethnic, political, or religious status quo—for, as noted earlier, a country will have both a narrative and an aspirational aspect to it. When it comes to change, however, patriots are more likely to be reformers than revolutionaries.[17] John F. Kennedy's rousing "ask not what your country can do for you—ask what you can do for your country" captures the essence of this form of patriotism.[18] And in opposition to those advocating a blind or unthinking patriotism, Carl Schurz's previously quoted affirmation puts it succinctly: "My country, right or wrong; if right, to be *kept* right; and if wrong, to be *set* right."[19] Although such patriotism may elicit the supreme sacrifice of dying for one's country, it may also embrace a robust but loyal opposition.

I now offer three clarifications and qualifications that bear on my underlying conception of a country as an associational object.

(1) When I speak of a country or *patria*, and of patriotism as loyalty to one's *patria*, I do not want to fix the idea of the *patria* too narrowly. *Patriae* are usually thought to comprise clusters of factors including land, language or dialect, cultural traditions, and institutions structured by the kind of constitutional and juridical orders that emerged in the seventeenth and eighteenth centuries. However, in some form or

---

[17] Patriots are likely to be concerned particularly about cultural integrity and progress, environmental quality, political stability, and economic and social conditions. Generally, though, patriotic advocates for change will want to bring about change in a relatively orderly manner. See Joel Feinberg, *Harmless Wrongdoing: The Moral Limits of Criminal Law*, vol. 4 (New York: Oxford University Press, 1990), ch. 29.

[18] Inaugural Speech, January 20, 1961, www.famousquotes.me.uk/speeches/John_F_Kennedy/5.htm.

[19] Carl Schurz, remarks in the Senate, February 29, 1872, *Congressional Globe* 45 (1872): 1287, http://en.wikisource.org/wiki/U._S._Senate_Speeches_and_Remarks_of_Carl_Schurz/Sales_of_Arms_to_French_Agents_6.

other, "countries" have existed for millennia, and human flourishing does not need a modern "state" for its realization. That is partly because some of the central associative elements for human flourishing—family, ethnic group, village organizations, and religious communities, all integral parts of what we speak of as countries—have very ancient histories and probably did not require anything as elaborate as the modern state for their coordination and sustenance. Nevertheless, they needed *something*, as the contractarian artifice of a state of nature was designed to show.

Early in the *Politics*, Aristotle remarks that "man is by nature a political animal."[20] We have already noted Aristotle's methodological strategy, namely, that if you want to understand something's nature, you look at it when it is fully or ideally realized. It is Aristotle's view that humans come to realize themselves fully only in the context of a *polis* or city-state and not in some prepolitical association. What for Aristotle is a *polis* we might now think of as a country. So important is the *polis* for Aristotle that he is prepared to say that "the state (*polis*) is by nature clearly prior to the family and to the individual."[21] What Aristotle suggests here is that for the full development of the individual, for the individual's flourishing or achievement of *eudaimonia*, a framing social order and an individual's engagement with it is necessary. *Patriae* offer distinctive forms of social experience and participation, and only a social order as embracing as a *patria* is able to foster and hold together the variety of associational arrangements that are necessary for our full realization.[22] As I have suggested, the most stable and successful kind of *patria* will probably have a constitution, be governed by law, and be likely to include a set of administrative institutional structures to promulgate, adjudicate, and enforce them. It will mediate, put its stamp on, and support a wide range of flexible and distinctive cultural options and opportunities for participation. In addition, it will look outward as well as inward; it will be concerned about the security of its borders and its way of life against outside threats as well as about disruption from within.

So, in conceiving of patriotism as loyalty to one's country, I do not want to structure the *patria* too rigidly. It is simply loyalty to the overarching territory and social order of which one is a member, usually as a *citizen*. It may be something as small as the Athenian *polis*, and in theory it could even be something as expansive as the ancient amphictyony or modern European Union. One may have loyalties to both

---

[20] Aristotle, *Politics*, 1253a3.

[21] Ibid., 1253a19.

[22] Aristotle's point is not that we cannot have a good or satisfying life without political participation, but that a life in which political participation is included is likely to be more fully realized than one without. One might compare with this his views on friendship and of the superiority of virtue friendship over companion friendship.

France and the EU, just as one may have loyalties to the State of Queensland as well as to Australia. One may, of course, have a stronger or more demanding loyalty to one than to the other, and, as secessionists will insist, sometimes one may have to choose between them. Generally, though, one is connected to a *patria* by *citizenship*.

Might countries wither away? Well, the state, as providing a specific kind of structural glue, might wither away. It is, after all, like so many of the ways of ordering our social milieux, contingent on a range of considerations that could be other than they are. Angels do not need a state, though they might still have a *patria*. And people as we find them may become other than what they are. But I suspect that, even with all the interest in cosmopolitanism (and its many varieties), on the one hand, and anarchism, on the other, some form of *patria* will be with us for a long time to come. Certainly, countries have their moral dangers—chauvinism, jingoism, and internal repression being prime among them. But such excesses are not written into their fabric or into patriotism.[23]

(2) *Patriae* are historical continuants. As already noted, countries are dynamic entities. Their territorial boundaries and constitution may remain stable over a long period of time, but their characters are likely to display considerable variation, depending in part on leadership, migration, economic conditions, absence of war, and so forth.[24] Occasionally, a country may cease to exist and then be reconstituted, as was the case with Poland between 1795 and 1918. Writing about countries in more normative terms, Alasdair MacIntyre and Richard Rorty have characterized them as narratives or projects—not simply formal structures or static unities, but as ongoing political and cultural communities that to varying degrees live up to or fall short of the normative ways in which they imagine themselves.[25] A patriotism that is dedicated to the status quo is conservative in a way that patriotism—and probably any loyalty—is not meant to be. When Carl Schurz says that the patriot needs to *keep* or *set* right his country, he reflects this normative dynamic. Albert Hirschman provides a broader theoretical framework through his view that all institutions have a natural tendency to decline in respect of that for which they stand and that their recuperation requires the loyalty of their members and beneficiaries: only those who are loyal will be willing to invest the effort that is required to restore the institution to its varied

---

[23] Even though Thoreau, in his "Essay on Civil Disobedience," offers reasons for thinking otherwise, it might be argued that, as against a cosmopolitan order, a plurality of states may help to keep existing ones honest.

[24] We would, for example, give markedly different accounts of Australian patriotism in 1850, 1950, and 2000.

[25] See, especially, MacIntyre, *Is Patriotism a Virtue?*; Richard Rorty, *Achieving Our Country: Leftist Thought in Twentieth-Century America* (Cambridge, MA: Harvard University Press, 1998).

ideals or, more aspirationally, to progress it toward what it holds itself to be.[26] More generally, countries will see themselves as evolving on a number of fronts.

Soon after the events of 9/11, when it became a popular political strategy to tar critics of the George W. Bush administration with charges of disloyalty, "Dissent Is Not Disloyalty" bumper stickers began to appear. As the critics saw it, the form taken by the US response to terrorism was incompatible with values for which the country had historically stood, albeit only imperfectly realized, and their loyal opposition to counterterrorist tactics and the invasion of Iraq was intended to recall the country— and especially its political leadership—to the liberal democratic values enshrined in its Declaration of Independence, Constitution, aspirational public rhetoric, and a fair bit of its history.

Even though patriotism is not compatible with contempt for one's country, it may be compatible with a great deal of criticism of what one's country has become or has failed to become.[27] A case in point was the lively dispute in Israel over a 2009 *Los Angeles Times* op-ed written by Neve Gordon, Chair of the Politics Department at Ben Gurion University. Gordon called for a graduated boycott against Israel for its treatment of Palestinians. Even many liberal nationalists called him a traitor, and efforts were made to dismiss or demote him. Was he unpatriotic? I believe not. There is no reason why a Jew who has chosen to live and rear his family in Israel because he is glad to live in a country in which he can feel at home *as a Jew* should not feel patriotically indignant that under its current leadership and as a result of social polarization, the country has increasingly become, as he called it, an "apartheid regime" in need of tough love.[28] The key to continued patriotism is whether the patriotic critic believes his country to be redeemable or whether, instead, the offenses it has committed are too serious to be forgivable (as many German Jews thought). If one conceives of one's country as an ongoing project, with successes as well as failures, but nevertheless remains optimistic about it (and, probably, about one's ability to contribute to that project), one might speak of continued patriotic loyalty despite harsh criticism of the status quo.[29]

(3) Even if *patriae* are complex associative arrangements that are good—perhaps important—to have, it would not follow that every *patria* is a good one or that loyalty

---

[26] Albert O. Hirschman, *Exit, Voice and Loyalty: Response to Decline in Firms, Organizations, and States* (Cambridge, MA: Harvard University Press, 1970).

[27] I agree with Keller that there would be something very strange about a person who said: "I am a true, genuine patriot, but there is nothing much that I like about my country; there is nothing important about my country for which I feel any affection"; "Patriotism as Bad Faith," 574. See, however, Boxill, "Frederick Douglass's Patriotism."

[28] See the article on Neve Gordon: http://en.wikipedia.org/wiki/Neve_Gordon.

[29] As Keller seems to allow in "Patriotism as Bad Faith," 577.

to every *patria* is warranted. This applies particularly in relation to the state, which is generally a central element in a *patria*. A revolution or administrative collapse may jeopardize or destroy the *patria* as it was (or, perhaps in some cases, revive or re-create a *patria*). In this respect, *patriae* may not be so different from families. Familial relationships may be important to a good life, but the same may not hold for particular families or family members—for such as they are or as they may become. Some families are toxic or family members may be evil, and the loyalty that may be owed to them by virtue of their associational connection will not be deserved and ought to be forgone or overridden by other considerations.

The USSR was fundamentally flawed, the Third Reich's reinterpretation of "Deutschland über alles" was deeply misguided, and acceptable expression of loyalty was made exceedingly difficult by the conditions they created.[30] And so, from the claim that patriotism is justified, even obligatory, it would not follow that it is acceptable no matter what or that it is obligatory tout court. Particular countries—as expressed through their constitutions and state apparatuses—may forfeit their claim to the loyalty of their citizens as, presumably, the American colonists believed that England did in the latter part of the eighteenth century. No doubt there will be considerable disagreement about what a country has to do to forfeit the loyalty of its citizens or to make revolution justifiable—that is, the kind of revolution that will transform it into a significantly different or "new" country.[31] But we would not have to resolve that to agree that some particular *patria* might lose either its legitimacy or any moral claim to the loyalty of its members.

CLARIFYING THE STATUS OF PATRIOTIC LOYALTY

The argument thus far might be taken to suggest only that patriotic loyalty is permissible. Is more warranted? Contingently, I believe that we can argue not only that patriotism may be a good thing but also that it is something that most of us *should* cultivate. For most twenty-first-century liberals, flourishing requires not only a large variety of associative involvements but also their effective coordination, support, and oversight. This gives us the basic ingredients for some sort of instrumental argument in favor of support for a larger civic order as represented by a *patria*. If we add to this that the complex of associational ties is held together as some sort of unity—that is, as a broadly conceived way of life embedded within and sustained by a country—then

---

[30] One might, indeed, characterize as patriots those who sought to assassinate Hitler.

[31] There are clearly some significant ontological but normatively laden questions here about whether a territorially bound country at t1 is the same as or different from a country at t2 that has roughly the same territorial boundaries but is different in other respects. Back to Theseus's ship.

it is likely that we will view it not simply as instrumental but also as integral to our identity and therefore intrinsically valuable. In identifying with it, we thus come to see ourselves as having loyal obligations to it.

Of course, we may view our *patria* as less. But I suggest that, as would be the case were we to see friendships or familial or other intimate relations only as instrumentally valuable, we would be shortchanging them and be open to criticism for viewing them thus.

As a consequence, there is a prima facie obligation to serve one's country in the event that it is in need of defense. One may also have a prima facie obligation not to migrate to another country simply for reasons of personal advancement. No doubt the obligation is often weak, as it would not jeopardize the interests of the country one is leaving. In other cases, however, one's leaving may be part of a brain drain that seriously depletes a country of some of its most valuable and critical resources.[32]

Two subsidiary issues need some discussion at this point: (1) what are our patriotic obligations? and (2) how strong are they? In an extended discussion of patriotism, each would warrant more attention than is provided by the sketch that follows.

(1) At a minimum, patriotic obligations will require that one acts in ways that do not jeopardize one's country's interests. This is one reason that a person may have a patriotic obligation not to be part of a brain drain. And no doubt it rules out passing on national security information to an enemy country or, perhaps, to revolutionary forces within one's country. Positively, patriotism may require that one agree to defend one's country in the event that it is attacked, though I doubt whether this extends to being obligated to fighting in whatever wars one's country chooses to involve itself. Thus, I doubt whether it was a *patriotic* obligation for Australian or even US forces to serve in Iraq (whatever other argument one have might have given for their doing so).

These expectations pretty much follow from the view that loyalty is perseverance in the conditions that sustain an identity-contributing relationship or affiliation. Patriotism expects from us some form of self-sacrificial commitment to the well-being of one's country. That said, what one views as legitimate patriotic obligations will, to some extent, also be a function of the strength of the association that one has with one's country. Even though each person should ordinarily recognize some minimal patriotic obligations by virtue of what the country is for the person whose particular identity is enabled and enriched through it, any additional patriotic obligations are likely to reflect other, and perhaps more individual, dimensions of the association that exists. As with family relationships, the more that a particular family member means to one, the greater the burdens or obligations of loyalty are likely to

---

[32] Human resources may not be the only ones that it would be unpatriotic to "export." Profiteering citizens may export natural resources that will leave a country seriously depleted.

be. However, if one's country has failed in its coordinating and supportive function, as a child of African slaves or German Jew might feel, then little if nothing may be owed as a matter of patriotic obligation. For most of us, something by way of patriotic commitment ought to be expected and, given the entropic tendencies of institutions, some active and costly engagement in the maintenance of social and political life would seem to be a reasonable expectation.

Not every obligation that one has to a country will be a patriotic obligation, and not every failure to fulfill a patriotic obligation will constitute disloyalty. The obligation to pay taxes on earnings is an obligation, but not a patriotic one. It is more like a membership obligation and is an obligation shared with earners who are not members of a polity. Voting might ordinarily be seen as a membership, rather than a patriotic, obligation, though more costly forms of political participation may need to be patriotically motivated. Patriotic obligations will be those that arise from an identification that is formed—or that is expected to be forged—between a person and a particular country. They will cover a range of acts, some fairly symbolic, others quite sacrificial, ranging from ritual (though not necessarily uncritical) celebrations of its history to volunteering to defend it—acts that deflect us from the temptations of narrow self-servingness.

(2) From the fact that we have patriotic obligations, it does not follow that we should give them precedence over all other normative claims to which we may be subject. Even legitimate patriotic obligations may be overridden, and sometimes there may be difficult decisions to make about which of two obligations (including loyalty-based ones) should be given precedence. Sartre's example of the young man who is faced with a choice between attending to the needs of his ailing mother and joining the resistance is a case in point.[33] Even countries may make concessions to family commitments if, for example, others in the family have sacrificed their lives in their service.

In cases in which such normative conflicts arise, we need to engage in a process of judgment in which a range of considerations will need to be assembled and then traded off and balanced against each other. As we have claimed before, there is no algorithmic way of doing this. It is not possible to argue, as some have, that wider obligations take precedence over narrower obligations; a lot depends on the content of the obligations, issues of urgency, the consequences of giving precedence to one, and so on. It should, nevertheless, be possible to enumerate some of the factors that are likely to come into play and initiate a process in which they can be brought into play.[34]

---

[33] Jean-Paul Sartre, "Existentialism Is a Humanism" (1946), www.marxists.org/reference/archive/sartre/works/exist/sartre.htm.

[34] See chapter 7. Stanley Benn has a good sense of the complexities of judgment in *A Theory of Freedom* (Cambridge: Cambridge University Press, 1987), 296–297.

DOES PATRIOTISM ENCOURAGE BAD FAITH?

Although I have suggested that a country is the kind of associational object that ceteris paribus may rightly expect our patriotic commitment, another dimension of that commitment might give us pause. Simon Keller believes that the problem with patriotism lies not so much with countries as with loyalty. Loyalty to country, he suggests, inclines one to bad faith and is therefore "probably a vice."[35]

To spell this out at length would require an excursus on Keller's primarily attitudinal account of loyalty, which I have already discussed.[36] Suffice it to repeat that I consider loyalty to be constituted primarily by perseverance in the expectations involved in maintaining a particularistic association or relationship, especially in the face of self-serving temptations to compromise those expectations. Although Keller's account makes loyalty more vulnerable to corruption and manipulation than I am prepared to accept, I nevertheless agree with him that loyalty (and not only patriotic loyalty) is susceptible to bad faith. That, however, I see as a moral hazard of patriotism rather than as a reason to steer clear of it.

For Keller, being a patriot is more than being loyal to country. It is, he writes, "to have a serious loyalty to country, one that is not characterized by the phenomenology of choice, is essentially grounded in the country's being yours, and involves reference to (what are taken to be) valuable defining qualities of the country."[37] Parsing Keller's account, a patriot has a loyalty to country—that is, is emotionally committed to taking the country's side. More than that, however, a patriot has the serious commitment that involves a willingness to make significant sacrifices for it, such loyalty (or its specific coloration) is generally not chosen but determined by one's place of birth, and although it is rooted in the relationship one bears to it, it must also make reference to certain features of the country that are seen as having value "from the neutral point of view."[38]

How, then, does loyalty, and in particular patriotic loyalty, "constitutionally" incline one to what Sartre speaks of as bad faith—that is, to "hiding a displeasing truth or presenting truth as a pleasing falsehood"?[39] As I read Keller, more than one feature of patriotic loyalty contributes to this strong tendency, though they contribute in some sort of concert rather than independently. First of all, there is the fact that one does not generally have much choice about the specific object of one's patriotic

---

[35] Keller, "Patriotism as Bad Faith," 566. It may be, as Keller elsewhere suggests, that it is not patriotism that is the vice, but the loyalty that finds its expression in patriotism.
[36] See chapter 1, and Keller, *The Limits of Loyalty*, 21.
[37] "Patriotism as Bad Faith," 577.
[38] Ibid., 574.
[39] Quoted in ibid., 579.

loyalty—say, the United States or Australia; it becomes the object of our potential loyalty by virtue of our being born in it (or of our parents being citizens of it). An individual who thinks he or she ought to be patriotic does not then ask the question: Of which country?[40] The country is given. Second, patriotic identification is usually inculcated from a young age; an emotional bond is fostered and reinforced by means of certain propositions about the country's history and characteristics that are intended to constitute it as a source of pride.[41] What this results in, Keller believes, is a set of beliefs about one's country that, though believed to be true and to warrant patriotic loyalty, are largely impervious to challenge, and it is in the resistance to that challenge that the patriot's bad faith is manifested. And third, no doubt, is the fact that with identification there goes a commitment or attachment whose breach is likely to be painful. We will seek to avoid it.

My response is, first of all, to concede that patriotism is prone to manipulation and, moreover, is frequently manipulated. The educational systems and political apparatuses of most countries usually foster a relatively uncritical patriotism that makes their citizens vulnerable to a corrupted or blind patriotism and, in certain cases, even chauvinism and jingoism.

But is that vulnerability and its exploitation sufficient to make patriotism a vice rather than an easily manipulable and corrupted virtue? I believe the latter: (1) much of what contributes to patriotic connection has little to do with the kinds of normative beliefs about a country that trouble Keller, (2) a good deal of patriotic discourse is aspirational in a way that is supportive of criticism, and (3) although patriotism is quite compatible with having one's eyes open with respect to one's country, we should not see all resistance to criticism as signaling bad faith.

(1) Although there is a contingency about countries, they are not easily dispensable. Our countries generally provide an important cultural, historical, and secure context for our living and flourishing. More than their instrumental value for us, they constitute important sources of meaning and identification.

Critical to Keller's position is his view that "truly patriotic loyalty is entangled with a conception of the beloved country as having certain valuable characteristics, characteristics that make it, in some minimal way at least, genuinely worthy of patriotic loyalty."[42] Such characteristics will "have value from the neutral point of view." There may be such characteristics, but Keller's account of patriotism asks us to look in the wrong place. A significant part of what draws us to *our* country, rather than to *patria* in some amorphous sense, are features that have no special significance from some

---

[40] Ibid., 568.
[41] Ibid., 581.
[42] Ibid., 574.

neutral point of view but are very specific to the country and have relatively little resonance for people from other countries. It is often these that give countries their distinctive character and make the patriot feel that her country is special in a way that other countries are not. To take a trivial but vivid example, the Australian connection to and fondness for Vegemite is unlikely to be shared by others. It is almost certainly an acquired taste and one that Australians acquire from a very young age. Yet it has an iconic status in Australian identity. Many other ways of seeing, feeling, thinking, and being that are distinctively Australian are also acquired in much the same way and are strongly associated with specifically Australian patriotism. Think of Australian forms of humor, its culture of mateship and being laid back, its outdoorsy and can-do attitudes, its sporting traditions and literary culture, its convict past, and so forth. Think of how much, even in what is reputedly the most metropolitan country in the world, the Australian psyche is informed by its landscapes and bushland. A nice example of this can be found in Dorothea Mackellar's "My Country," a poem that many Australians learn in childhood as part of their enculturation.[43] Notably free from chauvinism and jingoism, this paean to Australia is written in the recognition that what makes Australians distinctively and particularly Australian is something for which others cannot be expected to have much feeling. Consider the first two stanzas, in which Mackellar contrasts what helps to inform British patriotism with her own:

> The love of field and coppice, of green and shaded lanes,
> Of ordered woods and gardens is running in your veins.
> Strong love of grey-blue distance, brown streams and soft, dim skies—
> I know but cannot share it, my love is otherwise.
>
> I love a sunburnt country, a land of sweeping plains,
> Of ragged mountain ranges, of droughts and flooding rains.
> I love her far horizons, I love her jewel-sea,
> Her beauty and her terror—the wide brown land for me!

Of course, there is far more than landscape to patriotism. It may include important features of social life, such as the country's political traditions. But these may be valued not simply because of their "value from some neutral point of view," such as their liberal democratic character, but because of the particular shape and form that those liberal democratic traditions have acquired over the years. Thus, an Australian may identify her political traditions as special to her without ipso facto denigrating

---

[43] See www.dorotheamackellar.com.au/archive/mycountry.htm. The poem was commenced in London, as an expression of homesickness.

US political traditions—also characterizable as liberal democratic. What is broadly valuable about those political traditions from some neutral point of view may not make them distinctively valuable in a patriotic sense.

(2) Many patriotic declarations also have an idealistic or aspirational character—that is, they constitute benchmarks against which the actual country can be measured. Most likely these will map or reflect universalist moral values—such as the rule of law, democratic institutions, cultural vibrancy, and so on. This is particularly true of a country such as the United States, which is structured around ideals rather than ethnicity and ancient history. In a primarily migrant country, what binds its citizens, apart from various cultural distinctives, are—in this case—liberal democratic ideals. These constitute a means to critique the status quo—calls for the country to be made right as well as kept right—without abandoning the patriotism. No doubt blindness is often involved—particularly when "American exceptionalism" is invoked. Still, it is notable that Katharine Lee Bates's beloved "America the Beautiful" does not hold back from Schurz's call to repair its flaws:

> O beautiful for pilgrim feet,
> Whose stern, impassioned stress
> A thoroughfare for freedom beat
> Across the wilderness!
> America! America!
> God mend thy every flaw,
> Confirm thy soul in self control,
> Thy liberty in law.[44]

(3) And finally, I accept that patriotism will to some degree be informed by a set of founding and later historical myths—idealized and even falsified stories of hardship, heroism, and triumph—and that these are often inappropriately represented to exemplify values "from the neutral point of view."

What should we say about such myths? First of all, blind patriots may well refuse to accept murky truths about their country's past. Just as those who think that morality will be threatened if belief in God is called into question, there are those who think that patriotism requires that one avert one's eyes from serious historical engagement and perpetuate the sanitized myths of early schooling lest the country be corrupted and weakened from within. I hold no brief for blind patriotism. But it is

---

[44] Katharine Lee Bates's "America the Beautiful," http://kids.niehs.nih.gov/lyrics/america. htm. On Bates, see Lynn Sherr, *America The Beautiful: The Stirring True Story behind Our Nation's Favorite Song* (New York: PublicAffairs, 2001).

also a myth that learning the truth about one's country will necessarily undermine one's patriotism. One may stay resolutely patriotic at the same time as one acknowledges the failures and crimes of the past (and present). Indeed, acknowledging those failures and crimes may enable an equally strong but more mature patriotism to develop—one that is less conservative and more reformist.

Some initial resistance to reports of the bad doings of one's country is to be expected. Resistance will occur whenever trust has been created and that trust is then challenged. Whenever an associative bond is challenged—whether it concerns one's spouse, child, friend, or profession—there will be such resistance. Trust created would not be trust were one not to display an initial predisposition to take the side of that in which one has one's trust.[45] That said, criticism is no reason for an automatic or knee-jerk rejection of its validity. If an Australian patriot is presented with information about the settlement of his country and of its military history—that is, the treatment of early convicts, the early and ongoing situation of its Indigenous peoples, and the foolish debacles of Gallipoli and Vietnam—this may sit uncomfortably with stories of early exploration, drovers, and wartime heroism. It may take a bit to confront these, just as it may take a bit to confront negative stories one hears about a friend or family member. But to be and remain a patriot, one need not reject such stories out of hand or hide one's head in the sand. It is fully compatible with one's being a patriot to ensure that what one hears is seriously, thoughtfully, and not maliciously intended. At the same time, an educated and thoughtful patriot—any educated and thoughtful patriot—will probably realize that a good deal of every national history is written from a particular viewpoint and that it is all too likely that some of her country's historical hagiography will be overblown.[46]

The real worry is not patriotism but the manipulation of patriotism (and other loyalties) by the powers that be (and others) to reinforce and further their much more limited and often partisan goals. The manipulation takes place in a number of ways. One is to rigidify patriotism to mean patriotic loyalty to the current regime rather than patriotic loyalty to the larger narrative or project that constitutes one's country. A second way is to characterize dissent as disloyalty, rather than recognizing the legitimacy of a loyal opposition. A third way is to encourage the kind

---

[45] Keller tendentiously contrasts our readiness to believe such stories of other countries with our reluctance to believe such stories of our own. It may be the case that we should not be too ready to believe them in either case. But in the case in which some form of trust has already been established, there is good reason to be demanding about contrary evidence. That does not gainsay our potential for blindness. What is needed is open-mindedness, and that is consistent with trust. See Jason Baehr, "The Structure of Open-Mindedness," *Canadian Journal of Philosophy* 41, no. 2 (2011): 191–213.

[46] This is likely to be true of any associational commitment, whether it is one's family, one's friends, one's religious group, one's profession, or one's place of employment.

of bad faith that Keller sees as endemic to patriotism. And this can be done by controlling curricula and media in various ways. Each manipulative strategy is, alas, prevalent.

But we might ask: Are these manipulations of patriotism (and other loyalties) so prevalent and, given the disparity of power between a country's formal apparatus and its citizens, so virulent that we do better to discourage patriotism altogether than to develop a more informed patriotism? Callan poses that question in "Love, Idolatry, and Patriotism." Although he casts his discussion in terms of love of country and how blinding love can be,[47] the argument is as easily framed in terms of loyalty and its susceptibility to manipulation. Callan opines that "if humanity could make a bargain with God to make patriotism disappear, so that all its harms evaporated along with its benefits, maybe we should take the deal."[48] However, he goes on to argue, "no such bargain is on offer." We live in a world in which patriotism is and will remain a fact of our lives, and we do better to cultivate what he calls an innocent patriotism than simply to suffer the costs of an idolatrous one. Love, trust, and loyalty—indeed, almost any virtue—may be manipulated by others. The moral burden we confront, as persons of moral character and not simply as patriots, is to ensure that our virtues are not corrupted by pernicious influences.

CONCLUSION: THE CONVERGENCE OF PATRIOTISM AND NATIONALISM

I have discussed patriotism and nationalism separately and have attempted to make a modest case for each. The case for nationalism is somewhat less compelling than the case for patriotism, though if we have a recognizable nationality, it may be important to us. Nevertheless, it is less important that we have a particular nationality than that we have a country, and though, no doubt, some of us may flourish without a country to call our own, or without patriotism toward one that is our own, if we do so we are to some extent free riders on a social arrangement that has a distinctive coloration and for most of us offers a uniquely stabilizing and unifying environment.

In practice, nationalism and patriotism are often found together, and in rare cases, they practically coincide. The usual case, though, is one in which having a particular nationality may strengthen one's ties to a country, especially if the country sustains ways of life that are associated with that nationality.

---

[47] Love and trust may also be eye-opening. See Susan Wolf's 2010 Phi Beta Kappa Romanell lecture: "Loving Attention: Lessons in Love from *The Philadelphia Story*," in *Understanding Love through Philosophy, Film, and Fiction*, ed. Susan Wolf and Christopher Grau (New York: Oxford University Press, 2014), ch. 17.

[48] "Love, Idolatry, and Patriotism," 525–526.

I now want to bring the two closer together and to suggest that the traditional normative opposition of patriotism and nationalism and preference, if at all, for the former often fails to understand both the character of a viable patriotism and the value of nationalism. There are problematic ways of understanding the connection. Earlier I drew attention to John Stuart Mill's notorious argument that free institutions are hard to sustain if a country is made up of different nationalities: "Among a people without fellow-feeling, especially if they read and speak different languages, the united public opinion, necessary to the working of representative government, cannot exist." And "It is in general a necessary condition of free institutions that the boundaries of governments should coincide in the main with those of nationalities."[49] Although Mill recognizes that this is not always possible because of intermingling that has occurred, he seeks to make as much virtue as possible out of this. His preferences, however, are clear. Assimilation is generally the better way to go: "Experience proves that it is possible for one nationality to merge and be absorbed in another," adding, contentiously, "when it was originally an inferior backward portion of the human race the absorption is greatly to its advantage." It is not that Mill favors the homogenization of human life—and certainly not at the individual level—but he thinks that there are important social advantages to the mellowing of contrasts and enrichment of a preexisting status quo: "What really tends to the admixture of nationalities, and the blending of their attributes and peculiarities in a common union, is a benefit to the human race."

Although Mill's own preferences reek of nineteenth-century colonialism, the problem with which he grappled—that of developing a stable political culture—remains. My discussion in this and the previous chapter has not been intended to lead in the direction of an either-or solution but in the direction of both-and. Just as strong ethnocultural nationalism is prone to move in the direction of invidious exclusion, so formalistic patriotism, as represented in the "abstract procedures and principles" that are sometimes taken to comprise Jürgen Habermas's "constitutional patriotism,"[50] is

---

[49] John Stuart Mill, *Representative Government*, ch. 16, "Of Nationality, as connected with Representative Government."

[50] Jürgen Habermas, *The New Conservatism: Cultural Criticism and the Historian's Debate* (Cambridge: Polity, 1989), 261; also "Citizenship and National Identity: Some Reflections of the Future of Europe," *Praxis International* 12, no. 1 (1992): 1–19. However, as Anna Stilz has persuasively argued, Habermas's account of constitutional patriotism is probably to be articulated as a much fuller and particularized democratic project—something that a person can value for the particular local form that it takes—and not simply a bare structure of universalizable political principles. See her *Liberal Loyalty: Freedom, Obligation, and the State* (Princeton, NJ: Princeton University Press, 2009), ch. 6. As such, a person may value—as part of her patriotic heritage—the particulars of her polity without seeing them as being of value from some neutral point of view. Even so, I think that such patriotism is cast too narrowly.

likely to be too thin to bind a people together. Neither the United States nor Switzerland exemplifies the latter. Multicultural societies, of the integrated or relatively separate kinds that you find in the US and Switzerland, respectively, expend a good deal of energy to create, celebrate, and maintain a supervening "American way of life" or "Swissness." Rather than eschewing both patriotism and nationalism, we need something of each. What is needed—and it is implicit in the territorialness of nationalism and the cultural dimensions of patriotism—is some form of spatial delineation or overarching tradition that moves the nationalist in the direction of the liberal patriot and the patriot in the direction of the liberal nationalist. As Margaret Canovan points out, this convergence is achieved in much the same way in each case: both national identity and citizenship are often perpetuated through birth.[51] The identity of a second generation is inherited from the new country of their migrant parents—the former now become bearers of the new culture to which their parents came. If their parents came to the United States, then baseball and Thanksgiving will be *theirs*, along with the constitutional values to which they have been taught to pledge their allegiance. This need not require the abandonment of their national ties but their subsumption within the larger ties of a country that—aspirationally, at least—proclaims its multiculturalism.

[51] Margaret Canovan, "Patriotism Is Not Enough," *British Journal of Political Science* 30 (2000): 425–428.

14

GOD

We ought, therefore, to do a thing not because God wills it, but because it is righteous and good in itself—and it is because it is good in itself that God wills it and demands it of us.[1]

Theology sits at the window with a painted visage and sues for philosophy's favor, offering it her charms.[2]

At various points in this study, the question—indeed, the problem—of absolutism has been raised. In what is taken to be one of its deeply conservative dimensions, loyalty is often framed as an absolute demand. He who is not with me is against me. Are there loyalties that cannot be overridden, loyalties to which there cannot be any exception? If they are demanded, how reasonable are such demands? Can such loyalties be accommodated within a broadly liberal framework, or is there, at bottom, a deep tension between the demand for loyalty and the liberal expectation of freedom of conscience? I tackle some of these questions via the issue of religious loyalty.

INTRODUCTION

My approach is not without its own problems. Religious loyalties open a distinctive can of worms that quickly threatens to become unmanageable. There is barely an issue that is not vigorously contested. The intelligibility, let alone the identity and existence, of the title referent is problem enough. And of course, religious loyalties need

---

[1] Immanuel Kant, *Lectures on Ethics*, trans. Louis Infield (New York: Harper & Row, 1963), 22.
[2] Søren Kierkegaard, *Fear and Trembling*, trans. Walter Lowrie (Princeton, NJ: Princeton University Press, 1941), Preliminary Expectoration, www.religion-online.org/showbook. asp?title=2068.

not be construed simply as loyalty to God but can accommodate the loyalties that are developed to and within various religious communities (yet another contested category). Here surely there is more than ample room for the bad faith that Keller thinks is endemic to patriotism.

Furthermore, the problem of absolutism may not require any reference to God. Nevertheless, plausible absolutes are not easy to come by in moral practice or theory, albeit not for lack of effort. Deliberately killing the innocent has often been touted as an absolute prohibition,[3] and this is sometimes reflected in debates over abortion, in which double-effect arguments are marshaled to shore up what are seen as the prohibition's crumbling edges. The prohibition against torture also has some claim to being absolute, though ticking bomb arguments remain a test of resolve. The ancient maxim, *pereat coelum fiat justitia*—let justice be done, though the heavens fall—was originally intended to be taken seriously, though in recent literature it is more often cited as a *reductio*. Certain theoretical abstractions (for example, the greatest happiness of the greatest number) have also represented themselves in ways that look absolute, though again not usually as matters of absolute loyalty. Only Royce's ultimate and deeply problematic moral principle of "loyalty to loyalty" comes close to absolutism.[4] Nearer to loyalties of the standard kind have been attempts by some political, religious, and other groups to garner an exceptionless overriding commitment to their ends—an absolute loyalty to party, country, or community.

Although the loyalty of the samurai may have its modern-day admirers, most practical demands for absolute loyalty can be seen as manipulative and corruptive. Thus the blue wall of silence associated with policing is often interpreted to mean that "one should never, ever hurt another cop." This tendency, which is reinforced by making loyalty–disloyalty an exclusive duality, is one of the things that gives loyalty (and often policing) a bad name.

One might, nevertheless, ask whether there could be cases in which a particular kind of loyalty could reasonably be said to have an absolute claim on one. And religious loyalty—at this point understood as loyalty to God—might seem to be as plausible a candidate as any, if not in actuality, then at least as a hypothetical limiting

---

[3] "If someone really thinks, *in advance*, that it is open to question whether such an action as procuring the judicial execution of the innocent should be quite excluded from consideration—I do not want to argue with him; he shows a corrupt mind" (G. E. M. Anscombe, "Modern Moral Philosophy," *Philosophy* 33, no. 124 (January 1958): 17).

[4] For interesting recent discussions, see Simon Keller, *The Limits of Loyalty* (Cambridge: Cambridge University Press, 2007); and Mathew A. Foust, *Loyalty to Loyalty: Josiah Royce and the Genuine Moral Life* (New York: Fordham University Press, 2012).

case. On many accounts, God (almost by definition) is seen as having a more extensive claim on one than any other associative object—an absolute claim in fact.[5]

THE *AKEDAH*

We are provided with what appears to be such a case in Genesis 22—the story of
the *akedah*[6] (binding) of Isaac—a narrative that has exercised religious believers and
scholars for many centuries in Jewish, Christian, and (in a different version) Islamic
religious traditions. Indeed, because the story has foundational significance for the
three great monotheistic religions, a normative challenge lies at their very roots and
has proven a source of continuous perplexity, awe, or criticism. The twists and turns
of that discussion are instructive, and I use it here to explore some of the issues raised
by claims to absolute loyalty.

Although some would view the story simply as one of Abraham's preparedness to
obey God's command, I think it important to understand it no less as the expression
of loyalty to an associative other. The story is not about a simple Milgram-like obedience to authority but about the character and extent of Abraham's faith in God. What
is central is Abraham's trust in the God to whom he has covenanted himself and with
whom he is intimately related (as "a friend"), not simply his compliance with the
demands of an authority figure.[7] As we shall see, in other contexts (the story of the
destruction of Sodom), Abraham shows himself willing to contest God's plans. And
so, whatever we want to say about the *akedah*, it is not the story of someone with a
record of passive obedience.

---

[5] We might of course wonder what could possibly ground such a claim—Creation? Perfect
goodness? Omnipotence? Special relationship? Each has its following, though for reasons that
should become clear, an extended discussion of each can probably be bracketed.

[6] Within Jewish tradition, there is, in addition to the Genesis account, an extensive rabbinic
commentary that alters or questionably fills in details of that account, and I shall largely bypass
that discussion. Particularly illuminating, though, are Shalom Spiegel, *The Last Trial. On the
Legends and Lore of the Command to Abraham to Offer Isaac as a Sacrifice: The Akedah*, trans.
and intro. Judah Goldin (New York: Pantheon, 1979); and Jerome I. Gellman, *Abraham! Abraham! Kierkegaard and the Hasidim on the Binding of Isaac* (Aldershot, UK: Ashgate, 2003). In
the Qur'anic version, the son is not identified (Qur'an 37:99–113), though Islamic tradition
generally identifies him as Ishmael, and the occasion is memorialized annually in the holiday
of *Īd al-'hAḍḥá* (Eid al Adha). See Louis A. Berman, *Akedah: The Binding of Isaac* (Lanham,
MD: Rowman and Littlefield, 1997), ch. 22.

[7] God's approach to Abraham takes the form of a request ("Take, I pray you"—Gen. 22:2)
rather than that of a coercive or authoritarian command. Abraham is free to refuse or even
debate the issue. That said, friendship with God is not egalitarian in the way that other friendships tend to be. Later in the story it is Abraham's "obedience" and "fear of God" that are
praised. See chapter 9, note 8.

The textual context of the Judeo-Christian biblical version of the story has some bearing on how it is to be interpreted and therefore on how the challenge of claims to absolute loyalty might be met.[8] In Genesis 12, we are told that God called Abram/Abraham to leave his ancestral home and go to a land that he would be shown, where he and his multitudinous descendants would make a name for themselves and be a blessing to "all the tribes of the earth." The fly in the ointment here is that Abraham has no heir. His wife Sarai/Sarah is barren and post-menopausal, and a child that her maidservant bears for him does not qualify. Unrepeatably—miraculously, one might say—Sarah is promised and subsequently bears a son, Isaac.

At some later point, God puts Abraham to the test. We are not told the exact reason, though the postlude to the story (Genesis 22:15–18) strongly suggests that it is to test Abraham's fitness for the foundational role he has been called to play. Abraham is requested to take "his only child Isaac, whom [he loves]" and to sacrifice him as a burnt offering on a mountain some days' journey away in the land of Moriah. As we have the story, Abraham offers no protest and sets out early the next morning on an ass, with Isaac, two servants, and wood he prepares for the offering. A little short of the mountain, the servants are told to wait with the ass, while Abraham and Isaac continue to the mountain "to worship" and then return. Isaac carries the wood and Abraham carries the fire and knife. Along the way, Isaac inquires about the lamb for the offering. He is told: "My son, God himself will provide the lamb for the burnt offering." That's all. On arrival, Abraham builds an altar, arranges the wood on it, binds Isaac, places him on top, and takes the knife to kill him. At that point, we are told, an angelic messenger from God tells Abraham to desist. Abraham has passed the test: it is now known that he "fears God," for he has not withheld from God his only son. Abraham then notices a ram caught in a bush by its horns, and this is offered in place of Isaac. The original promise in Abraham's call is then reaffirmed and even enhanced by the angelic messenger, and Abraham makes his way back to the servants.

That's it. There are many questions we might want to ask about the story—what Abraham and Isaac were thinking, how old Isaac was, whether he struggled, how Abraham knew that God was actually speaking to him, whether he told anyone else (and, if not, why not), whether Isaac returned with Abraham, and so on. But we have to do without such details, even though much of the traditional commentary has been happy to speculate about them. With or without them, it is not difficult

---

[8] I propose to take at face value the text as we now have it. There have been various form-critical and other attempts to see the current text as a construction from earlier and diverse sources, with variant meanings. Without ruling out such possibilities, they are probably too diverse and contested to discuss here.

to see why the story has been seen as challenging, perplexing, and even offensive to many, and why, at least given the status that its telling has within the religious traditions of which it is a part, it has attracted ongoing parsing, commentary, and debate.[9]

There are at least two presumptions behind the story's challenge: first, that God actually spoke to Abraham—that is, Abraham was not mistaken about the source or substance of what he was asked to do. The story does not give us license to separate Abraham's belief that God was speaking to him and calling him to sacrifice his son from what was actually the case. Otherwise we might have expected Abraham to doubt whether the voice calling him was the voice of God rather than of Satan posing as God. Second, we are to presume that Abraham was not only aware of the divine prohibition against shedding innocent blood[10] but also of the divine aversion to child sacrifice and would have rejected the practice himself.[11] Thus we must presume that Abraham was aware of the moral significance of what it was he was asked to do. Sandwiched between Abraham's initial call and the call for Isaac's sacrifice is a story (that of Sodom and Gomorrah) designed to show not only that Abraham has a keen sense of the unacceptability of the shedding of innocent blood but also that his God is sensitive to that view.[12] Neither Abraham nor his God has previously been shown to be insensitive to moral considerations—and certainly not of this magnitude. Despite this, Abraham prepares to do what is asked of him.

[9] The fact that we are not made privy to the mind of Abraham—indeed, the fact that the author seems uninterested in what was going on in it—should not be taken to imply that Abraham had no mind on what was being asked of him or that we cannot make reasonable inferences to some of what was going on in his mind. We should not disregard the deliberateness of Abraham's actions in response or the import of the two statements he makes (about returning with Isaac and God's provision). It was clearly a request that burdened him. More speculative, however, are the comments of those who see Abraham as struggling to evacuate himself of his love for Isaac so that he can be focused entirely on God. See Gellman, *Abraham! Abraham!* 3–6.

[10] See Genesis 4:8–12; 9:5–6.

[11] Although it is clear from other parts of the tradition that child sacrifice is strongly rejected (see, for example, Lev. 18:21; 20:1–8; Deut. 12:31; 18:10; 2 Kings 13:27; 16:3; 17:17, 31; 21:6; 23:10; 2 Chron. 28:3; 33:6; Jer. 7:31; 19:5; 32: 35; Ezek. 20:26, 31; Isa. 57:4–5; Mic. 6:7), some writers have used the *akedah* to establish what was later clearly stated and thus to differentiate Abrahamic religion from that of some of its neighbors. I do not think that this latter suggestion makes sense of the story.

[12] Genesis 18. True, the point is put not in terms of the wrongness of killing the innocent but of the injustice of destroying the innocent along with the guilty. But that does not appear to constitute a morally relevant difference. The Sodom incident, moreover, casts doubt on those (Christian) commentators who seek to account for the *akedah* by arguing that, by virtue of his being born in sin, Isaac had no claim not to be killed and that God had every right to ask Abraham to be the agent of the punishment that was already his due.

To the outsider, someone not otherwise persuaded by the broader religious context of which the story is a part, the story's immediate effect is most likely to repel and appall.[13] It is repellent that God would ask Abraham to sacrifice his son and appalling that Abraham should comply. If ever a case illustrated the unacceptability of absolute loyalty, this surely is it. Even if we allow that the request to Abraham was only a test, it might be thought morally obnoxious to subject someone—even or especially someone to whom one was intimately related—to such a test. Is this a fair burden to place on a relationship? Or, if that is not the best way to represent it, is it fair even of God to place this kind of burden on another?[14]

Philosophically, one might see the story as a particular resolution of a *Euthyphro*-type dilemma, in which the question to be answered is whether God commands something because it is right or whether it is made right because God commands it.[15] Some will say: Because *God* commanded it, it must have been right—that is a moral prerogative that God (though no one else) has.[16] But construing it that way sits awkwardly with the story of Sodom and Gomorrah, for there God appears to act both scrutably and reasonably. Here, however, it seems counterintuitive and perplexing. If, following Kant, one says that God commands only what is (independently) right, then we have every reason to ask why that is so in this particular case, for the impression given is that the story does not speak well of either God or Abraham. True, it was *only* a test, and Abraham was kept from going through with it. But it looks like an unreasonable demand of loyalty and a blind exercise of it.

Yet the story's place within the tradition suggests that it is intended to speak well of both. Religious believers will want to avoid the unwelcome option of Socrates's challenge by saying that God qua God would command only what is right; they will therefore be obligated to explain how that is so. The onus is strongly on them to make that challenge good. Later I suggest some possibilities.

---

[13] By way of contrast, some have used the story to valorize sending one's children to war. See Carol Delaney, *Abraham on Trial: The Social Legacy of Biblical Myth* (Princeton, NJ: Princeton University Press, 1998); Yael Feldman, *Glory and Agony: Isaac's Sacrifice and National Narrative* (Stanford, CA: Stanford University Press, 2010).

[14] To ask this question is to make certain presumptions about how Abraham might or ought to have responded to such a request and therefore about how burdensome he found or ought to have found such a request to be. We are not told. However, we are given every reason to think that Abraham loved his son and did not seek to stifle that love. And so it makes some sense to think that the request was experienced as, at the very least, an exceptionally demanding one. At the same time, Abraham is characterized as having a particularly intimate relationship with God.

[15] *Euthyphro*, 10a.

[16] One common ploy has also been to argue that God has the moral authority to take human life. In any circumstances?

KIERKEGAARD'S *FEAR AND TREMBLING*

Although many attempts have been made to render the story intelligible and palatable, few have been as challenging and influential as Søren Kierkegaard's pseudonymous "defense" in *Fear and Trembling*.[17] I shall focus primarily on Kierkegaard's discussion and some of the questions it raises. Kierkegaard is awed by Abraham's faith. His immediate concern, however, is not to come to terms with the moral challenge it presents. Instead, he ascribes to the story a normative force that challenges those who would philosophize religious faith. His particular bête noire is popular Danish Hegelianism, in which, ultimately, the inward, subjective, and religious dimension of life must answer to the outer, public, and philosophical. Kierkegaard construes Abraham's act of loyal responsiveness to God as a countercase to the neo-Hegelian philosophical dialectic, with its methodological ambitions for reaching a final, universal truth. It is Abraham, the individual "knight of faith," Kierkegaard believes, who exposes the restricted scope of ethical universalism and exemplifies the priority of individual/solitary faith over conventional morality. It is the theology of his teacher, Hans Martensen, that, as Kierkegaard sees it, prostitutes itself to philosophy.[18]

In discussing Abraham's response to God, Kierkegaard draws a distinction among three ways of living out one's life: the aesthetic, the ethical, and the religious. Crudely put, the aesthetic focuses on individual sensory experience, whether base or refined, whereas the ethical is concerned with life matters that are publicly accessible to reason and is directed to the realization of a common good. And though the religious, like the aesthetic, is concerned with an individual's personal experience, its vital concern is that individual's solitary personal encounter with "the absolute." In *Fear and Trembling*, Kierkegaard's main focus is the ethical-religious distinction.

It is not easy to grasp Kierkegaard's account of the religious phase, of living by faith. His expression is often obscure, and, he would no doubt want to argue, we have been captured by Hegelian modes of thinking in which the religious has to be encompassed by the ethical. That is, we believe we must be able to give an account of religious truth in terms that are "universal" or publicly accessible. Nevertheless, although Kierkegaard is often seen as one of the great moving forces of existentialism,

---

[17] I will continue to refer to Kierkegaard as the speaker rather than Johannes de silentio, although I am aware that some commentators place considerable store on the fact of its pseudonymity as well as the particular name that Kierkegaard gave its "author." There may be some basis for this in Kierkegaard's posthumously published *The Point of View for My Work as an Author*. This then raises its own interpretive challenges. However, I believe that, for present purposes, I can safely bracket these questions.

[18] See Jon Stewart, *Kierkegaard's Relations to Hegel Reconsidered* (Cambridge: Cambridge University Press, 2003), esp. ch. 7.

it is to be doubted whether the leap into the absurd or the leap to faith of which he speaks should be interpreted as the "criterionless choice" of some later existentialist thinking. In some respects, his focus is closer to (though not identical with) the personal projects of Bernard Williams's individual whose authenticity and life's worth are threatened by a certain type of universalism. Unlike Williams's individual, however, the driving force behind Kierkegaard's knight of faith is not some project or cause that may be open to public scrutiny, but an individual person who putatively stands alone in his relationship to another—specifically, an encounter with the absolute or God. Kierkegaard's leap is the qualitatively distinctive commitment that a person makes to the object of faith, in which that person's dealings have come to be characterized and determined by trust: God will provide.

Abraham's compliance with God's request is religious in more than one sense. It is religious in respect of the categories that are appropriate to what he sets out to do. He is asked to give his all to the God to whom he has committed himself. And so his acceptance of what God asks of him is characterized as a resolve to *sacrifice* Isaac, not *murder* him. Moreover, what he does is structured by his commitment to the God who called him and in whose promise he has lived out his life. This commitment is essentially religious. But it is not this kind of religiosity that Kierkegaard is concerned to distinguish when he speaks of living by faith. He speaks scathingly of the person who, having heard a "cheap" sermon on Abraham, announces that he is now going to show his faith by sacrificing his son.[19]

How, we might want to ask, can Kierkegaard—let alone Abraham—assure us of the singularity, authenticity, and legitimacy of Abraham's faith rather than its being a misguided cloaking of murder in the garments of sacrifice? Mere use of the language of sacrifice is not enough. Apart from anything else, the religious tradition that Abraham is said to represent is as opposed to child sacrifice as it is to murder. Nobility of intention does not here suffice. The father who kills his child to spare it from what he thinks will be the miseries of contemporary life does not escape condemnation because his motivation is admirable. In doing what he does, he still intends the death of the child, and there is a burden on him to provide a justification for that, not simply a compassionate motive. Assuming that Abraham's call is a special case, it is not an emulation of Abraham to sacrifice (or be willing to sacrifice) one's child to God or out of some grand motive. And so the neo-Hegelian challenge that Kierkegaard must address is to distinguish the genuineness of the call to Abraham from one that is spurious—from an inner compulsion that seeks to "justify" whatever atrocity it demands. How can Kierkegaard avoid the Hegelian demand for some public affirmation?

[19] Delaney details a copycat case in *Abraham on Trial*, ch. 2.

According to Kierkegaard, *Abraham's* faith has to be understood in distinctive terms. In the "Exordium," Kierkegaard offers and critiques several interpretations of the *akedah* that he considers inadequate—interpretations prompted by the intrinsic challenge of the story—yet that, because they are attempts to make it rationally intelligible, ultimately fail to come to terms with it. They fail to grasp the true character of Abraham's faith and, consequently, what makes him a knight of faith. That faith, Kierkegaard asserts, requires a "teleological suspension of the ethical," a movement about which we will soon have more to say.

The knight of faith, Kierkegaard continues, is to be distinguished from his closest relative, the "knight of infinite resignation," who, in being confronted with the command that came to Abraham, comes to terms with the fact that compliance with it will result in his inability to realize that which he most desires. Yet his desire for the object of his deepest desire remains unabated, even though it is now detached from any expectation that it will be realized. For Kierkegaard, such infinite resignation is the necessary prelude to faith, whose knight, having given up the object of desire as impossible, then "absurdly" reclaims it by believing that he will obtain it. Such is the faith of Abraham.

It is this last movement—the movement of faith—that Kierkegaard sees as impossible for himself, and that fills him with awe. He psychologizes Abraham's response in a way that is not clearly represented in the original text. Kierkegaard wants us to feel the full burden (*angest*) of Abraham's test. It was not a momentary pain he experienced in being called to give up his son, but an extended period of loss-cum-hope. There is not just the initial resolve, the choice about whether to go the ethical or religious path, but three days in which he must implement his decision. It is a choice that he must make and put into effect *on his own*. He (apparently) seeks no counsel from others and, except in the most general terms, tells no one what he is about to do. He is on his own before God.

Not only was Abraham's "leap of faith" burdensome but, writes Kierkegaard, it had no communicable rationale to it. It was "absurd." Unlike Jephthah's sacrifice of his daughter, Agamemnon's sacrifice of Iphigenia, and Brutus's execution of his sons—sacrifices whose rationales can be grasped, whether or not we accept them—Abraham's act cannot be characterized in universalistic, publicly intelligible terms. He is not about to sacrifice Isaac in order to fulfill a vow to God, save the nation, or display impartial justice. Sacrificing Isaac is the negation of everything to which Abraham aspires. It is through Isaac that God's promise is to be fulfilled, and it is Isaac whom God is now asking him to give up. It is simply handing back everything to God, the surrender of everything that gives a point to his life journey. Nevertheless, Kierkegaard contends, Abraham's suspension of the ethical is also teleological: he must absurdly believe God's promise while fulfilling God's demand that would make its realization impossible. He must trust God in a way that makes him prepared to act in a manner that is completely contrary to everything that appears to undergird that trust.

I have two general worries about Kierkegaard's treatment of the *akedah*.

One concerns Kierkegaard's use of the story to refute neo-Hegelian pretensions that sought to bring the religious within the ambit of the ethical–rational–universal. No doubt it is a remarkable and challenging story, but not only is its purpose not philosophical but also it is somewhat distorting to characterize it in a way that serves the particular philosophical purposes that Kierkegaard has in mind. Perhaps that is a bit unfair, because the philosophical purpose to which Kierkegaard puts the story is no less than the refusal to encompass Abraham's response to God's call within the categories of philosophy. Nevertheless, resort to the language of absurdity, the leap to faith, paradox, and even the "teleological suspension of the ethical" represents ways of construing the story that risk obscuring and altering what may be its simpler point. Even without its Hegelian target and construed more generally as exemplifying the primacy of faith over reason, it imports into the story a distorting purpose. The second worry has to do with what Kierkegaard sees as the exemplary character of Abraham's faith—as something we might desire for ourselves but will for the most part fail to emulate. This use of the *akedah* tends to overlook its distinctive, unique, and foundational place within the religious traditions in which it figures. It may be admired but, in its more ethically challenging aspects, should not be seen as something to be replicated by all those who interpret their lives in terms of the tradition for which Abraham is deemed the father. A special situation may make special demands.

Let me expand on these points. First of all, the faith that Abraham displays is not most helpfully characterized in simple propositional terms as the conjunction of two incompatible beliefs:

1. God has told me to destroy the vehicle of my hope; and
2. I believe that God will ensure that my hope is realized.

Although it is arguable that the language of revelation and encounter to which Kierkegaard resorts takes him beyond this propositional representation—a position I am prepared to accept—nevertheless, the anti-Hegelian thrust of Kierkegaard's exposition leads him to adopt ways of speaking that heighten the story's paradoxical and moral challenge.

Faith—including religious faith—is not characterized most helpfully as a propositional attitude, even though it may be associated with certain propositional attitudes. Rather, it is to be construed as the trust that arises out of and reflects a particularistic relationship. According to the story, Abraham is called by God to follow him—a relationship that includes the promise that Abraham will become the founder of a great nation. Abraham responds affirmatively to this call. In the context of the relationship thus formed, God shows himself to be both capable and just—as one might hope from someone having pretensions to deity. Barren Sarah gives birth to the promised son, and in the judgment on Sodom and Gomorrah God shows himself to be sensitive to considerations of justice. Abraham's own performance is a bit spotty—he treats Hagar and Ishmael badly and displays a disconcerting timidity and self-servingness in his wanderings through others' territory by passing Sarah off as his sister. God has to extricate him from the consequences of his behavior.[20] In his treatment of Hagar, too, God must intervene.

In the context of his tried and long-standing relationship—in which God's trustworthiness has already been established but Abraham's has not—Abraham finds his loyalty and trust put to the test. The critical question is whether his trust can bear the burdens of the test. As the story has it, Abraham remains loyal and trusting despite the apparently outrageous demand that is made of him. What does he expect? All that we are told is that he says he will return with Isaac and that, with respect to the offering, "God will provide." Perhaps there is some significance in Abraham's response to Isaac's question. It is not "You are the lamb" but the gnomic "God will provide the lamb." Abraham has not given up hope that something will occur to enable the promise to be fulfilled. And yet Abraham is in no position to know what that something will be. All he has to go on is the integrity of the relationship. The New Testament author of the Letter to the Hebrews asserts that Abraham believed that God would raise Isaac from the dead. Maybe it was an option that occurred to Abraham, but it was hardly one for which there was a precedent or for which he could have provided some empirical evidence. We, the readers, are made privy to the bigger picture, in which Abraham is being tested, and as latter-day readers we know that if Abraham passes the test God will provide not only by intervening at the last minute but also by providing a ram substitute for Isaac. But all Abraham had to go on was what up to that point he had reason to believe his God to be.

The extreme or ultimate loyalty that Abraham is called upon to show is singular by virtue of the special place he has as "father of the faith"—whether we take that to be Judaism, Christianity, or Islam.[21] Although there is little doubt that each tradition views the faith of Abraham as a matter of great significance, it is questionable that the faith Abraham showed in responding to the test is intended as something that

---

[20] See Genesis 12:10–20; 20; 21:8–21.

[21] I am less certain about Islam, which both in its name—submission—and practice focuses more consciously on what it sees as Abraham's obedience.

others might emulate.[22] It has a particularity that sets it apart: Abraham is called to be a father of a special people; he is called in unpromising circumstances in that his wife is barren and so there is no obvious heir; God then enables Sarah to bear the son through whom the call is to be realized. But the question arises: Is Abraham up to the distinctive and essentially religious task for which he has been called? The test is to determine whether Abraham is fit: is he prepared to surrender to God all that God has given him, to put his trust wholly in the God who has called him?—not an unreasonable expectation of someone who is called to such a role.[23]

To contemporary ears, Kierkegaard's characterization of Abraham's faith as involving "the teleological suspension of the ethical" is suggestive but not altogether persuasive. Even though there is an active debate about the so-called overridingness of moral considerations, given the other legitimate demands that may be made upon us, in the case of the *akedah* the ethical demands seem sufficiently compelling to trump others. We can grant that what Kierkegaard has primarily in mind in referring to "the ethical" is the socially sanctioned morality of neo-Hegelian philosophy, but we do not need to interpret it so narrowly. Abraham sets out to fulfill God's request to sacrifice Isaac, and though he trusts that God will intervene or provide, apart from the relationship in which he stands to God, he has no particular reason to believe that it will avoid the sacrifice of Isaac. What Abraham's compliance shows is his willingness, as a loyal believer, to trust that what he is asked of God will turn out all right in the end—even if what he is asked to do appears to undercut that very possibility. Although it puts loyalty to God before loyalty to family, a position that might be defended, it also appears to allow that trust to transcend the bounds of what is morally acceptable.

MOVING BEYOND KIERKEGAARD

The foregoing reflections on Kierkegaard do not remove the paradox or ethical tension that Kierkegaard seems to relish, but I think they help to shift the discussion in a more helpful direction. The remarks that follow are intended to reinforce that shift in several ways.

First, we may want to construe Abraham's response to God in a way that diminishes the strong bifurcation of the religious and ethical that Kierkegaard's division encourages. Any particularistic relationship of trust is likely to take us into uncharted

---

[22] Interestingly, the New Testament does not single out Abraham's faith as exemplary in a way that the faith of martyrs and others is not. What is special about the response of Abraham is the context of his call, not the exceptional quality of his faith.

[23] In its outcome, the story is no doubt also meant to say something about the trustworthiness of the God in whom trust is to be placed—that is, that God *will* provide.

and perilous waters, in which we are called to set aside appearances in the name of the trustworthiness of the object of trust. In the *akedah*, Abraham's commitment to God, grounded as it has been up to that time in various evidences of God's righteousness— "shall not the judge of all the earth do right?"—is now being taken to a further level as Abraham is asked to move into morally hazardous territory. God wishes the child of promise to be sacrificed to him as an expression of his devotion. The God who promised and provided now tests the integrity of Abraham's trust, by "recalling" the gift through which the promise was to be realized. That is no trivial expectation. Even though Isaac was not any child that Abraham might have had, but the child of promise, it is repeatedly made clear in the text that this is a child that Abraham loves.

Note, though, that Abraham is not being asked to respond to the bare command of someone characterized simply by power or authority but rather to one who—in the Sodom announcement and other events—has displayed a certain moral character, sometimes in the face of Abraham's own moral weakness. The question is whether Abraham's loyalty is robust enough for the role that he is called to assume as the father of a great people. The question for trust is as follows: Has Abraham been given any reason—apart from the immediate request—to believe that the God he has followed from Haran, the God who has made specific promises to him, the God who has shown himself able to provide an heir, and the God who has shown himself to be just and watchful over him will now show himself to be other than what he has had reason to believe he is? True, that does not diminish the magnitude and apparent moral incomprehensibility of what he is now being asked to do. But it provides a distinctive context for the request and indicates that what is at issue is Abraham's trust and God's trustworthiness rather than (simply) God's power and Abraham's obedience.

To the extent that this is so, the religious demand on Abraham is not so much a violation of the ethical as a call to a different ethical demand, one embedded in the trust created by a relationship that has been grounded in ethically infused expectations. It is, perhaps, with reason that Kierkegaard speaks not so much of the "overriding" or "superseding" as of the "suspension" of the ethical, and not so much of the mere suspension of the ethical as its "teleological" suspension. Nevertheless, Kierkegaard's terminology is disconcerting, even given its seemingly anti-Hegelian focus. There are hints of this in Kierkegaard himself, hints that have some of their more contemporary expressions in the debate over universalism and particularism. We need to keep in mind that Kierkegaard's primary concern in *Fear and Trembling* is the prevailing Danish Hegelianism in its demand that the religious believer subject himself to public norms directed to the fulfillment of a common good. As I suggested earlier, there are significant similarities between Kierkegaard's rejection of what he views as the inauthenticity of neo-Hegelian ethics and Bernard Williams's concern about the personal destructiveness of giving primacy to universalistic moral theories. The choice that Abraham makes to stand before God in a singular relationship of trust, responsive to the connection that he has forged with him, has some parallels to Williams's choice of ground projects that give human life its meaning and worth. As Calvin Schrag puts it, "What is suspended in Kierkegaard's teleological suspension is not the ethical mode of existence but the ethical as a universal moral requirement."[24] As Williams chooses to make a distinction between the moral life and the good one, Kierkegaard wants to distinguish between two conceptions of the ethical, one in which the individual "determines his relation to the absolute by his relation to the universal" and the other in which the individual "determines his relation to the universal by his relation to the absolute." As he puts it, it does not "follow from this that ethics should be entirely abolished, but it receives an entirely different expression."[25]

The point, perhaps, is this. Faith as loyal trust is not something "beyond" ethics, but a significant dimension of it. Indeed, if we think of the core of ethics as the conditions under which we relate to each other, then trust will enter into ethics at two levels—our relations to each other as fellow human beings and our special relations to others as particularistic associates (friends, families, and so forth). In the latter case, in which we tend to make ourselves more vulnerable to others, trust will have a heightened role. Faith as trust may have its base in publicly determinable events and experiences, but when established as faith—Kierkegaard's "leap"—it calls us beyond the base on which it was erected, and we are made vulnerable to the associative other. We may find ourselves disappointed, misguided, or betrayed.

Second, although friendship and other intimate relationships are not blind, they may make demands on us to which we would not be inclined to respond positively absent the relationship. Consider the situation in which a close friend is accused of a horrible crime and in which the evidence so far gathered seems to point to the friend's guilt. But the friend professes to you that he is entirely innocent and asks for your trust. What are you to do? You can imagine—given what you have seen of the evidence—that a jury would convict him. But you know your friend well, and it does not appear, given what you know, that he would do that of which he has been accused. It would be—so far as you are able to tell—completely out of character. That, of course, does not show that he could not have done it: people act out of character frequently enough. But your loyalty and trust are now tested by a lot of hard evidence. If your loyalty is not to be blind, there must be some point at which you will have to

[24] Calvin O. Schrag, "Note on Kierkegaard's Teleological Suspension of the Ethical," *Ethics* 70, no.1 (October 1959): 67.
[25] Kierkegaard, *Fear and Trembling*, ch. 4.

be willing to say: "I was wrong. He did it, and I feel betrayed." But if you know your friend well and have every reason to believe that he has spoken truthfully to you (since that has been part of the relationship), it may not be unreasonable for you to loyally stick with him when most others have no reason to do so. Unlike them, you have a reason—you have a well-formed relationship that makes it reasonable that you trust him, at least for now.

The analogy, of course, is far from perfect. Your friend is not asking you to do what appears to be a heinous act. And Abraham is not just dealing with a close friend—he is dealing with God, and religious encounters are inherently more problematic than straightforwardly ethical encounters with other human beings. To the outsider at least, there is much more room for self-deception and mistake. Assume, though, as I have for the purpose of this discussion, that the facts are as the story indicates. As such, the story illustrates the way in which particularistic relationships may create their own ethical expectations that, certainly to an outsider, but even to an insider, may stand in a problematic relation to universalistic moral requirements. Nevertheless, barring contingencies, such tensions are unlikely to be permanent. At some point, the loyalty will be shown to be justified or misplaced. And in the case of the *akedah*, we are told, the request was a test that was resolved after a few difficult days. Isaac was not sacrificed, even though Abraham's faith was such that for the God he had come to serve, he was prepared to go forward as God had asked.

Third, it may be instructive to the case I am making to speculate what would have happened had Abraham gone through with the sacrifice and there was no resurrection or other restoration of the promise. One possibility would have been for Abraham to have retained his faith in God. God had demanded the sacrifice of him, and that was it: God gave and God had taken away. Abraham's loyalty would have been absolute. But loyalty that continued after such a repugnant outcome would not only have been absolute; it would have also been blind. Different though his life might have been from then on, it would have been a life in which his loyalty had not wavered. Absolute indeed, but morally perverse. On my own reading of the story, however, had things not turned out somewhat as they did, Abraham would have been devastated. Had the sacrifice been made and God not resurrected Isaac or in some other way made good on the promise, Abraham would—and should—have felt betrayed by the God in whom he had so completely placed his trust. The Abraham who asserted that he and Isaac would return after worshipping and who trusted that God would provide for the sacrifice would have been shattered by what had come to be (and what he had done).

Fourth, as I have already suggested, there is an important insider-outsider dimension to the *akedah*—not only how the situation would have presented itself to

Abraham and someone observing the events[26] but also how the situation might be represented by the religious believer and nonreligious. What the young men accompanying Abraham might have thought had they continued up the mountain (that Abraham was crazy?) was not what Abraham would have been thinking, given the relation in which he stood to the God who had called him to act in a particular way. We should not be surprised to find a similar difference between the religious believer and skeptic reviewing the story—though of course we can make no inference about the correctness of one vis-à-vis the other. The religious believer is likely to see in the story a confirmation of the trustworthiness of the God in whom his faith rests; the skeptic might be partially mollified but continue to believe that there was something profoundly immoral on the part of both parties in the story. Somewhat like the person who conditionally trusts the innocent protestations of the close friend, despite the daunting accumulation of evidence, trust may show a good deal of resilience. It may be misplaced—but will be maintained beyond the point at which nonassociated others will be prepared to go. Only subsequent events—if even those, sometimes—will enable us to determine who was right.

CONCLUSION

My conclusion from this, then, is not that absolute loyalties may sometimes be legitimate and that the story of Abraham represents one such case. It is, rather, the opposite. Even in this "limiting" case, in which God seeks wholehearted loyalty in circumstances that appear to transgress moral boundaries and absolutize itself, such loyalty is legitimately given only against a background of circumstances in which it makes some sense to give it. Were it not to have been a test, were Abraham not to have considered that God would provide and that he would return with Isaac after worshipping, were Abraham not to have trusted that the judge of all the earth would act rightly, were Abraham not to have had a strong sense of the larger mission to which he had been called and for which God's provision (of Isaac) had been made, even in the face of what seemed from where he stood to be the abandonment of everything he stood for, then his loyalty would have been blind and perverse. Such is generally the case with absolute loyalties, whether religious, political, or institutional. The story of Abraham is not so much an encouragement to them, but a cautionary tale about how much needs to be in place for an associative commitment to flirt with absolute expectations.

---

[26] There is a great deal of discussion about how Sarah did or didn't figure in the events. Insofar as the story offers any clues, I suspect that the reason probably relates to this distinction. The story is about Abraham's faith in God, something he must resolve on his own. More interesting—though this does not get as much attention—is Isaac's sense of what is going on.

CONCLUDING NOTE

Why is loyalty such a problematic virtue? The simplest and most general answer is that it often keeps bad company. Loyalty is a virtue of association—a normative glue that binds a person to a particular associational object. Because the associational object may vary in its character, loyalty, as costly perseverance in the conditions that undergird that bond, can easily go astray if the associational object is deeply flawed. On its own, loyalty is no more able to determine the worthiness of its object than sincerity or conscientiousness, though a virtuous person, governed by *phronesis*, will seek to ensure that loyalty is not misplaced. Its vulnerability to bad company, however, should not lead us to dismiss its importance for maintaining good company.

Loyalty's problematic character is reinforced by the fact that, as an associative bond, it involves some form of trust in its object, and, like love, affection, and other associative bonds, views them from the inside rather than the outside. Just as the perspectives of a religious believer and friend are different from those of an anthropologist and sociologist of religious belief and friendship, the perspective of the loyalist is first and foremost that of the insider. Yet the wall of separation between inside and outside is a porous one, and the loyalist need not be imprisoned within. One of our distinctively human powers is the ability to step outside while remaining inside—of open-mindedness in trust, open to reviewing our commitments while remaining true to them.

It was a great strength of the ancients that they did not approach virtues in an isolated fashion but as a cluster of practical traits, moderating each other and securing the virtuous against tendencies inimical to their individual and collective human flourishing. True, the membership of that cluster is a matter of ongoing debate, but insofar as we accept the importance of associative relationships, loyalty is almost certain to figure.

It is regrettable that the altogether admirable emphasis on human individuality, so impressively and engagingly articulated in chapter 3 of Mill's *On Liberty*, has been associated with a failure to acknowledge the communal or associative dimensions of our human flourishing. No doubt, the glorification of the human individual and insistence on the separateness of individuals was a salutary reaction against tyranny, whether by despots, "the majority," or even the group. But, as in loyalty's case, the misuse and corruption of important dimensions of our well-being should not blind us to their better angels. The fine balance and interpenetration of individuality and community constitutes an ongoing but necessary challenge.

The human task, as distinct from the philosophical one, is to root ourselves in relationships, institutions, and associations that are not only conducive to and elements of our well-being but also have inner resources that will enable them to remain that way. It was to encourage that understanding of loyalty that I sought to highlight the place of a loyal opposition—to secure loyalty against those would improperly absolutize it. Of course, as I endeavored to show, even a loyal opposition may not always be enough. Associational objects can forfeit their claim to our loyalty, and, in such cases, it is no disloyalty to abandon them. Our flourishing may be bound up with our bonds to others, but not any and every bond will do or always do.

Where should our loyalties be placed? That is not a question to which there is a clearly defined liberal answer: most generally, in relationships and institutions that contribute in various ways to our human flourishing. I have focused on a range of associative objects—friends, families, organizations, professions, national, patrial, and religious groups—that are commonly considered objects for our serious loyalties and reviewed some of the conditions under which it is valuable for and even incumbent on us to develop loyalties in relation to them. I make no claims about the completeness of my listing, even though some of them are cast in very broad terms, but hope that I have given some account of why, commonly, some of their incarnations become legitimate, even obligatory, objects of our loyalty.

If the foregoing seems obvious, that may not be a bad thing. It has not been my purpose to develop some radically new account of loyalty but to develop in detail why Pettit and others have seen loyalty as central to commonsense morality and to rescue loyalty from both its proponents and critics via an assessment of its problematic character. Novelty, even in ethics, has a place, yet I remain mindful of J. L. Austin's observation that

> our common stock of words embodies all the distinctions men have found worth drawing, and the connections they have found worth marking, in the lifetime

of many generations: these surely are likely to be more numerous, more sound, since they have stood up to the long test of survival of the fittest, and more subtle, at least in all ordinary and reasonable practical matters, than any that you or I are likely to think up in our armchair of an afternoon—the most favourite alternative method.[1]

[1] J. L. Austin, "A Plea for Excuses," in *Philosophical Papers*, ed. J. O. Urmson and G. J. Warnock (Oxford: Oxford University Press, 1961), 130.

REFERENCES

Adams, Robert M. "The Virtue of Faith." In *The Virtue of Faith and Other Essays in Philosophical Theology*, 9–24. New York: Oxford University Press, 1987.

Aeschylus. *Agamemnon*. Translated by E. D. A. Morshead. http://classics.mit.edu/Aeschylus/agamemnon.html.

Agassi, Joseph. "The Last Refuge of the Scoundrel." *Philosophia* 4, no. 2–3 (1974): 315–317.

Aldington, Richard. *The Colonel's Daughter: A Novel*. New York: Doubleday, 1931.

Allen, R. T. "Rational Autonomy: The Destruction of Freedom." *Journal of Philosophy of Education* 16, no. 2 (1982): 199–207.

Allen, R. T. "When Loyalty No Harm Meant." *Review of Metaphysics* 43, no. 2 (1989): 281–294.

Anscombe, (G. E. M.) Gertrude Elizabeth Margaret. "Modern Moral Philosophy." *Philosophy* 33, no. 124 (1958): 1–19.

Applbaum, Arthur Isak. "Professional Detachment: The Executioner of Paris." *Harvard Law Review* 109, no. 2 (1995): 458–486.

Applbaum, Arthur Isak. "Are *Lawyers* Liars? The Argument of Redescription." *Legal Theory* 4, no.1 (1998): 63–91.

Aquinas, Thomas. *Summa Theologiae Theologica*. Translated by Fathers of the English Dominican Province. www.ccel.org/ccel/aquinas/summa.html.

Ariès, Philippe. *Centuries of Childhood*. London: Cape, 1962.

Aristotle. *Complete Works of Aristotle, Volume 2: The Revised Oxford Translation*. Edited by J. Barnes. Princeton, NJ: Princeton University Press, 1984.

Augustine. *The Good of Marriage*. Translated by Charles T. Wilcox. New York: Fathers of the Church, 1955.

Austin, John L. "A Plea for Excuses." In *Philosophical Papers*, edited by James O. Urmson and Geoffrey J. Warnock, 123–152. Oxford: Oxford University Press, 1961.

Austin, John L. *Sense and Sensibilia*. Oxford: Oxford University Press, 1962.

Axinn, Sidney. "Loyalty and the Limits of Patriotism." In *Political Realism and International Morality: Ethics in the Nuclear Age*, edited by Kenneth Kipnis and Diana T. Meyers, 239–250. Boulder, CO: Westview, 1987.

Axinn, Sidney. "Thoughts in Response to Fr. John C. Haughey on Loyalty in the Workplace." *Business Ethics Quarterly* 4, no. 3 (1994): 355–357.

Badhwar, Neera Kapur, ed. *Friendship: A Philosophical Reader*. Ithaca, NY: Cornell, 1993.

Baehr, Jason. "The Structure of Open-Mindedness." *Canadian Journal of Philosophy* 41, no. 2 (2011): 191–213.

Barker, Peter. "Wends, Serbs or Sorbs? The British Foreign Office and the Sorbs of Lusatia (1942–47)." *German Life and Letters* 48, no. 3 (1995): 362–370.

Barker, Peter. "From Wendish-Speaking Germans to Sorbian-Speaking Citizens of the GDR: Contradictions in the Language Policy of the SED." In *Finding a Voice: Problems of Language in East German Society and Culture*, edited by Graham Jackman and Ian F. Roe, 39–54. Amsterdam: Rodopi, 2000.

Baron, Marcia. *The Moral Status of Loyalty*. Dubuque, IA: Kendall/Hunt, 1984.

Baron, Marcia. "Impartiality and Friendship." *Ethics* 101 (1991): 839–842.

Bates, Katharine Lee. "America the Beautiful." http://kids.niehs.nih.gov/lyrics/america.htm.

Beatty, Joseph. "Him or Me?" *American Philosophical Quarterly* 23, no. 3 (1986): 231–241.

Benn, Piers. "Forgiveness and Loyalty." *Philosophy* 71, no. 277 (1996): 369–383.

Benn, Stanley. *A Theory of Freedom*. Cambridge: Cambridge University Press, 1987.

Benner, Erica. "Is There a Core National Doctrine?" *Nations and Nationalism* 7, no. 2 (2001): 158–159.

Berman, Louis A. *Akedah: The Binding of Isaac*. Lanham, MD: Rowman and Littlefield, 1997.

The Bible. New Revised Standard Version. Division of Christian Education of the National Council of the Churches of Christ in the United States of America, 1989.

Blamires, Harry. *The Christian Mind*. London: S.P.C.K., 1963.

Bloch, Herbert A. *The Concept of Our Changing Loyalties: An Introductory Study into the Nature of the Social Individual*. New York: Columbia University Press, 1934.

Blum, Lawrence. "Friendship as a Moral Phenomenon," in *Friendship: A Philosophical Reader*, edited by Neera Kapur Badhwar, 192–210. Ithaca, NY: Cornell, 1993.

Blustein, Jeffrey. *Parents and Children: The Ethics of the Family*. New York: Oxford University Press, 1982.

Blustein, Jeffrey. *Care and Commitment: Taking the Personal Point of View*. New York: Oxford University Press, 1991.

Boswell, James. *The Life of Samuel Johnson, LL.D.* London: Macmillan, 1900.

Bouville, Mathieu. "Is Diversity Good? Six Possible Conceptions of Diversity and Six Possible Answers." *Science and Engineering Ethics* 14, no. 1 (2008): 51–63.

Boxill, Bernard R. "Frederick Douglass's Patriotism." *Journal of Ethics* 13, no. 4 (2009): 301–317.

Brighouse, Harry, and Adam Swift. "Parents' Rights and the Value of the Family." *Ethics* 117 (2006): 80–108.

Brighouse, Harry, and Adam Swift. "Legitimate Parental Partiality." *Philosophy & Public Affairs* 37, no. 1 (2009): 43–80.

Bruck, Connie. "Rudolph Giuliani." *American Lawyer* 11, no. 3 (1989): 99+.

Bryant, Sophie. "Loyalty." In *Encyclopedia of Religion and Ethics*, edited by James Hastings, vol. 8, 183–188. Edinburgh: T. & T. Clarke, 1915.

Burgess, Ann Wolbert, Lynda Lytle Holmstrom, and Maureen P. McCausland. "Divided Loyalty in Incest Cases." In *Sexual Assault of Children and Adolescents*, edited by Ann Wolbert Burgess, A. Nicholas Groth, Lynda Lytle Holmstrom, and Suzanne M. Sgroi, 115–126. Lexington, MA: Lexington Books, 1978.

Butler, Joseph. *Fifteen Sermons Preached at the Rolls Chapel*. Cambridge: Hilliard & Brown, 1827. http://anglicanhistory.org/butler/rolls/.

Callan, Eamonn. "Love, Idolatry, and Patriotism." *Social Theory and Practice* 32, no. 4 (2006): 525–546.

Callan, Eamonn. "The Better Angels of Our Nature: Patriotism and Dirty Hands." *Journal of Political Philosophy* 18, no. 3 (2010): 249–270.

Canovan, Margaret. "Patriotism Is Not Enough." *British Journal of Political Science* 30 (2000): 413–432.

Carr, David. "Chastity and Adultery." *American Philosophical Quarterly* 23, no. 4 (1986): 363–371.

Carville, James. *We're Right, They're Wrong: A Handbook for Spirited Progressives.* New York: Simon & Schuster, 1996.

Carville, James. *Stickin': The Case for Loyalty.* New York: Simon & Schuster, 2000.

Center for Professional Responsibility, American Bar Assocation. *Model Rules of Professional Conduct.* Chicago: American Bar Association, 2007.

Chan, Sin Yee. "Paternalistic Wife? Paternalistic Stranger?" *Social Theory and Practice* 26, no. 1 (2000): 85–101.

Chesterton, Gilbert K. "A Defence of Patriotism." In *The Defendant* (1901). www.cse.dmu.ac.uk/~mward/gkc/books/The_Defendant.html.

Church of England. *Book of Common Prayer.* www.cofe.anglican.org/worship/liturgy/commonworship/texts/marriage/marriage.html.

Cicero. *Laelius de Amicitia (On Friendship).* Translated by Evelyn Shirley Shuckburgh. www.gutenberg.org/ebooks/2808.

Clark, Stephen R. L. "Good Dogs and Other Animals." In *In Defense of Animals*, edited by Peter Singer, 41–51. New York: Harper & Row, 1985.

CNN. *The Situation Room*, September 23, 2009. http://transcripts.cnn.com/TRANSCRIPTS/0909/23/sitroom.02.html.

Cochran, Ruth B. "Some Problems with Loyalty: The Metaethics of Commitment." *Dialectics and Humanism* 17, no. 3 (1990): 201–210.

Cocking, Dean, and Jeanette Kennett. "Friendship and the Self." *Ethics* 108, no. 4 (April 1998): 502–527.

Cocking, Dean, and Jeanette Kennett. "Friendship and Moral Danger." *Journal of Philosophy* 97 (2000): 278–296.

Cocking, Dean, and Justin Oakley, "Indirect Consequentialism, Friendship, and the Problem of Alienation." *Ethics* 106 (1995): 86–111.

Confucius, *Analects* (Lún Yŭ. www.confucius.org/lunyu/lange.htm.

Connor, James. *The Sociology of Loyalty.* New York: Springer, 2007.

Conrad, Joseph. *Collected Works.* http://ebooks.adelaide.edu.au/c/conrad/joseph/index.html.

Cooper, John M. "Aristotle on the Forms of Friendship." *Review of Metaphysics* 30, no. 4 (1977): 619–648.

Cooper, John M. "Friendship and the Good in Aristotle." *Philosophical Review* 86, no. 3 (1977): 290–315.

Cooper, John M. "Friendship." In *Encyclopedia of Ethics*, Volume 1, edited by L. Becker, 388–91. New York: Garland, 1991.

Cooper, John M. "Political Animals and Civic Friendship," reprinted in *Friendship: A Philosophical Reader*, edited by Neera Kapur Badhwar, 303–326. Ithaca, NY: Cornell University Press, 1993.

Cooper, John M. "The Unity of Virtue." *Social Philosophy & Policy* 15, no. 1 (1998): 233–274.

Cooper, John M. *Reason and Emotion: Essays on Moral Psychology and Ethical Theory.* Princeton, NJ: Princeton University Press, 1999.

Costigan Jr., George P. "The Full Remarks on Advocacy of Lord Brougham and Lord Chief Justice Cockburn at the Dinner to M. Berryer on November 8, 1864." *California Law Review* 19, no. 5 (1931): 521–523.

Cottingham, John. "Ethics and Impartiality." *Philosophical Studies* 43, no. 1 (1983): 83–99.

Crick, Bernard. "Two Theories of Opposition." *New Statesman*, June 18, 1960, 882–883.

Davie, William. "Hume on Monkish Virtues." *Hume Studies* 25, no. 1–2 (1999): 139–154.

Davis, Michael. "Thinking Like an Engineer: The Place of a Code of Ethics in the Practice of a Profession." *Philosophy & Public Affairs* 20, no. 2 (1991): 150–167.

Davis, Michael. "Some Paradoxes of Whistleblowing." *Business and Professional Ethics Journal* 15, no. 1 (1996): 3–19.

Death in Brunswick. DVD. Directed by John Ruane. Roadshow Entertainment (Australia). 1991.

Decatur, Stephen. "Toast Given at Norfolk," April, 1816. Reported in Niles's *Weekly Register* (Baltimore), April 20, 1816. Reproduced in *Respectfully Quoted: A Dictionary of Quotations* (2010), Library of Congress, Congressional Research Service.

DeGeorge, Richard T. "Ethical Responsibilities of Engineers in Large Organizations: The Pinto Case." *Business & Professional Ethics Journal* 1, no. 1 (1981): 1–14.

DeGeorge, Richard T. *Business Ethics*, 3rd ed. New York: Macmillan, 1990.

Delaney, Carol. *Abraham on Trial: The Social Legacy of Biblical Myth*. Princeton, NJ: Princeton University Press, 1998.

De Maria, William. "Whistleblowing—International Bibliography" (1995), University of Queensland. www.bmartin.cc/dissent/documents/DeMaria_bib.html.

Dewey, John. *Human Nature and Conduct: An Introduction to Social Psychology*. London: Allen & Unwin, 1922.

Dickens, Charles. *Bleak House*. 1852–1853. www.gutenberg.org/ebooks/1023.

Dictionnaire étymologique de la langue latine: histoire des mots, 4th ed. Edited by Alfred Ernout and Antoine Meillet. Paris: Librairie C. Klincksieck, 1959.

Disraeli, Benjamin. *Lord George Bentinck: A Political Biography*. London: Routledge, 1858.

Duska, Ronald. "Whistleblowing and Employee Loyalty." In *Contemporary Issues in Business Ethics*, edited by Joseph DesJardins and John McCall. Belmont, CA: Wadsworth, 1985.

Ehrenreich, Barbara. "Family Values." In *The Worst Years of Our Lives: Irreverent Notes from a Decade of Greed*. New York: Harper Collins, 1991.

Ewin, R. E. *Co-operation and Human Values: A Study of Moral Reasoning*. Brighton, UK: Harvester, 1981.

Ewin, R. E. "Loyalty: The Police." *Criminal Justice Ethics* 9, no. 2 (1990): 3–15.

Ewin, R. E. "Loyalty and Virtues." *Philosophical Quarterly* 42, no. 169 (1992): 403–419.

Ewin, R. E. "Corporate Loyalty: Its Objects and Its Grounds." *Journal of Business Ethics* 12, no. 5 (1993): 387–396.

Ewin, R. E. "Loyalties, and Why Loyalty Should be Ignored." *Criminal Justice Ethics* 12, no. 1 (1993): 36–42.

"Faithful Old Dog Awaits Return of Master Dead for Seven Years." *Asahi Shimbun*, October 4, 1933.

Feinberg, Joel. *Harmless Wrongdoing: The Moral Limits of Criminal Law*, vol. 4. New York: Oxford University Press, 1990.

Feldman, Yael. *Glory and Agony: Isaac's Sacrifice and National Narrative*. Stanford, CA: Stanford University Press, 2010.

Fink, Sheri. "Tortured Profession: Psychologists Warned of Abusive Interrogations, Then Helped Craft Them." *ProPublica*, May 5, 2009. www.propublica.org/article/tortured-profession-psychologists-warned-of-abusive-interrogations-505.

Fisher, David H. "Loyalty, Tolerance, and Recognition: Aspects of Morality in a Multicultural Society." *Journal of Value Inquiry* 31, no.3 (1997): 339–351.

Fitzgerland, John T., ed. *Friendship, Flattery and Frankness of Speech: Studies on Friendship in the New Testament World*. Leiden: E. J. Brill, 1996.

Fletcher, George. *Loyalty: An Essay on the Morality of Relationships*. New York: Oxford University Press, 1993.

Foord, Archibald Smith. *His Majesty's Opposition 1714–1830*. Oxford: Clarendon, 1964.

Foot, Philippa. *Virtues and Vices*. Oxford: Oxford University Press, 1978.

Foust, Mathew A. *Loyalty to Loyalty: Josiah Royce and the Genuine Moral Life*. New York: Fordham University Press, 2012.

Fox, Ellen L. "Paternalism and Friendship." *Canadian Journal of Philosophy* 23, no. 4 (1993): 575–594.

Freedman, Monroe. *Lawyers' Ethics in an Adversary System*. Indianapolis, IN: Bobbs Merrill, 1975.

Freedman, Monroe, and Abbe Smith. *Understanding Lawyers' Ethics*, 3rd ed. New York: Matthew Bender, 2004.

Fried, Charles. *Order and Law: Arguing the Reagan Revolution—A Firsthand Account*. New York: Simon & Schuster, 1991.

Fuller, Lon L. "The Philosophy of Codes of Ethics." In *Moral Responsibility and the Professions*, edited by Bernard Baumrin and Benjamin Freedman. New York: Haven, 1984.

Gabriel, Richard A. *To Serve with Honor: A Treatise on Military Ethics and the Way of the Soldier*. Westport, CT: Greenwood, 1982.

Gallie, Walter B. "Essentially Contested Concepts." *Proceedings of the Aristotelian Society* 56 (1955–1956): 167–198.

Galsworthy, John. *Loyalties: A Drama in Three Acts*. New York: Charles Scribner's Sons, 1922.

Gaus, Gerald F. *The Modern Liberal Theory of Man*. New York: St. Martin's Press, 1983.

Gellman, Jerome I. *Abraham! Abraham! Kierkegaard and the Hasidim on the Binding of Isaac*. Aldershot, UK: Ashgate, 2003.

Gellner, Ernest. *Nations and Nationalism*. Ithaca, NY: Cornell University Press, 1983.

Gert, Bernard. *Morality: A New Justification of the Moral Rules*. New York: Oxford University Press, 1988.

Gewirth, Alan. *Reason and Morality*. Chicago: University of Chicago Press, 1978.

Gewirth, Alan. "Ethical Universalism and Particularism." *Journal of Philosophy* 85, 6 (1988): 283–302.

Gilmour, Bill (MP for Comox-Alberni). Press Release: "Her Majesty's Loyal Opposition." www.parl.gc.ca/HousePublications/Publication.aspx?DocId=2332524&Language=E&Mode=1#16829.

Giuliani, Rudy, with Ken Kurson. *Leadership*. New York: Miramax Books/Hyperion, 2002.

Glazer, Myron Peretz, and Penina Migdal Glazer. *The Whistleblowers: Exposing Corruption in Government and Industry*. New York: Basic Books, 1989.

Godwin, William. *Enquiry Concerning Political Justice and Its Influence on Morals and Happiness*, 3rd ed., edited by F. E. L. Priestley. Toronto: Toronto University Press, 1946.

Godwin, William. *St Leon; A Tale of the Sixteenth Century (1799)*. http://gutenberg.net.au/ebooks06/0605711.txt.

Goman, Carol Kinsey. *The Loyalty Factor: A Management Guide to the Changing Dynamics of Loyalty in the Workplace*. New York: Donald I. Fine, 1991.

Gomberg, Paul. "Patriotism Is Like Racism." *Ethics* 101 (1990): 144–150.

Green, Leslie. "Loyalty, Security and Democracy." In *National Security: Surveillance and Accountability in a Democratic Society*, edited by Peter Hanks and John D. McCamus. Quebec: Éditions Yvon Blais, 1989.

Greenawalt, Kent. *Conflicts of Law and Morality*. Oxford: Clarendon, 1987.

Greene, Graham. *The Virtue of Disloyalty*. London: Bodley Head, 1972.

Gromm, Michael. "The Battle of Horno." http://slavia.8m.com/horno-p.htm.

Grote, John. *An Examination of the Utilitarian Philosophy*, edited by Joseph Bickersteth Mayor. Cambridge: Deighton, 1870.

Habermas, Jürgen. *The New Conservatism: Cultural Criticism and the Historian's Debate*. Cambridge: Polity, 1989.

Habermas, Jürgen. "Citizenship and National Identity: Some Reflections of the Future of Europe." *Praxis International* 12, no. 1 (1992): 1–19.

Hardimon, Michael O. "Role Obligations." *Journal of Philosophy* 91, no. 7 (1994): 333–363.

Hare, (R. M.) Richard M. *Moral Thinking: Its Levels, Method and Point*. Oxford: Clarendon, 1981.

Hare, (R. M.) Richard M. *The Morality of Freedom*. Oxford: Clarendon, 1986.

Hart, (H. L. A.) Herbert L. A. "Are There Any Natural Rights?" *Philosophical Review* 64, no. 2 (1955): 175–191.

Harvard University. "Policies Relating to Research and Other Professional Activities within and outside the University." www.fas.harvard.edu/~research/greybook/policies.html.

Haun, Pamela A. "The Marital Privilege in the Twenty-First Century." *University of Memphis Law Review* 32 (2001): 137–178.

Hazard Jr., Geoffrey C. "Triangular Lawyer Relationships: An Exploratory Analysis." *Georgetown Journal of Legal Ethics* 1, no. 1 (1987): 15–42.

Hegel, (G. W. F.) Georg. *Philosophy of Right*. Translated by Thomas Malcolm Knox. Oxford: Oxford University Press, 1967.

Heinz, John H., and Edward O. Laumann. *Chicago Lawyers: The Social Structure of the Bar*. New York: Russell Sage Foundation, 1982.

Held, Virginia. *The Ethics of Care: Personal, Political, Global*. New York: Oxford University Press, 2006.

Hickley, Catherine. "Germany's Sorb Minority Fights to Save Villages From Vattenfall." *Bloomberg.com*, December 18, 2007. www.bloomberg.com/apps/news?pid=20601088& sid=aCW1fh0XInBE&refer=muse.

Hirschman, Albert O. *Exit, Voice, and Loyalty: Response to Decline in Firms, Organizations, and States*. Cambridge, MA: Harvard University Press, 1970.

Hirschman, Albert O. "Exit, Voice, and Loyalty: Further Reflections and a Survey of Recent Contributions." *Social Science Information* 13, no. 1 (1974): 7–26.

Hobsbawm, Eric. *Nations and Nationalism since 1780: Programme, Myth, Reality*. Cambridge: Cambridge University Press, 1990.

Hockin, Thomas A. "The Roles of the Loyal Opposition in Britain's House of Commons: Three Historical Paradigms." *Parliamentary Affairs* 25, no. 1 (1971): 50–68.

Höpfl, H .M. "Isms." *British Journal of Political Science* 13, no. 1 (1983): 1–17.

Horton, John. *Political Obligation*. London: Macmillan, 1992.

Hume, David. *Treatise of Human Nature*. Edited by L. A. Selby-Bigge. Oxford: Clarendon, 1888.

Hume, David. *An Enquiry Concerning the Principles of Morals*. Edited by Tom L. Beauchamp. Oxford: Oxford University Press, 1998.

Instructions for the Government of Armies of the United States in the Field (1863). General Order No. 100. http://avalon.law.yale.edu/19th_century/lieber.asp.

Itoh, Mayum. *The Truth of the Life and Legend of the Most Famous Dog in Japan*. Amazon: 2013, Kindle edition.

Jahn, Beate. "Barbarian Thoughts: Imperialism in the Philosophy of John Stuart Mill." *Review of International Studies* 31, no. 3 (July 2005): 599–618.

Jennings, W. Ivor. *Cabinet Government*. Cambridge: Cambridge University Press, 1936.

Johns v. Smyth, 176 F. Supp. 949 (1959).

Judge, Edwin A. "St Paul as a Radical Critic of Society." *Interchange* 16 (1974): 191–203.

Kant, Immanuel. *Lecture-Notes on Pedagogy*. In *Kant's Educational Theory*. Translated and edited by Edward Franklin Buchner. Philadelphia: Lippincott Company, 1904. http://ia600407.us.archive.org/15/items/cu31924032702981/cu31924032702981.pdf.

Kant, Immanuel. *Groundwork of the Metaphysic of Morals*. Translated by Herbert (H. J.) Paton. New York: Harper & Row, 1956.

Kant, Immanuel. *Lectures on Ethics*. Translated by Louis Infield. New York: Harper & Row, 1963.

Kant, Immanuel. "Lecture on Friendship." In *Lectures on Ethics*. Translated by Louis Infield. New York: Harper and Row, 1963.

Kasachkoff, Tziporah. "Explaining and Justifying." *Informal Logic* 10, no. 1 (1988): 21–30.

Kasachkoff, Tziporah, and Isaac Nevo. "Is It Wise to Teach Our Students to Follow the Argument Wherever It Leads?" *Teaching Philosophy* 29, no. 2 (2006): 157–172.

Keller, Simon. "Patriotism as Bad Faith." *Ethics* 115 (2005): 563–592.

Keller, Simon. *The Limits of Loyalty*. Cambridge: Cambridge University Press, 2007.

Kelly, Thomas. "Following the Argument Where It Leads." *Philosophical Studies* 154, no. 1 (2011): 105–124.

Kennedy, John F. Inaugural Speech, January 20, 1961. www.famousquotes.me.uk/speeches/John_F_Kennedy/5.htm.

Kierkegaard, Søren. *Fear and Trembling*. Translated by Walter Lowrie. Princeton, NJ: Princeton University Press, 1941. www.religion-online.org/showbook.asp?title=2068.

Kierkegaard, Søren. *Works of Love*. Translated by Howard V. Hong and Edna H. Hong. New York: Harper & Row, 1962.

Kierkegaard, Søren. *The Point of View for My Work as an Author*. Edited by Benjamin Nelson. London: Joanna Coulter, 1978.

Kleinig, John. "Conceptual Cannibalism: The Social Scientific Appropriation of Ordinary Discourse." *International Journal of Applied Philosophy* 6, no. 2 (1991): 1–12.

Kleinig, John. *The Ethics of Policing*. Cambridge: Cambridge University Press, 1996.

Kleinig, John. "The Blue Wall of Silence: An Ethical Analysis." *International Journal of Applied Philosophy* 15, no. 1 (2001): 1–23.

Kleinig, John, and Nicholas G. Evans. "Human Flourishing, Human Dignity, and Human Rights." *Law and Philosophy* 32, no. 5 (2013): 539–564.

Kleinig, John, and Albert J. Gorman. "Professional Courtesies: To Ticket or Not to Ticket?" In *Handbook of Police Administration*, edited by James Ruiz and Don Hummer, 193–205. New York: Taylor & Francis, 2007.

Kleinig, John, Simon Keller, and Igor Primoratz. *The Ethics of Patriotism: A Debate* (Malden, MA: Wiley Blackwell, 2014).

Kolers, Avery H. "Dynamics of Solidarity." *Journal of Political Philosophy* 20, no. 4 (2012): 365–383.

Konvitz, Milton. "Loyalty." In *Encyclopedia of the History of Ideas*, vol. 3, edited by Philip P. Wiener, 108–116. New York: Scribner, 1973.

Kovesi, Julius. *Moral Notions*. London: Routledge & Kegan Paul, 1967.

Kraus, Karl. *Half Truths and One-and-a-Half Truths: Selected Aphorisms*, edited and translated by Harry Zohn. Montreal, Quebec: Egendra, 1976.

Kraut, Richard. *Socrates and the State*. Princeton, NJ: Princeton University Press, 1984.

Kupfer, Joseph. "Can Parents and Children Be Friends?" *American Philosophical Quarterly* 27, no. 1 (1990): 15–26.

Ladd, John. "Loyalty." In *The Encyclopedia of Philosophy*, vol. 5, edited by Paul Edwards, 97–98. New York: Macmillan and Free Press, 1967.

Latimer, Matt. *Speech-less: Tales of a White House Survivor*. New York: Crown, 2009.

Lawson, Guy, and William Oldham. *The Brotherhoods: The True Story of Two Cops Who Murdered for the Mafia*. New York: Scribner, 2006.

Lear, Jonathan. *Love and Its Place in Nature*, 2nd ed. New Haven, CT: Yale University Press, 1998.

Levin, Michael. *J. S. Mill on Civilization and Barbarism*. London: Routledge, 2004.

Li, Chenyang. "Shifting Perspectives: Filial Morality Revisited." *Philosophy East and West* 47, no. 2 (1997): 211–232.

Locke, John. *Two Treatises of Government*. Edited by Thomas Hollis. London: A. Millar et al., 1764. http://oll.libertyfund.org/?option=com_staticxt&staticfile=show.php%3Ftitle=222.

Locke, John. *An Essay Concerning Human Understanding*. In *The Works of John Locke in Nine Volumes*, 12th ed., vol. 1. London: Rivington, 1824. http://oll.libertyfund.org/index.php?option=com_staticxt&staticfile=show.php%3Ftitle=761&Itemid=28.

Luban, David. "The Adversarial System Excuse." In *The Good Lawyer: Lawyers' Roles and Lawyers' Ethics*, edited by David Luban. Totowa, NJ: Rowman & Allanheld, 1984.

Luban, David. *Lawyers and Justice: An Ethical Study*. Princeton, NJ: Princeton University Press, 1988.

Maas, Frank. *Serpico*. New York: Viking, 1973.

Maas, Peter. *Underboss: Sammy the Bull Gravano's Story of Life in the Mafia*. New York: HarperCollins, 1997.

MacIntyre, Alasdair. *Is Patriotism a Virtue?* Lawrence: University of Kansas Press, 1984.

MacIver, Robert Morrison, and Charles Hunt Page. *Society: An Introductory Analysis*. New York: Rinehart, 1949.

Mackellar, Dorothea. "My Country." Originally published as "Core of My Heart." *Spectator*, September 5, 1908: 17. www.dorotheamackellar.com.au/archive/mycountry.htm.

Marcuse, Herbert. "Repressive Tolerance." In *A Critique of Pure Tolerance*, edited by Robert Paul Wolff, Barrington Moore Jr., and Herbert Marcuse, 95–137. Boston: Beacon, 1969.

Margalit, Avishai. "The Moral Psychology of Nationalism." In *The Morality of Nationalism*, edited by Robert McKim and Jeff McMahan, 74–87. Oxford: Oxford University Press, 1977.

Martin, Brian. "Illusions of Whistleblower Protection." *UTS Law Review* 5 (2003): 119–130.

Martin, Josef (pseudonym). *To Rise above Principle: Memoirs of an Unreconstructed Academic Dean*. Urbana: University of Illinois Press, 1988. http://henryhbauer.homestead.com/files/trapfull.pdf.

Martin, Mike W. "Whistleblowing: Professionalism, Personal Life, and Shared Responsibility for Safety in Engineering." *Business and Professional Ethics Journal* 11, no. 2 (1992): 21–40.

Marx, Karl, and Friedrich Engels. *The Communist Manifesto*, part 2. 1848. www.anu.edu.au/polsci/marx/classics/manifesto.html.

McChrystal, Michael K. "Professional Loyalties: A Response to John Kleinig's Account." *American Philosophical Association Newsletters, Newsletter on Philosophy and Law*, 98, no. 1 (1998): 83–90.

McConnell, Terrence. *Gratitude*. Philadelphia: Temple University Press, 1993.

Mercedes Benz Advertisement. *New York Times Magazine*, April 18, 1999, 115.

Milgram, Stanley. *Obedience to Authority: An Experimental View.* New York: Harper, 1974.

Mill, John Stuart. *Representative Government* (1861). www.constitution.org/jsm/rep_gov. htm.

Mill, John Stuart. *Utilitarianism and On Liberty,* 2nd ed. Edited by Mary Warnock. Malden, MA: Blackwell, 2003.

Minogue, Kenneth. "Loyalty, Liberalism and the State." In *Lives, Liberties and the Public Good: New Essays in Political Theory for Maurice Cranston,* edited by George Feaver and Frederick Rosen, 203–227. New York: St. Martin's Press, 1987.

Monro, D. H. "Archbishop Fénelon versus My Mother." *Australasian Journal of Philosophy* 28, no. 3 (1950): 154–173.

Montaigne, Michel de. "Of Moderation." In *Essays of Montaigne,* vol. 2. Translated by Charles Cotton and revised by William Carew Hazlett. New York: Edwin C. Hill, 1910. http://oll.libertyfund.org/?option=com_staticxt&staticfile=show.php%3Ftitle=108&ch apter=219681&layout=html&Itemid=27.

Morris, John D. "New Nader Group Seeking Tipsters; Asks Professionals to 'Blow Whistle' on Employers." *New York Times,* January 1, 1971, 32.

Nathanson, Stephen. *Patriotism, Morality, and Peace.* Lanham, MD: Rowman & Littlefield, 1993.

Nathanson, Stephen. "Nationalism and the Limits of Global Humanism." In *The Morality of Nationalism,* edited by Robert McKim and Jeff McMahan, 176–187. New York: Oxford University Press, 1997.

Nathanson, Stephen. Personal communication from Stephen Nathanson, November 23, 1998.

National Aeronautics and Space Administration. "Challenger STS 51–L Accident." http:// history.nasa.gov/sts51l.html.

National Society for Professional Engineers. "Code of Ethics for Engineers." www.nspe.org/ Ethics/CodeofEthics/index.html.

Nielsen, George R. *In Search of a Home: The Wends (Sorbs) on the Australian and Texas Frontiers,* rev. ed. College Station: Texas A. & M. University Press, 1989.

Nightingale, J., ed. *Trial of Queen Caroline,* vol 2. London: J. Robins, 1820–1821.

Noddings, Nel. *Caring: A Feminine Approach to Ethics and Moral Education.* Berkeley: University of California Press, 1984.

Note, "Developments in the Law—Privileged Communications: I: The Development of Evidentiary Privileges in American Law." *Harvard Law Review* 98, no. 7 (1985): 1450–1471.

Oldenquist, Andrew. "Loyalties." *Journal of Philosophy* 79, no. 4 (1982): 173–193.

Oldenquist, Andrew. *The Non-Suicidal Society.* Bloomington: Indiana University Press, 1986.

Oldenquist, Andrew. "The Ethics of Parts and Wholes." *Criminal Justice Ethics* 12, no. 1 (Winter–Spring 1993): 43–47.

Orwell, George. "England Your England." February 19, 1941. www.netcharles.com/orwell/ essays/lion-and-unicorn1.htm.

Pang, He How, *Singapore: From Hope to Certainty.* Maroubra, Australia: Author, 2003.

Pettit, Philip. "The Paradox of Loyalty." *American Philosophical Quarterly* 25, no. 2 (1988): 163–171.

Pettit, Philip. "Republican Freedom and Contestatory Democratization." In *Democracy's Value,* edited by Ian Shapiro and Casiano Hacker-Cordón, 163–190. Cambridge: Cambridge University Press, 1999.

Pfeiffer, Raymond S. "Owing Loyalty to One's Employer." *Journal of Business Ethics* 11, no. 7 (1992): 535–543.

Plato. *The Collected Dialogues of Plato: Including the Letters.* Edited by Edith Hamilton and Huntington Cairns. Princeton, NJ: Princeton University Press, 1961.

Plutarch. *Moralia.* Translated by Arthur Richard Shilleto. London: George Bell and Sons, 1898. www.gutenberg.org/files/23639/23639-h/23639-h.htm.

Primoratz, Igor. "Patriotism—Morally Allowed, Required, or Valuable?" In *Nationalism and Ethnic Conflict: Philosophical Perspectives,* edited by N. Miscevic, 101–113. Chicago: Open Court, 2000.

Primoratz, Igor. "Patriotism: A Deflationary View." *Philosophical Forum* 23, no. 4 (2002): 443–458.

Putnam, Robert. *Bowling Alone: The Collapse and Revival of American Community.* New York: Simon & Schuster, 2000.

Racine, Jean. *La Thébaïde ou les Frères ennemis.* 1664. www.inlibroveritas.net/lire/oeuvre388.html.

Railton, Peter. "Alienation, Consequentialism, and the Demands of Morality." *Philosophy & Public Affairs* 13, no. 2 (1984): 134–171.

Ramsey, Paul. *The Patient as Person: Explorations in Medical Ethics.* New Haven, CT: Yale University Press, 1970.

Rashke, Richard L. *The Killing of Karen Silkwood: The Story behind the Kerr-McGee Plutonium Case,* 2nd ed. Ithaca, NY: Cornell University Press, 2000.

Rawls, John. "Legal Obligation and the Duty of Fair Play." In *Law and Philosophy,* edited by Sidney Hook, 3–18. New York: New York University Press, 1964.

Rawls, John. *A Theory of Justice.* Cambridge, MA: Belknap/Harvard University Press, 1971.

Reeves, Richard. "Patriotism Calls Out the Censor." *New York Times,* October 1, 2001, A23.

Renan, Ernest. "What Is a Nation?" (1882). www.cooper.edu/humanities/core/hss3/e_renan.html.

Richards, Norvin. "Paternalism toward Friends." In *Person to Person,* edited by George Graham and Hugh LaFollette, 235–244. Philadelphia: Temple University Press, 1989.

Roberts, Robert C. "Will Power and the Virtues." *Philosophical Review* 93, no. 2 (1984): 227–247.

Roehm, Michelle L., Ellen Bolman Pullins, and Harper A. Roehm Jr. "Designing Loyalty—Building Programs for Packaged Goods Brands." *Journal of Marketing Research* 39, no. 2 (2002): 202–213.

Rorty, Richard. *Achieving Our Country: Leftist Thought in Twentieth-Century America.* Cambridge, MA: Harvard University Press, 1998.

Rousseau, Jean Jacques. *Émile.* Translated by B. Foxley. London: J. M. Dent, 1974.

Royce, Josiah. *The Philosophy of Loyalty.* New York: Macmillan, 1908. www.archive.org/details/philosophyloyal00roycuoft.

Royce, Josiah. *The Problem of Christianity.* New York: Macmillan, 1913.

Sakenfeld, Katharine Doob. *Faithfulness in Action: Loyalty in Biblical Perspective.* Philadelphia: Fortress, 1985.

Sartre, Jean-Paul. "Existentialism Is a Humanism" (1946). www.marxists.org/reference/archive/sartre/works/exist/sartre.htm.

Scheffler, Samuel. "Individual Responsibility in a Global Age." *Social Philosophy and Policy* 12, no. 1 (1995): 219–236.

Scheffler, Samuel. "Relationships and Responsibilities." *Philosophy & Public Affairs* 26, no. 3 (Summer 1997): 189–209.

Schrag, Brian. "The Moral Significance of Employee Loyalty." *Business Ethics Quarterly* 11, no. 1 (2001): 41–66.

Schrag, Calvin O. "Note on Kierkegaard's Teleological Suspension of the Ethical." *Ethics* 70, no. 1 (1959): 66–68.

Schultz, Donald O., ed. *Critical Issues in Criminal Justice.* Springfield, IL: Charles C Thomas, 1975.

Schurz, Carl. "Remarks in the Senate, February 29, 1872." *Congressional Globe* 45 (1872): 1287. http://en.wikisource.org/wiki/U._S._Senate_Speeches_and_Remarks_of_Carl_Schurz/Sales_of_Arms_to_French_Agents_6.

Schwartz, Murray L. "The Zeal of the Civil Advocate." In *The Good Lawyer: Lawyers' Roles and Lawyers' Ethics*, edited by David Luban, 150–171. Totowa, NJ: Rowman & Allanheld, 1984.

Seneca. *Agamemnon.* Translated by Richard J. Tarrant. Cambridge: Cambridge University Press, 1977.

Shakespeare, William. *The Merchant of Venice: Folger Shakespeare Library.* London: Simon & Schuster, 2004.

Shelley, Mary Wollstonecraft. *Frankenstein.* New York: Pyramid, 1957.

Sherman, Nancy. *Making a Necessity of Virtue: Aristotle and Kant on Virtue.* Cambridge: Cambridge University Press, 1997.

Sherr, Lynn. *America the Beautiful: The Stirring True Story behind Our Nation's Favorite Song.* New York: PublicAffairs, 2001.

Shklar, Judith. *Ordinary Vices.* Cambridge, MA: Belknap/Harvard University Press, 1984.

Shklar, Judith. "Obligation, Loyalty, Exile." *Political Theory* 21, no. 2 (1993): 181–197.

Shogan, Debra. "Trusting Paternalism? Trust as a Condition for Paternalistic Decisions." *Journal of the Philosophy of Sport* 18 (1991): 49–58.

Sidgwick, Henry. *The Methods of Ethics.* New York: Macmillan, 1901.

Simmons, A. John. *Moral Principles and Political Obligations.* Princeton, NJ: Princeton University Press, 1979.

Smart, (J. J. C.) John Jameson Carswell, and Bernard Williams. *Utilitarianism: For and Against.* Cambridge: Cambridge University Press, 1973.

Smith, Anthony D. *Nationalism.* Cambridge: Polity, 2001.

Souryal, Sam S., and Brian W. McKay. "Personal Loyalty to Superiors in Public Service." *Criminal Justice Ethics* 15, no. 2 (1996): 41–58.

Spiegel, Shalom.*The Last Trial. On the Legends and Lore of the Command to Abraham to Offer Isaac as a Sacrifice: The Akedah.* Translated and introduced by Judah Goldin. New York: Pantheon, 1979.

Stewart, Jon. *Kierkegaard's Relations to Hegel Reconsidered.* Cambridge: Cambridge University Press, 2003.

Stilz, Anna. *Liberal Loyalty: Freedom, Obligation, and the State.* Princeton, NJ: Princeton University Press, 2009.

Stocker, Michael. "The Schizophrenia of Modern Ethical Theories." *Journal of Philosophy* 73, no. 14 (1976): 453–466.

Stone, Gerald. *The Smallest Slavonic Nation: The Sorbs of Lusatia.* London: Athlone, 1972.

Striking Distance. Directed by Rowdy Herrington. Columbia Pictures, 1993.

Tarasoff v. Regents of the University of California, 17 Cal. 3d 425, 551 P.2d 334, 131 Cal. Rptr. 14 (1976).

Taylor, Richard. *Love Affairs: Marriage and Infidelity*, rev. ed. Buffalo, NY: Prometheus, 1997.

Ten, Chin Liew. "Multiculturalism and the Value of Diversity." In *Multicultural Citizens: The Philosophy and Politics of Identity*, edited by Chandran Kukathas, 7–16. St. Leonards, Australia: Centre for Independent Studies, 1993.

Ten, Chin Liew, ed. *Multiculturalism and the Value of Diversity*. Singapore: Marshall Cavendish, 2004.

Thomas, Keith. "The Double Standard." *Journal of the History of Ideas* 20, no. 2 (1959): 195–216.

Thomas, Laurence. "Friendship." *Synthese* 72, no. 2 (1987): 217–236.

Thomas, Laurence. "Friendship and Other Loves." In *Friendship: A Philosophical Reader*, edited by Neera Kapur Badhwar, 48–64. Ithaca, NY: Cornell University Press, 1993.

Thompson, Dennis F. "The Institutional Turn in Professional Ethics." *Ethics & Behavior* 9, no. 2 (1999): 109–118.

Thoreau, Henry David. *Civil Disobedience and Other Essays*. Stilwell, KS: Dover, 1993.

Tōju, Nakae. *Nihon shisō taikei*, vol. 29. Tokyo: Iwanami Shoten, 1974.

Trianosky, Gregory W. "Virtue, Action, and the Good Life: Toward a Theory of the Virtues." *Pacific Philosophical Quarterly* 68, no. 2 (June 1987): 124–147.

Trotsky, Leon, John Dewey, and George Novak. *Their Means and Ours: Marxist versus Liberal Views on Morality*, 5th ed. New York: Pathfinder, 1973.

Twain, Mark. *Mark Twain's Notebook*. Edited by Albert Paine. New York: Harper, 1935.

Twain, Mark. *A Connecticut Yankee in King Arthur's Court* [1889]. London: Penguin, 1971.

Veblen, Thorsten. *Absentee Ownership and Business Enterprise in Recent Times: The Case of America*. New York: B. W. Huebsch, 1923.

Vest, George Graham. "Tribute to the Dog." Reprinted in "Faithful, Even in Death." *New York Times Magazine*, April 18, 1999, 72–73.

Waldron, Jeremy. "Special Ties and Natural Duties." *Philosophy & Public Affairs* 22, no. 1 (1993): 3–30.

Walzer, Michael. *Obligations: Essays on Disobedience, War, and Citizenship*. Cambridge, MA: Harvard University Press, 1970.

Watson, Gary. "Virtues in Excess." *Philosophical Studies* 46, no. 1 (1984): 57–74.

Weber, Max. "Politics as a Vocation." In *From Max Weber: Essays in Sociology*, edited by H. H. Gerth & C. Wright Mills, 77–128. New York: Oxford University Press, 1946.

Weisband, Edward, and Thomas M. Franck. *Resignation in Protest: Political and Ethical Choices between Loyalty to Team and Loyalty to Conscience in American Public Life*. New York: Grossman, 1975.

West, Ranyard. *Conscience and Society*. New York: Emerson, 1945.

Whitlock, Greg. "Concealing the Misconduct of One's Own Father: Confucius and Plato on a Question of Filial Piety." *Journal of Chinese Philosophy* 21, no. 2 (1994): 113–137.

Whitrod, Ray. In *The Age*, May 13, 1988.

Wikipedia Contributors. "Neve Gordon." http://en.wikipedia.org/wiki/Neve_Gordon.

Wilensky, Harold L. "The Professionalization of Everyone?" *American Journal of Sociology* 70, no. 2 (1964): 137–158.

Williams, Bernard. "Persons, Character and Morality." In *Moral Luck: Philosophical Papers 1973–80*, 1–19. Cambridge: Cambridge University Press, 1981.

Williams, Bernard. "Utilitarianism and Moral Self-Indulgence." In *Moral Luck: Philosophical Papers 1973–80*, 40–53. Cambridge: Cambridge University Press, 1981.

Williams, Bernard. *Ethics and the Limits of Philosophy*. London: Fontana, 1985.

Wilson, James Q. *The Moral Sense*. New York: Free Press, 1993.

Winkler, Eva C. "The Ethics of Policy Writing: How Should Hospitals Deal with Moral Disagreement about Controversial Medical Practices?" *Journal of Medical Ethics* 31 (2005): 559–566.

Wolf, Susan. "'One Thought Too Many': Love, Morality, and the Ordering of Commitment." In *Luck, Value, and Commitment: Themes from the Ethics of Bernard Williams*, edited by Ulrike Heuer and Gerald Lang, 71–92. New York: Oxford University Press, 2012.

Wolf, Susan. "Loving Attention: Lessons in Love from *The Philadelphia Story*." In *Understanding Love through Philosophy, Film, and Fiction*, edited by Susan Wolf and Christopher Grau. New York: Oxford University Press, 2014.

Wolfe, Alan. *Moral Freedom: The Impossible Idea That Defines the Way We Live Now*. New York: W. W. Norton, 2001.

Wolfram, Charles W. *Modern Legal Ethics*. St. Paul, MN: West, 1986.

Wren, Thomas E. "Whistle-Blowing and Loyalty to One's Friends." In *Police Ethics: Hard Choices in Law Enforcement*, edited by William C. Heffernan and Timothy Stroup, 25–43. New York: John Jay, 1985.

Zagzebski, Linda. *Virtues of the Mind: An Inquiry into the Nature of Virtue and the Ethical Foundations of Knowledge*. Cambridge: Cambridge University Press, 1996.

INDEX

An "*n*" after a locator indicates a footnote.